Sk·ip·Beat!

Shojo Beat

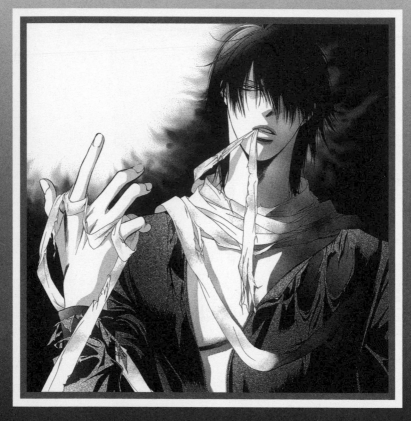

Skip·Beat!

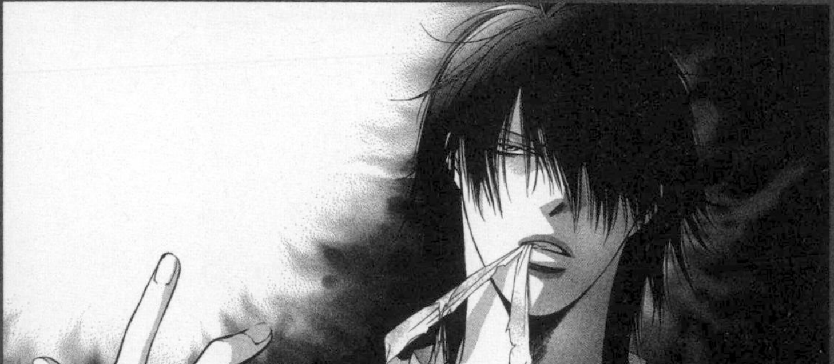

32

Story & Art by Yoshiki Nakamura

Skip·Beat!

Volume 32

CONTENTS

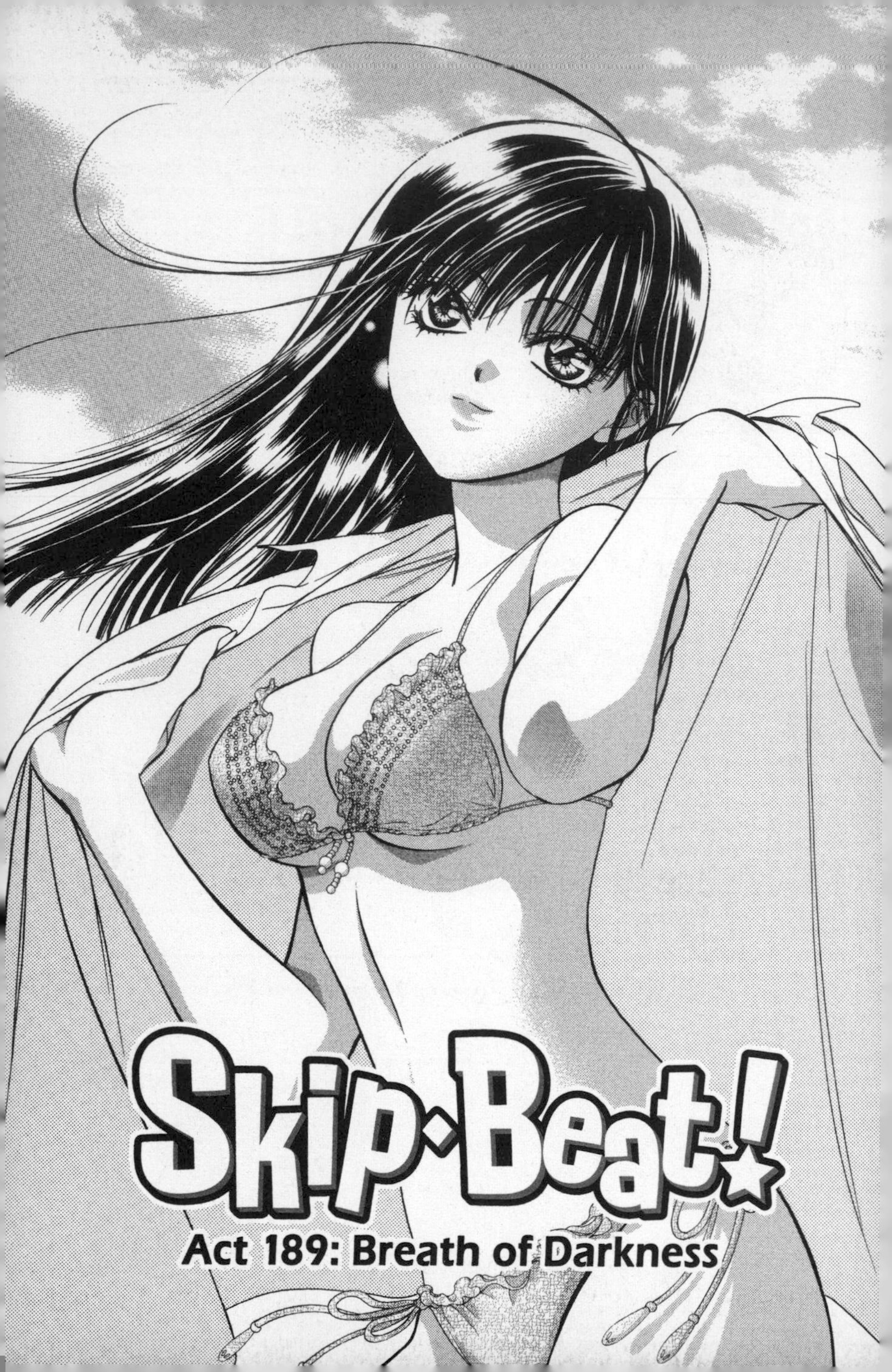
Skip·Beat!
Act 189: Breath of Darkness

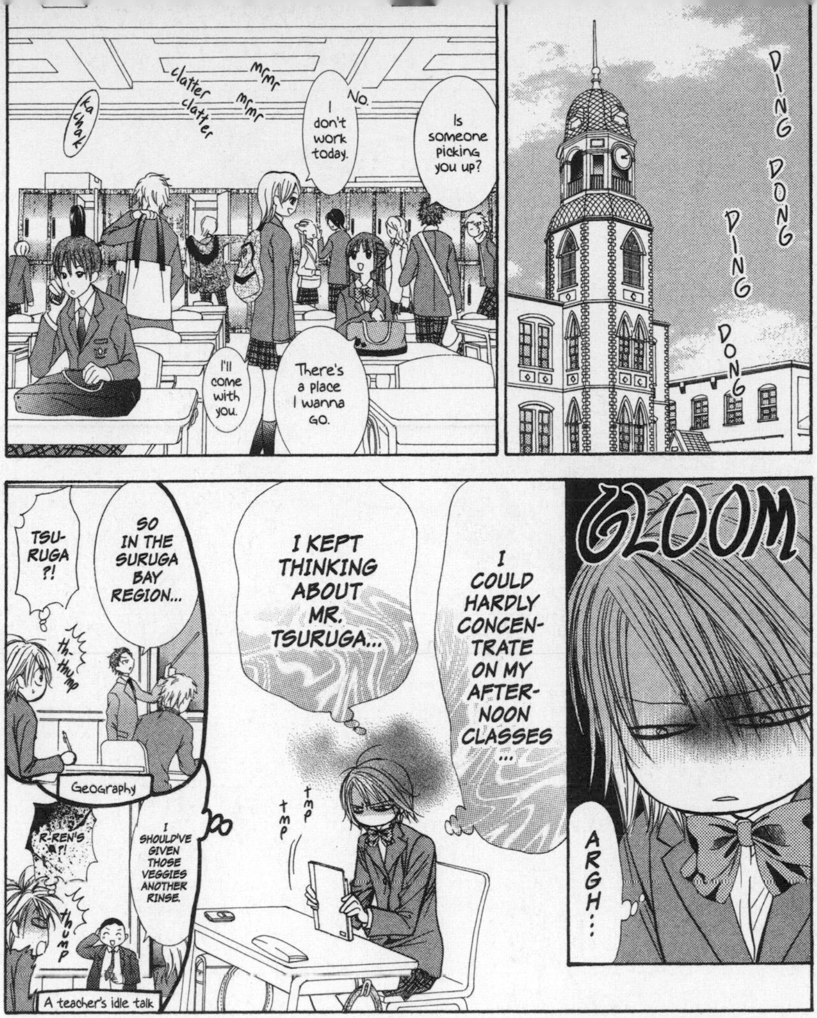
DING DONG
DING DONG
Is someone picking you up?
No. I don't work today.
mrmr mrmr
clatter clatter
ka chak
There's a place I wanna go.
I'll come with you.
GLOOM
ARGH...
I COULD HARDLY CONCENTRATE ON MY AFTERNOON CLASSES...
I KEPT THINKING ABOUT MR. TSURUGA...
tmp tmp
SO IN THE SURUGA BAY REGION...
TSU-RUGA?!
th-thump
Geography
I SHOULD'VE GIVEN THOSE VEGGIES ANOTHER RINSE.
R-REN'S?!
thump
A teacher's idle talk

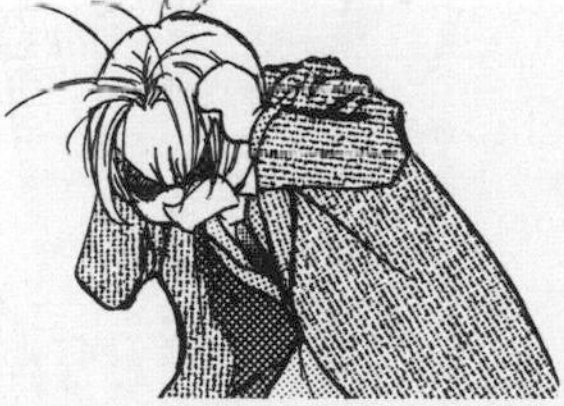

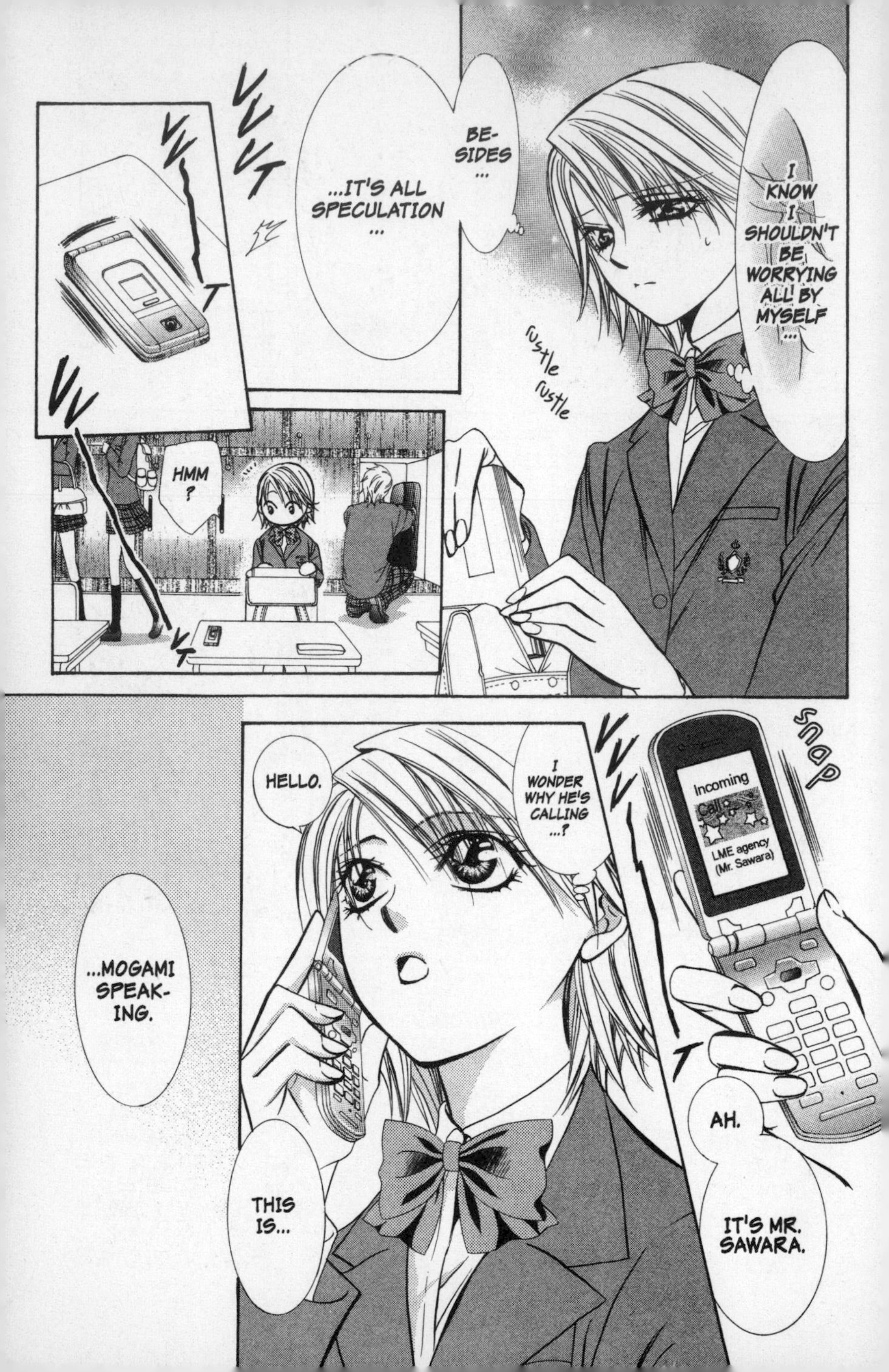
I KNOW I SHOULDN'T BE WORRYING ALL BY MYSELF...
rustle rustle
BE-SIDES...
...IT'S ALL SPECULATION...
VVVT
VVVT
HMM?
VVVT
snap
Incoming Call
LME agency (Mr. Sawara)
AH.
IT'S MR. SAWARA.
I WONDER WHY HE'S CALLING...?
HELLO.
THIS IS...
...MOGAMI SPEAK-ING.

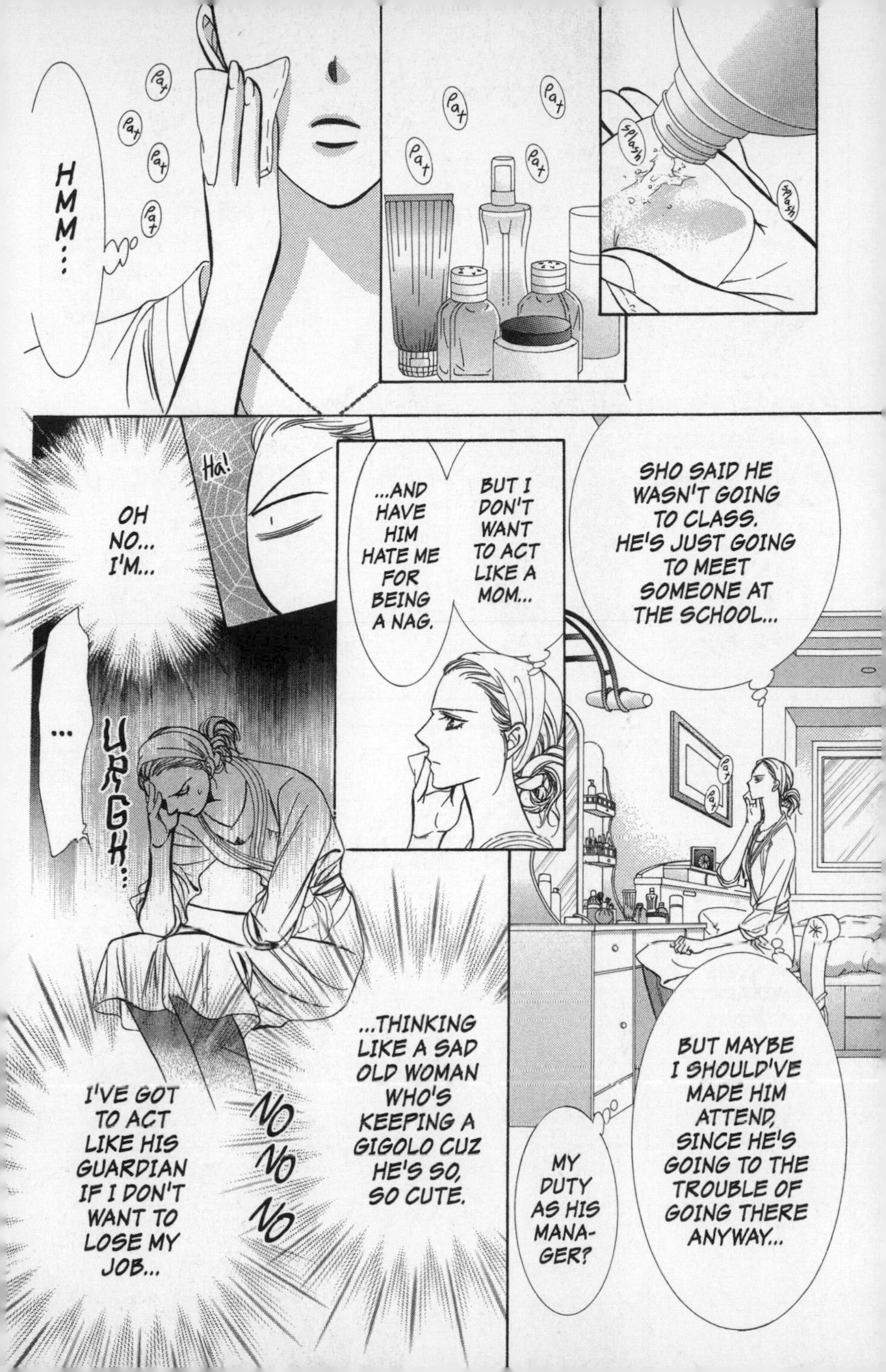
splash
splash
Pat
Pat
Pat
Pat
Pat
Pat
Pat
HMM...
SHO SAID HE WASN'T GOING TO CLASS. HE'S JUST GOING TO MEET SOMEONE AT THE SCHOOL...
Pat
Pat
BUT MAYBE I SHOULD'VE MADE HIM ATTEND, SINCE HE'S GOING TO THE TROUBLE OF GOING THERE ANYWAY...
MY DUTY AS HIS MANA-GER?
BUT I DON'T WANT TO ACT LIKE A MOM...
...AND HAVE HIM HATE ME FOR BEING A NAG.
Ha!
OH NO... I'M...
...
URGH...
...THINKING LIKE A SAD OLD WOMAN WHO'S KEEPING A GIGOLO CUZ HE'S SO, SO CUTE.
NO NO NO
I'VE GOT TO ACT LIKE HIS GUARDIAN IF I DON'T WANT TO LOSE MY JOB...

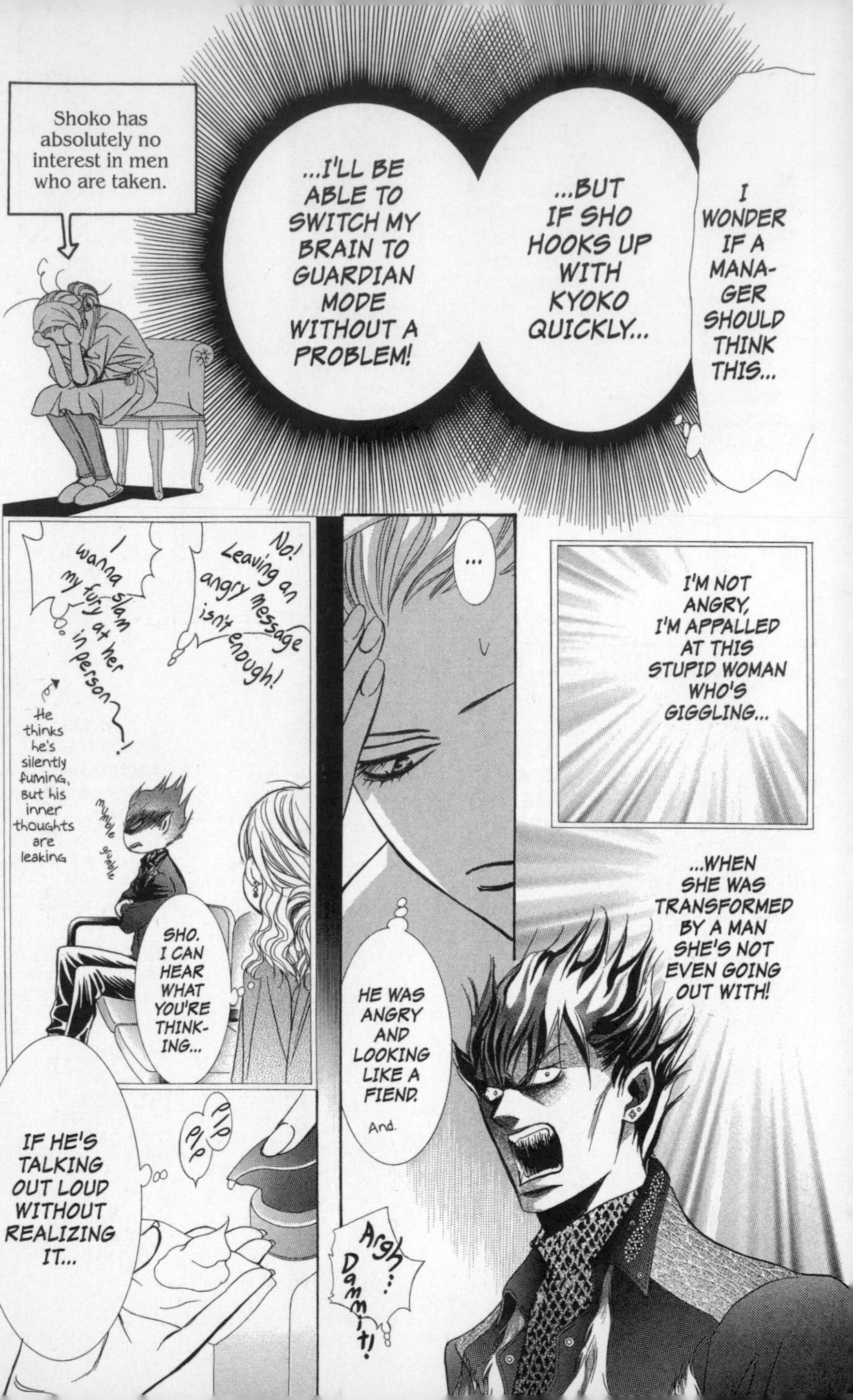
I WONDER IF A MANAGER SHOULD THINK THIS...
...BUT IF SHO HOOKS UP WITH KYOKO QUICKLY...
...I'LL BE ABLE TO SWITCH MY BRAIN TO GUARDIAN MODE WITHOUT A PROBLEM!
Shoko has absolutely no interest in men who are taken.
I'M NOT ANGRY, I'M APPALLED AT THIS STUPID WOMAN WHO'S GIGGLING...
...WHEN SHE WAS TRANSFORMED BY A MAN SHE'S NOT EVEN GOING OUT WITH!
...
HE WAS ANGRY AND LOOKING LIKE A FIEND.
And.
Argh... Dammit!
No! Leaving an angry message isn't enough!
I wanna slam my fury at her in person~!
He thinks he's silently fuming, but his inner thoughts are leaking
mumble grumble
SHO. I CAN HEAR WHAT YOU'RE THINKING...
pip pip
IF HE'S TALKING OUT LOUD WITHOUT REALIZING IT...

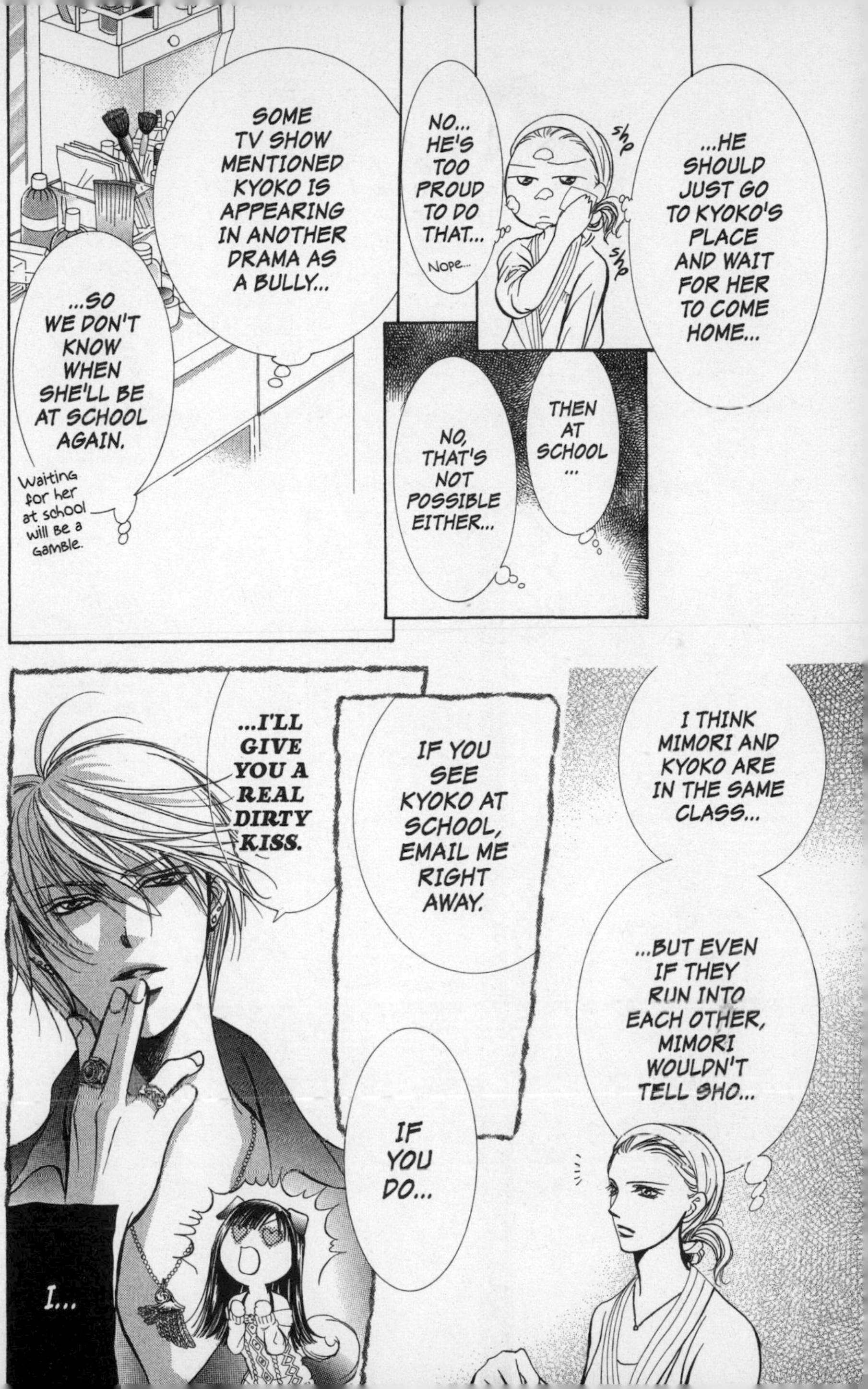
...HE SHOULD JUST GO TO KYOKO'S PLACE AND WAIT FOR HER TO COME HOME...
shp
shp
NO... HE'S TOO PROUD TO DO THAT...
Nope...
THEN AT SCHOOL...
NO, THAT'S NOT POSSIBLE EITHER...
SOME TV SHOW MENTIONED KYOKO IS APPEARING IN ANOTHER DRAMA AS A BULLY...
...SO WE DON'T KNOW WHEN SHE'LL BE AT SCHOOL AGAIN.
Waiting for her at school will be a gamble.
I THINK MIMORI AND KYOKO ARE IN THE SAME CLASS...
...BUT EVEN IF THEY RUN INTO EACH OTHER, MIMORI WOULDN'T TELL SHO...
IF YOU SEE KYOKO AT SCHOOL, EMAIL ME RIGHT AWAY.
IF YOU DO...
...I'LL GIVE YOU A REAL DIRTY KISS.
I...

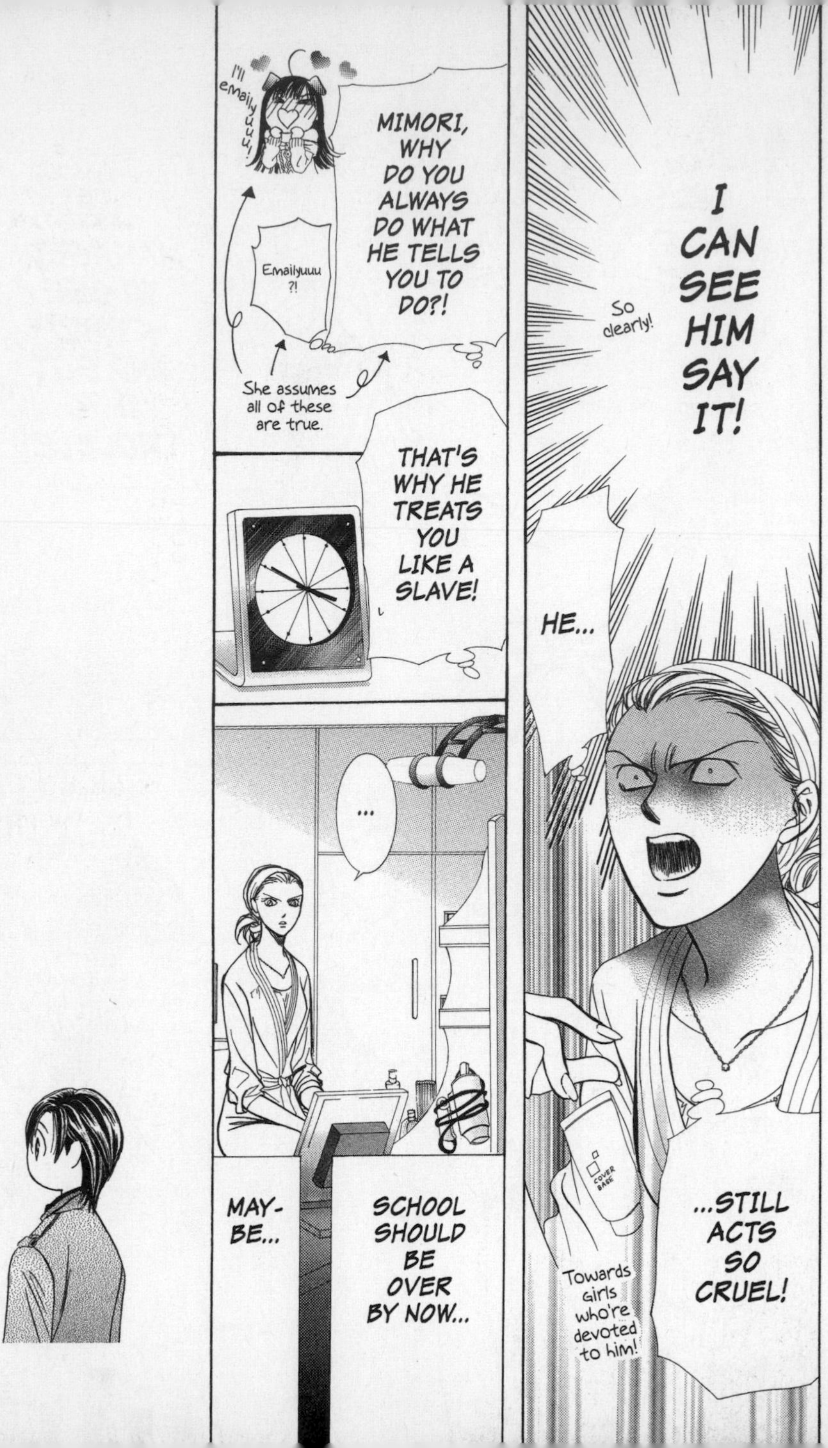
I CAN SEE HIM SAY IT!
So clearly!
HE...
...STILL ACTS SO CRUEL!
Towards girls who're devoted to him!
MIMORI, WHY DO YOU ALWAYS DO WHAT HE TELLS YOU TO DO?!
I'll emailyuuu!
Emailyuuu ?!
She assumes all of these are true.
THAT'S WHY HE TREATS YOU LIKE A SLAVE!
...
SCHOOL SHOULD BE OVER BY NOW...
MAY-BE...
COVER BASE

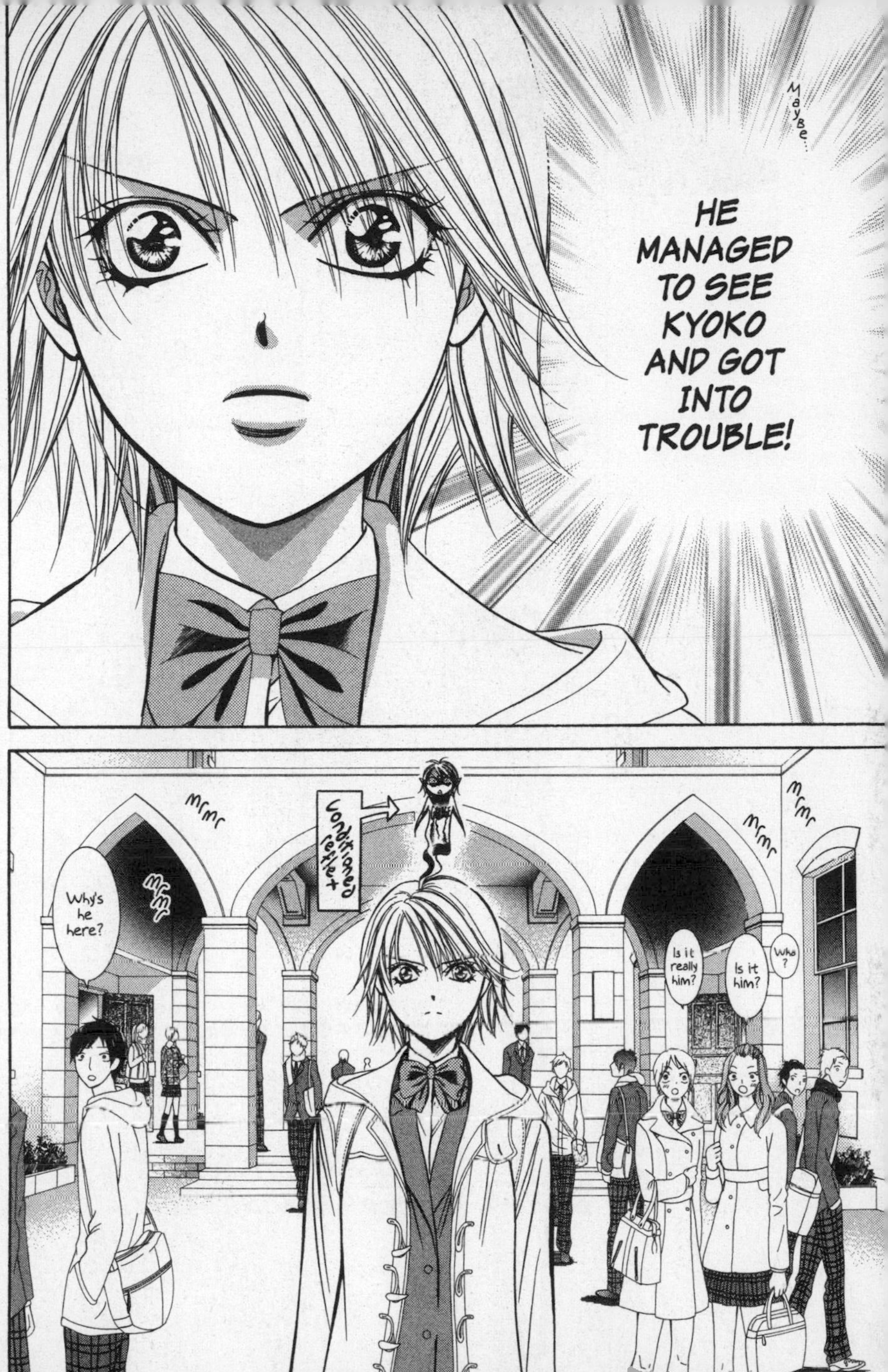
Maybe...
HE MANAGED TO SEE KYOKO AND GOT INTO TROUBLE!
mrmr
mrmr
Who?
Is it him?
Is it really him?
Conditioned reflex
mrmr
mrmr
Why's he here?

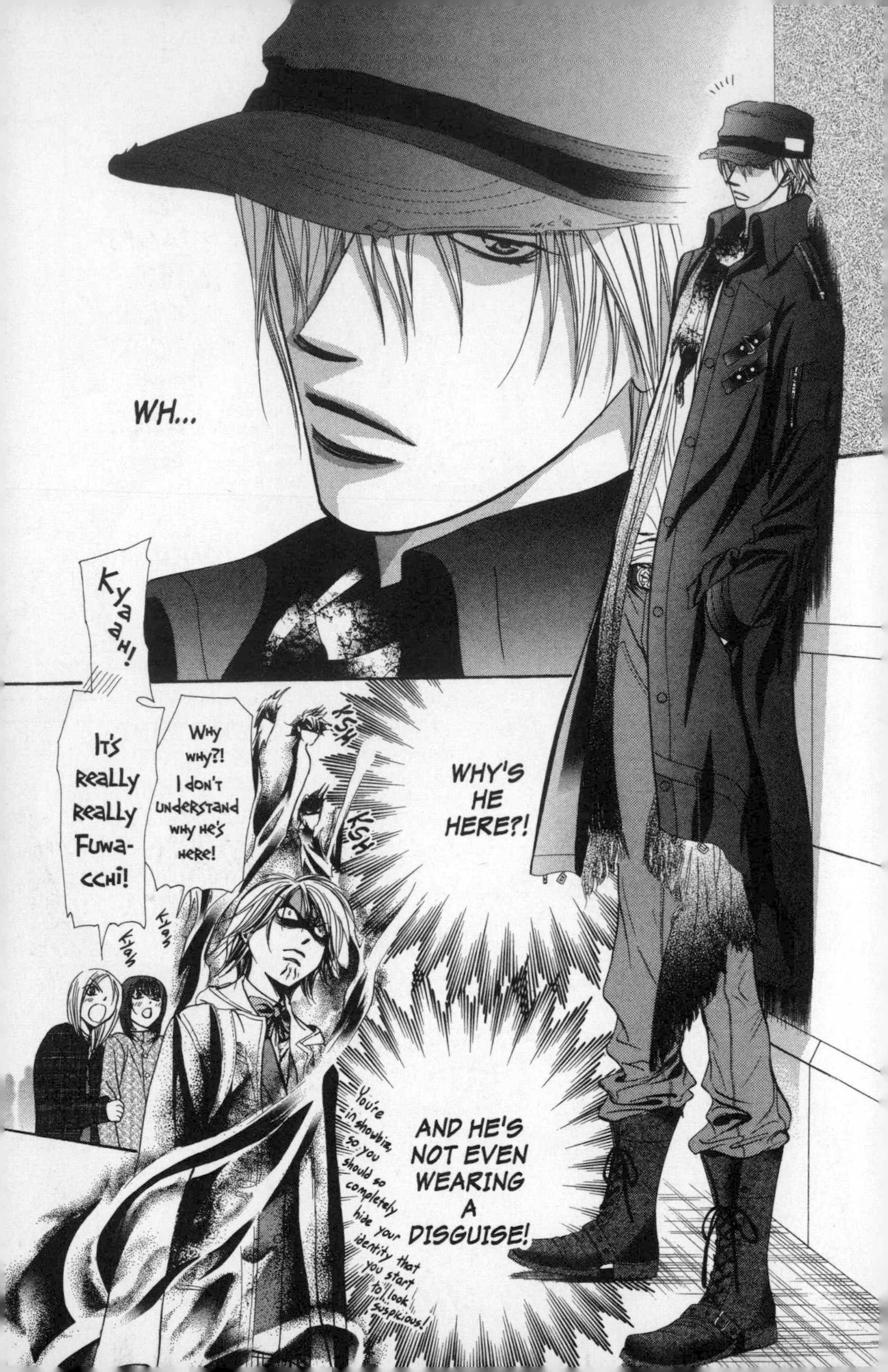

WH...
Kyaaah!
WHY'S HE HERE?!
KSH
KSH
Why why?! I don't understand why he's here!
It's really really Fuwa-cchi!
Kyah
Kyah
AND HE'S NOT EVEN WEARING A DISGUISE!
You're in showbiz, so you should so completely hide your identity that you start to look suspicious!

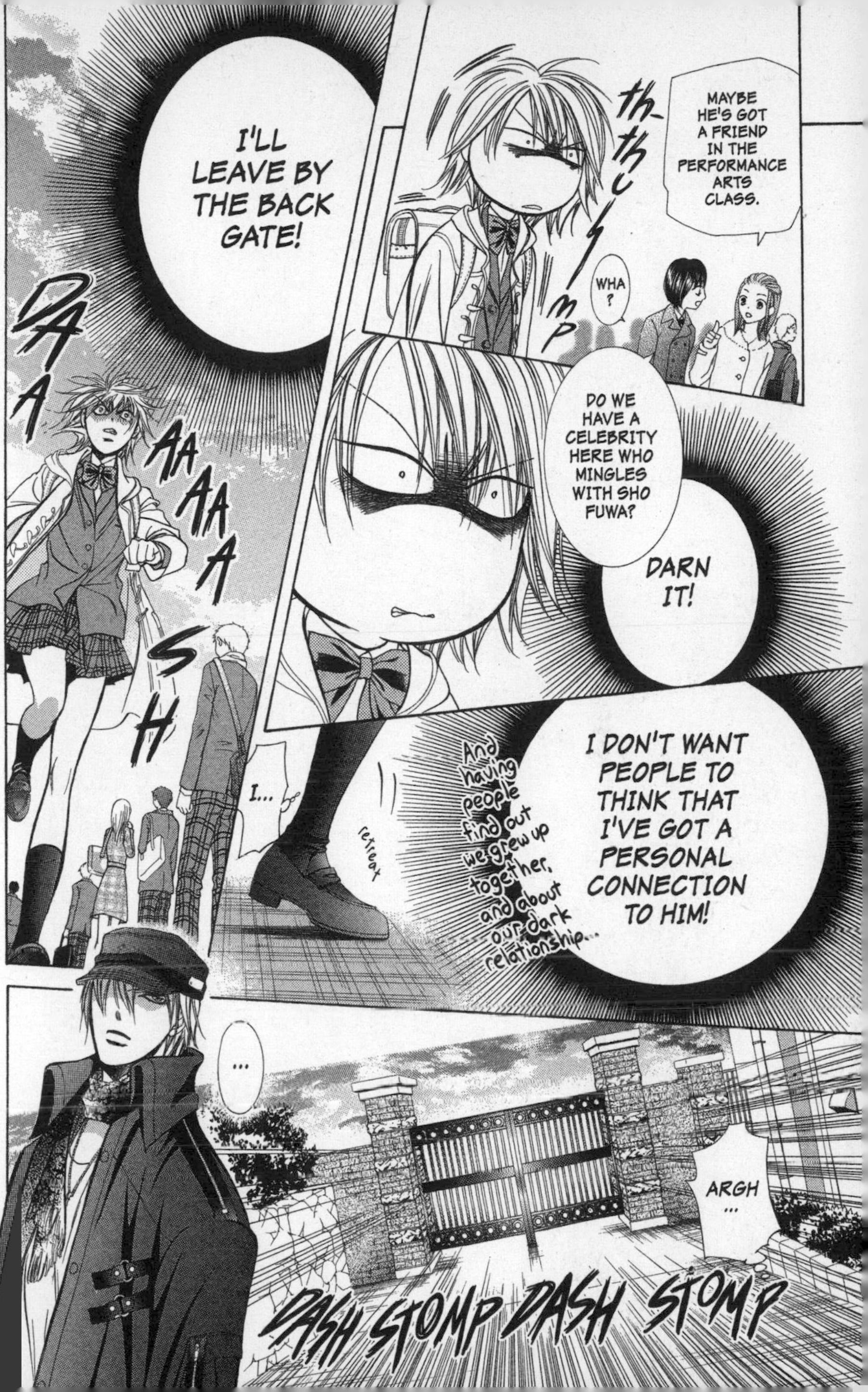
MAYBE HE'S GOT A FRIEND IN THE PERFORMANCE ARTS CLASS.
WHA?
DO WE HAVE A CELEBRITY HERE WHO MINGLES WITH SHO FUWA?
DARN IT!
I DON'T WANT PEOPLE TO THINK THAT I'VE GOT A PERSONAL CONNECTION TO HIM!
And having people find out we grew up together, and about our dark relationship...
retreat
I...
I'LL LEAVE BY THE BACK GATE!
DAAAAAAAAASH
ARGH...
...
DASH STOMP DASH STOMP

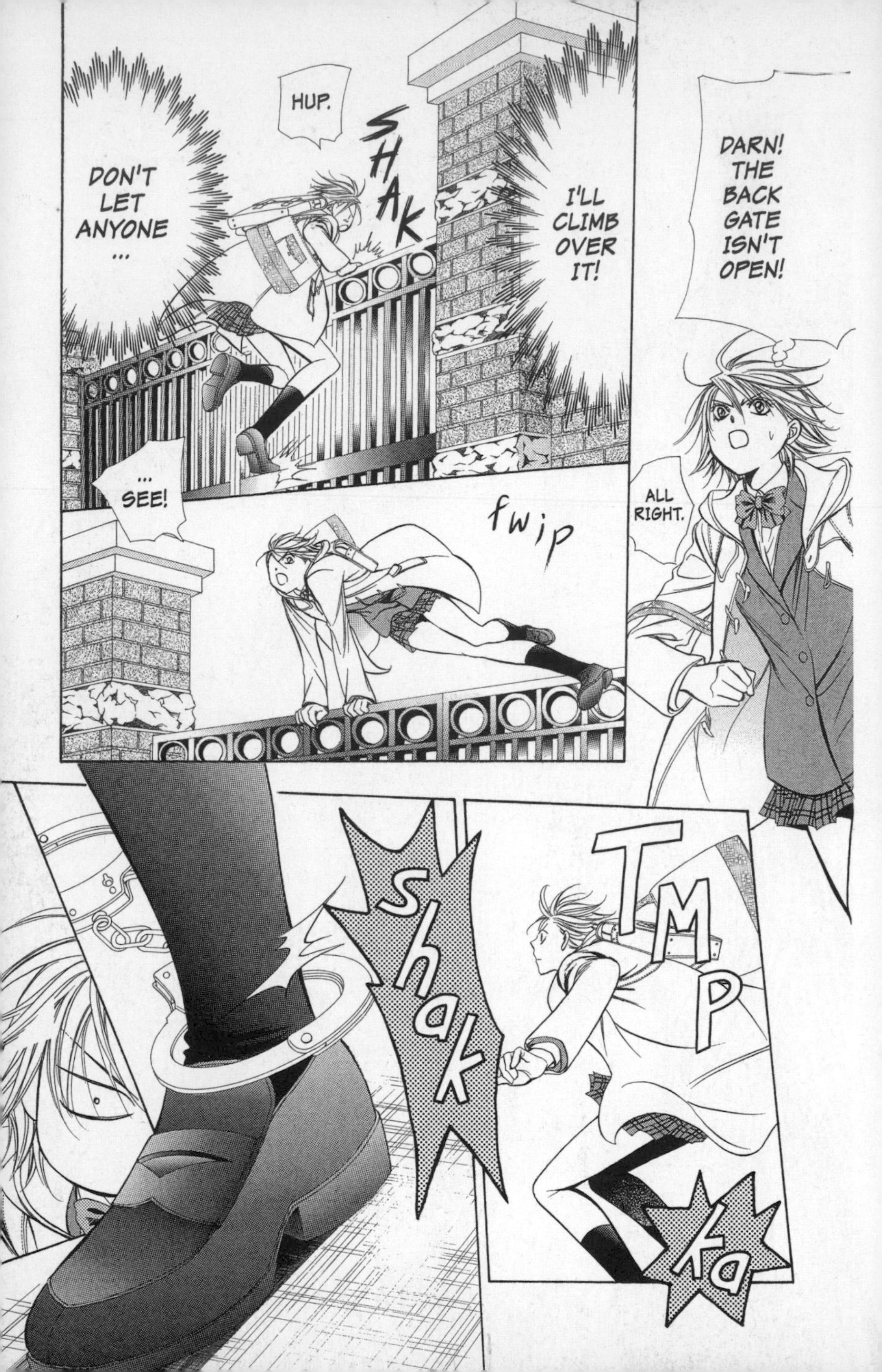
DARN! THE BACK GATE ISN'T OPEN!
ALL RIGHT.
I'LL CLIMB OVER IT!
HUP.
SHAK
DON'T LET ANYONE ...
... SEE!
fwip
TMP
ka
shak

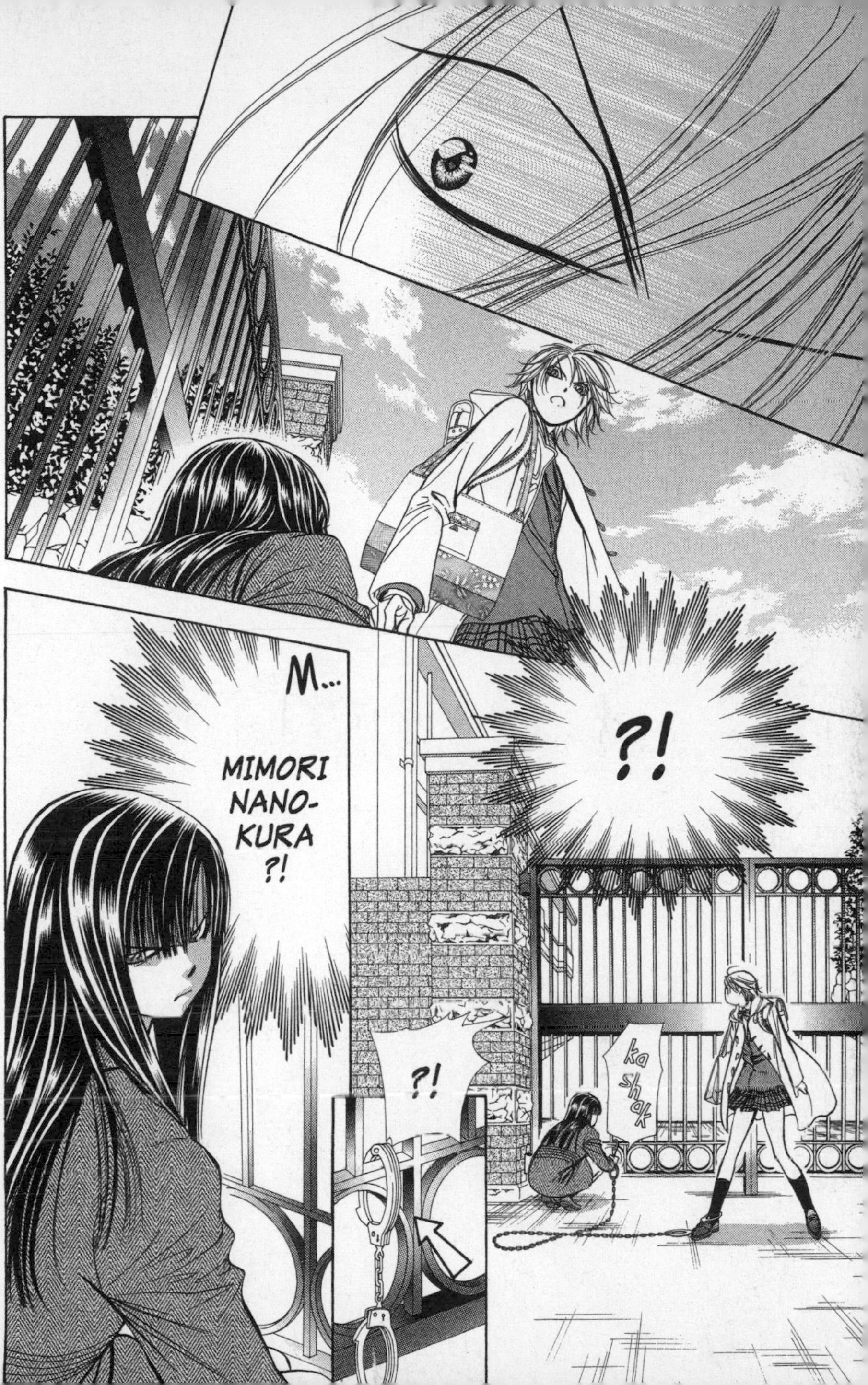
?!
M...
MIMORI NANO-KURA ?!
?!
ka shak

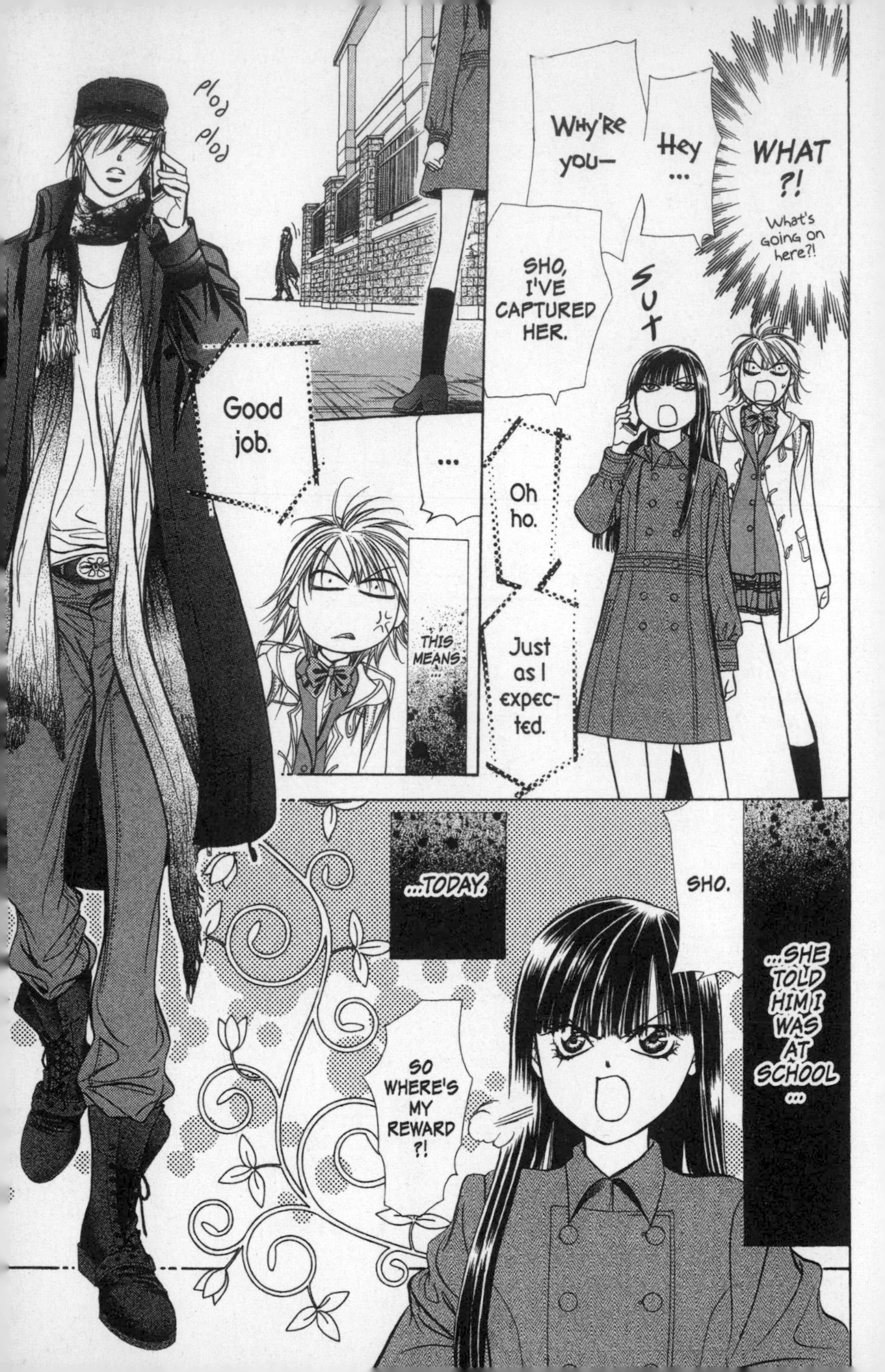
WHAT?!
What's going on here?!
Hey ...
Why're you—
SHO, I'VE CAPTURED HER.
SUT
Oh ho.
Just as I expected.
...
THIS MEANS ...
SHO.
...SHE TOLD HIM I WAS AT SCHOOL ...
...TODAY.
SO WHERE'S MY REWARD?!
plod plod
Good job.

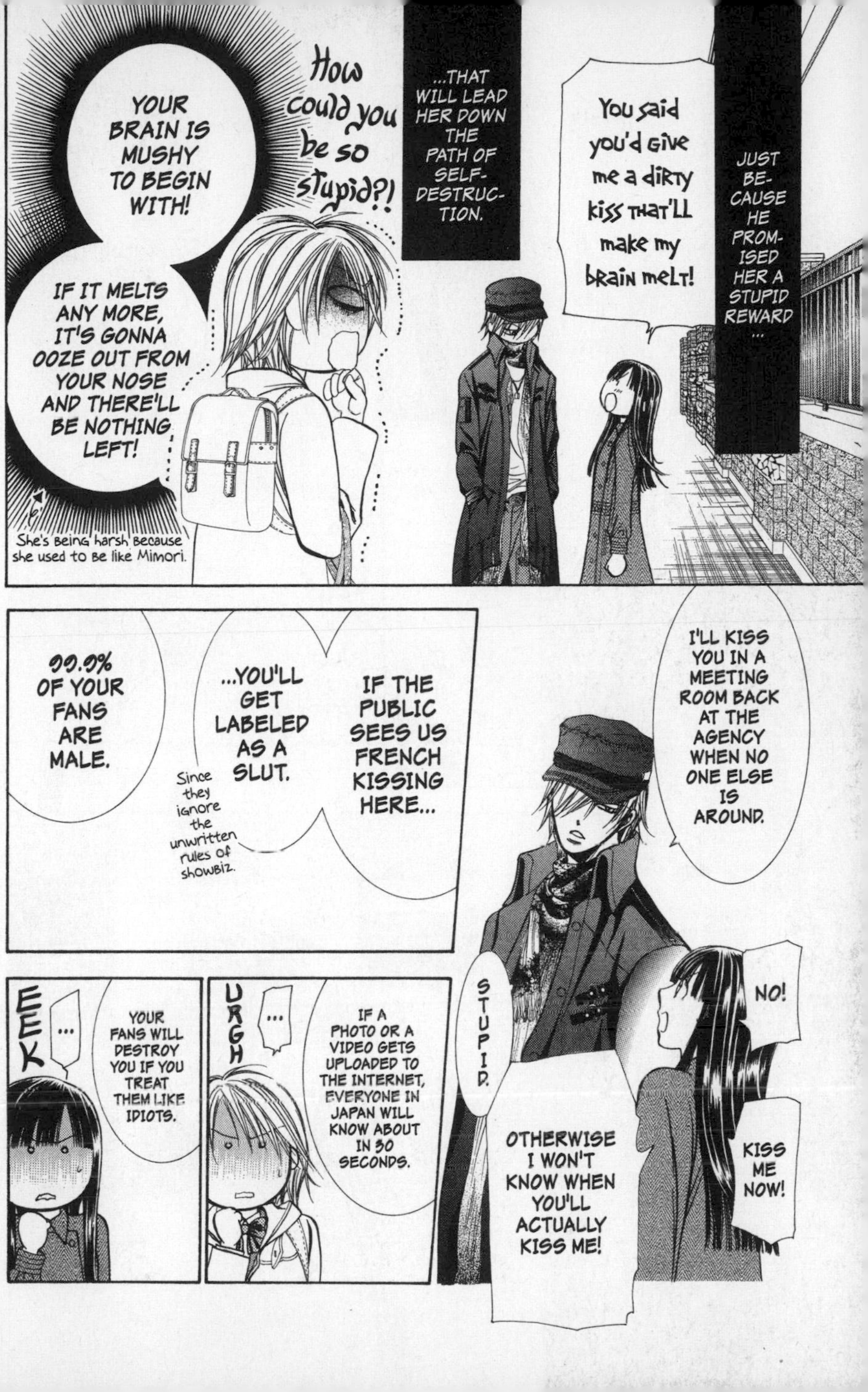
JUST BECAUSE HE PROMISED HER A STUPID REWARD...
You said you'd give me a dirty kiss that'll make my brain melt!
...THAT WILL LEAD HER DOWN THE PATH OF SELF-DESTRUCTION.
How could you be so stupid?!
YOUR BRAIN IS MUSHY TO BEGIN WITH!
IF IT MELTS ANY MORE, IT'S GONNA OOZE OUT FROM YOUR NOSE AND THERE'LL BE NOTHING LEFT!
She's being harsh because she used to be like Mimori.
I'LL KISS YOU IN A MEETING ROOM BACK AT THE AGENCY WHEN NO ONE ELSE IS AROUND.
NO!
KISS ME NOW!
OTHERWISE I WON'T KNOW WHEN YOU'LL ACTUALLY KISS ME!
STUPID.
IF THE PUBLIC SEES US FRENCH KISSING HERE...
...YOU'LL GET LABELED AS A SLUT.
99.9% OF YOUR FANS ARE MALE.
Since they ignore the unwritten rules of showbiz.
URGH
...
IF A PHOTO OR A VIDEO GETS UPLOADED TO THE INTERNET, EVERYONE IN JAPAN WILL KNOW ABOUT IN 30 SECONDS.
EEK
...
YOUR FANS WILL DESTROY YOU IF YOU TREAT THEM LIKE IDIOTS.

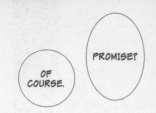

pout
...
Peep
Peep
ka chak
ka chak
rustle
rum-mage
HELLO.
Mimori?
Are you still in your class-room?
ka chak
ka chak
I'm here to pick you up, so come out now.
YEAH... OKAY.
bip
stare
WILL YOU REALLY KISS ME THE NEXT TIME I SEE YOU?
YEAH.
pat
pat
PROMISE?
OF COURSE.
I'M SORRY...
...I MADE YOU DO THIS TODAY.

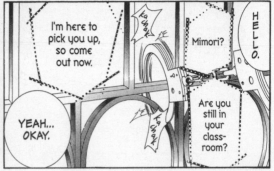

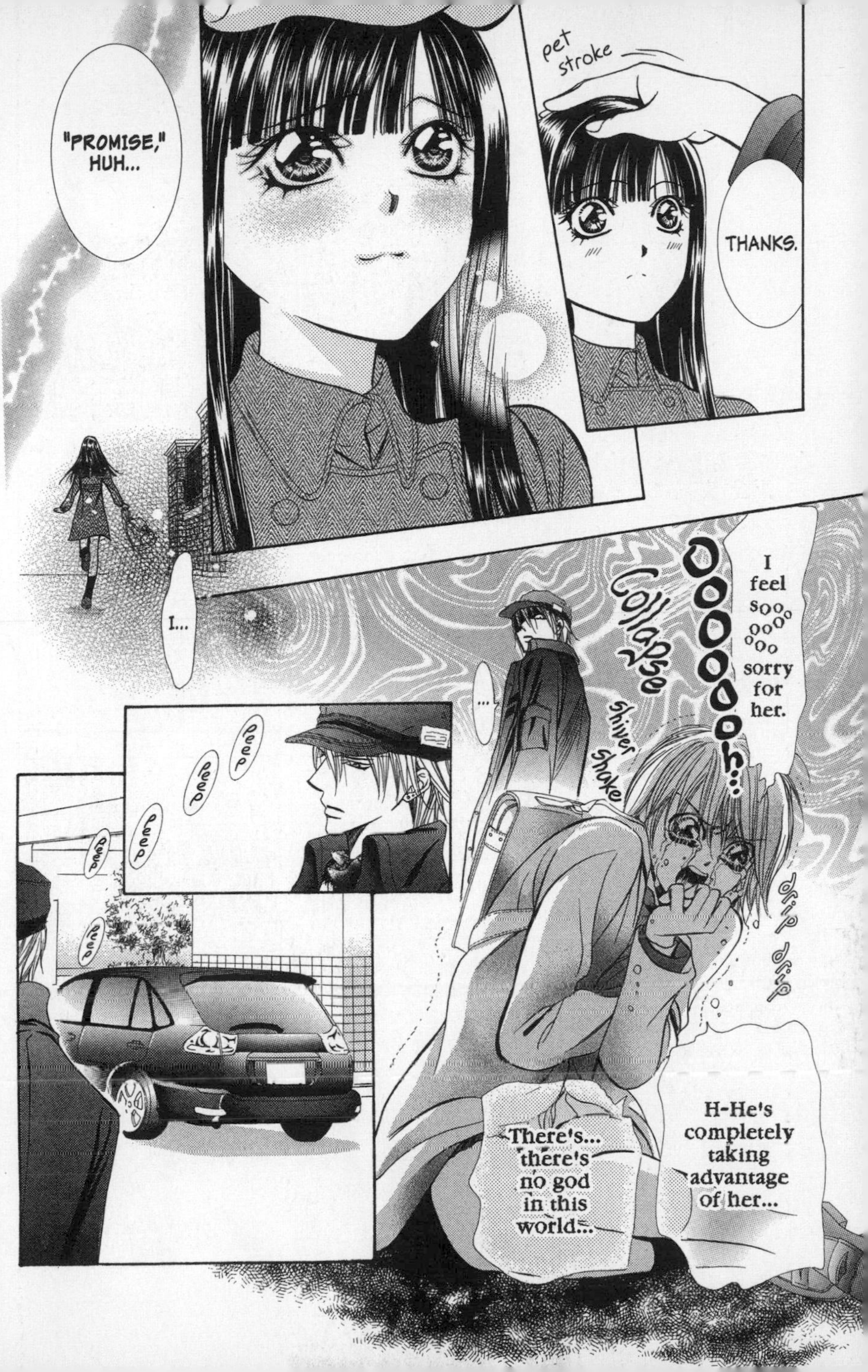

pet stroke
THANKS.
"PROMISE," HUH...
...
OOOOOOh...
I feel sooo ooo ooo sorry for her.
Collapse
shiver shake
drip drip
H-He's completely taking advantage of her...
There's... there's no god in this world...
I...
peep
peep
peep
peep
peep

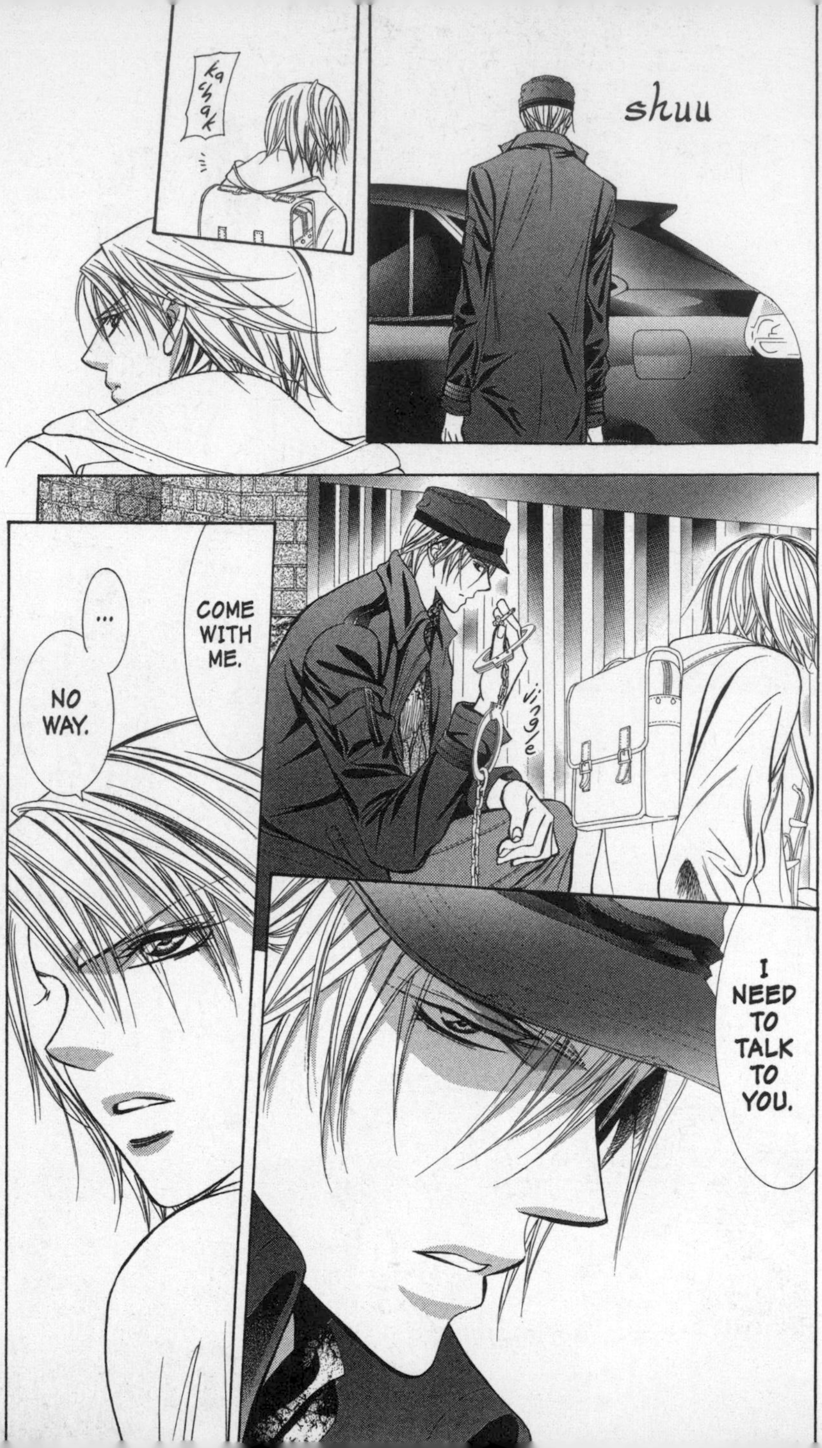
shuu
kachak
jingle
I NEED TO TALK TO YOU.
COME WITH ME.
...
NO WAY.

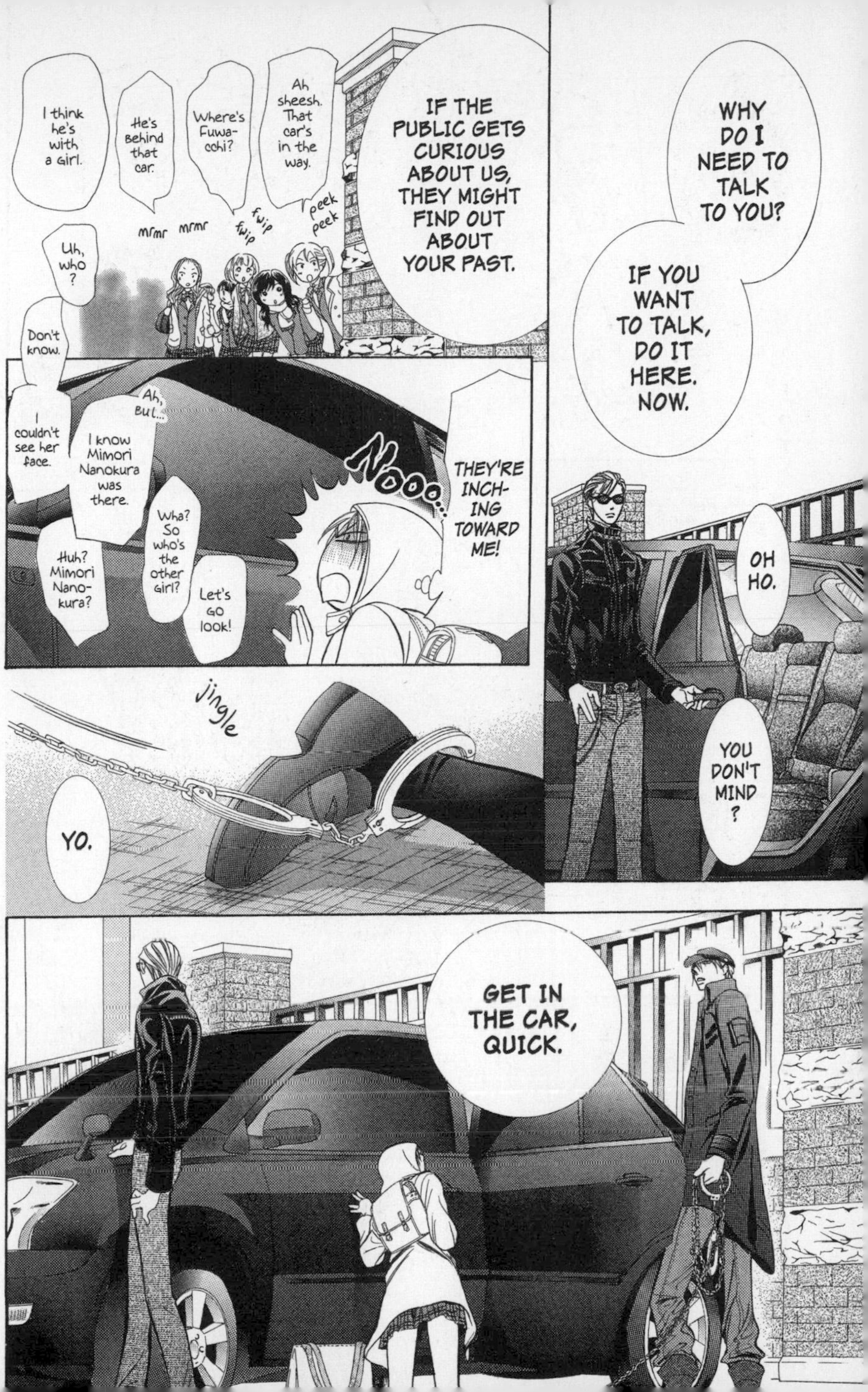
WHY DO I NEED TO TALK TO YOU?
IF YOU WANT TO TALK, DO IT HERE. NOW.
OH HO.
YOU DON'T MIND?
IF THE PUBLIC GETS CURIOUS ABOUT US, THEY MIGHT FIND OUT ABOUT YOUR PAST.
Ah sheesh. That car's in the way.
Where's Fuwa-cchi?
He's behind that car.
I think he's with a girl.
peek peek
fwip fwip
mrmr mrmr
Uh, who?
Don't know.
THEY'RE INCHING TOWARD ME!
Nooo...
Ah, But...
I know Mimori Nanokura was there.
I couldn't see her face.
Wha? So who's the other girl?
Huh? Mimori Nanokura?
Let's go look!
jingle
YO.
GET IN THE CAR, QUICK.

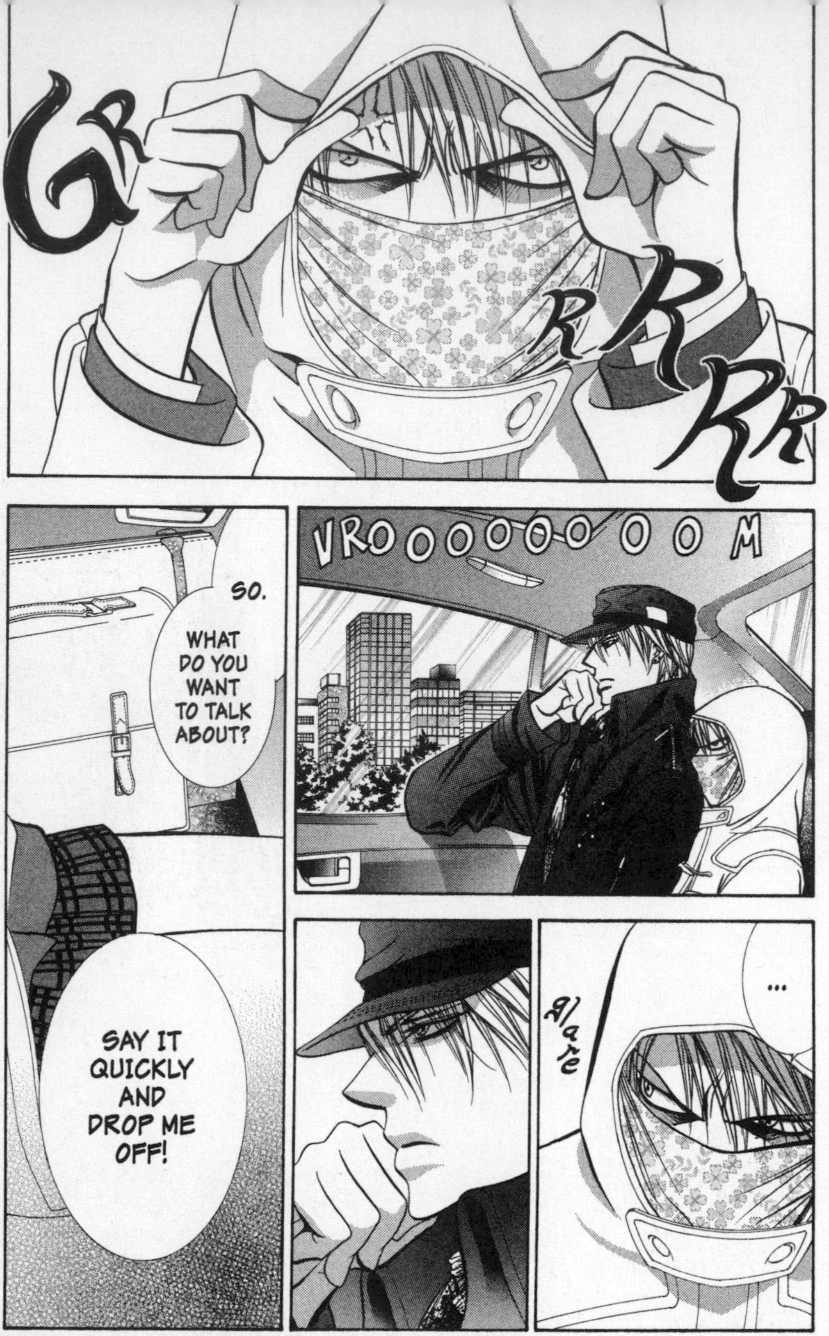
GRRRRRR
VROOOOOOOOM
SO.
WHAT DO YOU WANT TO TALK ABOUT?
glare
...
SAY IT QUICKLY AND DROP ME OFF!

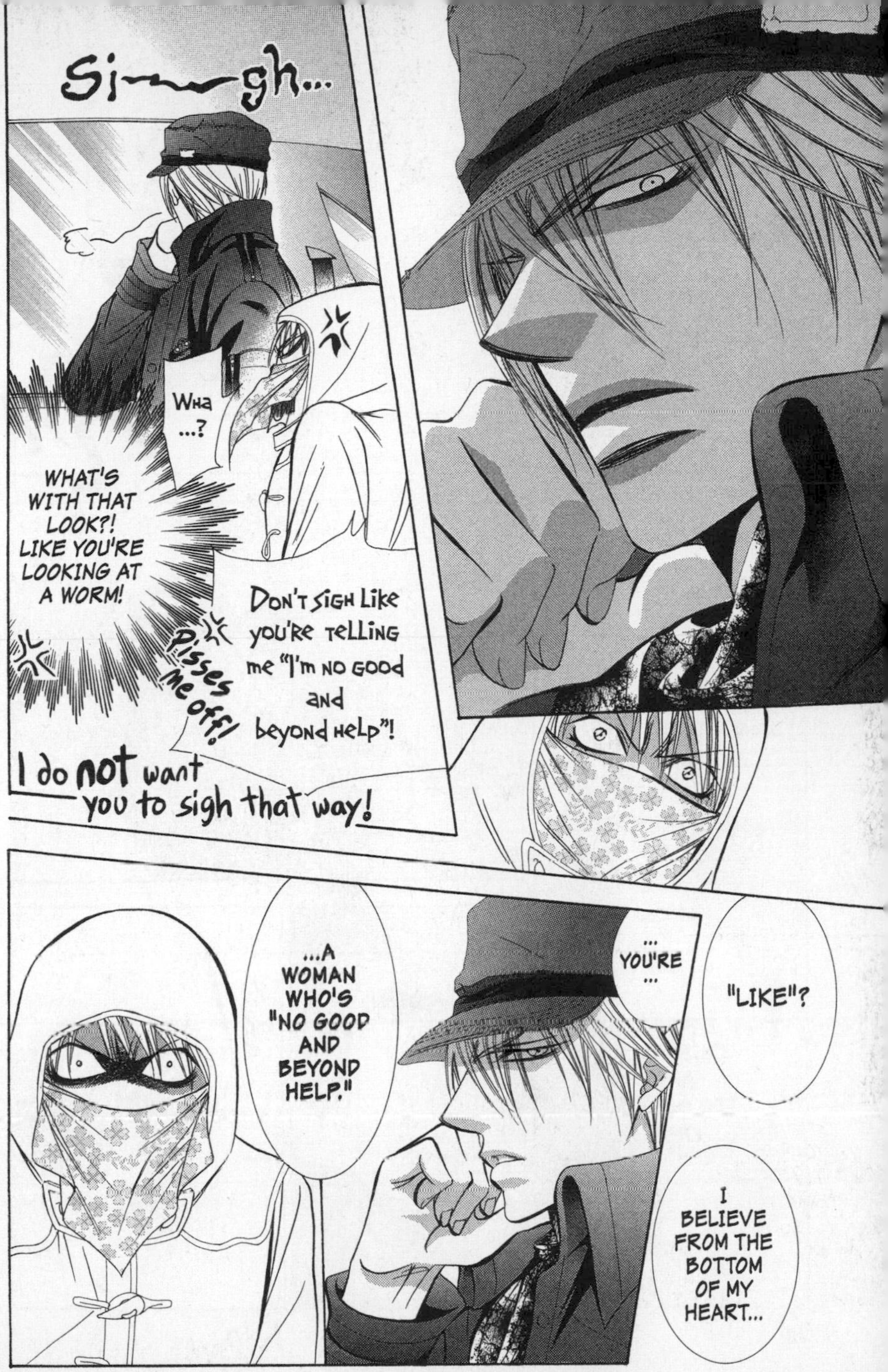

Si-gh...
Wha ...?
Don't sigh like you're telling me "I'm no good and beyond help"!
WHAT'S WITH THAT LOOK?! LIKE YOU'RE LOOKING AT A WORM!
Pisses me off!
I do not want you to sigh that way!
I BELIEVE FROM THE BOTTOM OF MY HEART...
"LIKE"?
... YOU'RE ...
...A WOMAN WHO'S "NO GOOD AND BEYOND HELP."

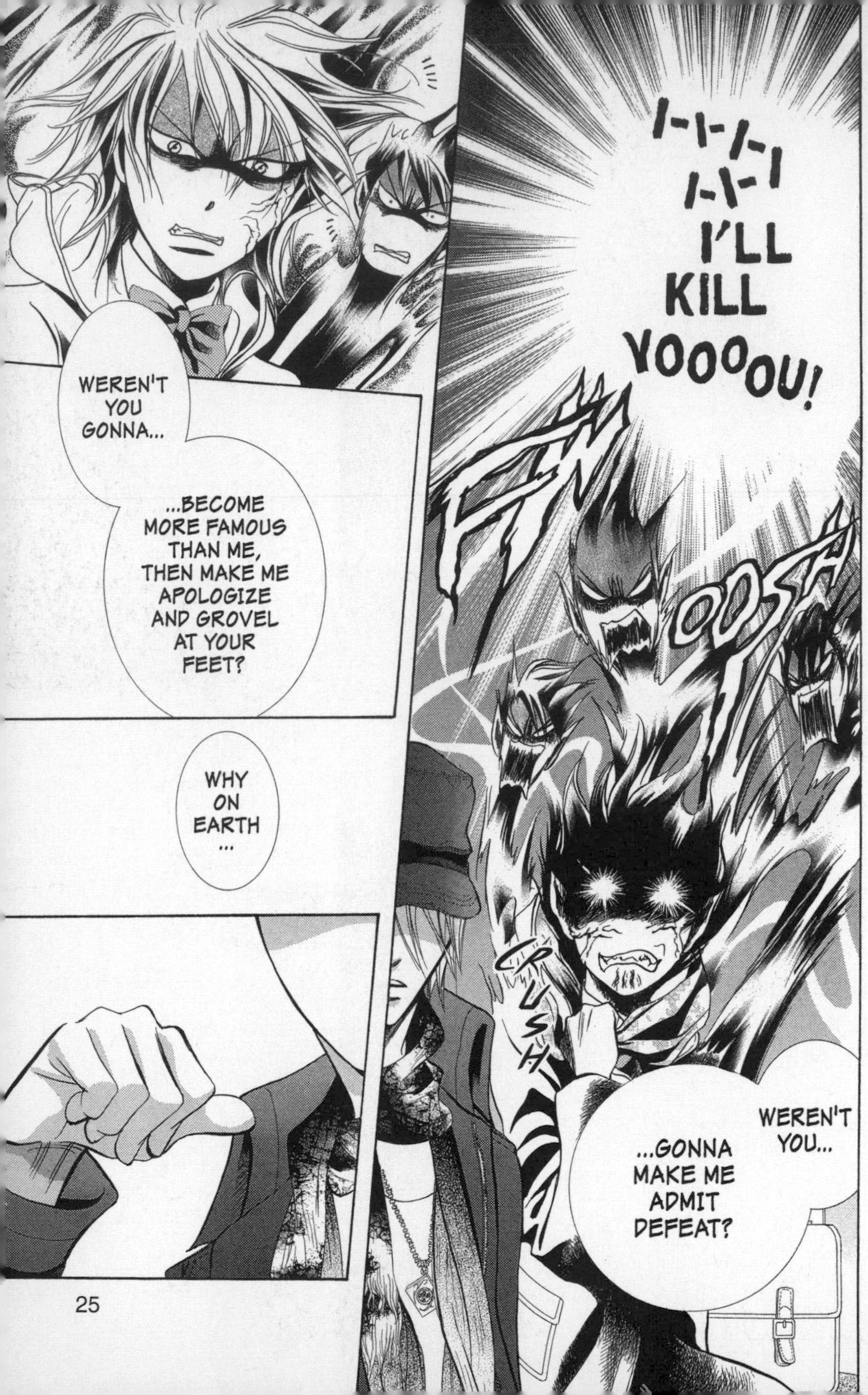
I-I-I-I I-I-I I'LL KILL YOOOOU!
FWOOSH
CRUSH
WEREN'T YOU...
...GONNA MAKE ME ADMIT DEFEAT?
WEREN'T YOU GONNA...
...BECOME MORE FAMOUS THAN ME, THEN MAKE ME APOLOGIZE AND GROVEL AT YOUR FEET?
WHY ON EARTH ...

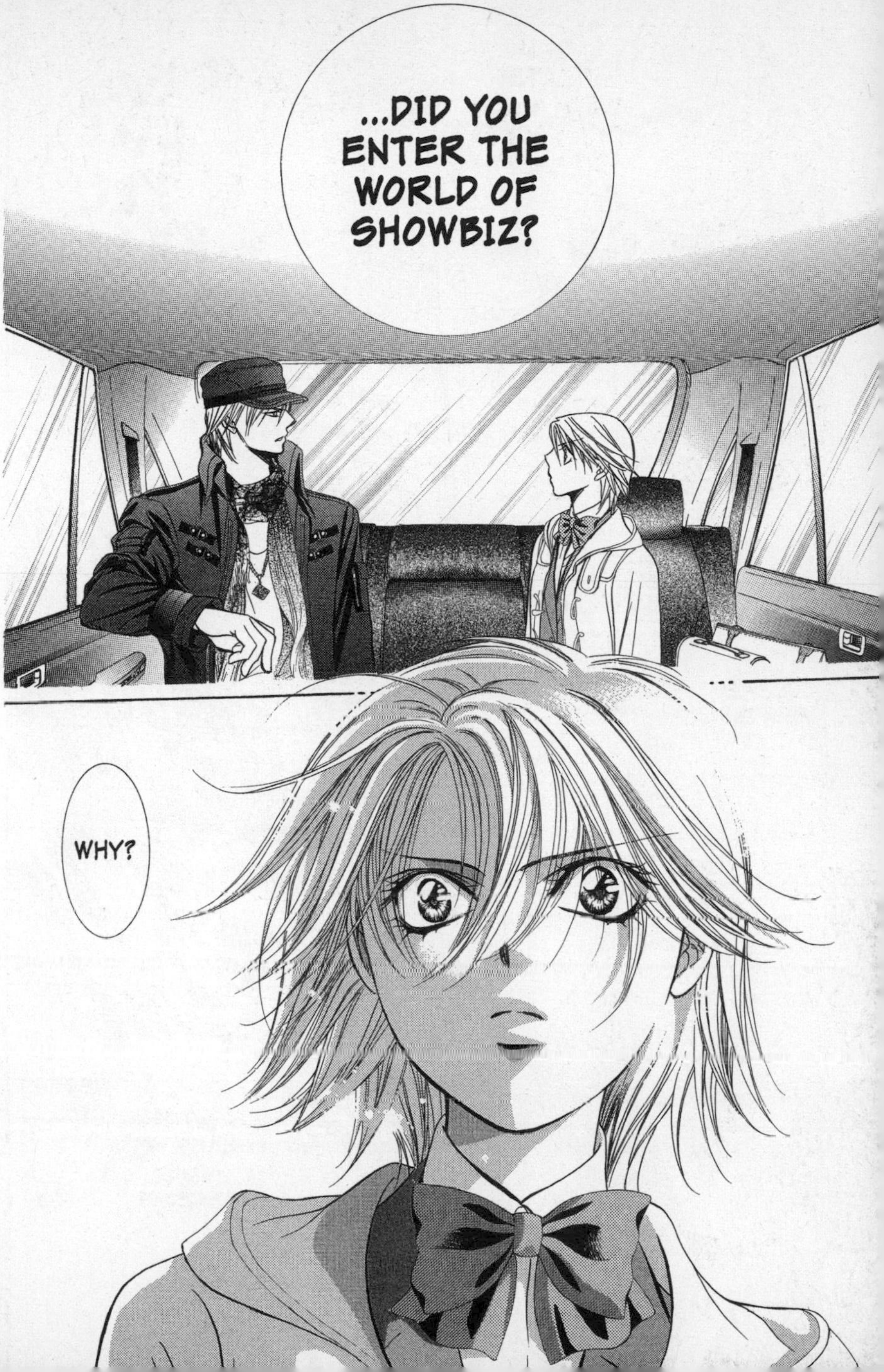
...DID YOU ENTER THE WORLD OF SHOWBIZ?
WHY?

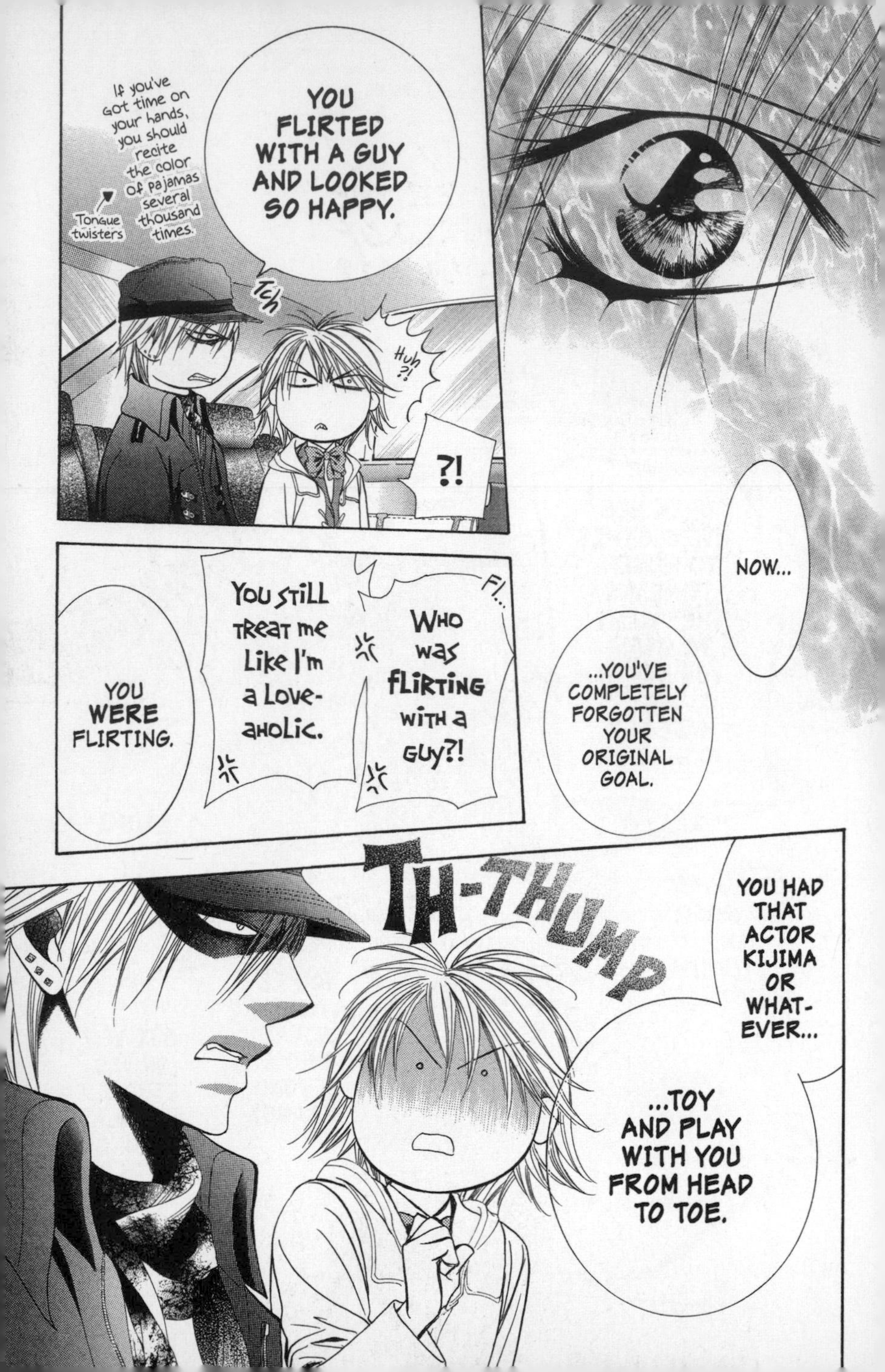
NOW...
...YOU'VE COMPLETELY FORGOTTEN YOUR ORIGINAL GOAL.
YOU FLIRTED WITH A GUY AND LOOKED SO HAPPY.
If you've got time on your hands, you should recite the color of pajamas several thousand times.
Tongue twisters
Tch
Huh?!
?!
Fl...
Who was flirting with a guy?!
You still treat me like I'm a love-aholic.
YOU WERE FLIRTING.
YOU HAD THAT ACTOR KIJIMA OR WHAT-EVER...
...TOY AND PLAY WITH YOU FROM HEAD TO TOE.
TH-THUMP

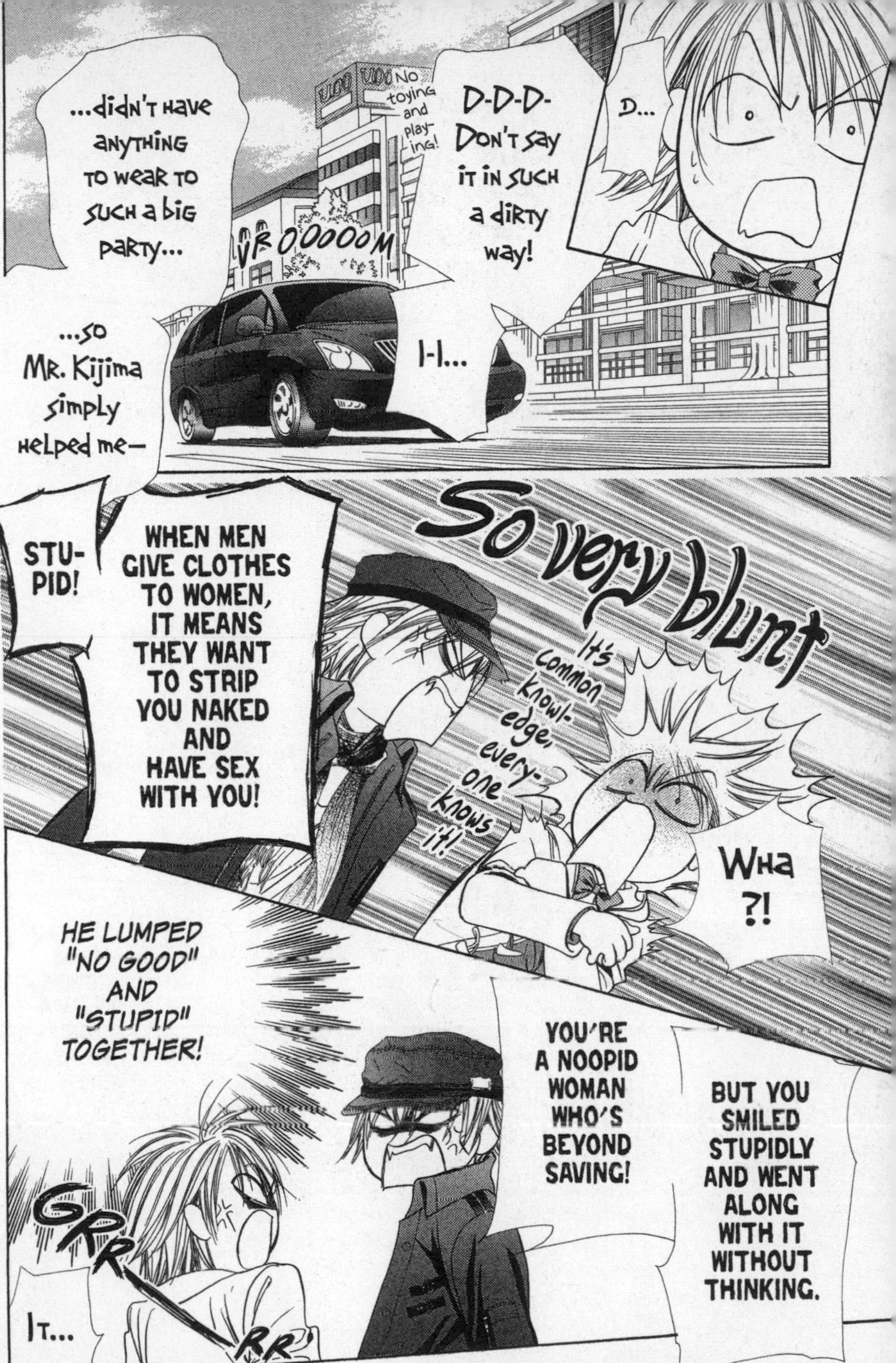
D...
D-D-D- Don't say it in such a dirty way!
No toying and playing!
I-I...
...didn't have anything to wear to such a big party...
VROOOOOM
...so Mr. Kijima simply helped me—
So very blunt
Wha ?!
It's common knowl-edge, every-one knows it!
WHEN MEN GIVE CLOTHES TO WOMEN, IT MEANS THEY WANT TO STRIP YOU NAKED AND HAVE SEX WITH YOU!
STU-PID!
BUT YOU SMILED STUPIDLY AND WENT ALONG WITH IT WITHOUT THINKING.
YOU'RE A NOOPID WOMAN WHO'S BEYOND SAVING!
HE LUMPED "NO GOOD" AND "STUPID" TOGETHER!
GRRRR
IT...

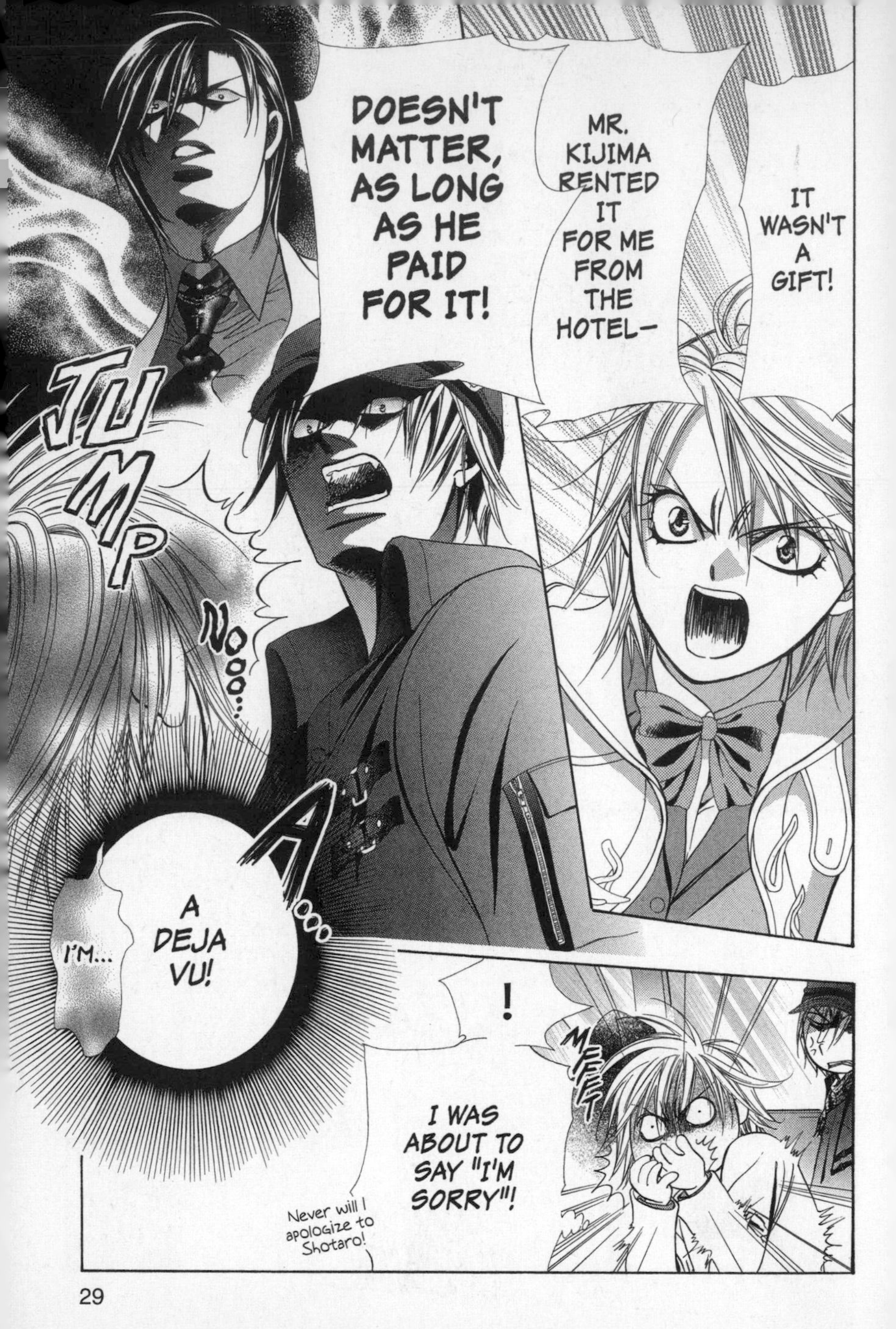
IT WASN'T A GIFT!
MR. KIJIMA RENTED IT FOR ME FROM THE HOTEL—
DOESN'T MATTER, AS LONG AS HE PAID FOR IT!
JUMP
NOOO...
AOOO
A DEJA VU!
I'M...
!
MFFT
I WAS ABOUT TO SAY "I'M SORRY"!
Never will I apologize to Shotaro!

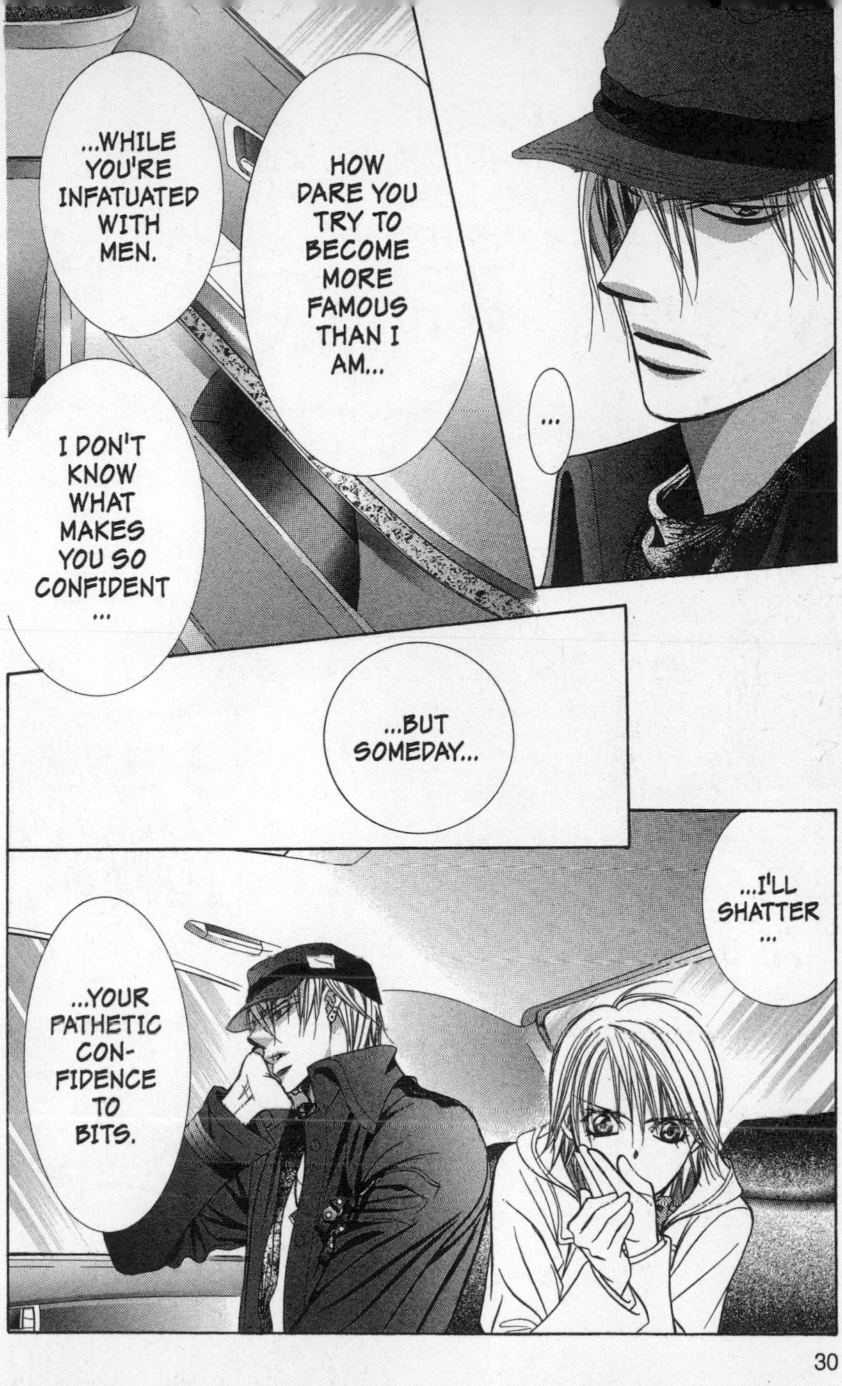
...
HOW DARE YOU TRY TO BECOME MORE FAMOUS THAN I AM...
...WHILE YOU'RE INFATUATED WITH MEN.
I DON'T KNOW WHAT MAKES YOU SO CONFIDENT...
...BUT SOMEDAY...
...I'LL SHATTER...
...YOUR PATHETIC CON-FIDENCE TO BITS.

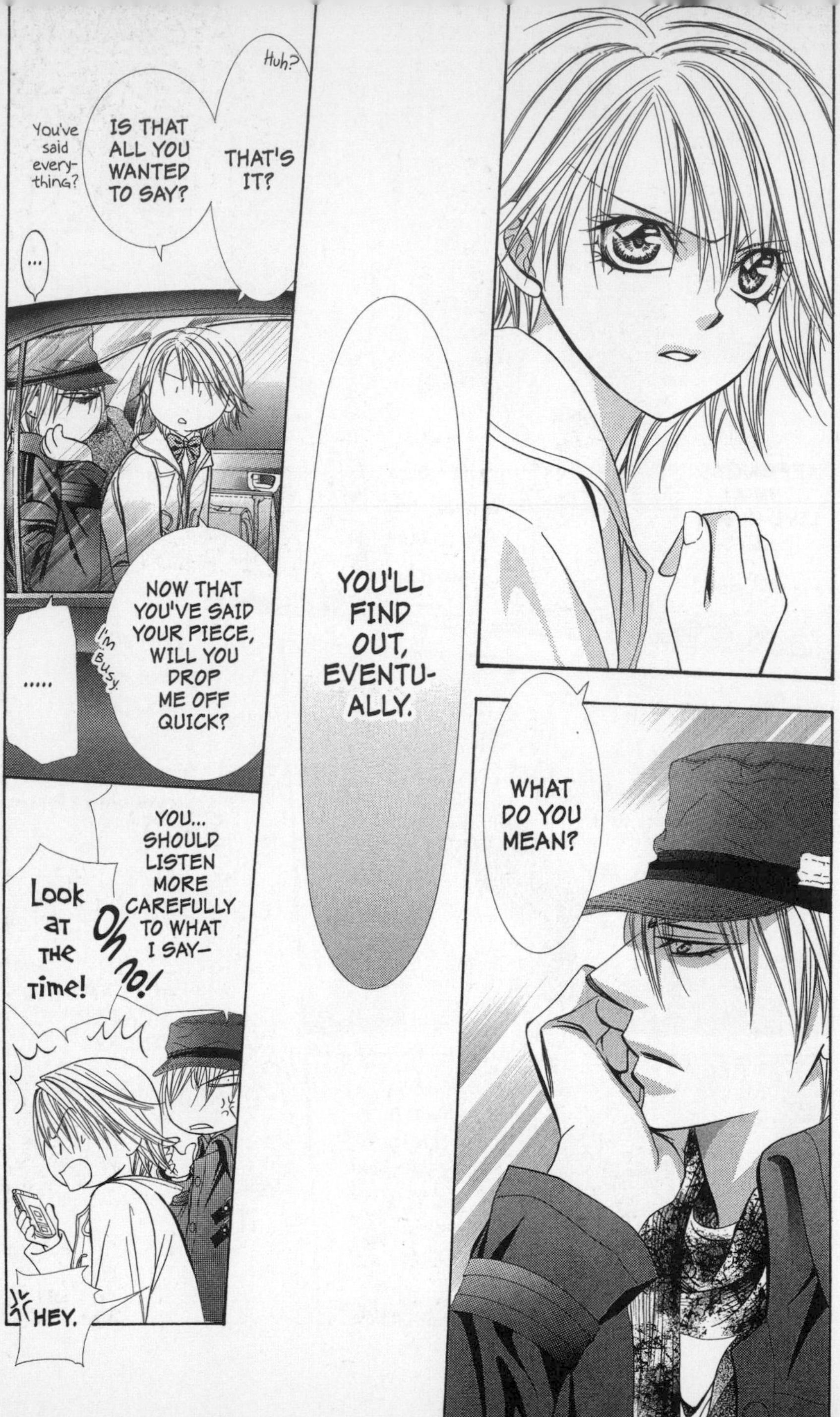

WHAT DO YOU MEAN?
YOU'LL FIND OUT, EVENTUALLY.
Huh?
THAT'S IT?
IS THAT ALL YOU WANTED TO SAY?
You've said every-thing?
...
NOW THAT YOU'VE SAID YOUR PIECE, WILL YOU DROP ME OFF QUICK?
I'm busy.
.....
YOU... SHOULD LISTEN MORE CAREFULLY TO WHAT I SAY—
Oh no!
Look at the time!
HEY.

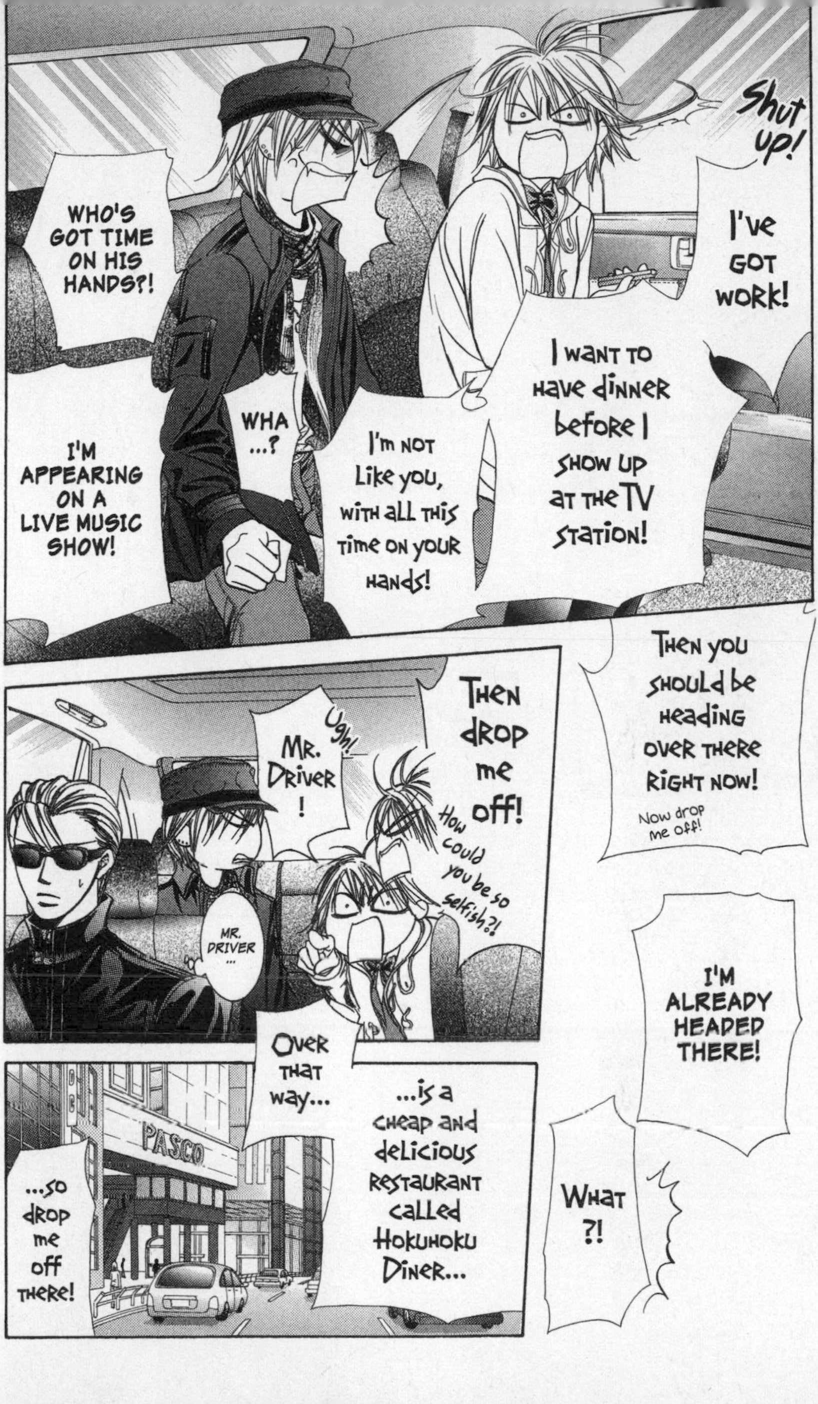
Shut up!
I've got work!
I want to have dinner before I show up at the TV station!
I'm not like you, with all this time on your hands!
Wha...?
Who's got time on his hands?!
I'm appearing on a live music show!
Then you should be heading over there right now!
Now drop me off!
I'm already headed there!
What ?!
Then drop me off!
Ugh!
Mr. Driver!
How could you be so selfish?!
Mr. Driver...
Over that way...
...is a cheap and delicious restaurant called Hokuhoku Diner...
PASCO
...so drop me off there!

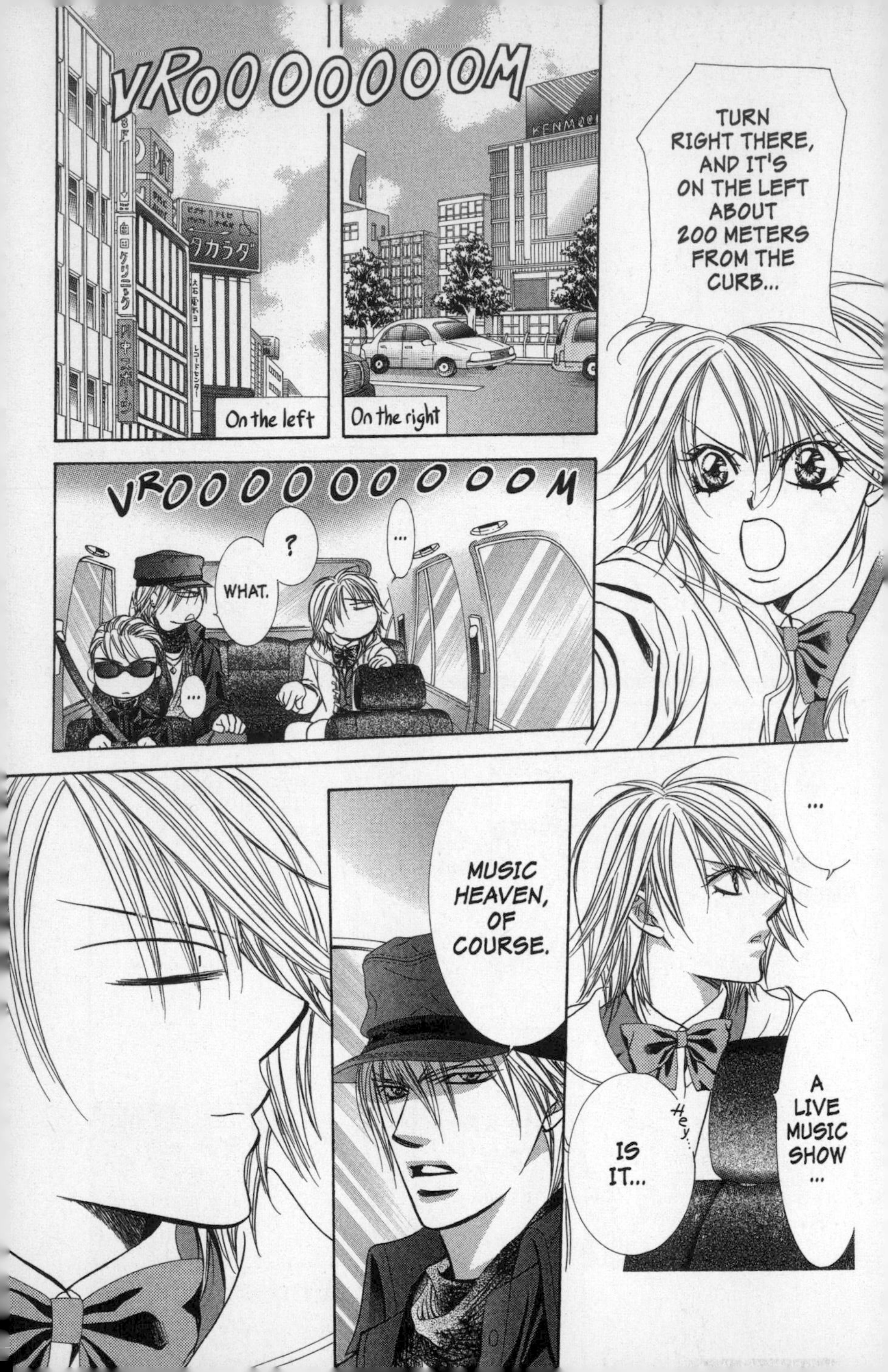
TURN RIGHT THERE, AND IT'S ON THE LEFT ABOUT 200 METERS FROM THE CURB...
VROOOOOOOM
On the right
On the left
VROOOOOOOOOOM
?
...
WHAT.
...
...
A LIVE MUSIC SHOW ...
Hey...
IS IT...
MUSIC HEAVEN, OF COURSE.

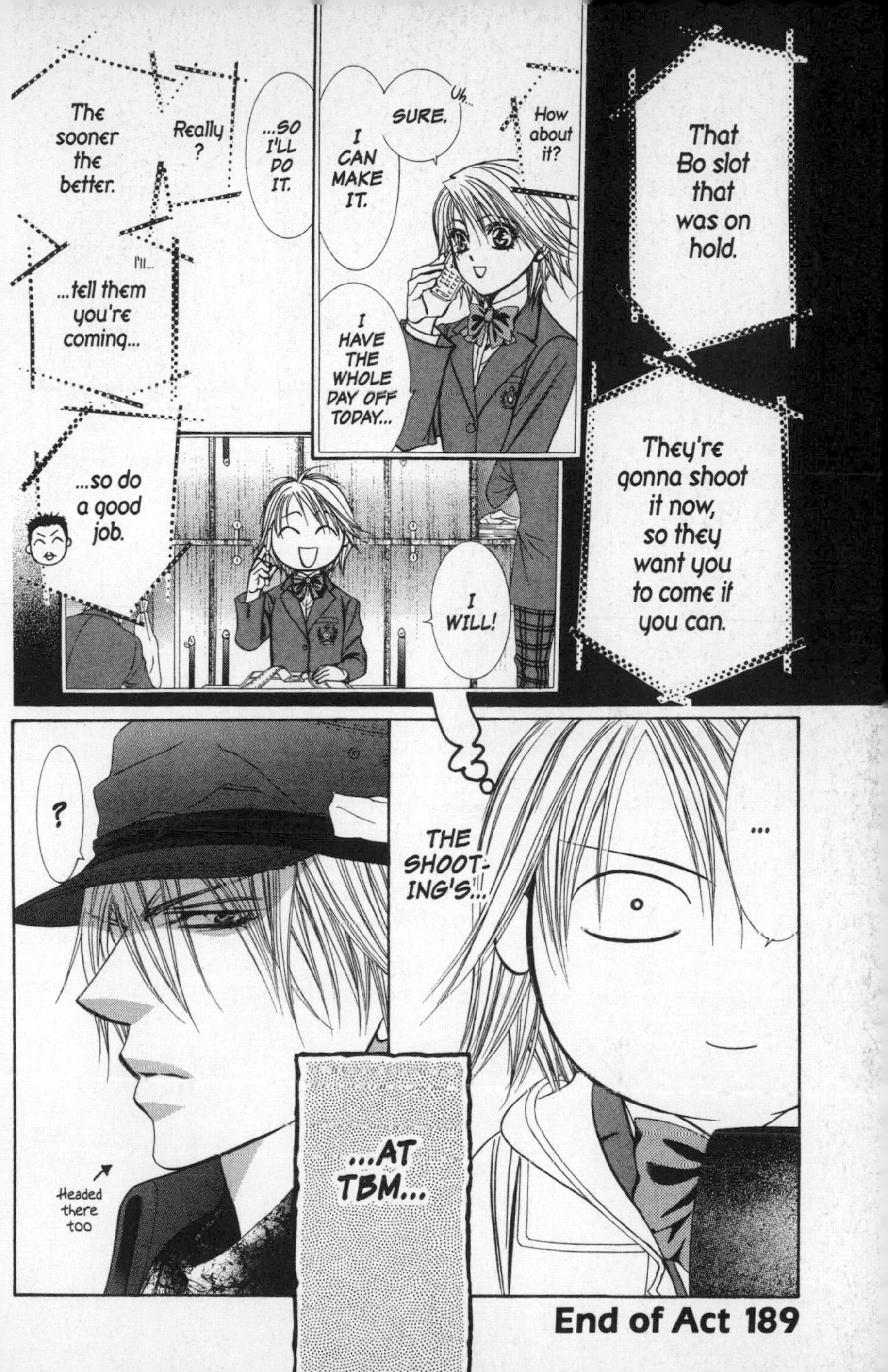
That Bo slot that was on hold.
They're gonna shoot it now, so they want you to come if you can.
How about it?
Uh...
SURE.
I CAN MAKE IT.
I HAVE THE WHOLE DAY OFF TODAY...
...SO I'LL DO IT.
Really?
The sooner the better.
I'll...
...tell them you're coming...
I WILL!
...so do a good job.
...
THE SHOOT-ING'S...
...AT TBM...
?
Headed there too

End of Act 189

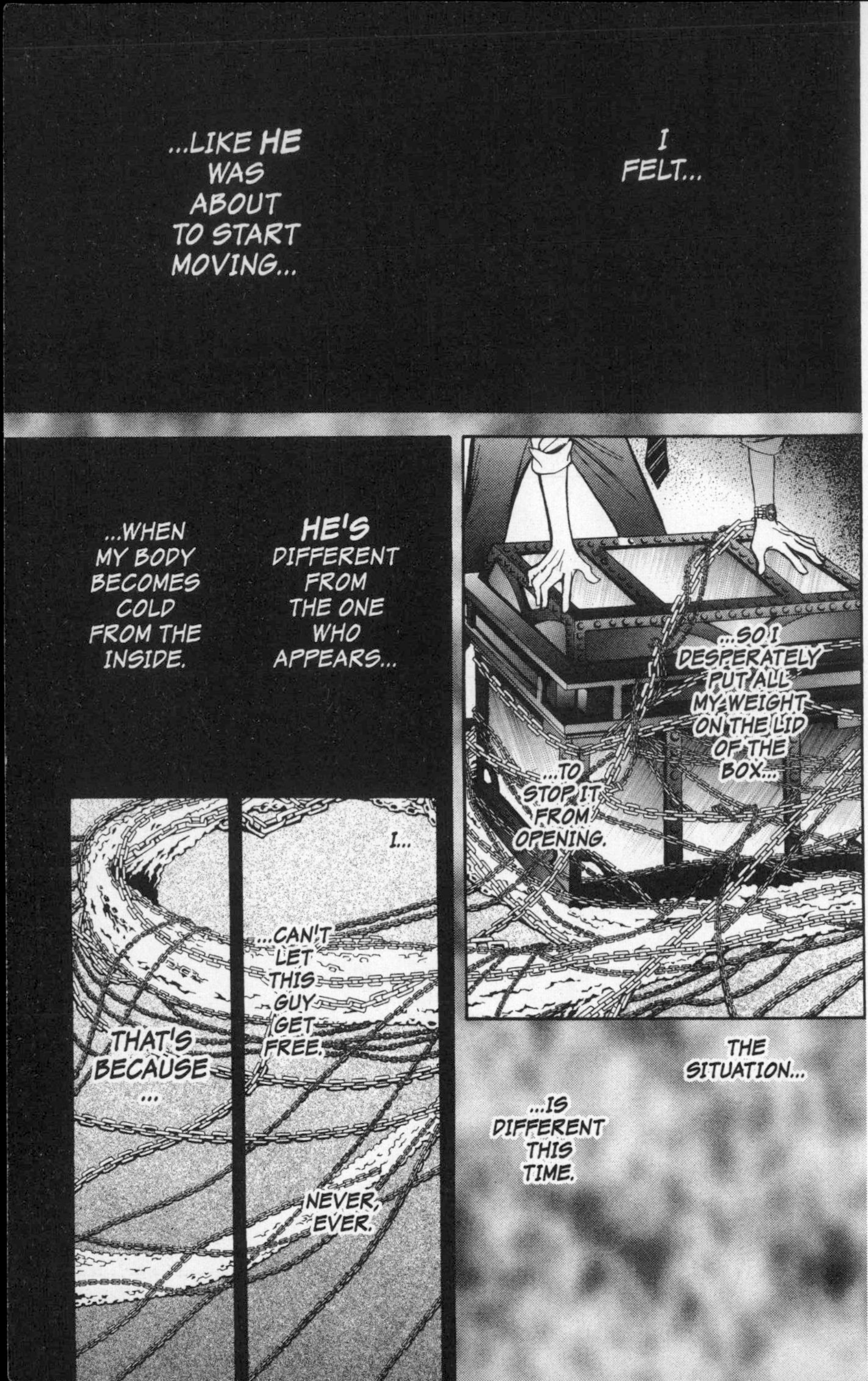
I FELT...
...LIKE HE WAS ABOUT TO START MOVING...
...SO I DESPERATELY PUT ALL MY WEIGHT ON THE LID OF THE BOX...
...TO STOP IT FROM OPENING.
HE'S DIFFERENT FROM THE ONE WHO APPEARS...
...WHEN MY BODY BECOMES COLD FROM THE INSIDE.
THE SITUATION...
...IS DIFFERENT THIS TIME.
I...
...CAN'T LET THIS GUY GET FREE.
NEVER, EVER.
THAT'S BECAUSE...

...SOMETHING TERRIFYING...
...COULD HAPPEN...
...IF HE GAINS HIS FREEDOM.
THIS TIME...
...HE'LL BARE HIS FANGS...

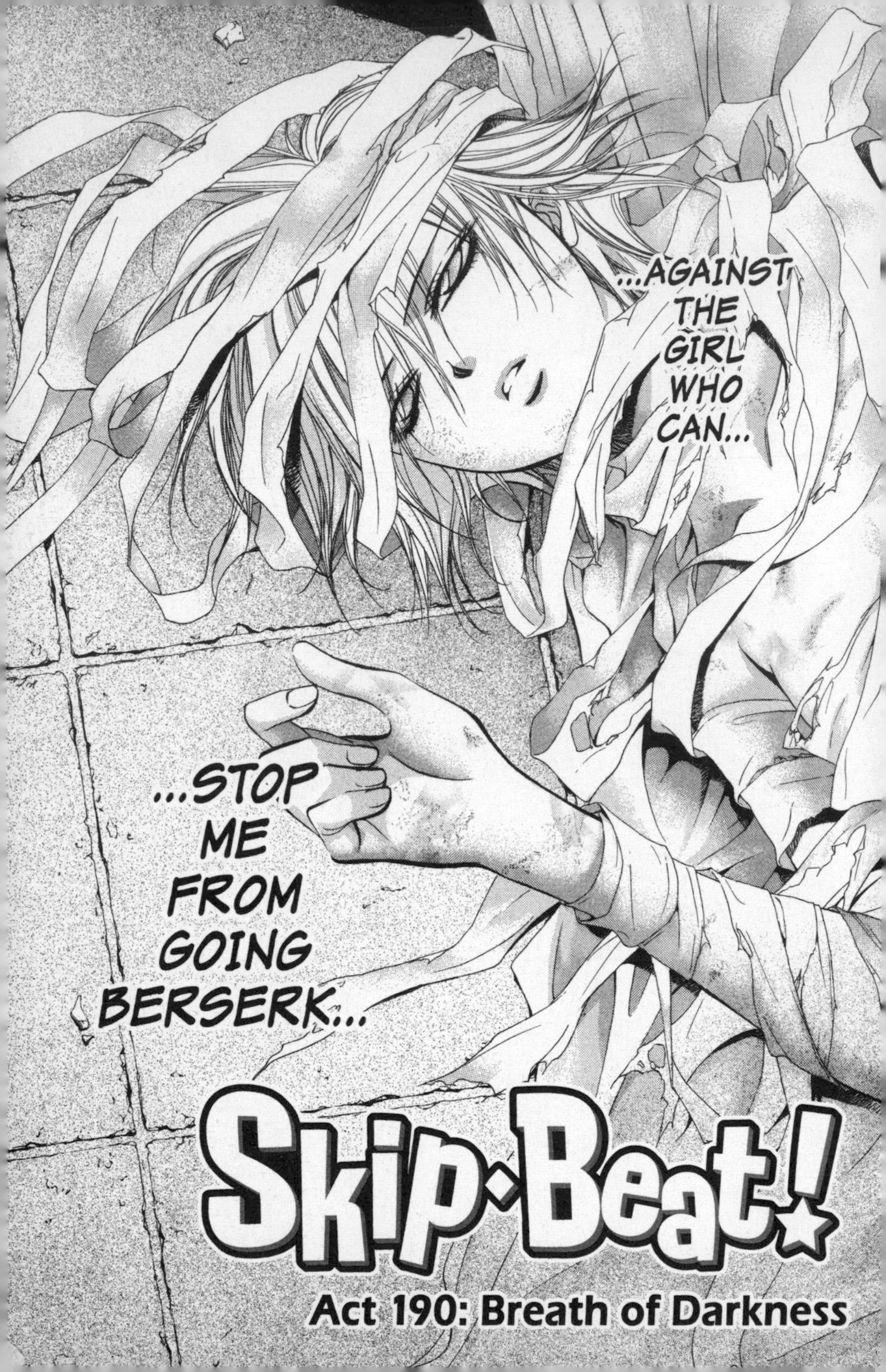
...AGAINST THE GIRL WHO CAN...
...STOP ME FROM GOING BERSERK...
Skip·Beat!
Act 190: Breath of Darkness

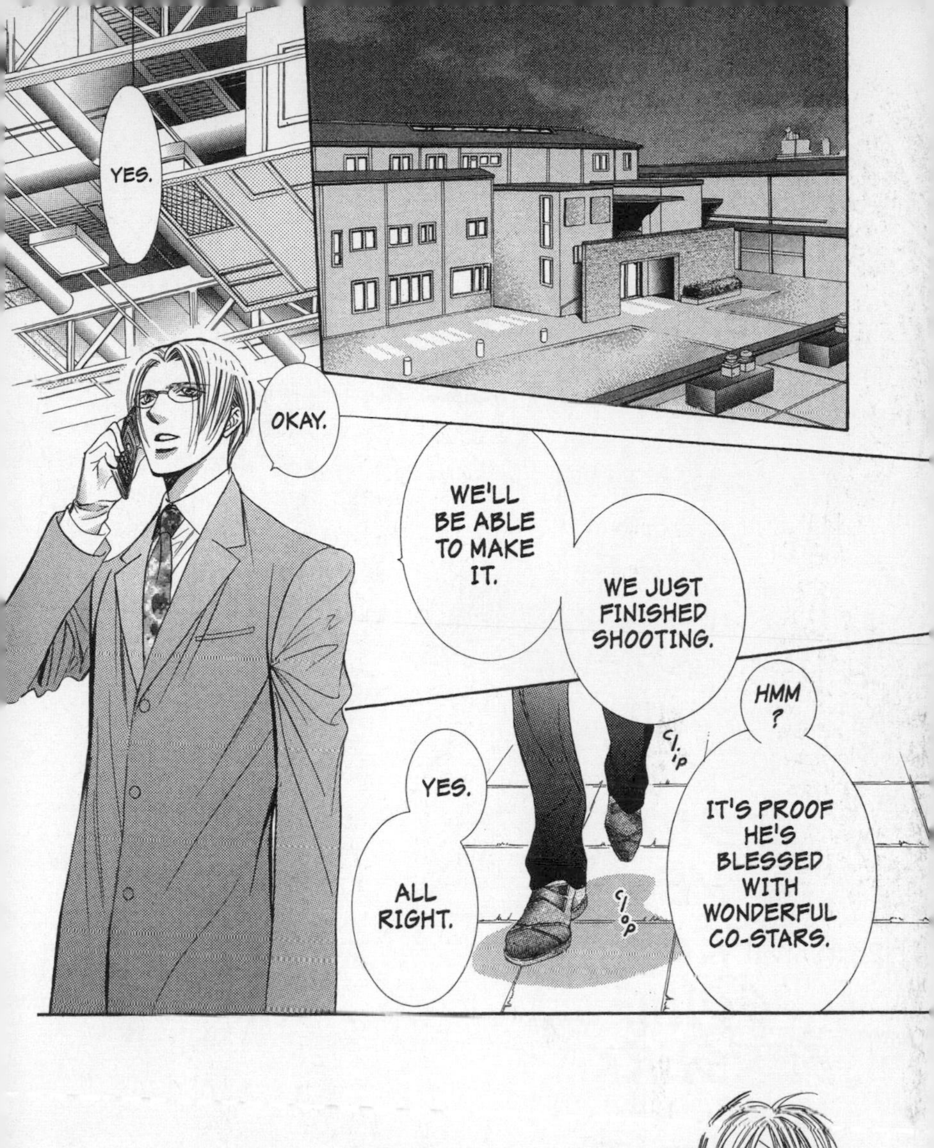
YES.
OKAY.
WE'LL BE ABLE TO MAKE IT.
WE JUST FINISHED SHOOTING.
HMM?
clip
IT'S PROOF HE'S BLESSED WITH WONDERFUL CO-STARS.
clop
YES.
ALL RIGHT.

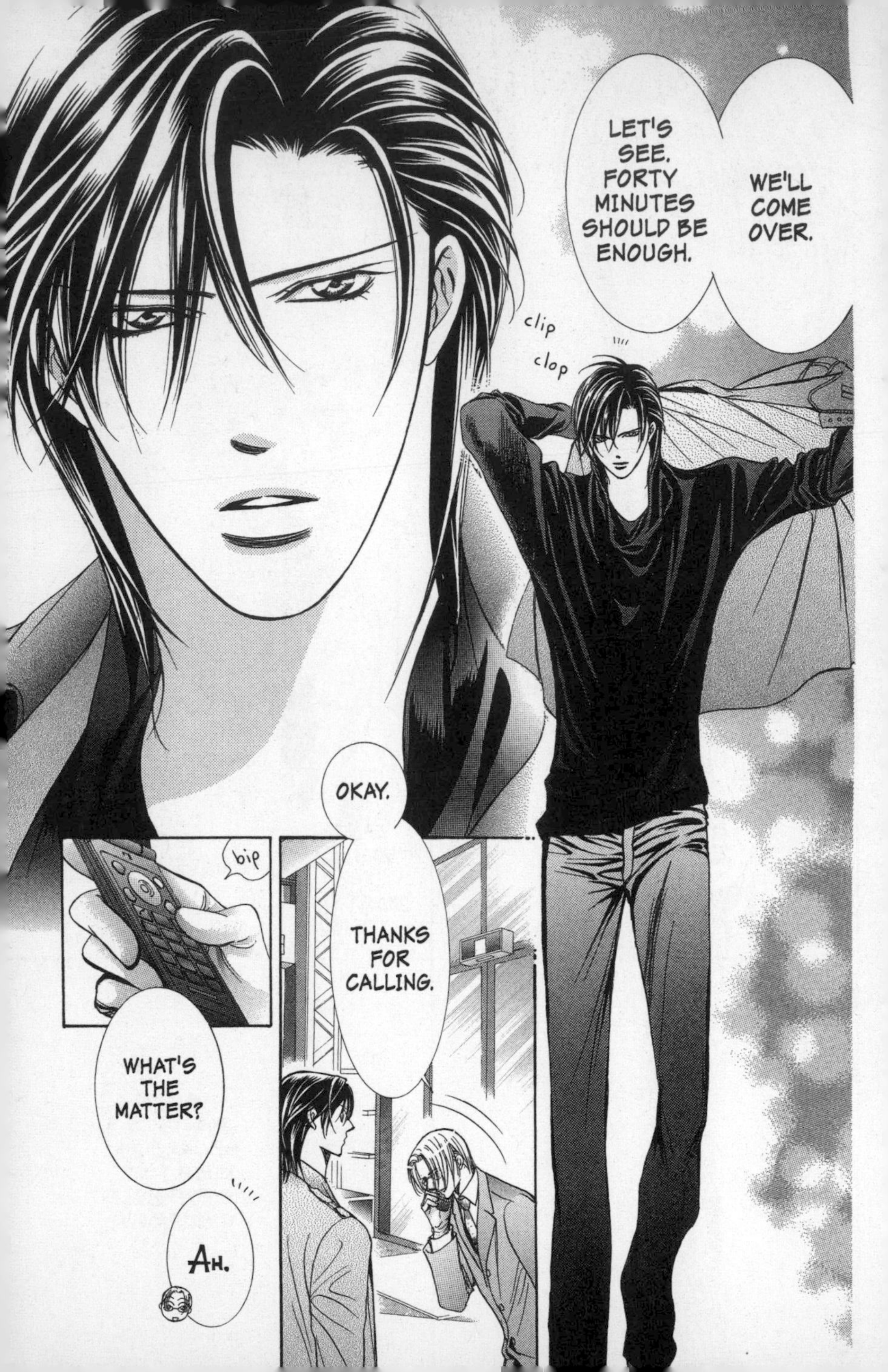

WE'LL COME OVER.
LET'S SEE. FORTY MINUTES SHOULD BE ENOUGH.
clip
clop
OKAY.
THANKS FOR CALLING.
bip
WHAT'S THE MATTER?
AH.

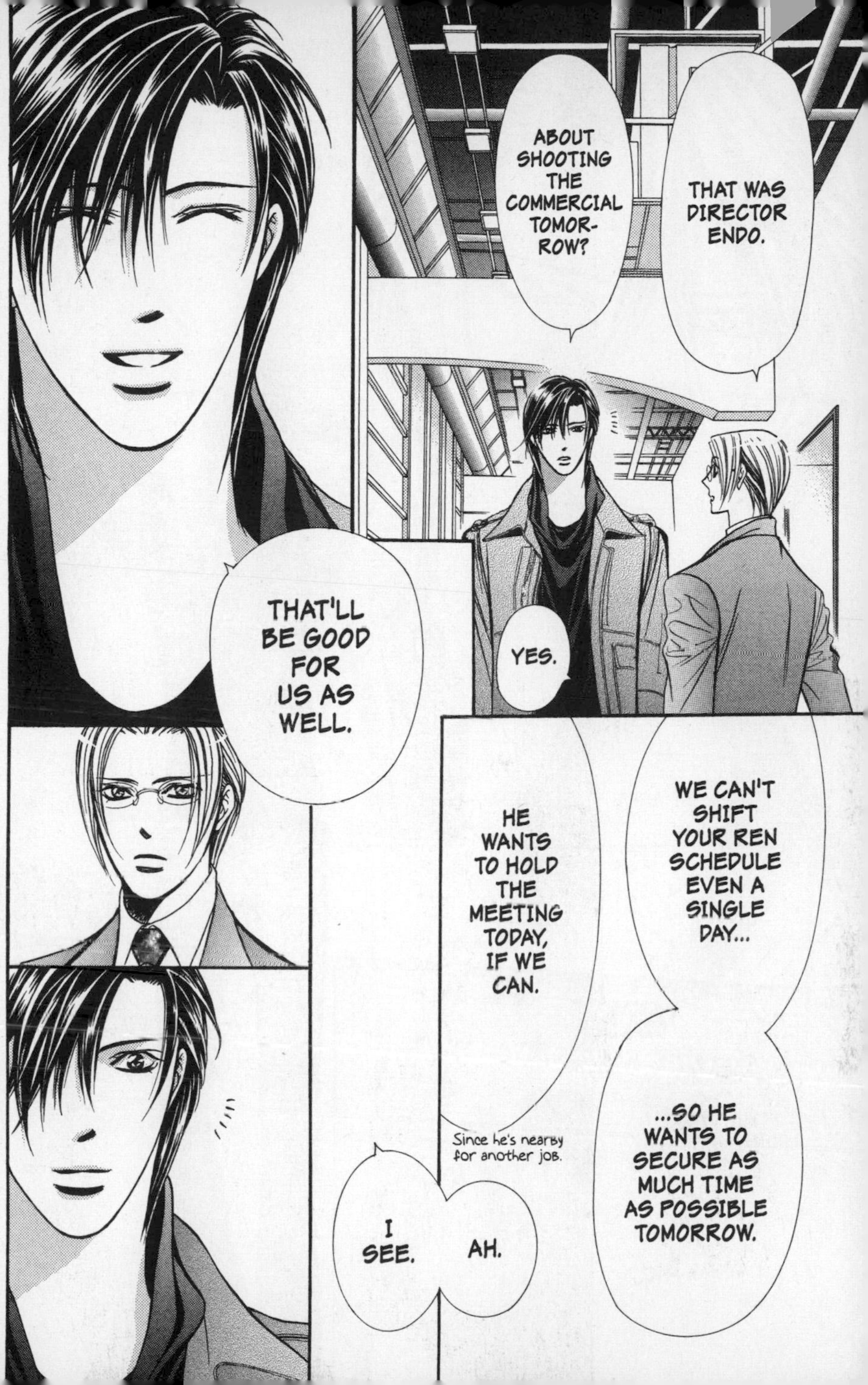
THAT WAS DIRECTOR ENDO.
ABOUT SHOOTING THE COMMERCIAL TOMOR-ROW?
YES.
WE CAN'T SHIFT YOUR REN SCHEDULE EVEN A SINGLE DAY...
...SO HE WANTS TO SECURE AS MUCH TIME AS POSSIBLE TOMORROW.
HE WANTS TO HOLD THE MEETING TODAY, IF WE CAN.
Since he's nearby for another job.
AH.
I SEE.
THAT'LL BE GOOD FOR US AS WELL.

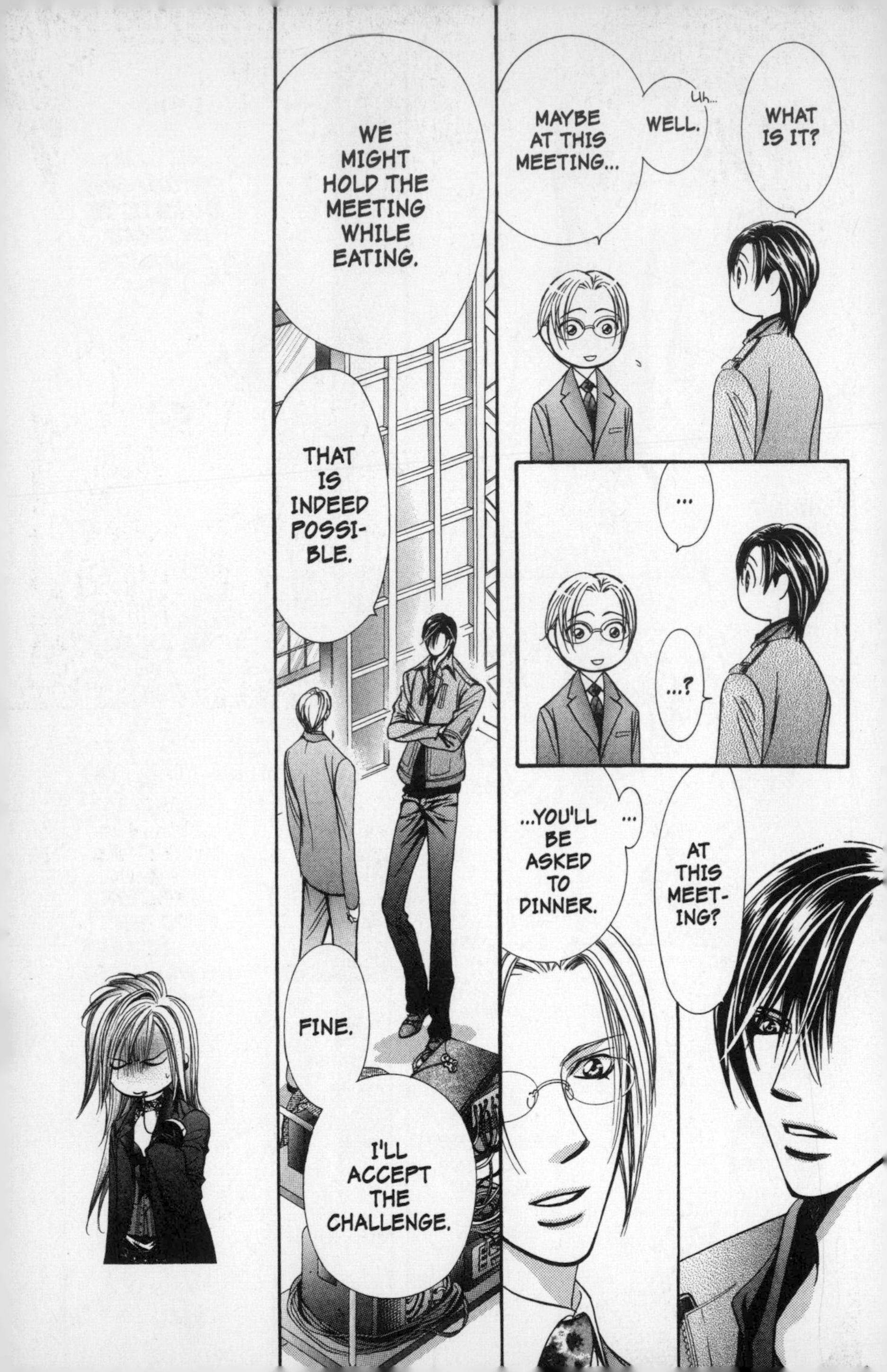
WHAT IS IT?
Uh...
WELL.
MAYBE AT THIS MEETING...
...
...?
AT THIS MEET-ING?
...
...YOU'LL BE ASKED TO DINNER.
WE MIGHT HOLD THE MEETING WHILE EATING.
THAT IS INDEED POSSI-BLE.
FINE.
I'LL ACCEPT THE CHALLENGE.

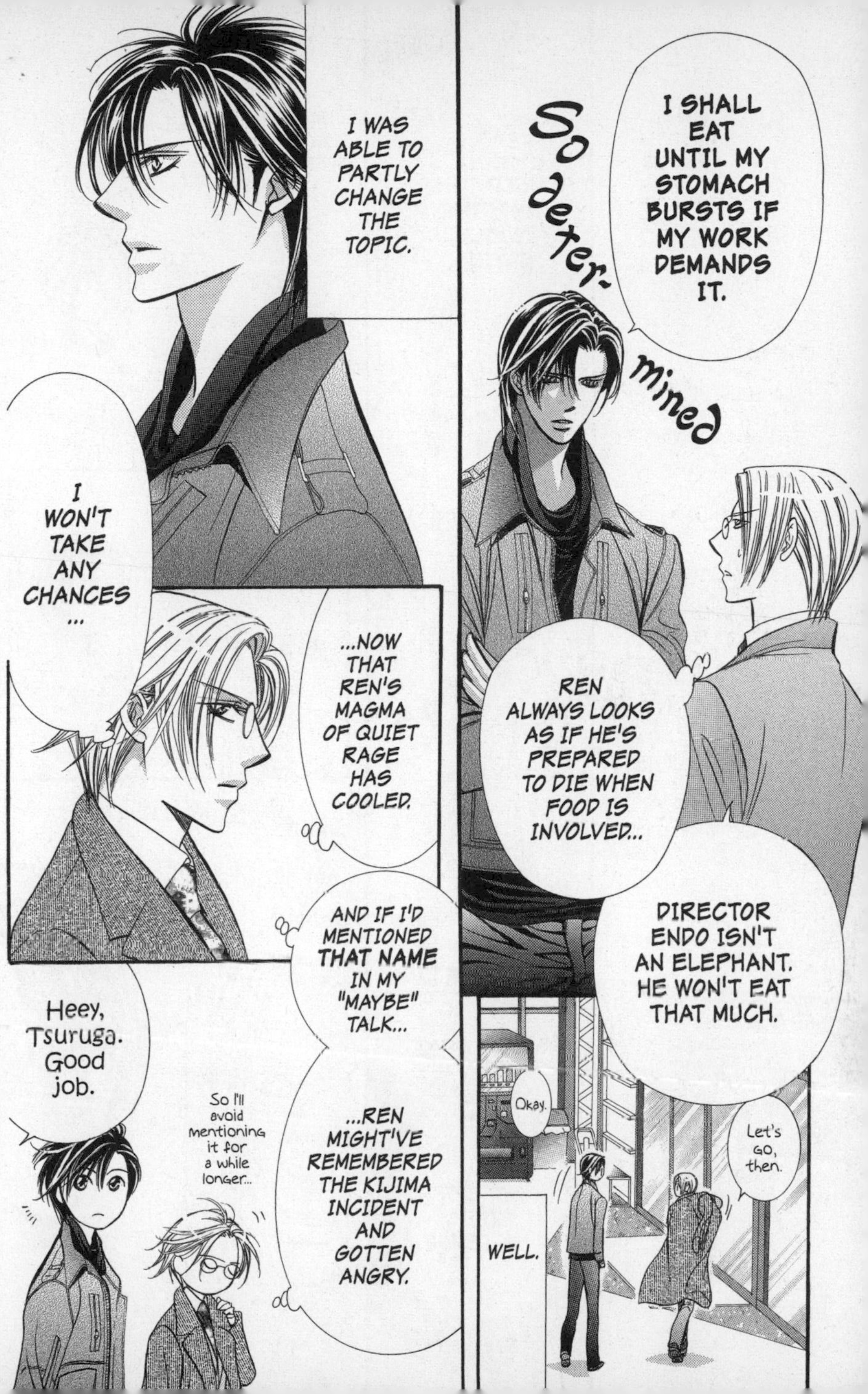
I SHALL EAT UNTIL MY STOMACH BURSTS IF MY WORK DEMANDS IT.
So deter-mined
REN ALWAYS LOOKS AS IF HE'S PREPARED TO DIE WHEN FOOD IS INVOLVED...
DIRECTOR ENDO ISN'T AN ELEPHANT. HE WON'T EAT THAT MUCH.
Let's go, then.
Okay.
WELL.
I WAS ABLE TO PARTLY CHANGE THE TOPIC.
I WON'T TAKE ANY CHANCES...
...NOW THAT REN'S MAGMA OF QUIET RAGE HAS COOLED.
AND IF I'D MENTIONED THAT NAME IN MY "MAYBE" TALK...
...REN MIGHT'VE REMEMBERED THE KIJIMA INCIDENT AND GOTTEN ANGRY.
Heey, Tsuruga. Good job.
So I'll avoid mentioning it for a while longer...

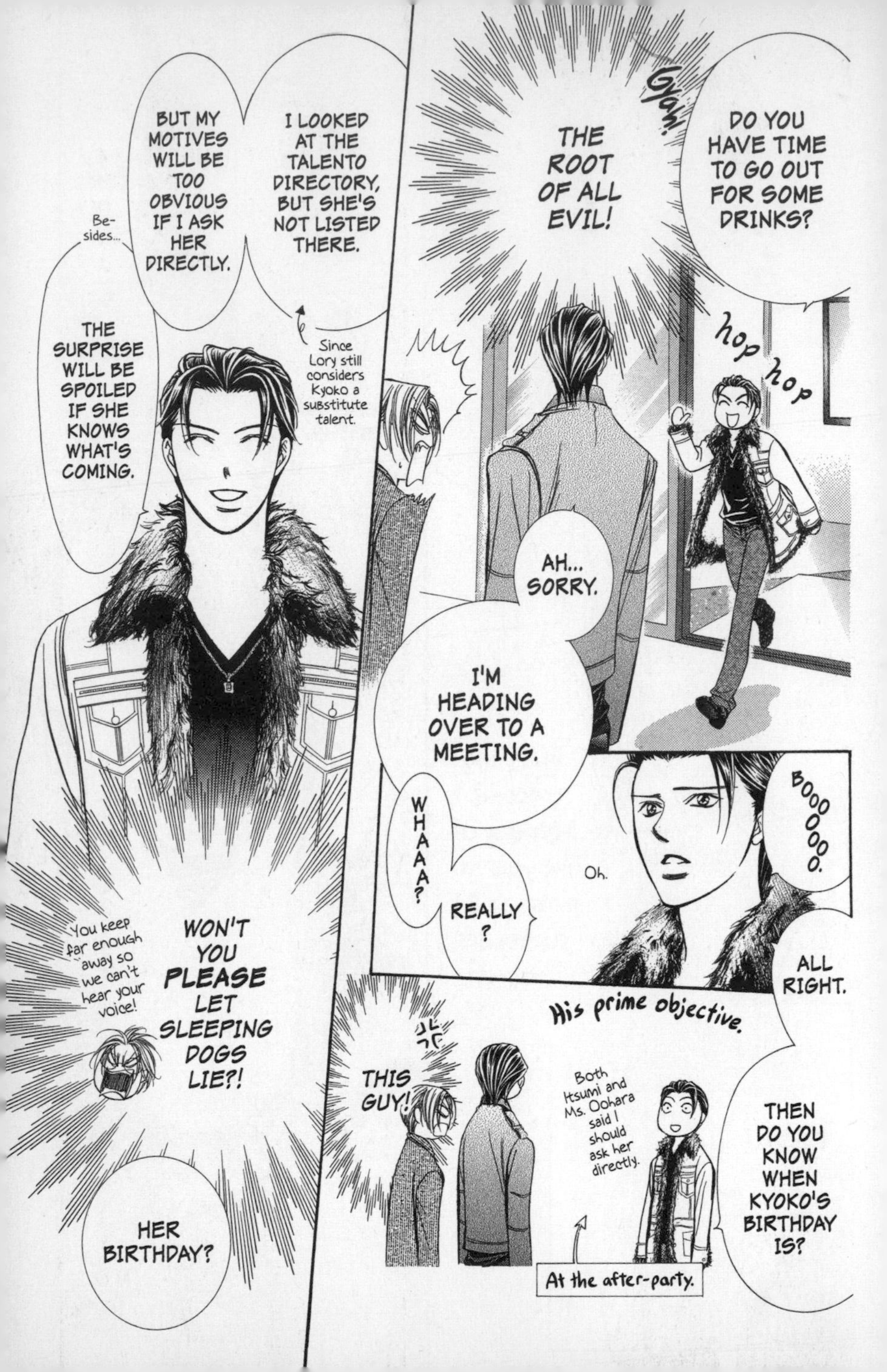
DO YOU HAVE TIME TO GO OUT FOR SOME DRINKS?
Gyah!
THE ROOT OF ALL EVIL!
hop hop
AH... SORRY.
I'M HEADING OVER TO A MEETING.
WHAAA?
REALLY?
BOOOOOOO.
Oh.
ALL RIGHT.
His prime objective.
THEN DO YOU KNOW WHEN KYOKO'S BIRTHDAY IS?
At the after-party.
Both Itsumi and Ms. Oohara said I should ask her directly.
THIS GUY!
I LOOKED AT THE TALENTO DIRECTORY, BUT SHE'S NOT LISTED THERE.
Since Lory still considers Kyoko a substitute talent.
BUT MY MOTIVES WILL BE TOO OBVIOUS IF I ASK HER DIRECTLY.
Be-sides...
THE SURPRISE WILL BE SPOILED IF SHE KNOWS WHAT'S COMING.
WON'T YOU PLEASE LET SLEEPING DOGS LIE?!
You keep far enough away so we can't hear your voice!
HER BIRTHDAY?

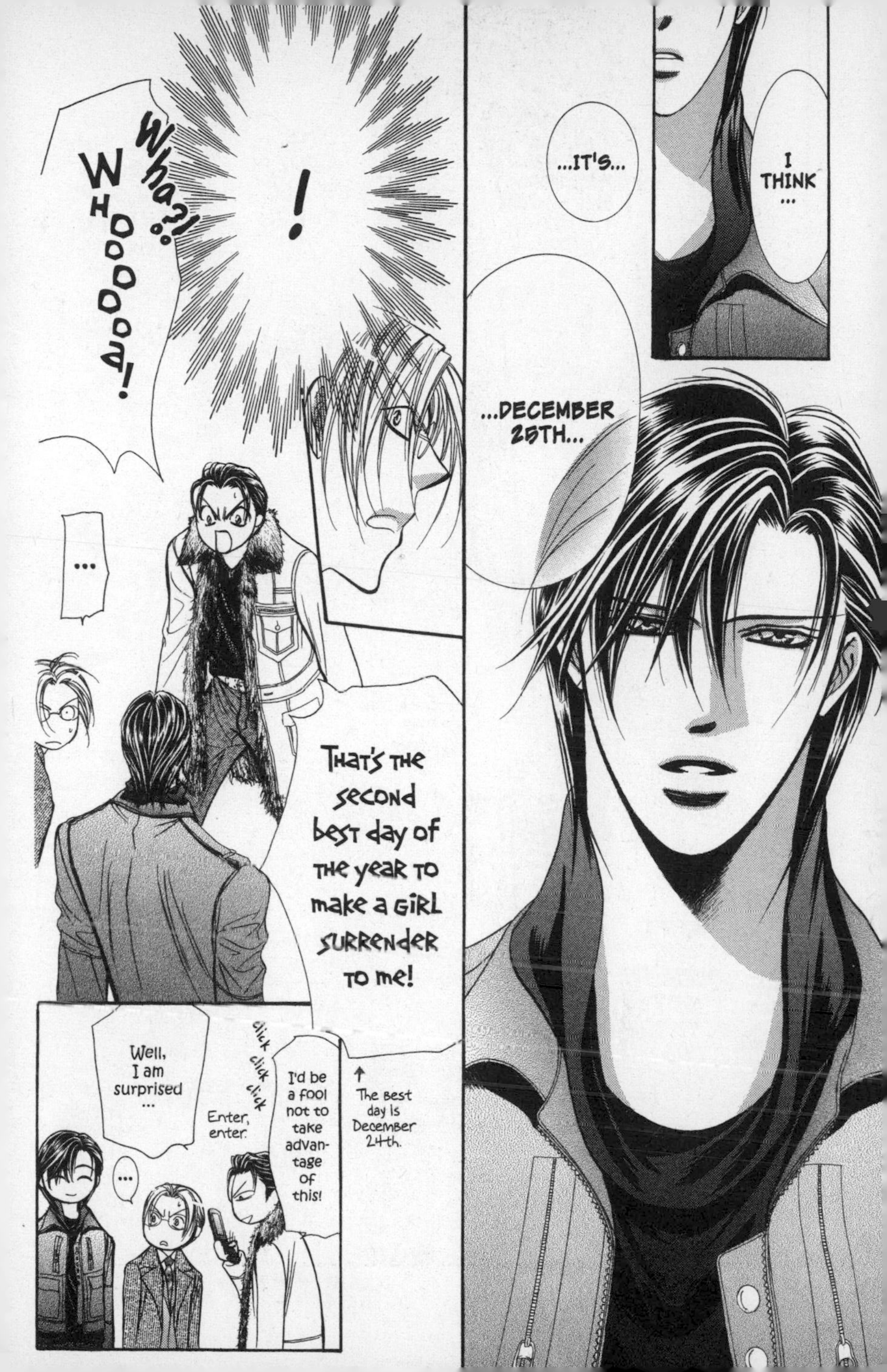
I THINK...
...IT'S...
...DECEMBER 25TH...
!
Wha?! WHOOOOOa!
That's the second best day of the year to make a girl surrender to me!
...
↑ The best day is December 24th.
I'd be a fool not to take advantage of this!
click click click
Enter, enter.
Well, I am surprised...
...

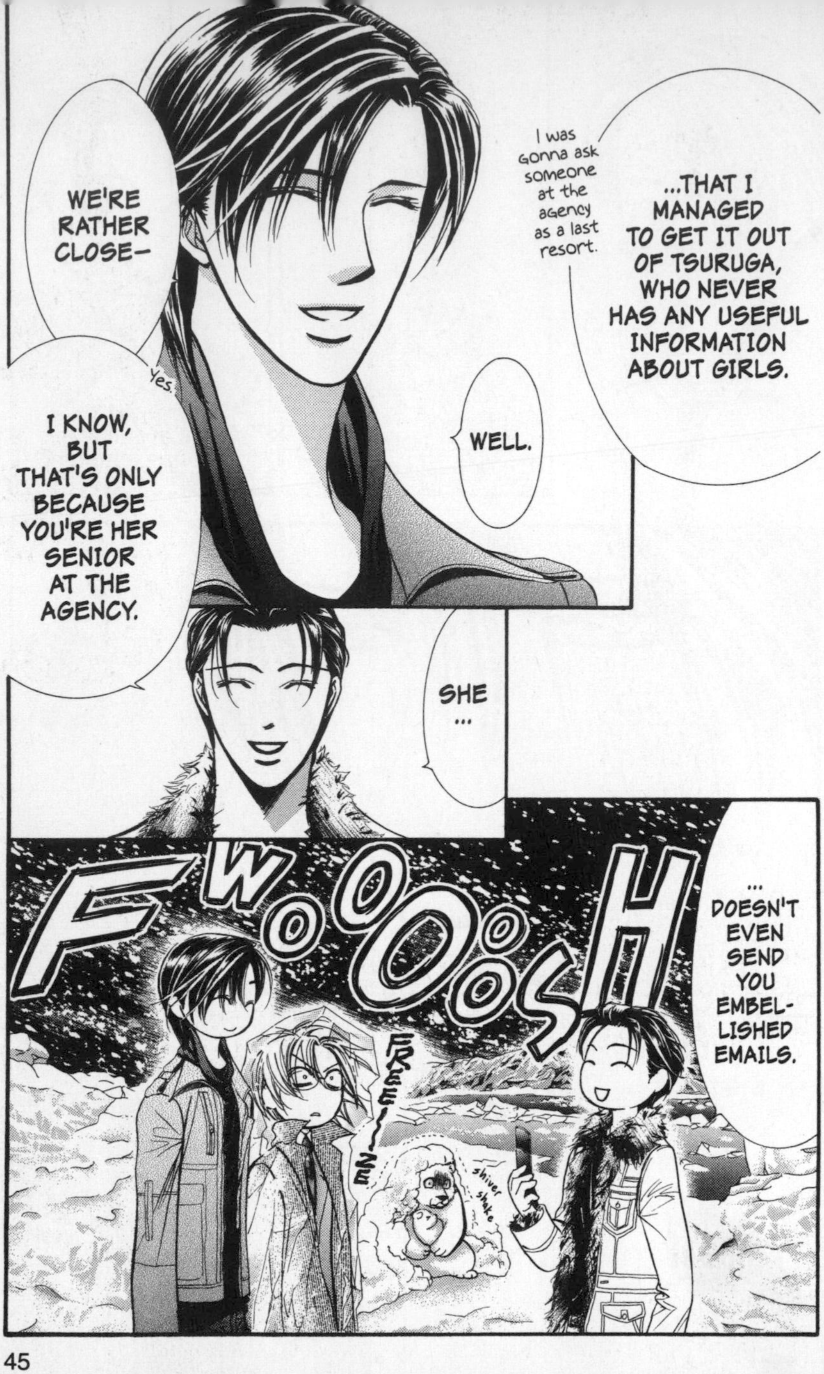

I was gonna ask someone at the agency as a last resort.
...THAT I MANAGED TO GET IT OUT OF TSURUGA, WHO NEVER HAS ANY USEFUL INFORMATION ABOUT GIRLS.
WE'RE RATHER CLOSE–
WELL.
Yes.
I KNOW, BUT THAT'S ONLY BECAUSE YOU'RE HER SENIOR AT THE AGENCY.
SHE ...
... DOESN'T EVEN SEND YOU EMBEL-LISHED EMAILS.
FWOOOOOSH
FREEEZE
shiver shake

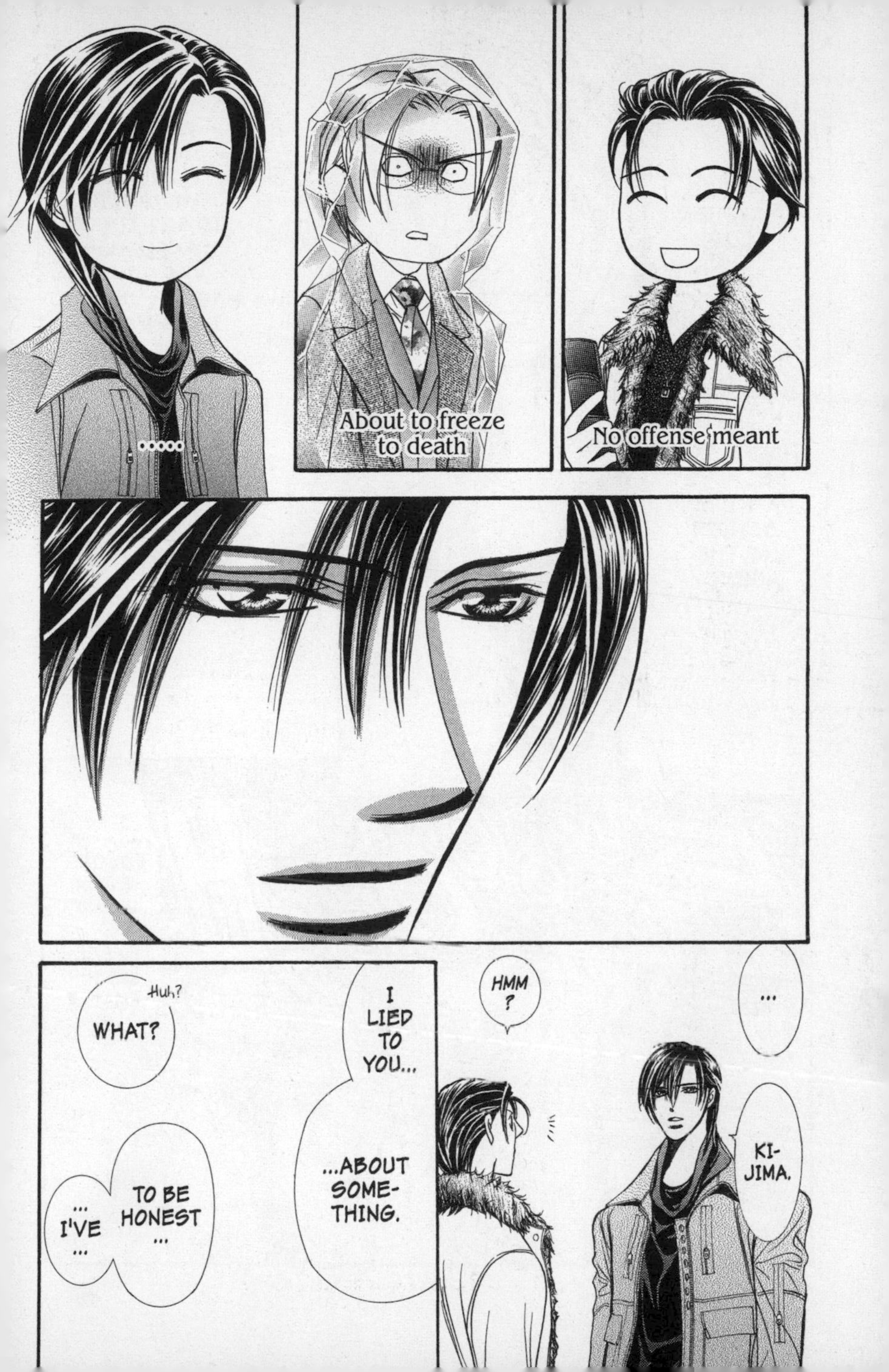
No offense meant
About to freeze to death
.....
...
KI-JIMA.
HMM?
TO BE HONEST ...
... I'VE ...
I LIED TO YOU...
...ABOUT SOMETHING.
Huh?
WHAT?

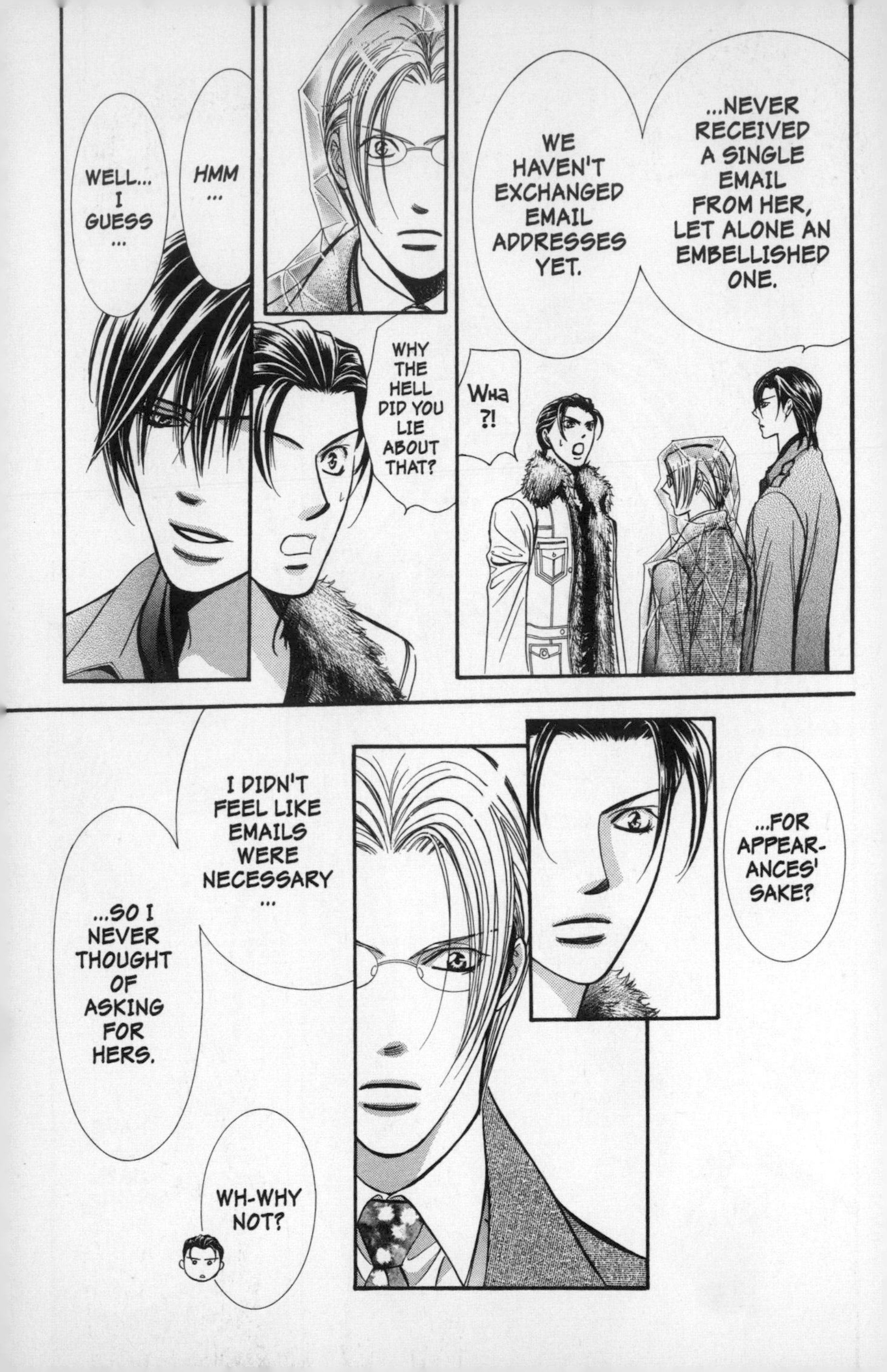
...NEVER RECEIVED A SINGLE EMAIL FROM HER, LET ALONE AN EMBELLISHED ONE.
WE HAVEN'T EXCHANGED EMAIL ADDRESSES YET.
Wha ?!
WHY THE HELL DID YOU LIE ABOUT THAT?
HMM ...
WELL... I GUESS ...
...FOR APPEARANCES' SAKE?
I DIDN'T FEEL LIKE EMAILS WERE NECESSARY ...
...SO I NEVER THOUGHT OF ASKING FOR HERS.
WH-WHY NOT?

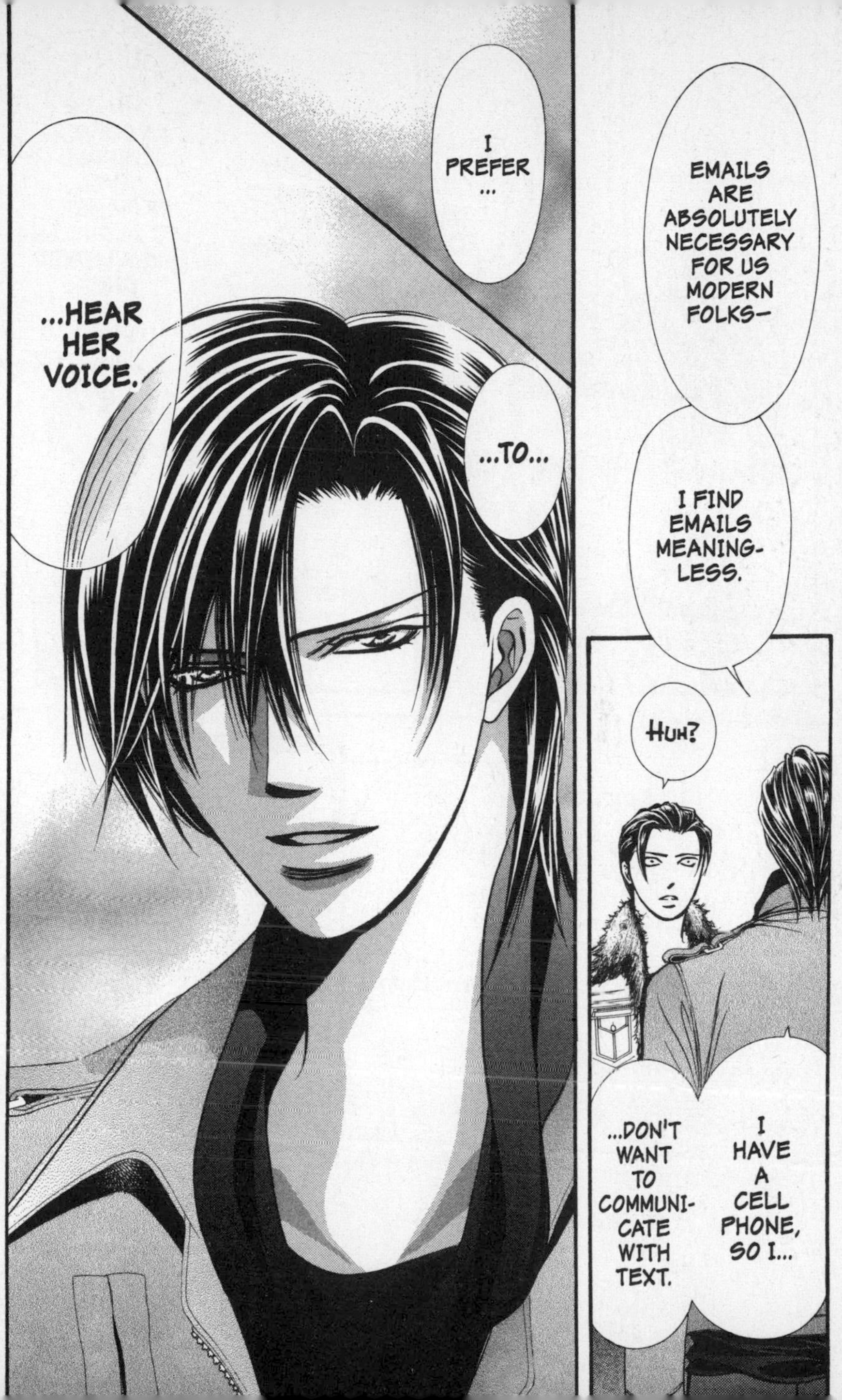
EMAILS ARE ABSOLUTELY NECESSARY FOR US MODERN FOLKS—
I FIND EMAILS MEANING-LESS.
HUH?
I HAVE A CELL PHONE, SO I...
...DON'T WANT TO COMMUNI-CATE WITH TEXT.
I PREFER...
...TO...
...HEAR HER VOICE.

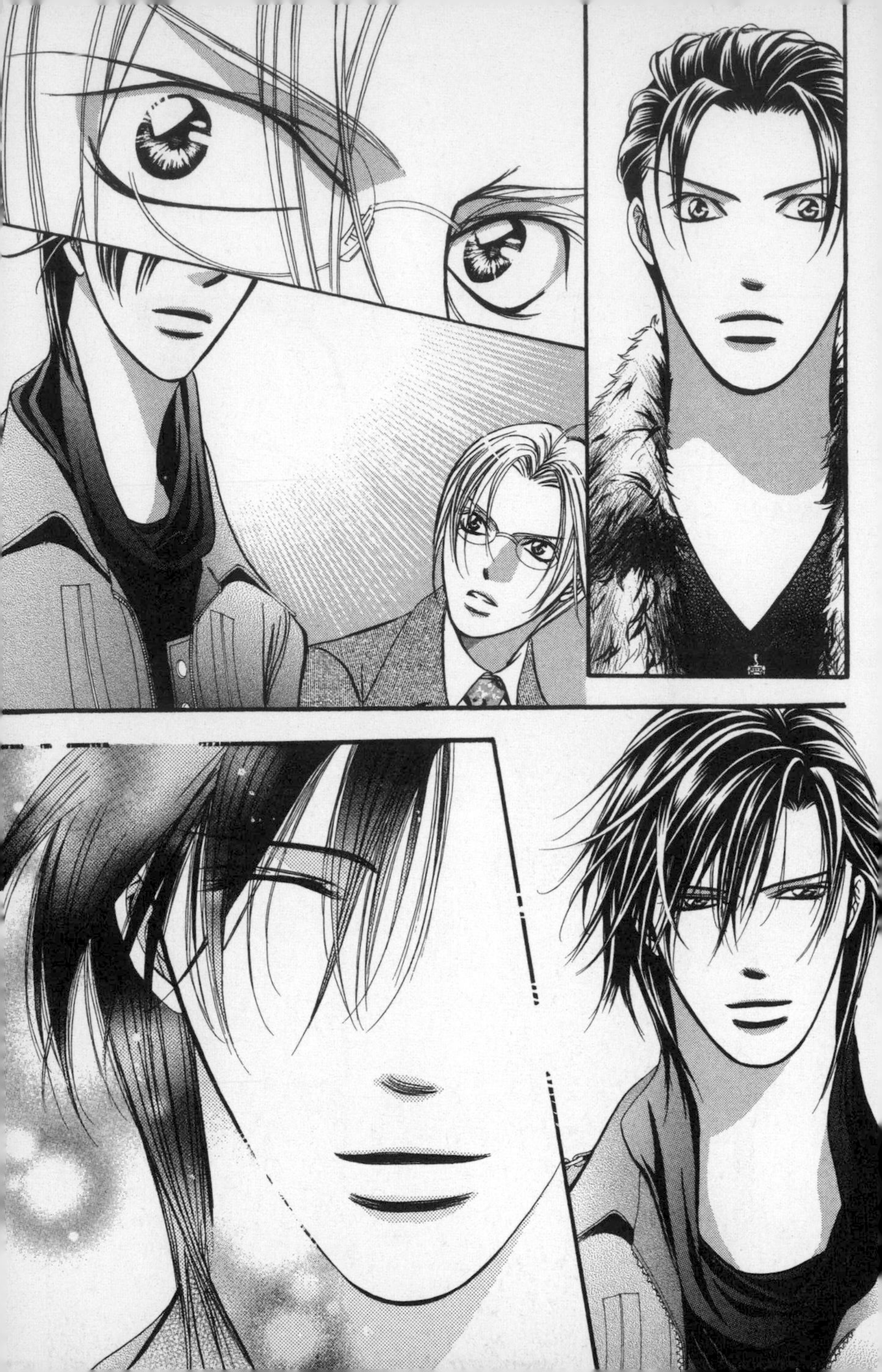

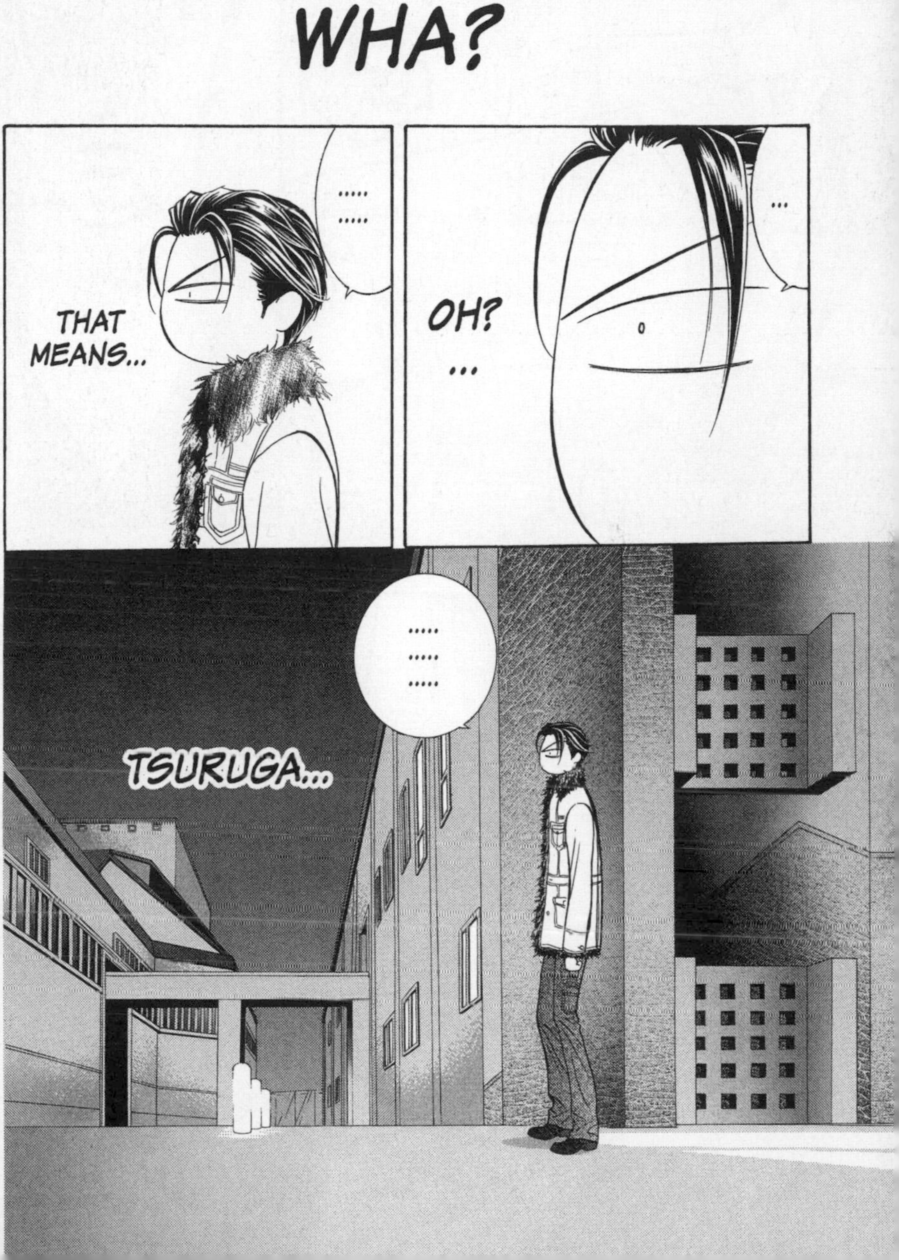
WHA?
...
OH? ...
....
THAT MEANS...
....
TSURUGA...

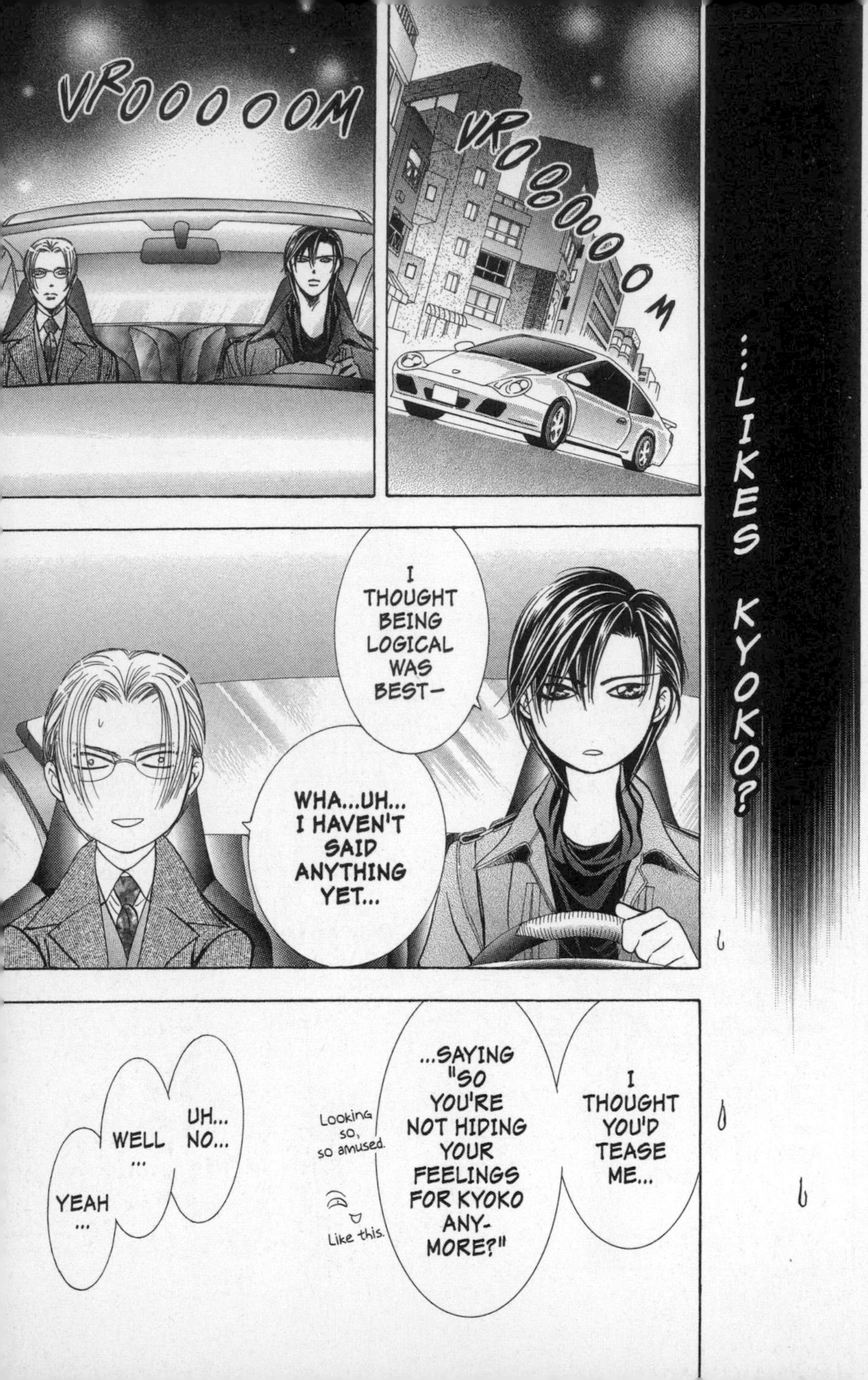
...LIKES KYOKO?
VROOOOOOOOM
VROOOOOM
I THOUGHT BEING LOGICAL WAS BEST–
WHA...UH... I HAVEN'T SAID ANYTHING YET...
I THOUGHT YOU'D TEASE ME...
...SAYING "SO YOU'RE NOT HIDING YOUR FEELINGS FOR KYOKO ANYMORE?"
Looking so, so amused.
Like this.
UH... NO...
WELL...
YEAH...

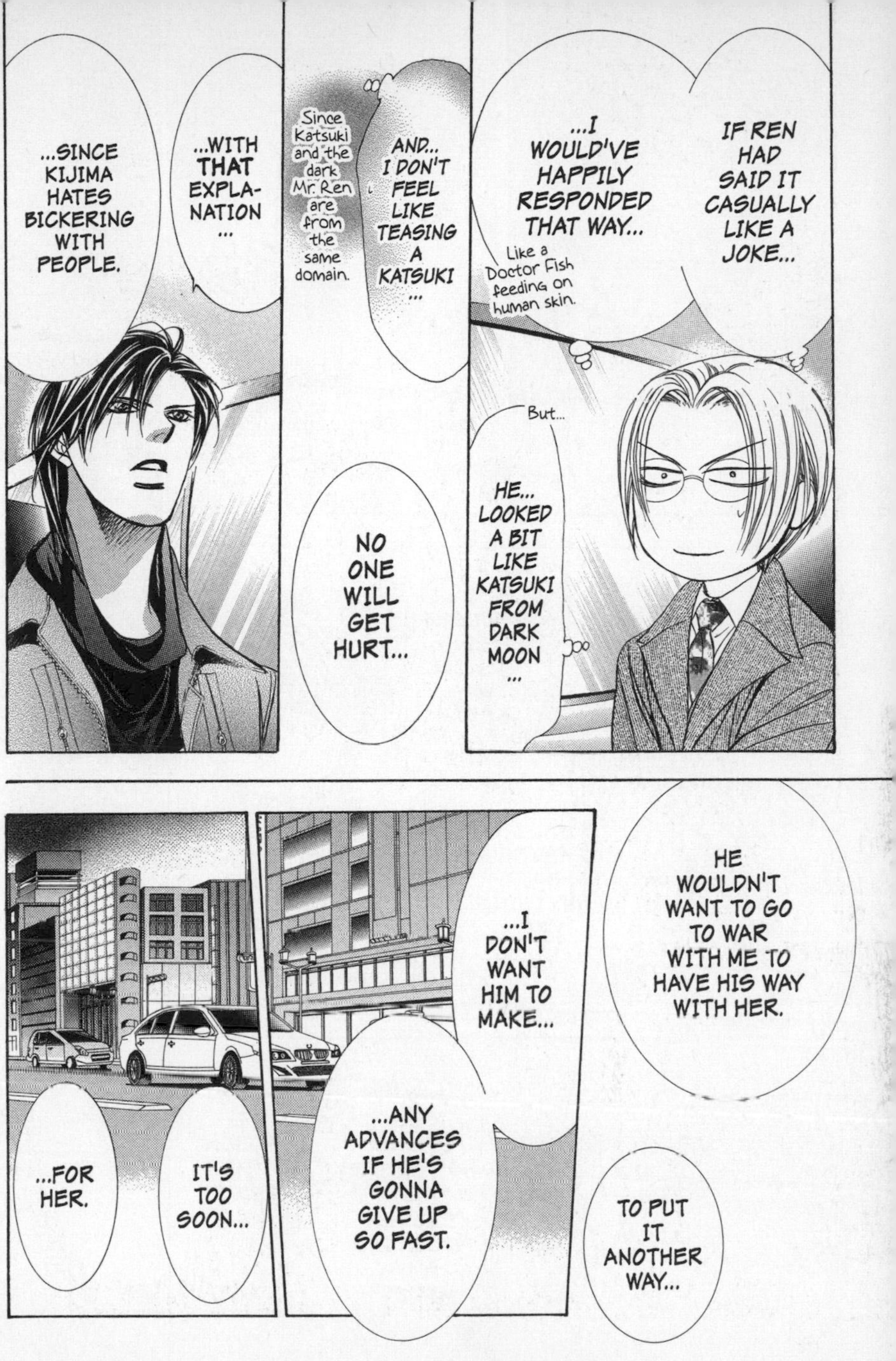
IF REN HAD SAID IT CASUALLY LIKE A JOKE...
...I WOULD'VE HAPPILY RESPONDED THAT WAY...
Like a Doctor Fish feeding on human skin.
But...
HE... LOOKED A BIT LIKE KATSUKI FROM DARK MOON...
AND... I DON'T FEEL LIKE TEASING A KATSUKI...
Since Katsuki and the dark Mr. Ren are from the same domain.
NO ONE WILL GET HURT...
...WITH THAT EXPLANATION...
...SINCE KIJIMA HATES BICKERING WITH PEOPLE.
HE WOULDN'T WANT TO GO TO WAR WITH ME TO HAVE HIS WAY WITH HER.
TO PUT IT ANOTHER WAY...
...I DON'T WANT HIM TO MAKE...
...ANY ADVANCES IF HE'S GONNA GIVE UP SO FAST.
IT'S TOO SOON...
...FOR HER.

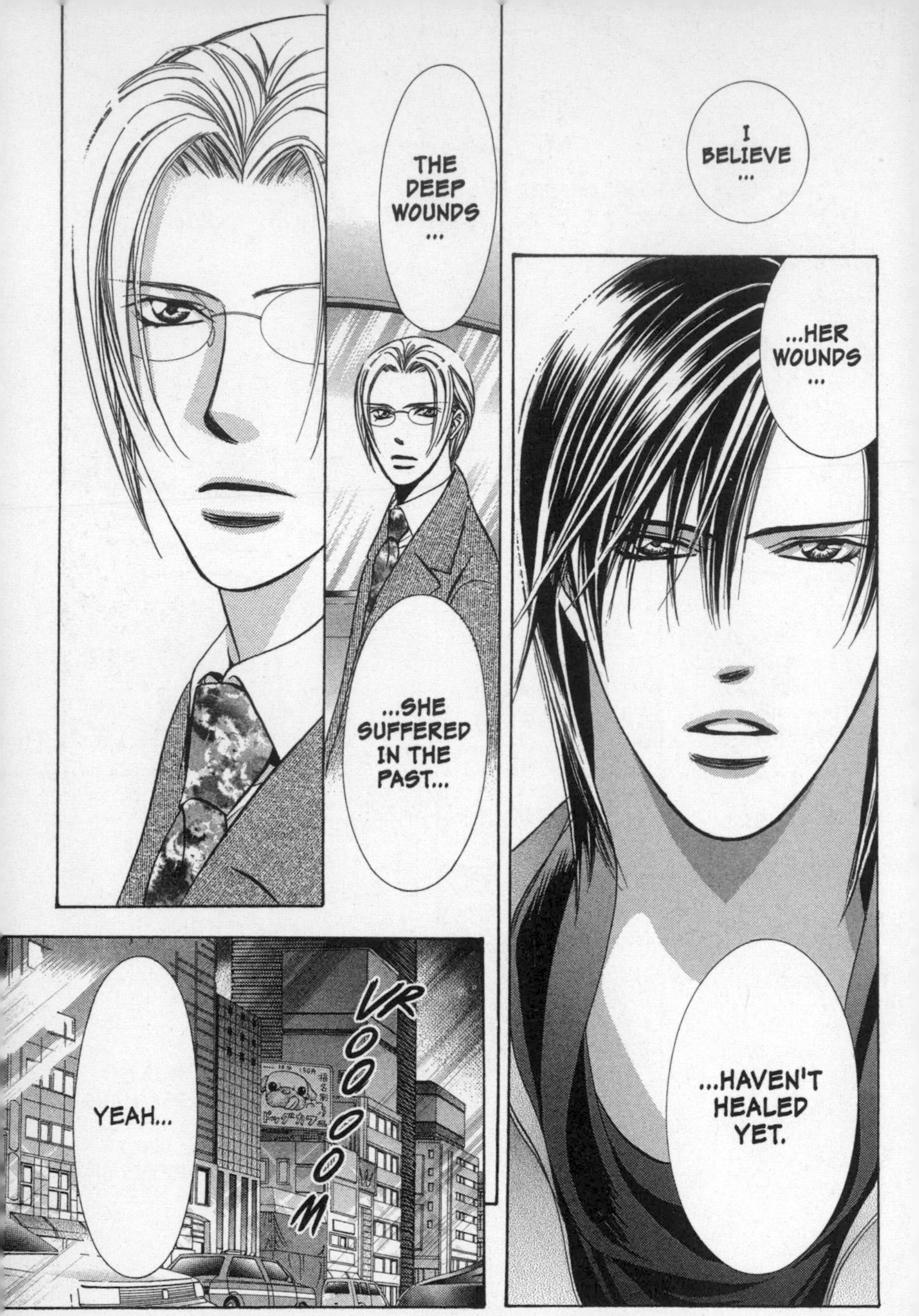
I BELIEVE ...
...HER WOUNDS ...
...HAVEN'T HEALED YET.
THE DEEP WOUNDS ...
...SHE SUFFERED IN THE PAST...
YEAH...
VROOOOOOM

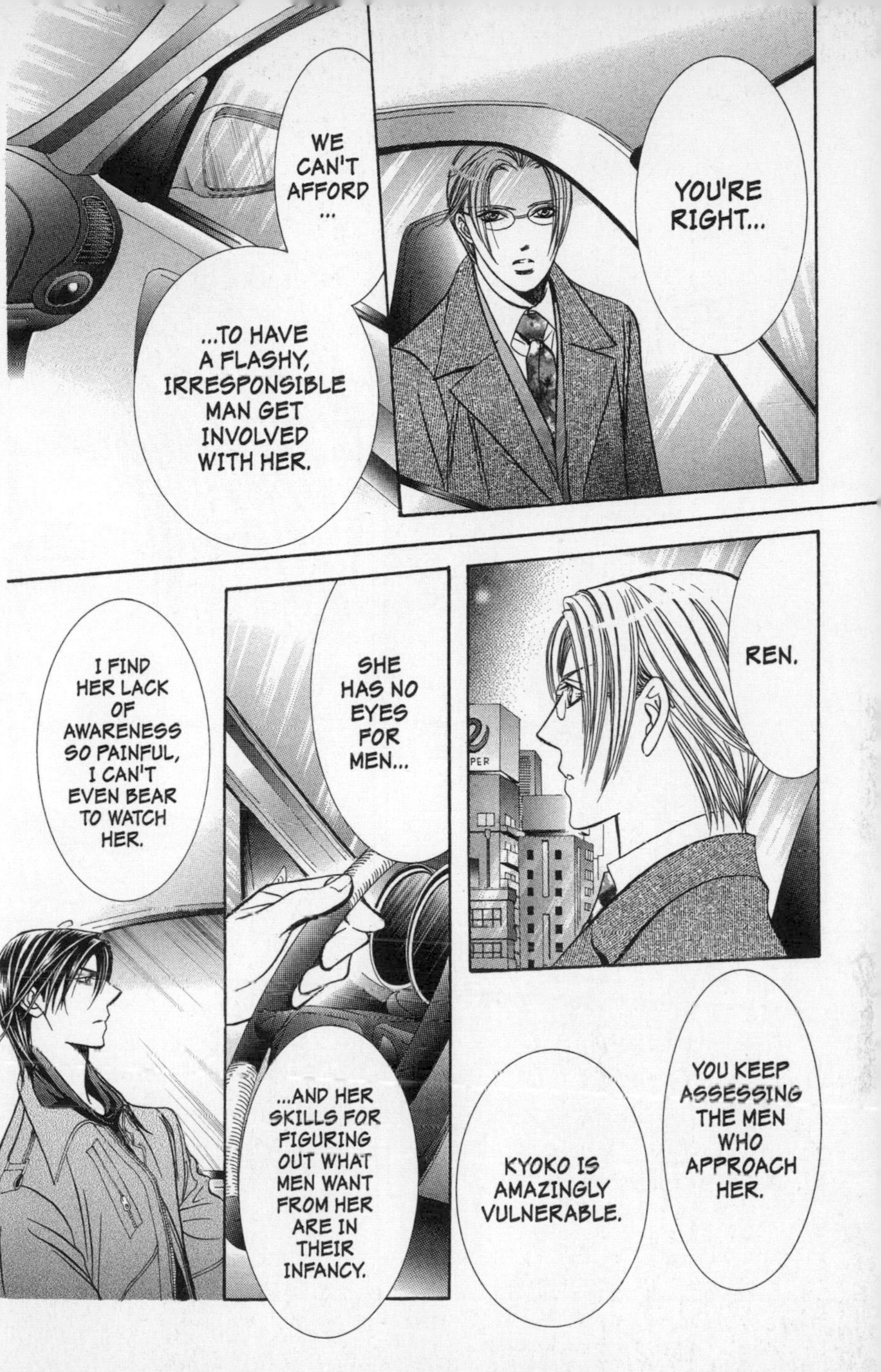
YOU'RE RIGHT...
WE CAN'T AFFORD ...
...TO HAVE A FLASHY, IRRESPONSIBLE MAN GET INVOLVED WITH HER.
REN.
YOU KEEP ASSESSING THE MEN WHO APPROACH HER.
KYOKO IS AMAZINGLY VULNERABLE.
SHE HAS NO EYES FOR MEN...
...AND HER SKILLS FOR FIGURING OUT WHAT MEN WANT FROM HER ARE IN THEIR INFANCY.
I FIND HER LACK OF AWARENESS SO PAINFUL, I CAN'T EVEN BEAR TO WATCH HER.

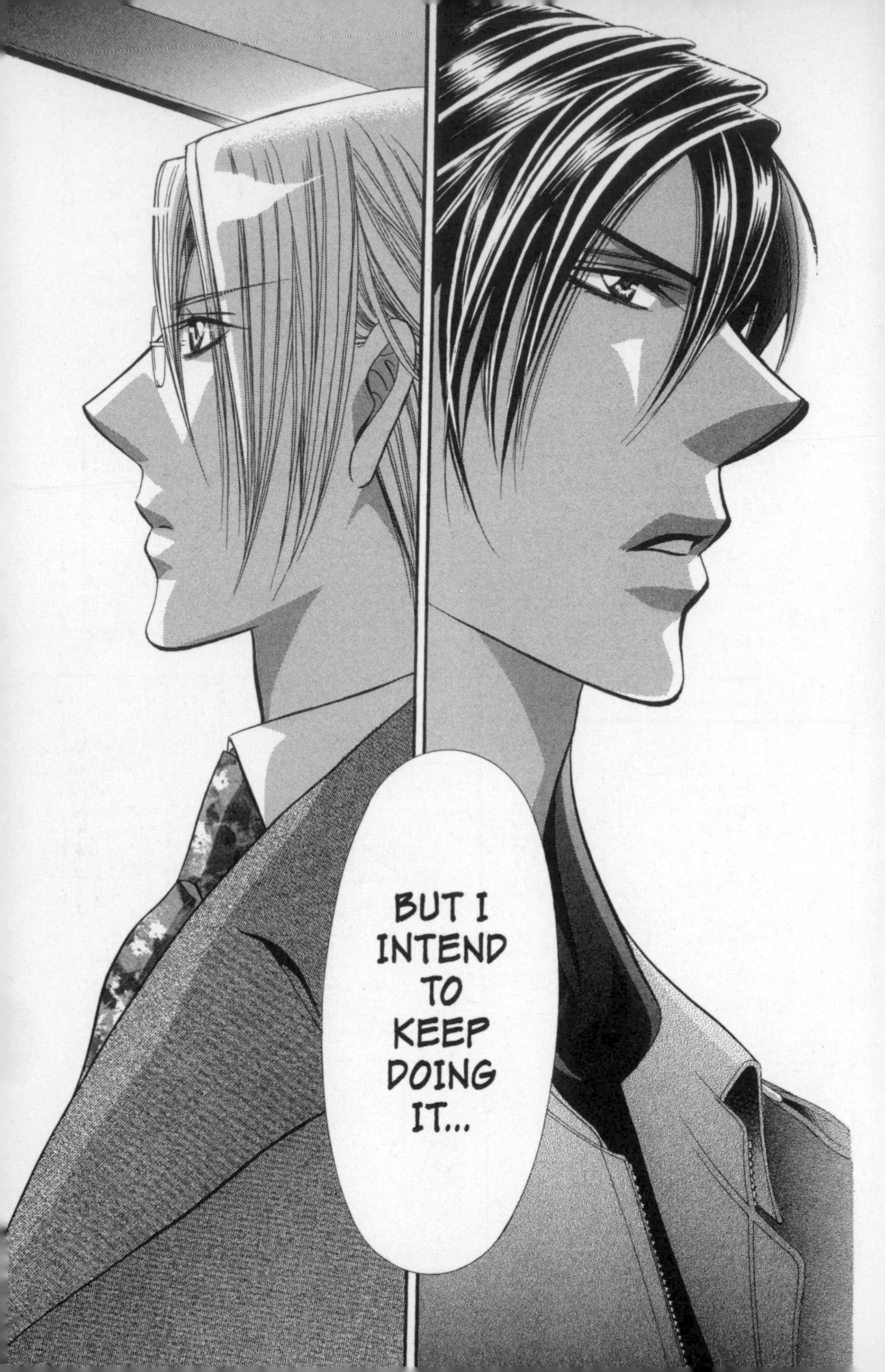
BUT I INTEND TO KEEP DOING IT...

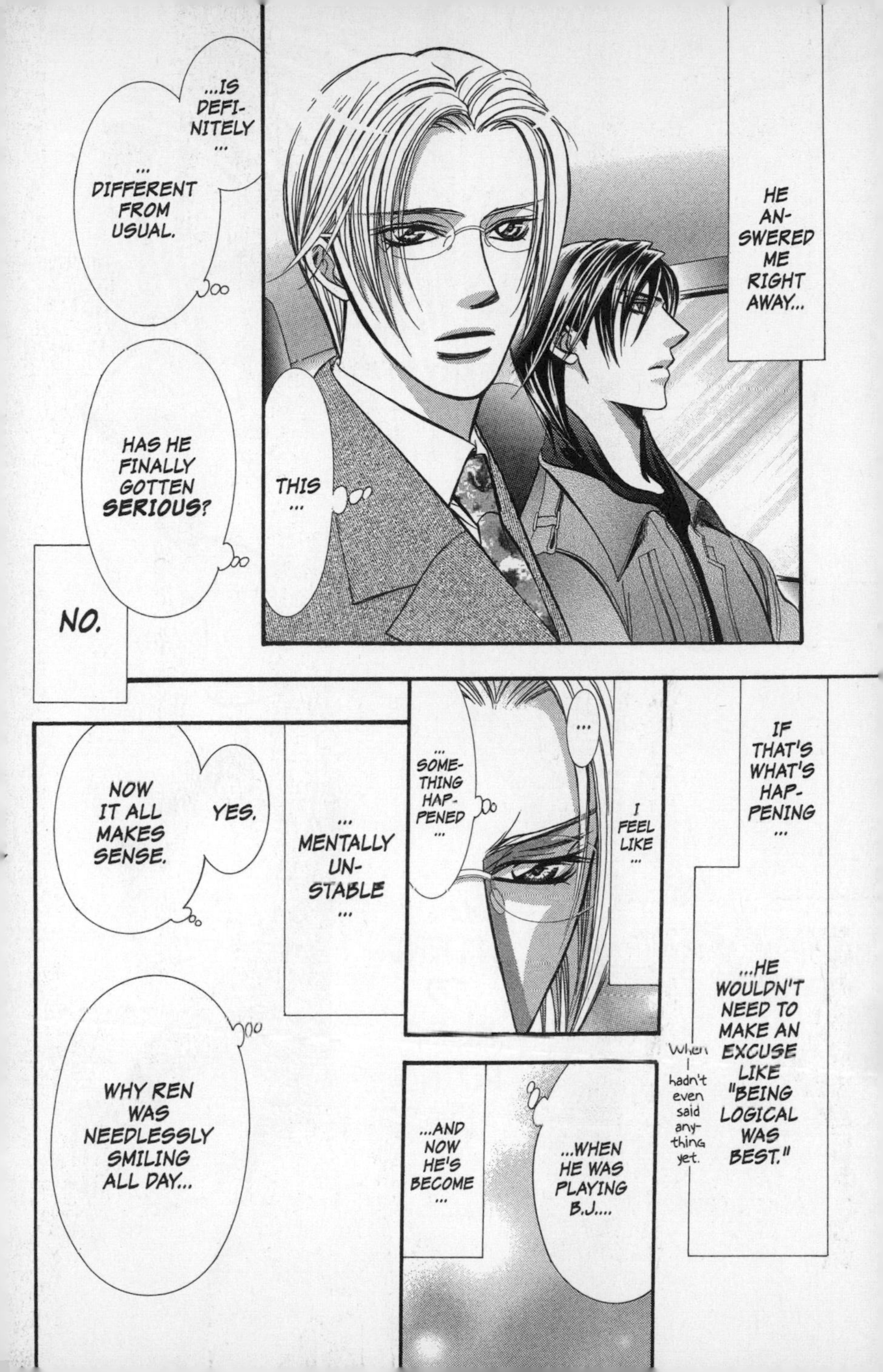
HE ANSWERED ME RIGHT AWAY...
THIS ...
...IS DEFINITELY ... ... DIFFERENT FROM USUAL.
HAS HE FINALLY GOTTEN SERIOUS?
NO.
IF THAT'S WHAT'S HAPPENING ...
...HE WOULDN'T NEED TO MAKE AN EXCUSE LIKE "BEING LOGICAL WAS BEST."
When I hadn't even said anything yet.
...
I FEEL LIKE ...
... SOMETHING HAPPENED ...
... MENTALLY UNSTABLE ...
YES.
NOW IT ALL MAKES SENSE.
...WHEN HE WAS PLAYING B.J....
...AND NOW HE'S BECOME ...
WHY REN WAS NEEDLESSLY SMILING ALL DAY...

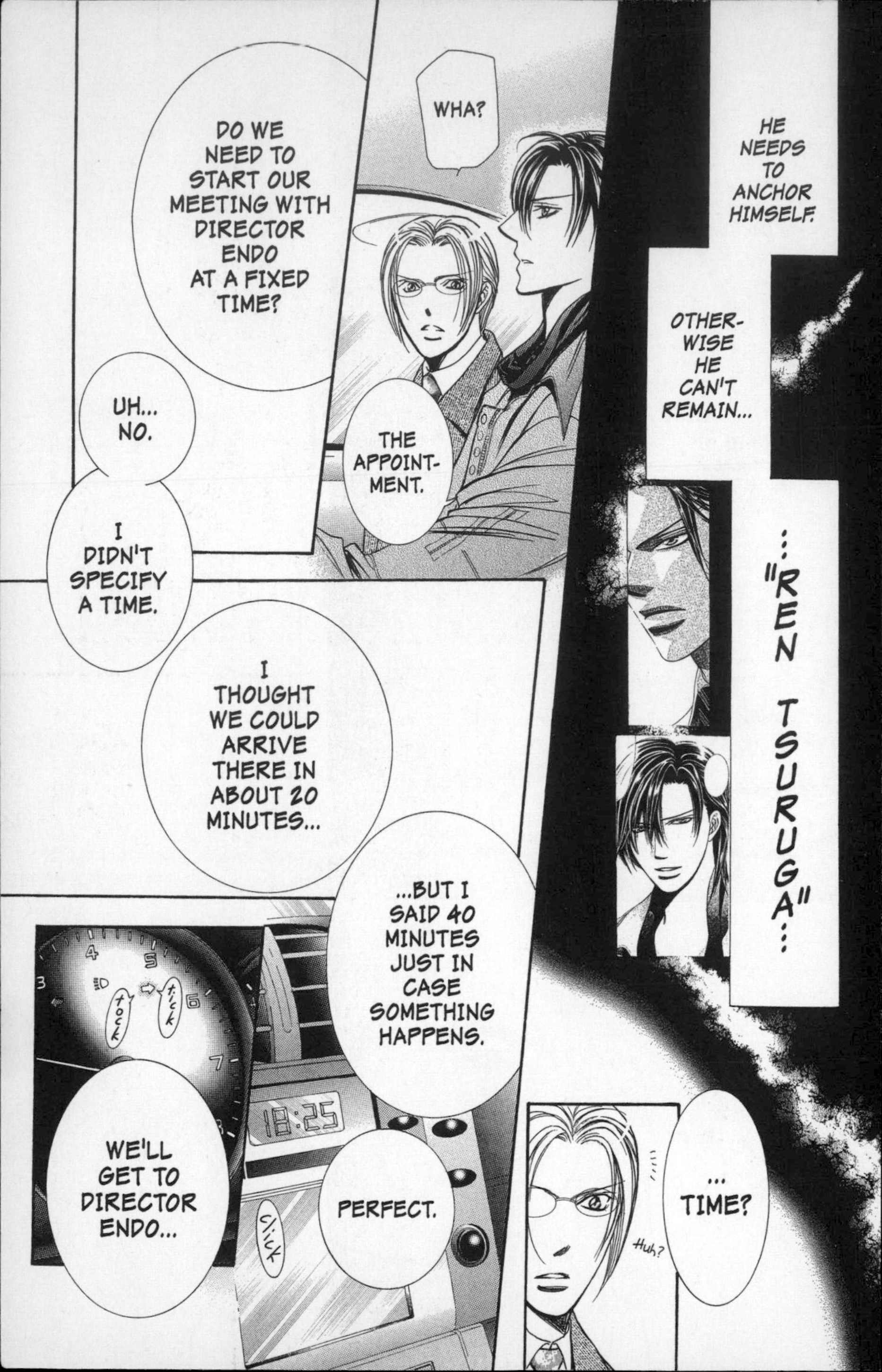
HE NEEDS TO ANCHOR HIMSELF.
OTHER-WISE HE CAN'T REMAIN...
..."REN TSURUGA"...
WHA?
DO WE NEED TO START OUR MEETING WITH DIRECTOR ENDO AT A FIXED TIME?
THE APPOINT-MENT.
UH... NO.
I DIDN'T SPECIFY A TIME.
I THOUGHT WE COULD ARRIVE THERE IN ABOUT 20 MINUTES...
...BUT I SAID 40 MINUTES JUST IN CASE SOMETHING HAPPENS.
... TIME?
Huh?
PERFECT.
click
18:25
tick
tock
WE'LL GET TO DIRECTOR ENDO...

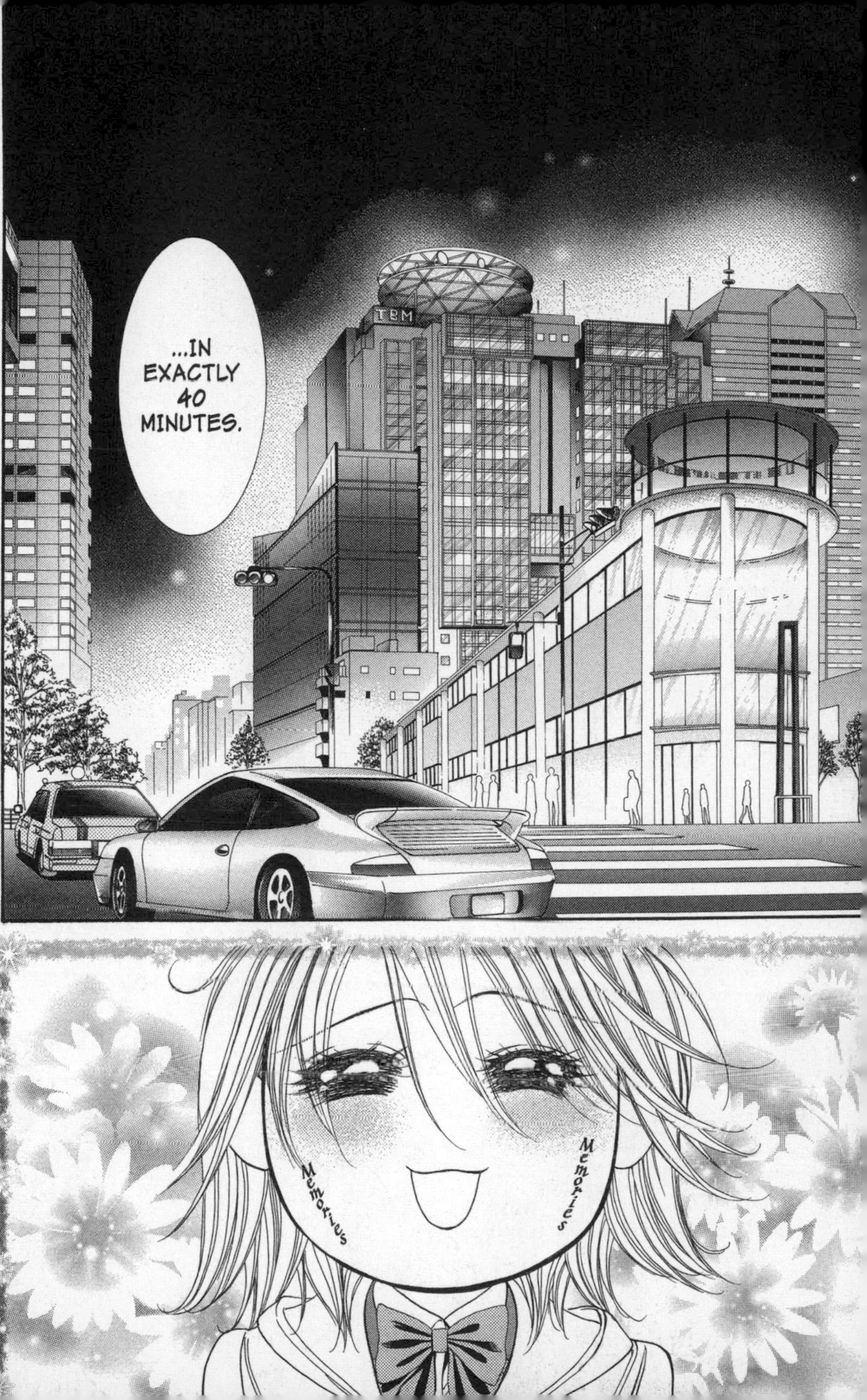
...IN EXACTLY 40 MINUTES.
TBM
Memories
Memories

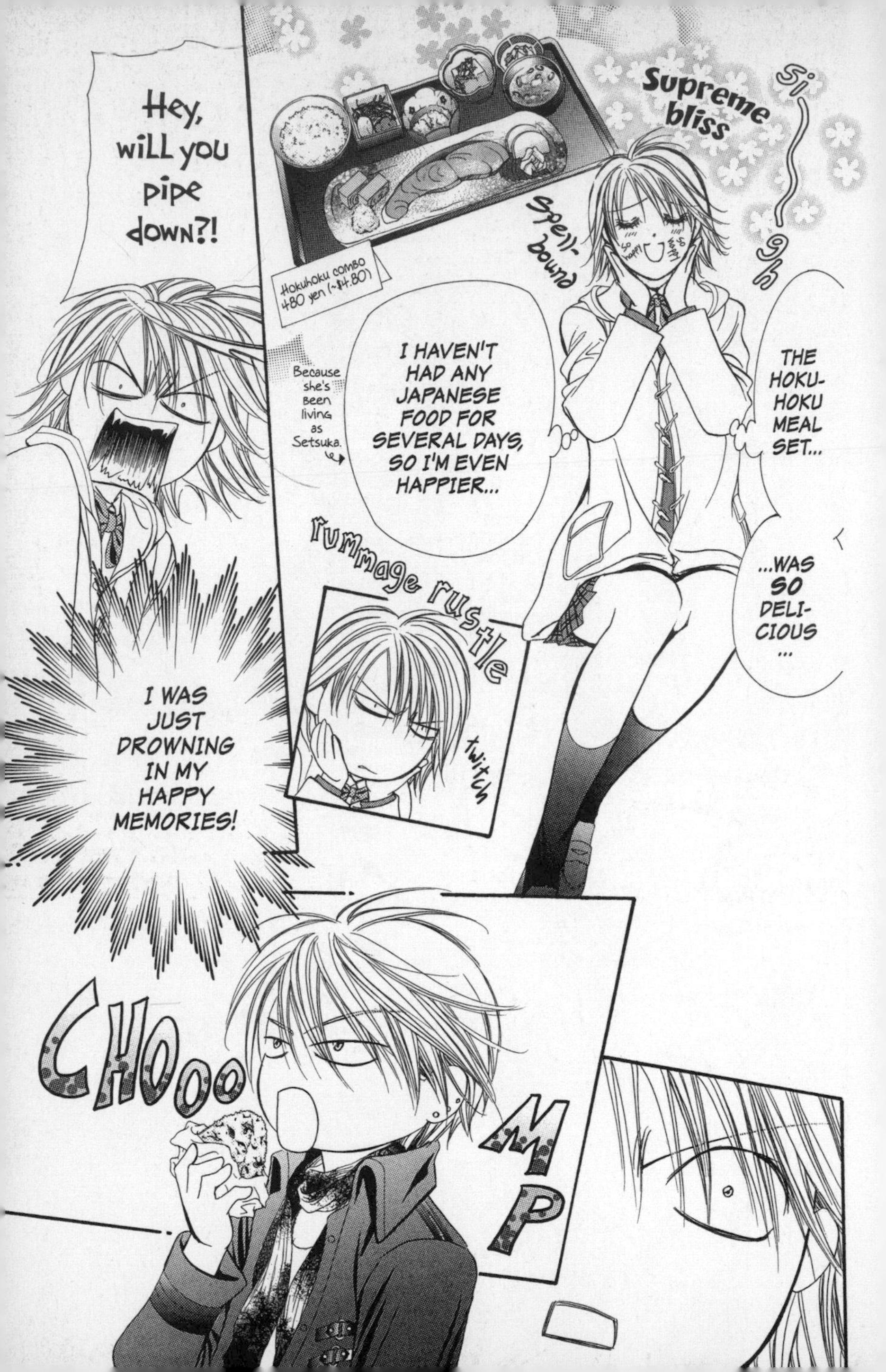
Supreme bliss
si—gh
Spell-bound
So happy
So happy
Hokuhoku combo 480 yen (~$4.80)
THE HOKU-HOKU MEAL SET...
...WAS SO DELICIOUS...
I HAVEN'T HAD ANY JAPANESE FOOD FOR SEVERAL DAYS, SO I'M EVEN HAPPIER...
Because she's been living as Setsuka.
rummage rustle
twitch
Hey, will you pipe down?!
I WAS JUST DROWNING IN MY HAPPY MEMORIES!
CHOOOMP

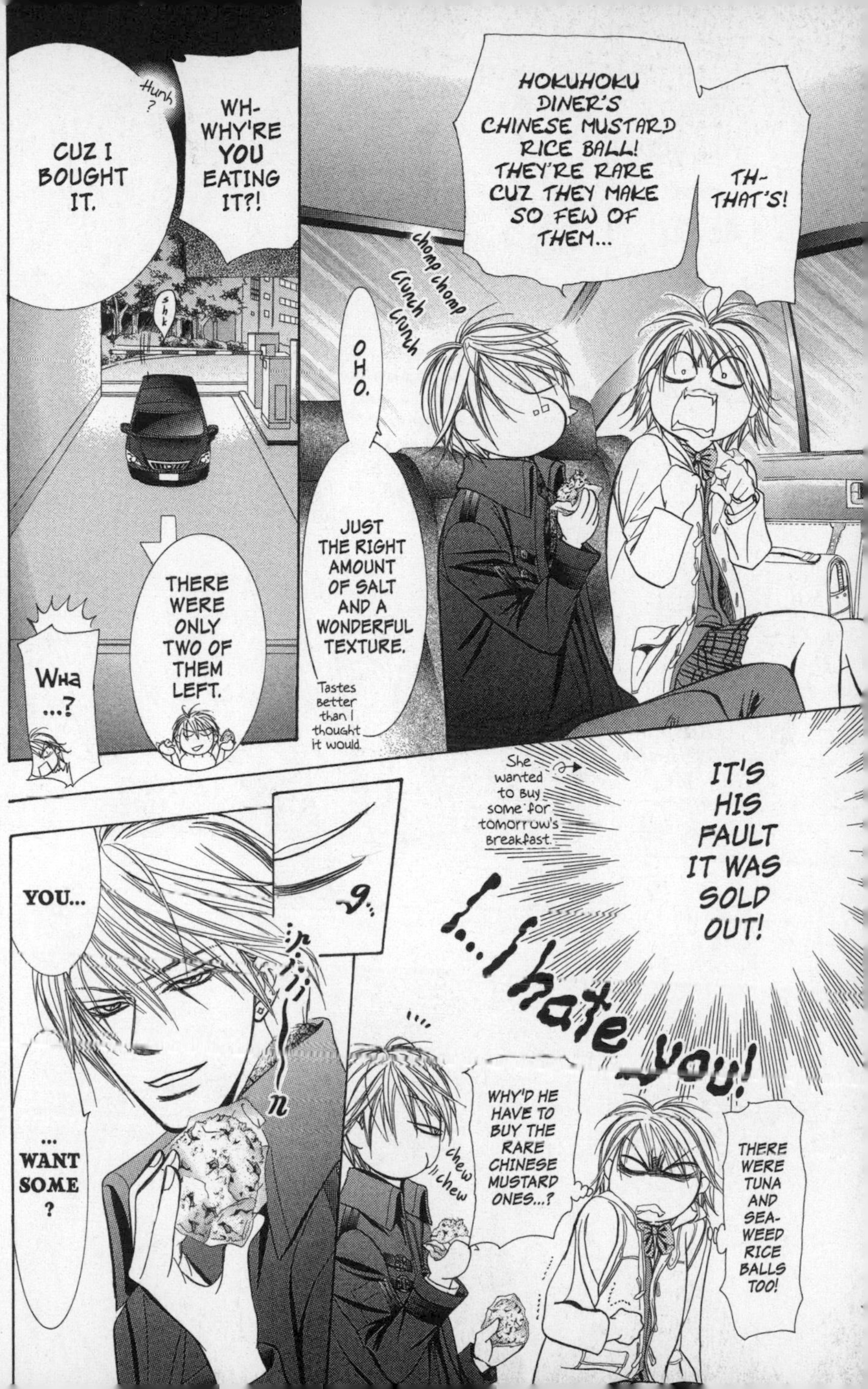
TH-THAT'S!
HOKUHOKU DINER'S CHINESE MUSTARD RICE BALL! THEY'RE RARE CUZ THEY MAKE SO FEW OF THEM...
chomp chomp
crunch crunch
OHO.
JUST THE RIGHT AMOUNT OF SALT AND A WONDERFUL TEXTURE.
Tastes better than I thought it would.
WH-WHY'RE YOU EATING IT?!
Hunh?
CUZ I BOUGHT IT.
shk
THERE WERE ONLY TWO OF THEM LEFT.
Wha ...?
IT'S HIS FAULT IT WAS SOLD OUT!
She wanted to buy some for tomorrow's breakfast.
I...I hate you!
THERE WERE TUNA AND SEA-WEED RICE BALLS TOO!
WHY'D HE HAVE TO BUY THE RARE CHINESE MUSTARD ONES...?
chew chew
...
g...
YOU...
...WANT SOME?

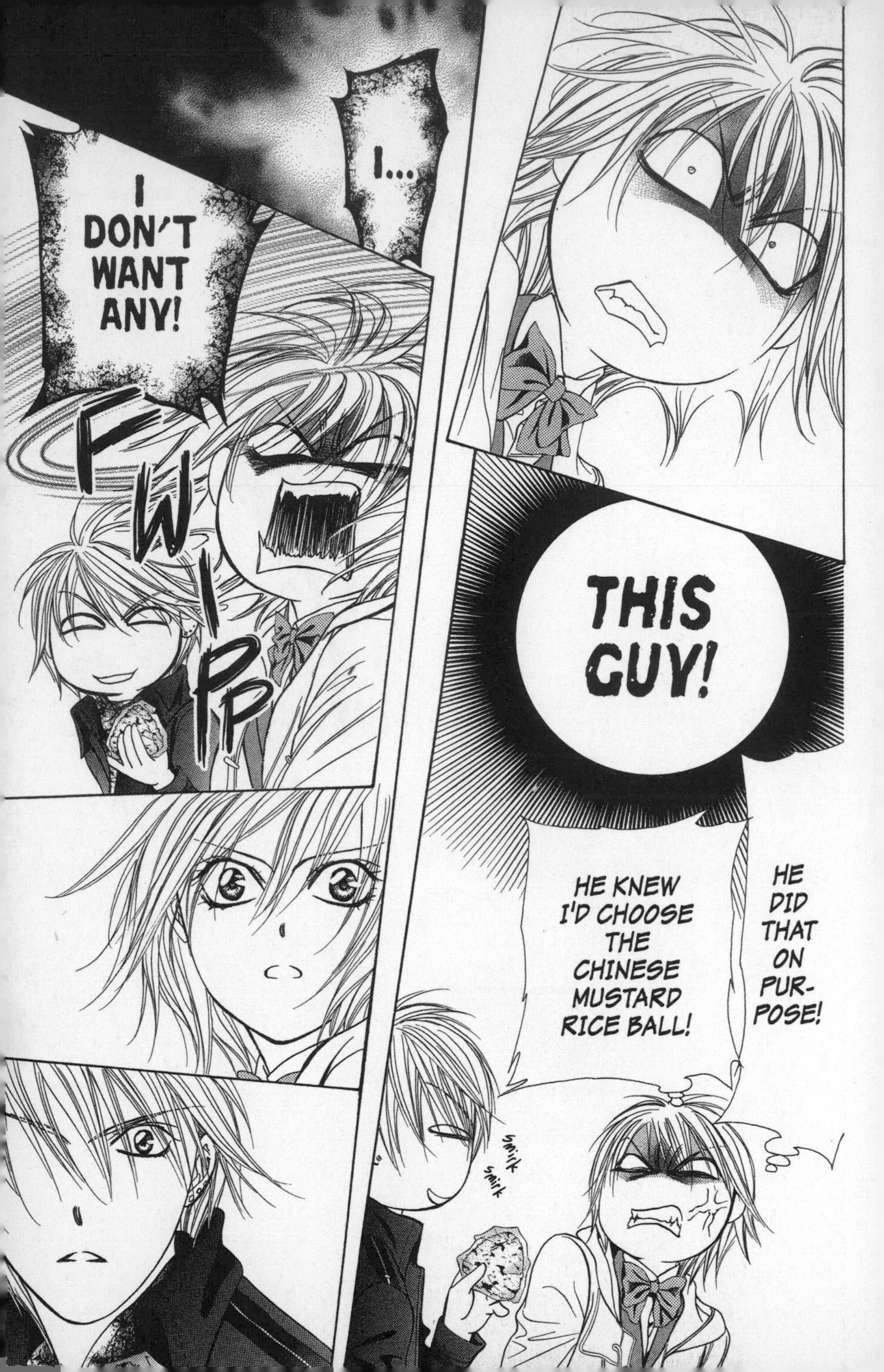
I...
I DON'T WANT ANY!
FWIPP
THIS GUY!
HE DID THAT ON PUR-POSE!
HE KNEW I'D CHOOSE THE CHINESE MUSTARD RICE BALL!
smirk smirk

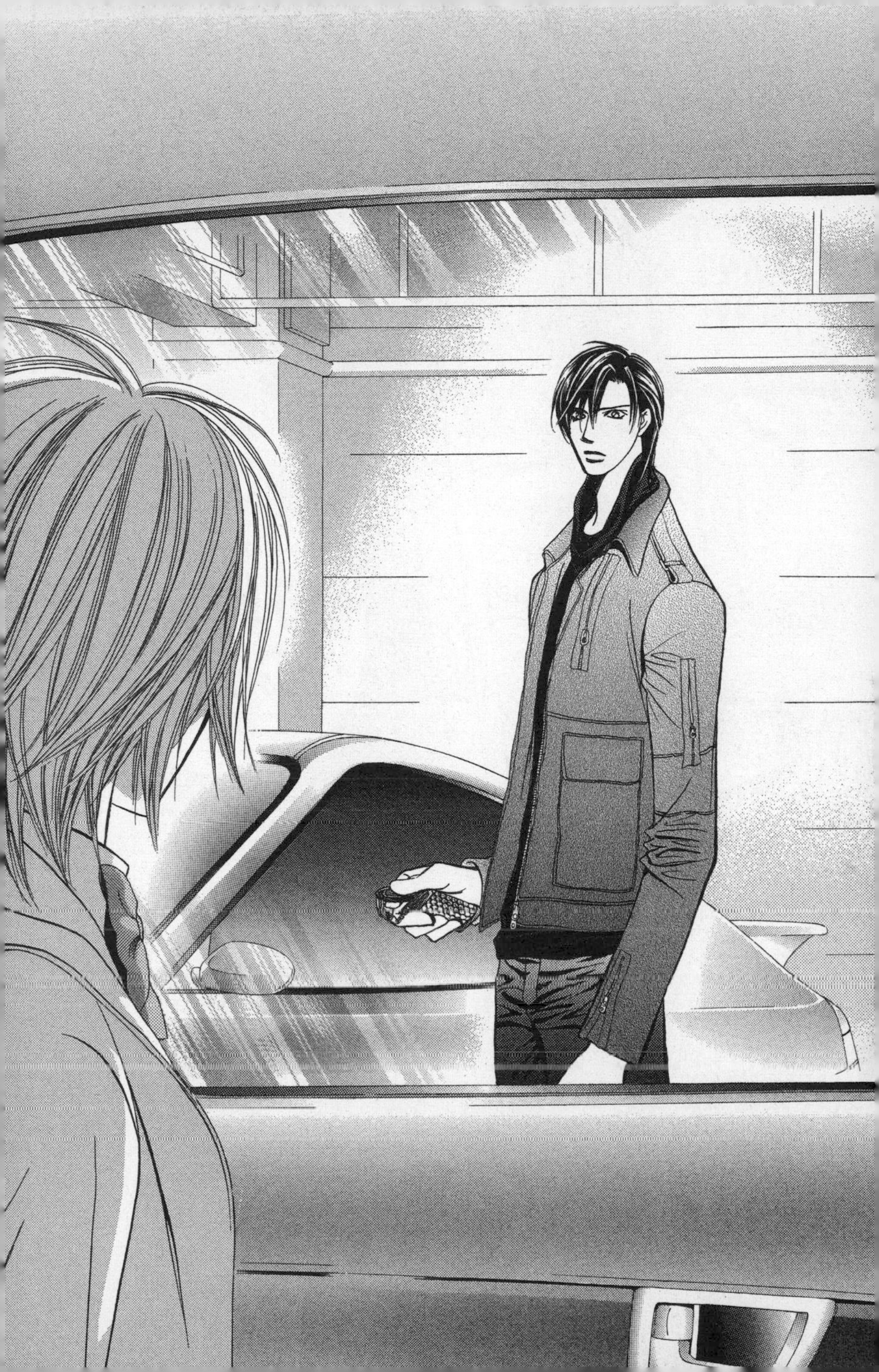

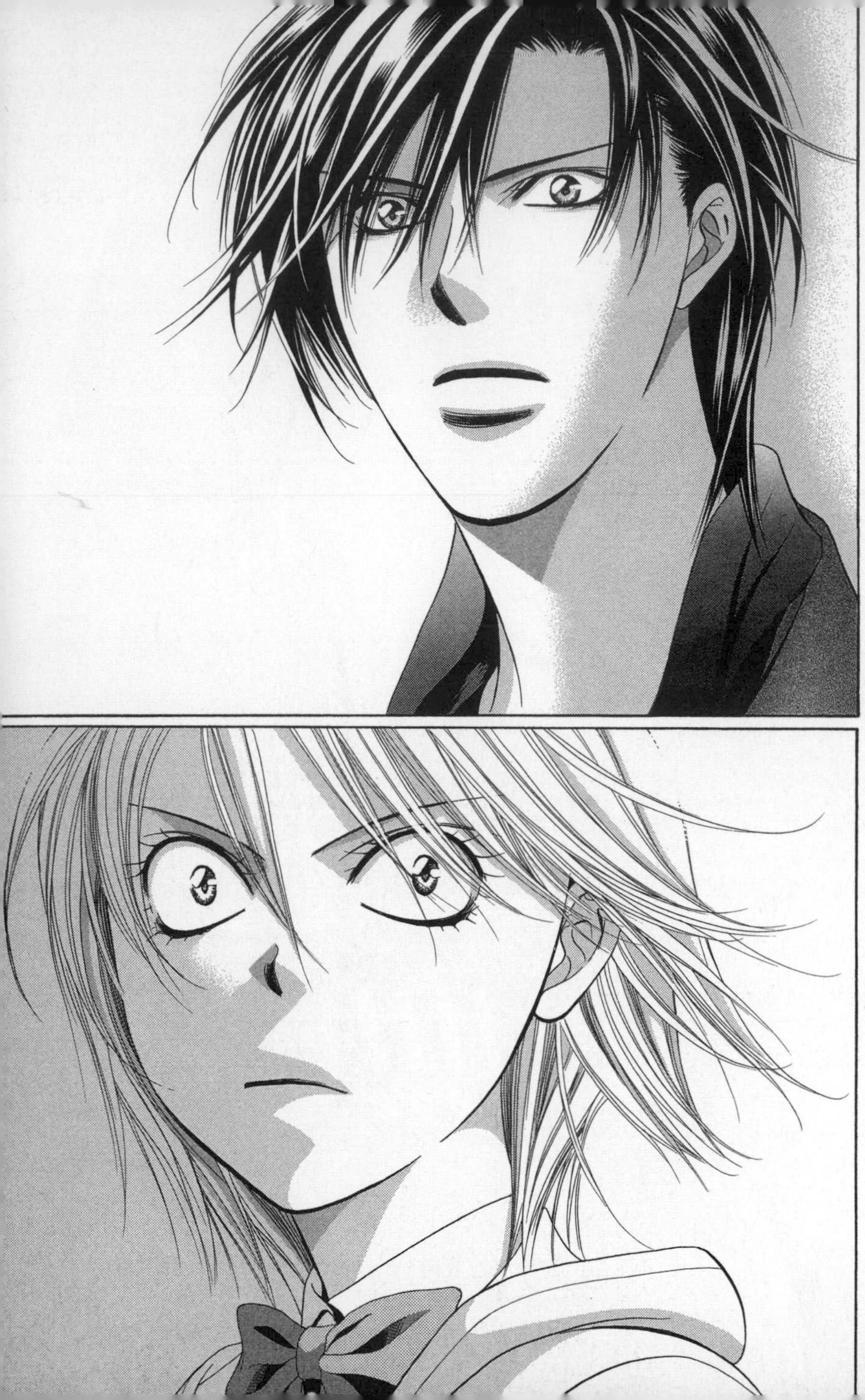

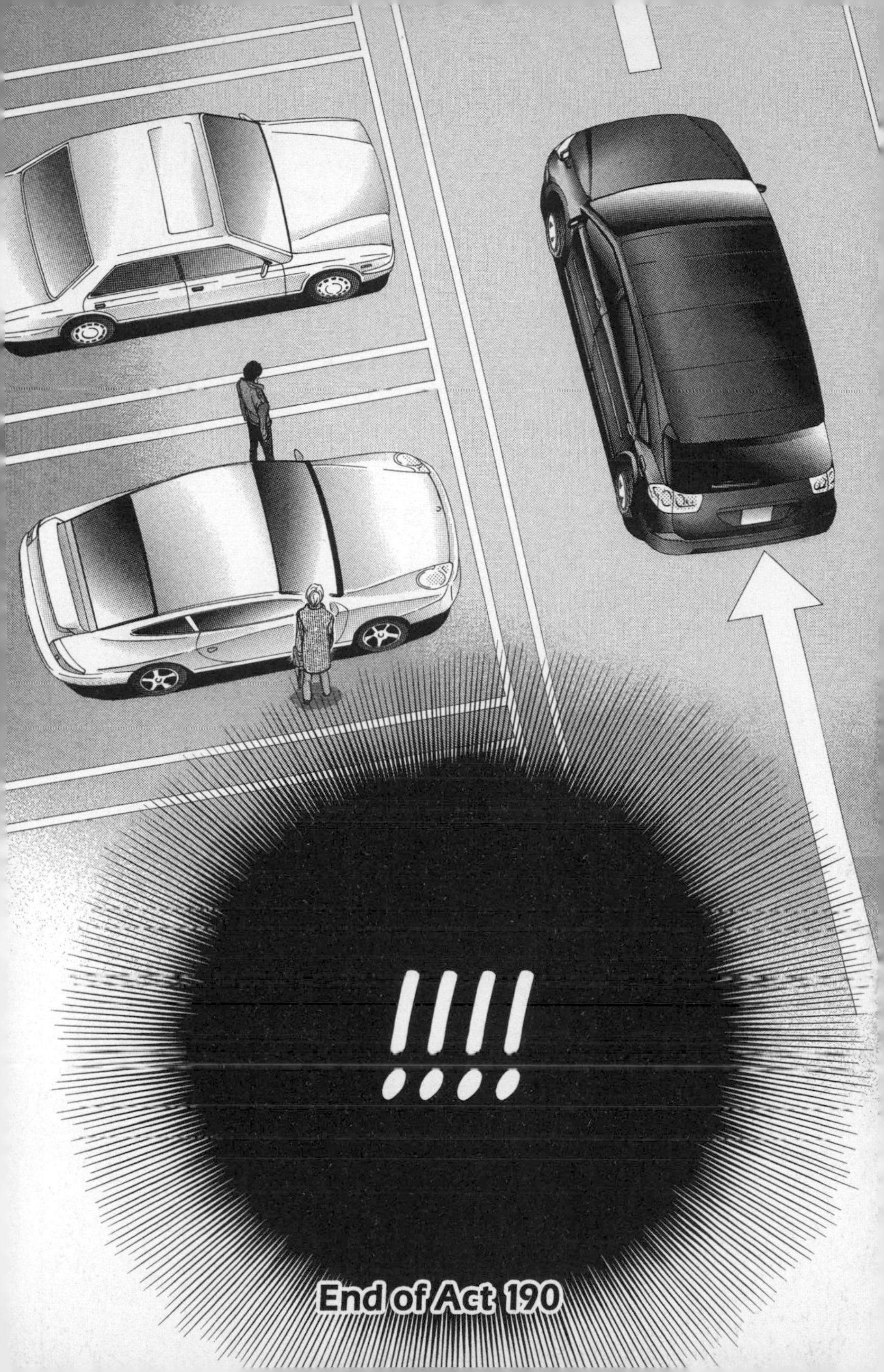
!!!!
End of Act 190

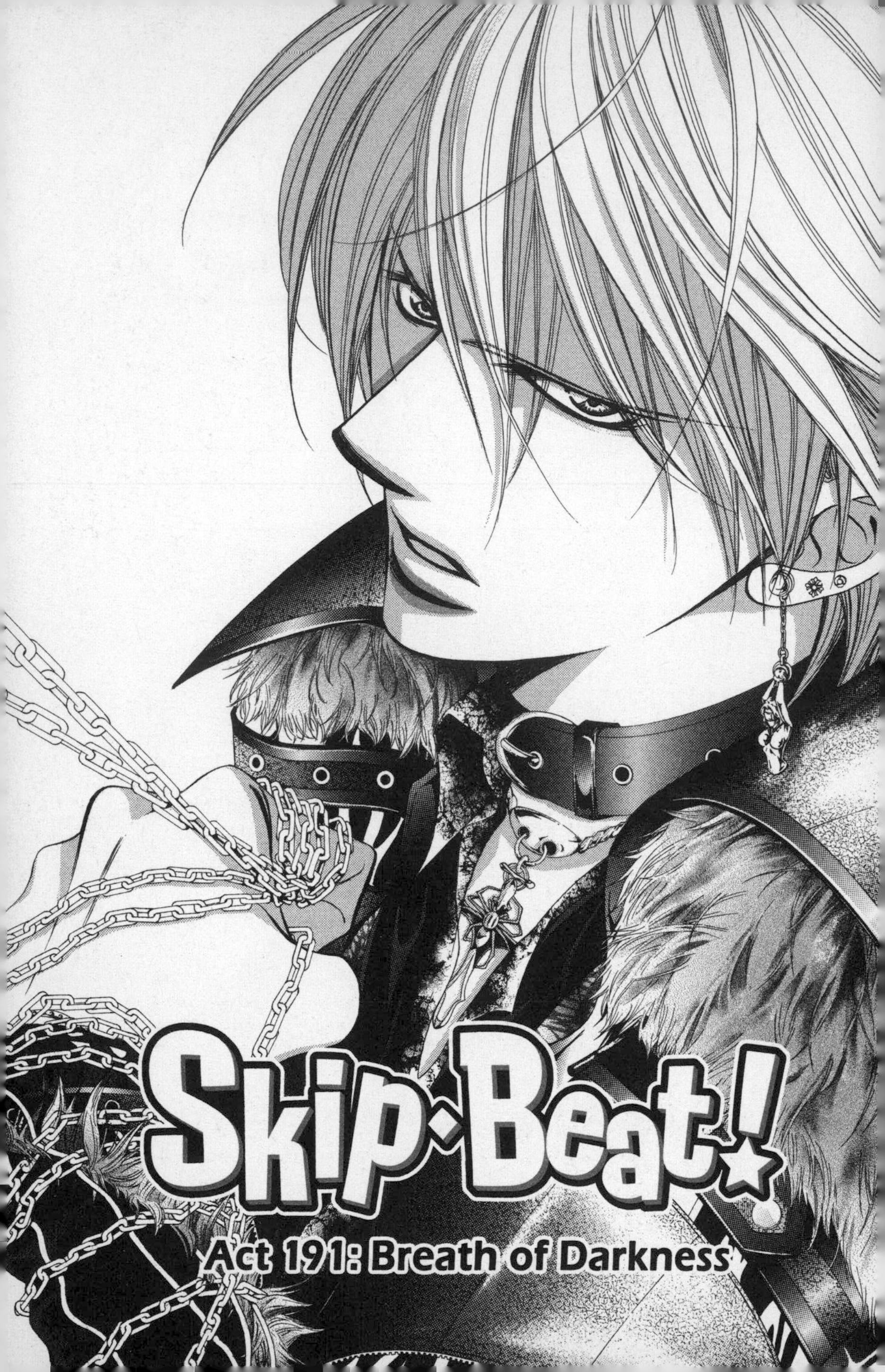
Skip·Beat!
Act 191: Breath of Darkness

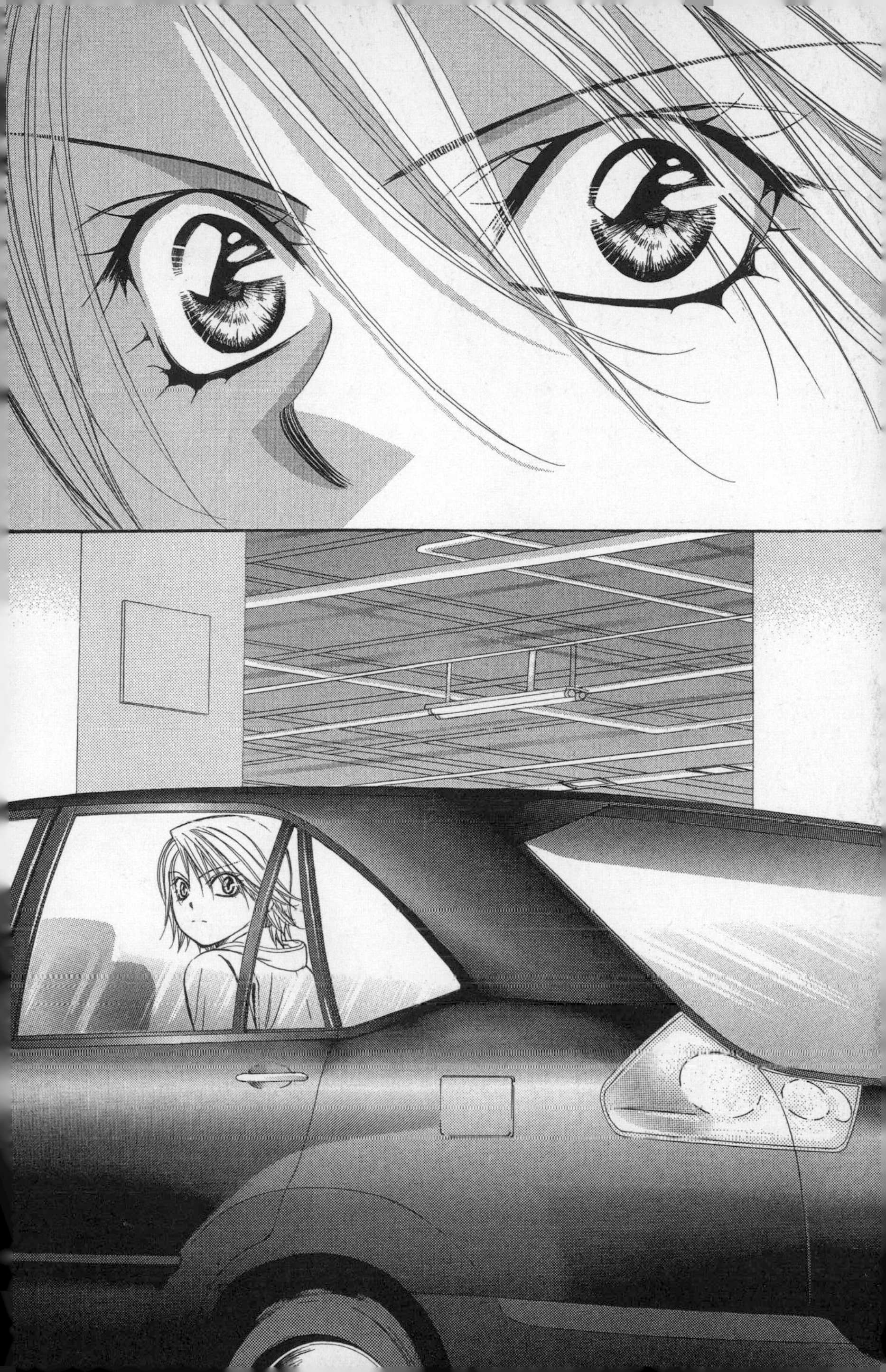

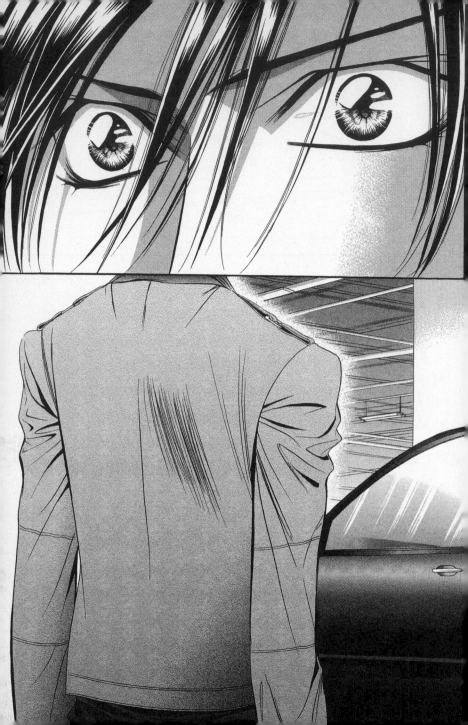

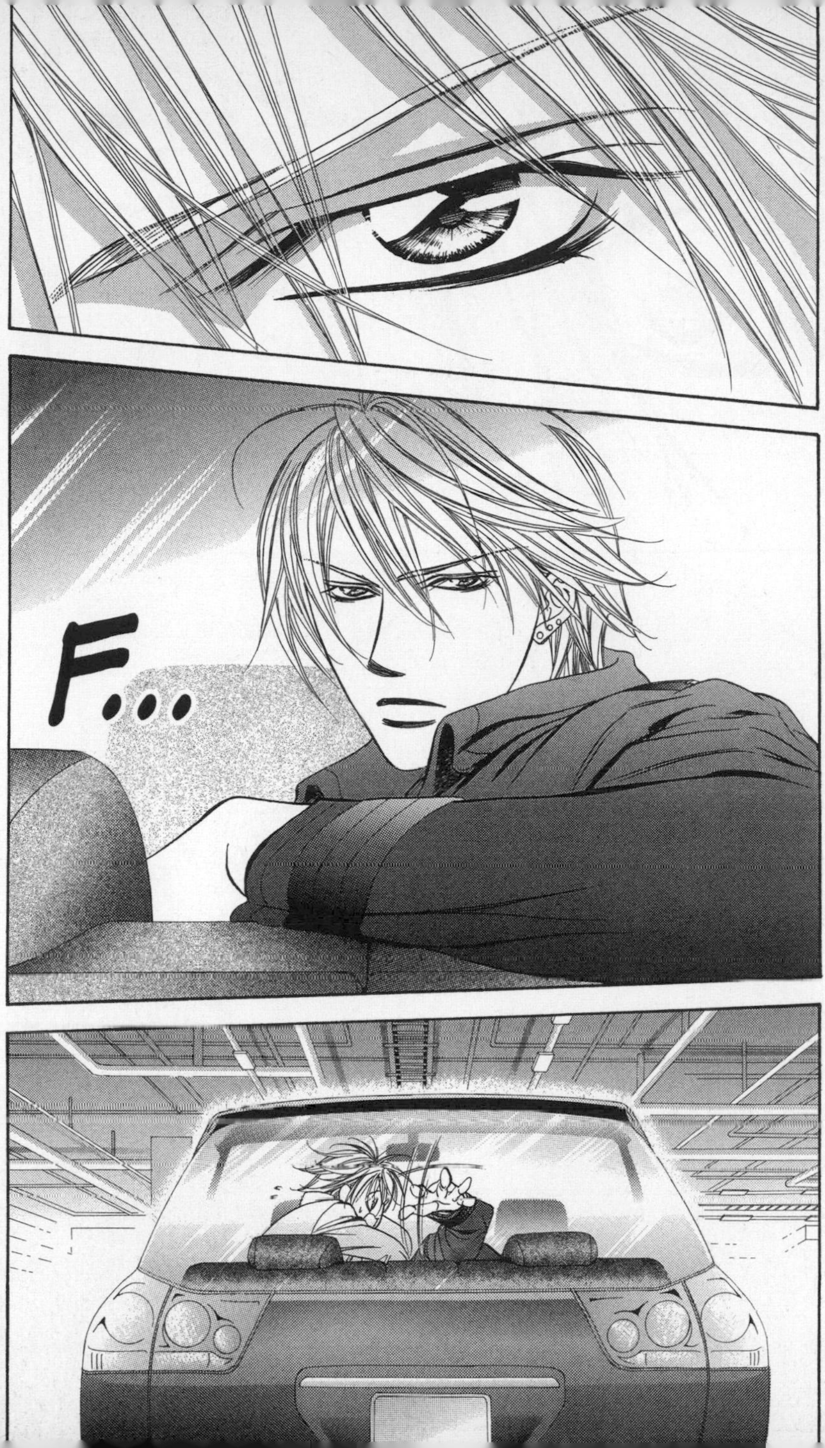
F...

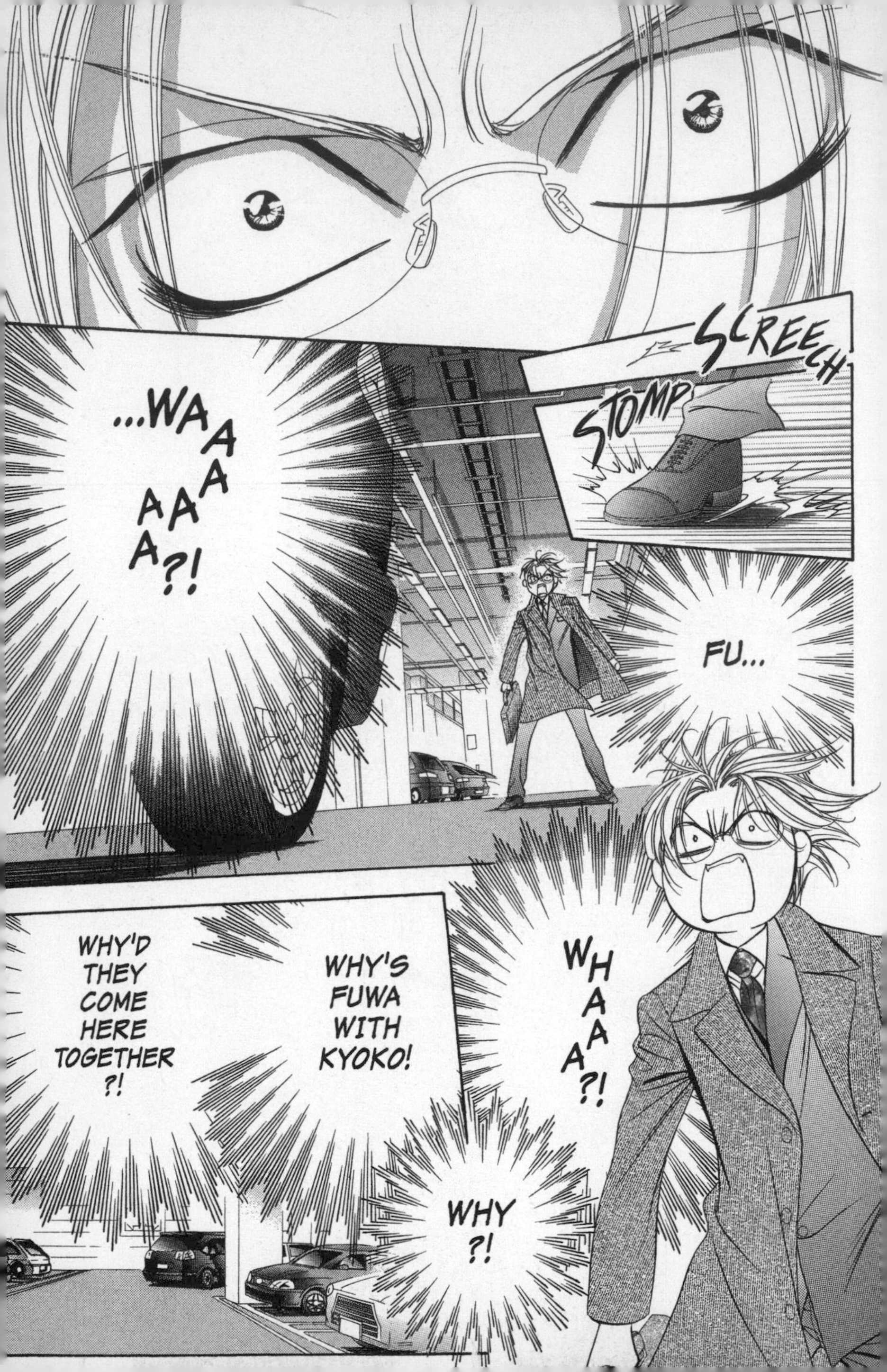
SCREECH
STOMP
...WAAAAAA?!
FU...
WHAAAA?!
WHY'S FUWA WITH KYOKO!
WHY'D THEY COME HERE TOGETHER?!
WHY?!

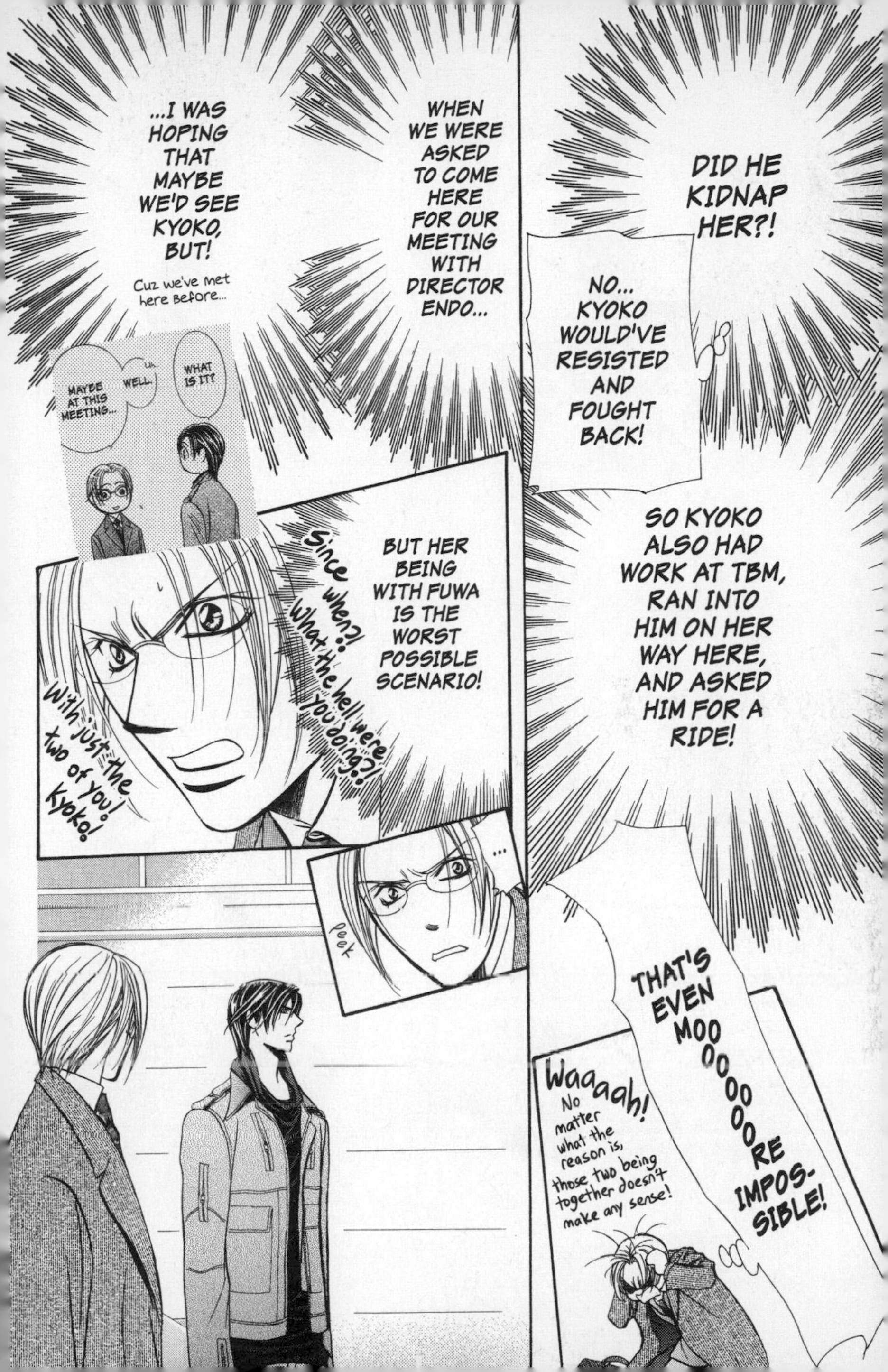
DID HE KIDNAP HER?!
NO... KYOKO WOULD'VE RESISTED AND FOUGHT BACK!
SO KYOKO ALSO HAD WORK AT TBM, RAN INTO HIM ON HER WAY HERE, AND ASKED HIM FOR A RIDE!
THAT'S EVEN MOOOOOOOOORE IMPOS-SIBLE!
Waaaah!
No matter what the reason is, those two being together doesn't make any sense!
WHEN WE WERE ASKED TO COME HERE FOR OUR MEETING WITH DIRECTOR ENDO...
...I WAS HOPING THAT MAYBE WE'D SEE KYOKO, BUT!
Cuz we've met here before...
WHAT IS IT?
Uh... WELL.
MAYBE AT THIS MEETING...
BUT HER BEING WITH FUWA IS THE WORST POSSIBLE SCENARIO!
Since when?! What the hell were you doing?!
With just the two of you! Kyoko!
...
Peek

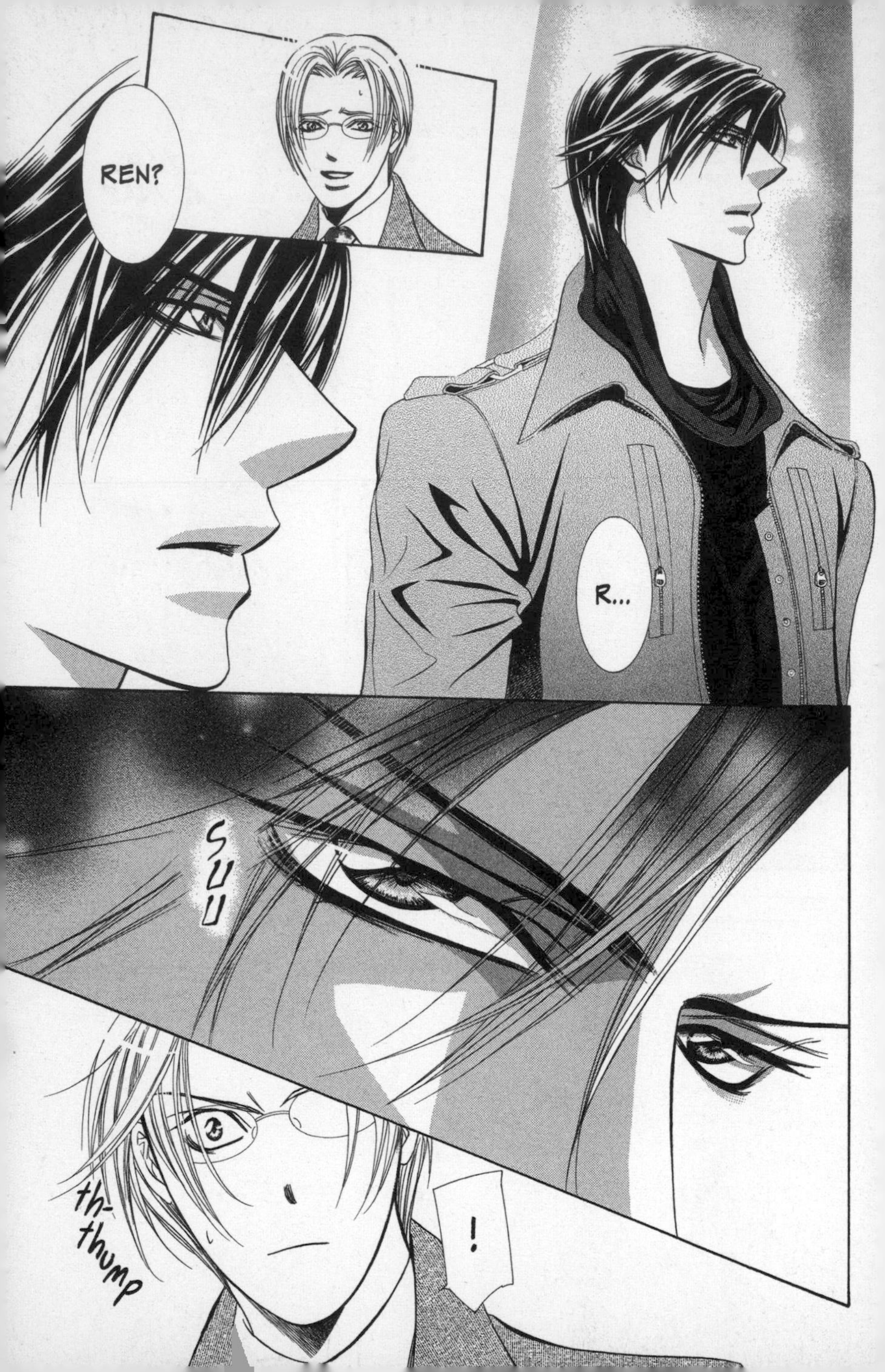
R...
REN?
SUUU
!
th-thump

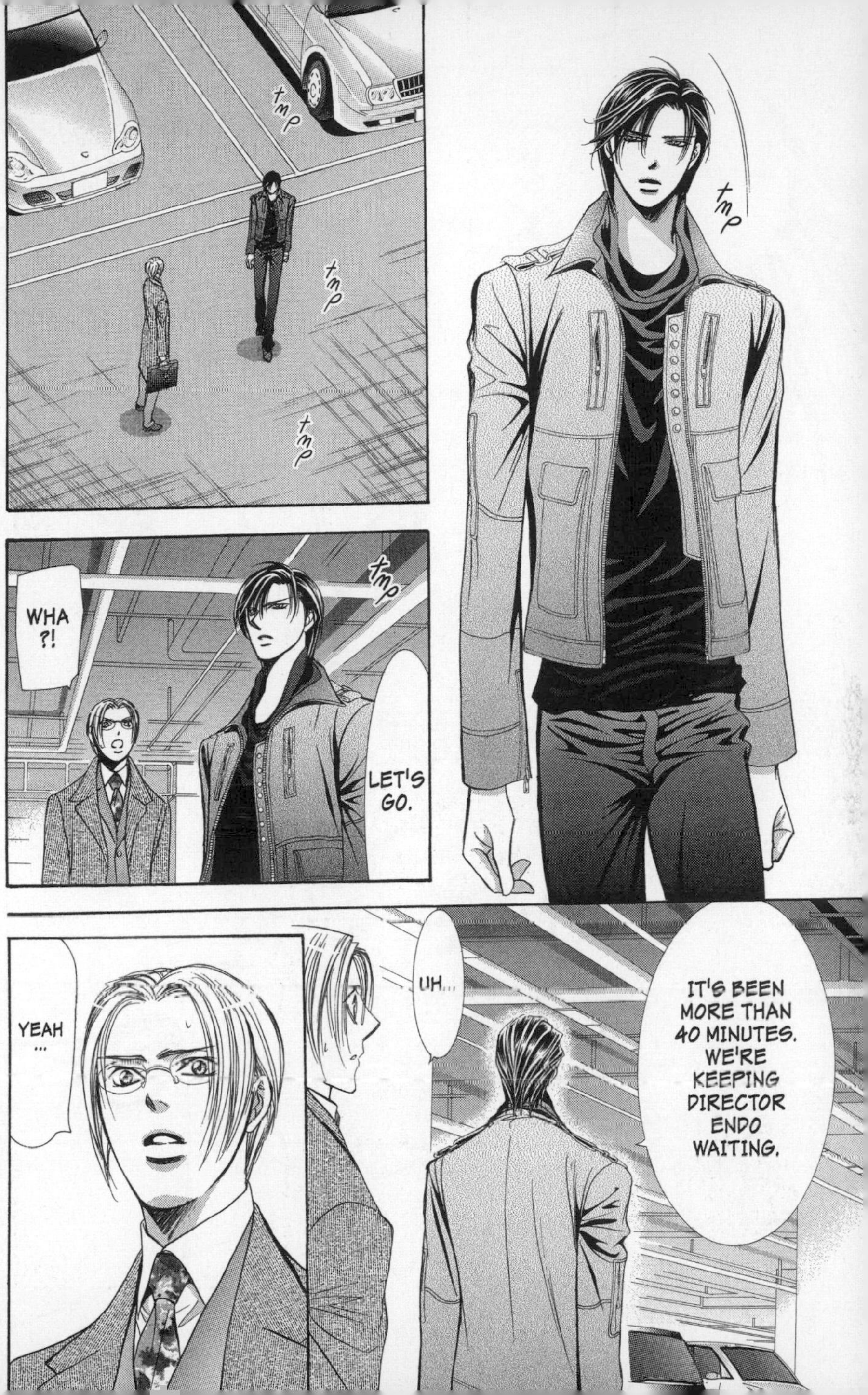

tmp
tmp
tmp
tmp
tmp
WHA ?!
LET'S GO.
IT'S BEEN MORE THAN 40 MINUTES. WE'RE KEEPING DIRECTOR ENDO WAITING.
UH...
YEAH ...

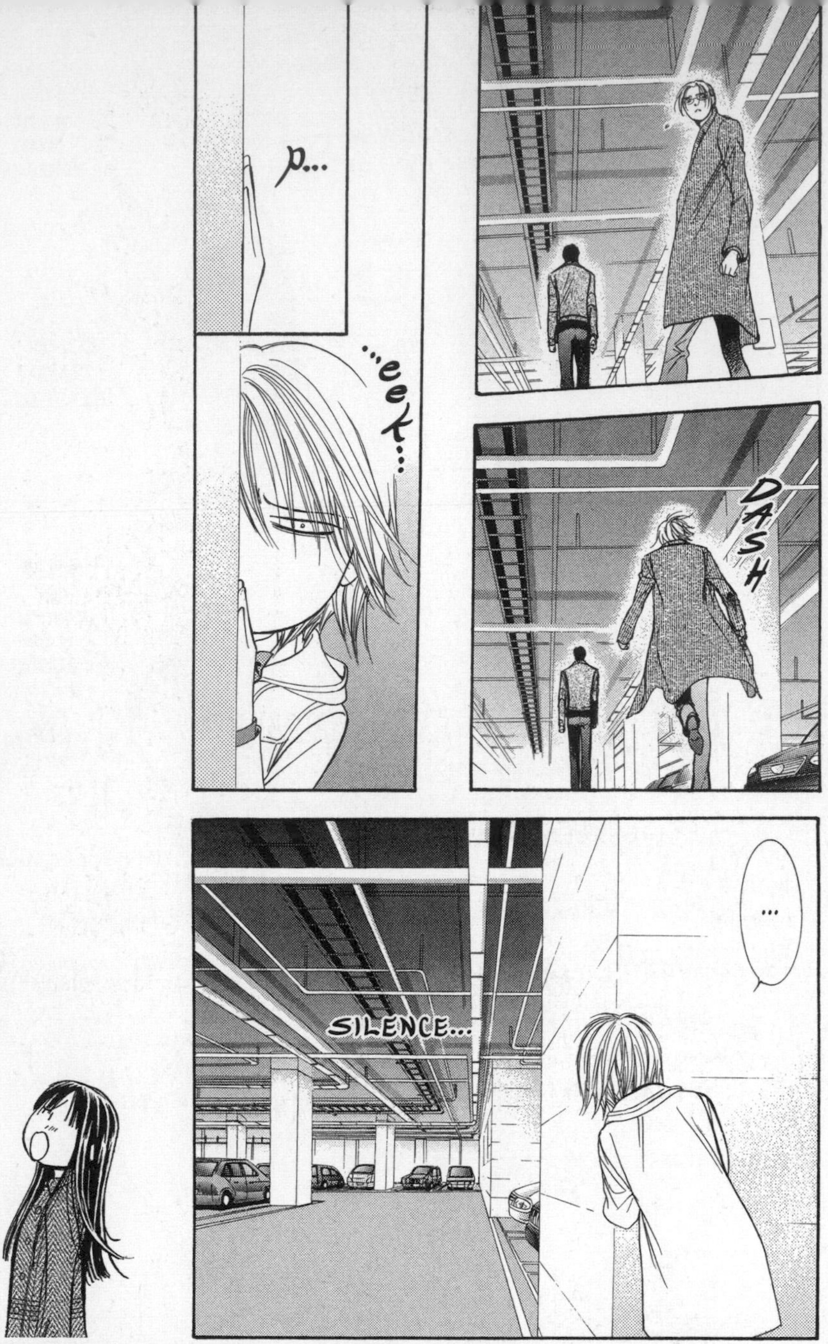
DASH
D...
...eek...
...
SILENCE...

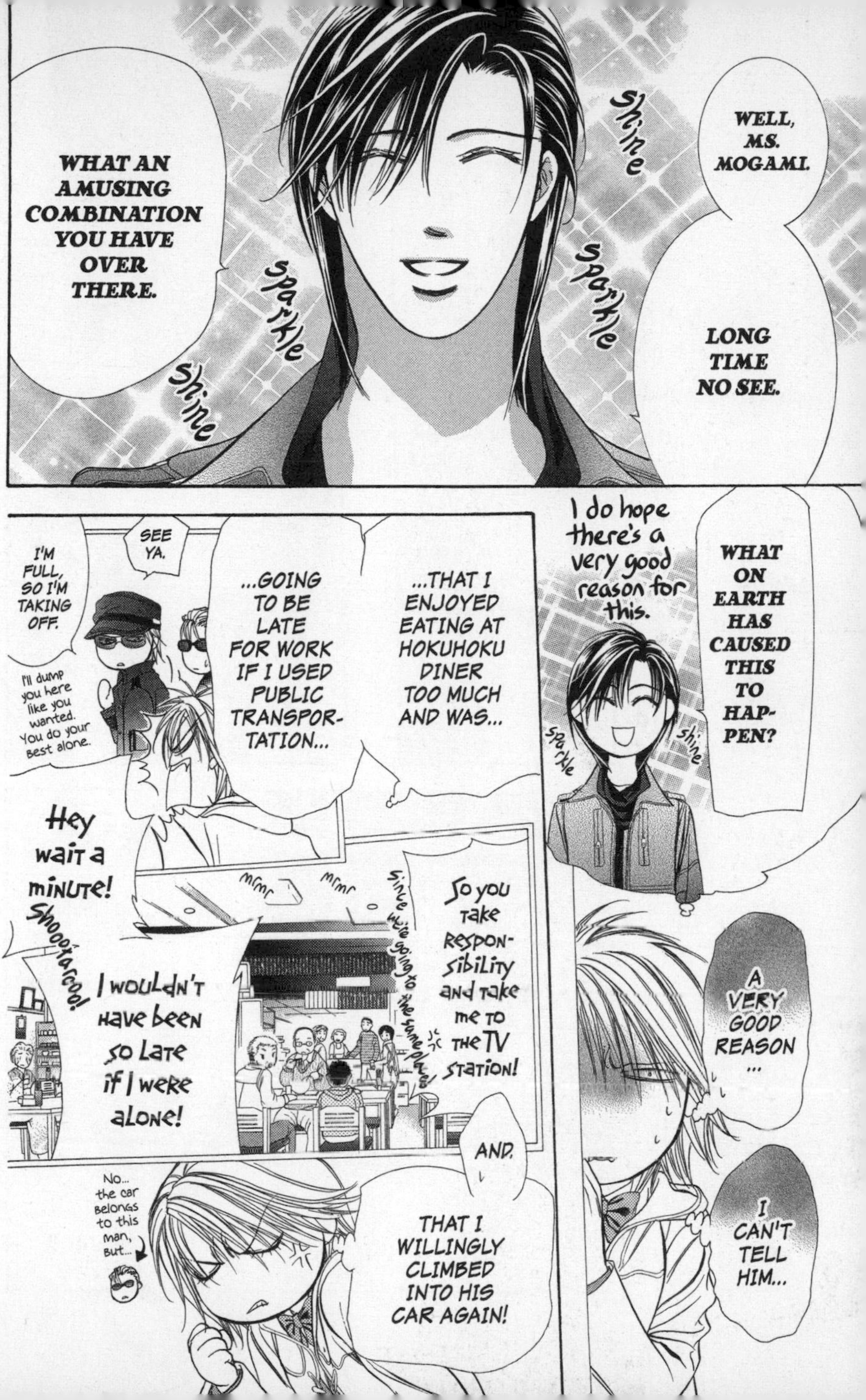
WELL, MS. MOGAMI.
LONG TIME NO SEE.
Shine
Sparkle
WHAT AN AMUSING COMBINATION YOU HAVE OVER THERE.
Sparkle
Shine
WHAT ON EARTH HAS CAUSED THIS TO HAPPEN?
I do hope there's a very good reason for this.
Shine
Sparkle
...THAT I ENJOYED EATING AT HOKUHOKU DINER TOO MUCH AND WAS...
...GOING TO BE LATE FOR WORK IF I USED PUBLIC TRANSPORTATION...
SEE YA.
I'M FULL, SO I'M TAKING OFF.
I'll dump you here like you wanted. You do your best alone.
So you take responsibility and take me to the TV station!
Since we're going to the same place!
mrmr
mrmr
Hey wait a minute!
Shoootaroo!
I wouldn't have been so late if I were alone!
A VERY GOOD REASON...
I CAN'T TELL HIM...
AND,
THAT I WILLINGLY CLIMBED INTO HIS CAR AGAIN!
No... the car belongs to this man, but...

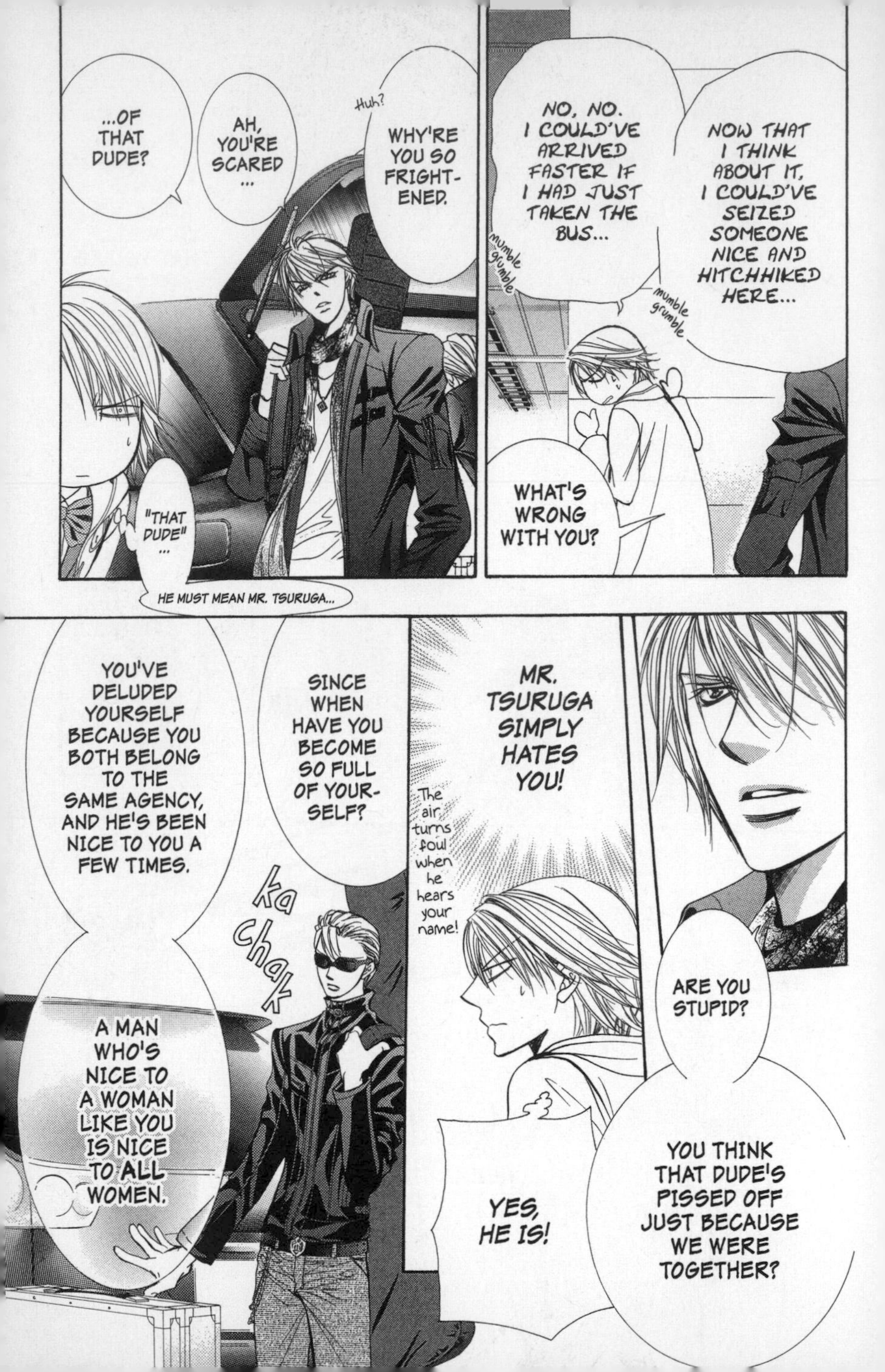
NOW THAT I THINK ABOUT IT, I COULD'VE SEIZED SOMEONE NICE AND HITCHHIKED HERE...
mumble grumble
NO, NO. I COULD'VE ARRIVED FASTER IF I HAD JUST TAKEN THE BUS...
mumble grumble
WHAT'S WRONG WITH YOU?
Huh?
WHY'RE YOU SO FRIGHT-ENED.
AH, YOU'RE SCARED ...
...OF THAT DUDE?
"THAT DUDE" ...
HE MUST MEAN MR. TSURUGA...
ARE YOU STUPID?
YOU THINK THAT DUDE'S PISSED OFF JUST BECAUSE WE WERE TOGETHER?
MR. TSURUGA SIMPLY HATES YOU!
The air turns foul when he hears your name!
YES, HE IS!
SINCE WHEN HAVE YOU BECOME SO FULL OF YOUR-SELF?
YOU'VE DELUDED YOURSELF BECAUSE YOU BOTH BELONG TO THE SAME AGENCY, AND HE'S BEEN NICE TO YOU A FEW TIMES.
ka chak
A MAN WHO'S NICE TO A WOMAN LIKE YOU IS NICE TO ALL WOMEN.

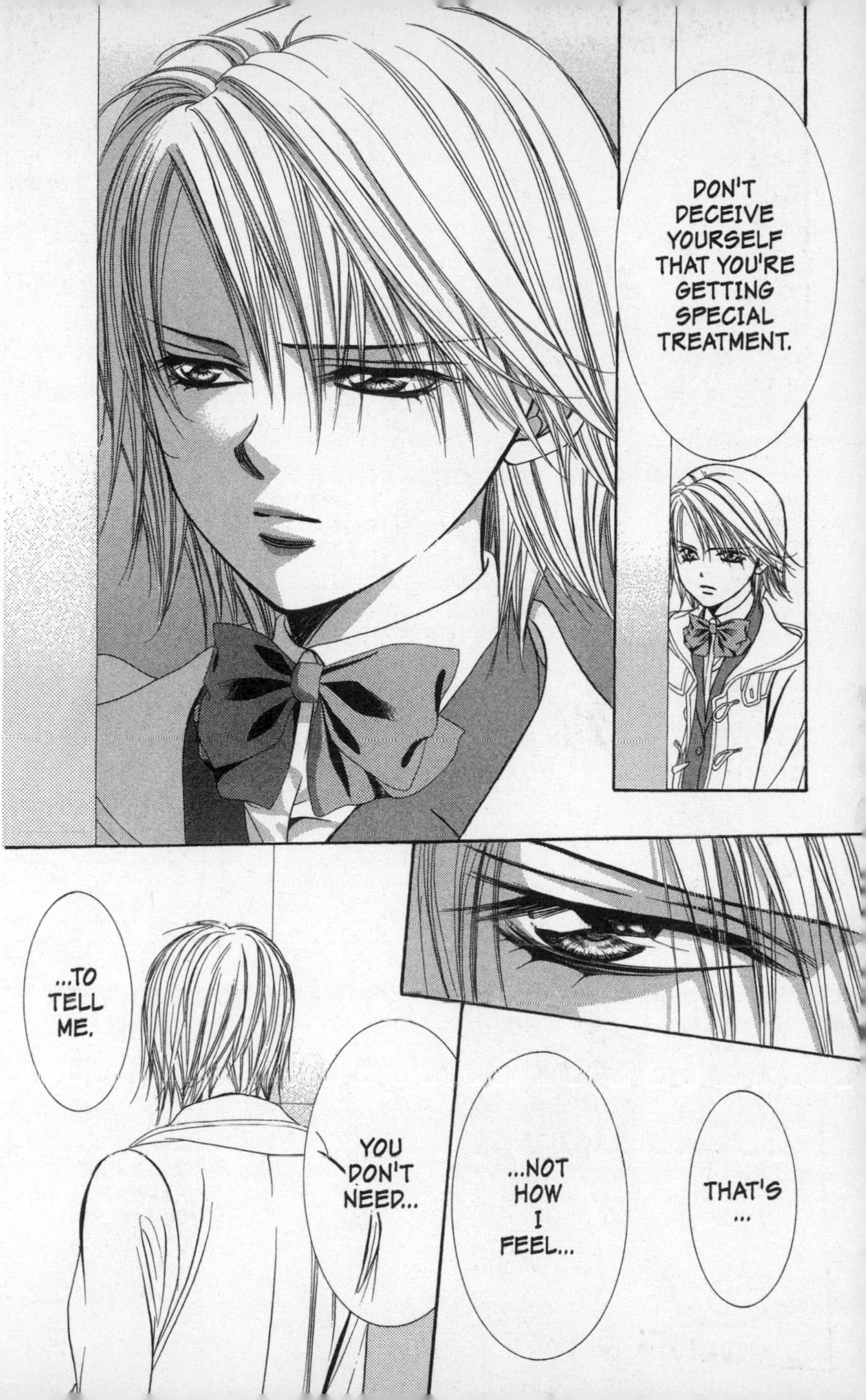
DON'T DECEIVE YOURSELF THAT YOU'RE GETTING SPECIAL TREATMENT.
THAT'S...
...NOT HOW I FEEL...
YOU DON'T NEED...
...TO TELL ME.

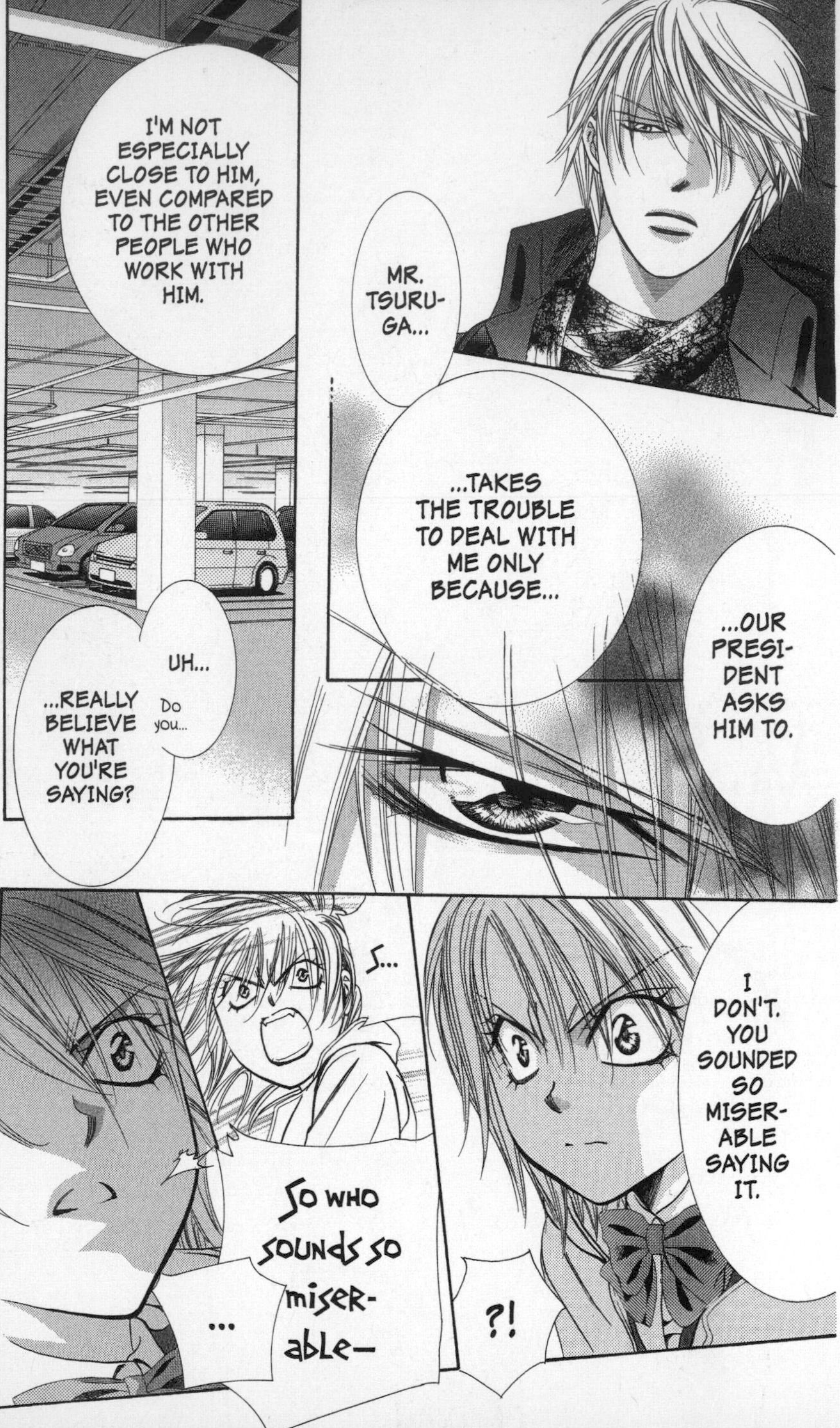
MR. TSURU-GA...
...TAKES THE TROUBLE TO DEAL WITH ME ONLY BECAUSE...
...OUR PRESI-DENT ASKS HIM TO.
I'M NOT ESPECIALLY CLOSE TO HIM, EVEN COMPARED TO THE OTHER PEOPLE WHO WORK WITH HIM.
UH...
Do you...
...REALLY BELIEVE WHAT YOU'RE SAYING?
I DON'T. YOU SOUNDED SO MISER-ABLE SAYING IT.
?!
S...
So who sounds so miser-able—
...

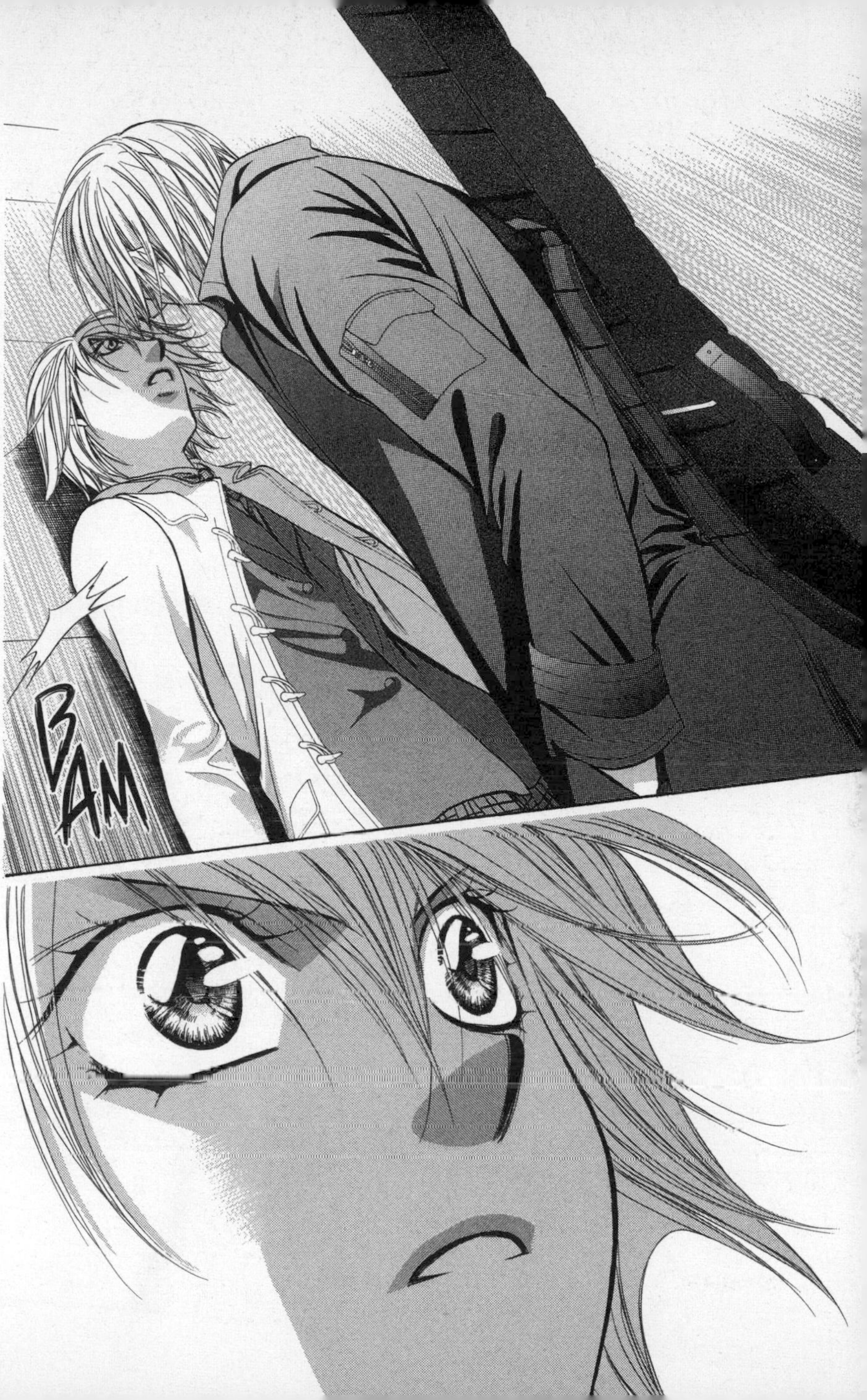
BAM

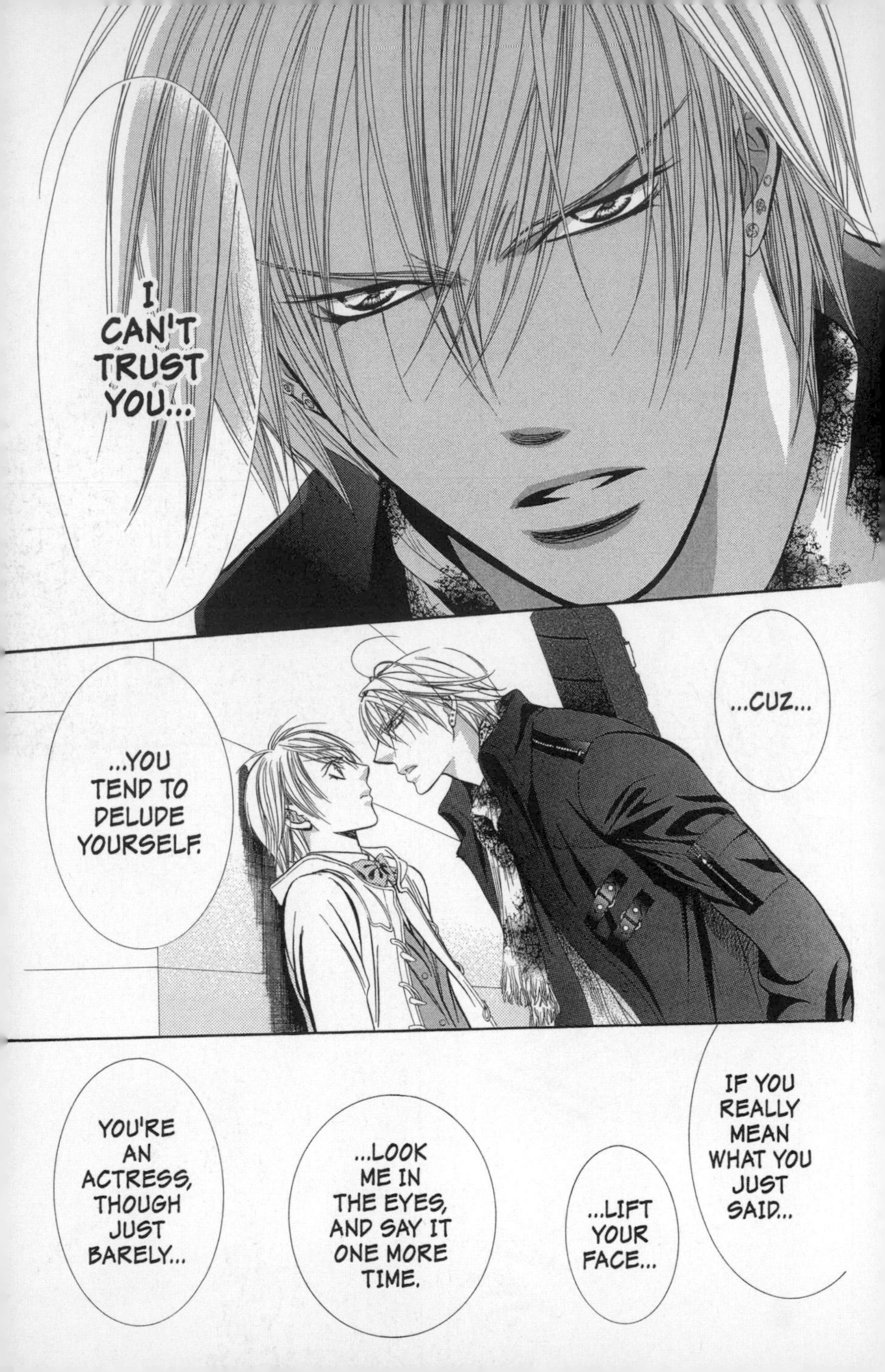
I CAN'T TRUST YOU...
...CUZ...
...YOU TEND TO DELUDE YOURSELF.
IF YOU REALLY MEAN WHAT YOU JUST SAID...
...LIFT YOUR FACE...
...LOOK ME IN THE EYES, AND SAY IT ONE MORE TIME.
YOU'RE AN ACTRESS, THOUGH JUST BARELY...

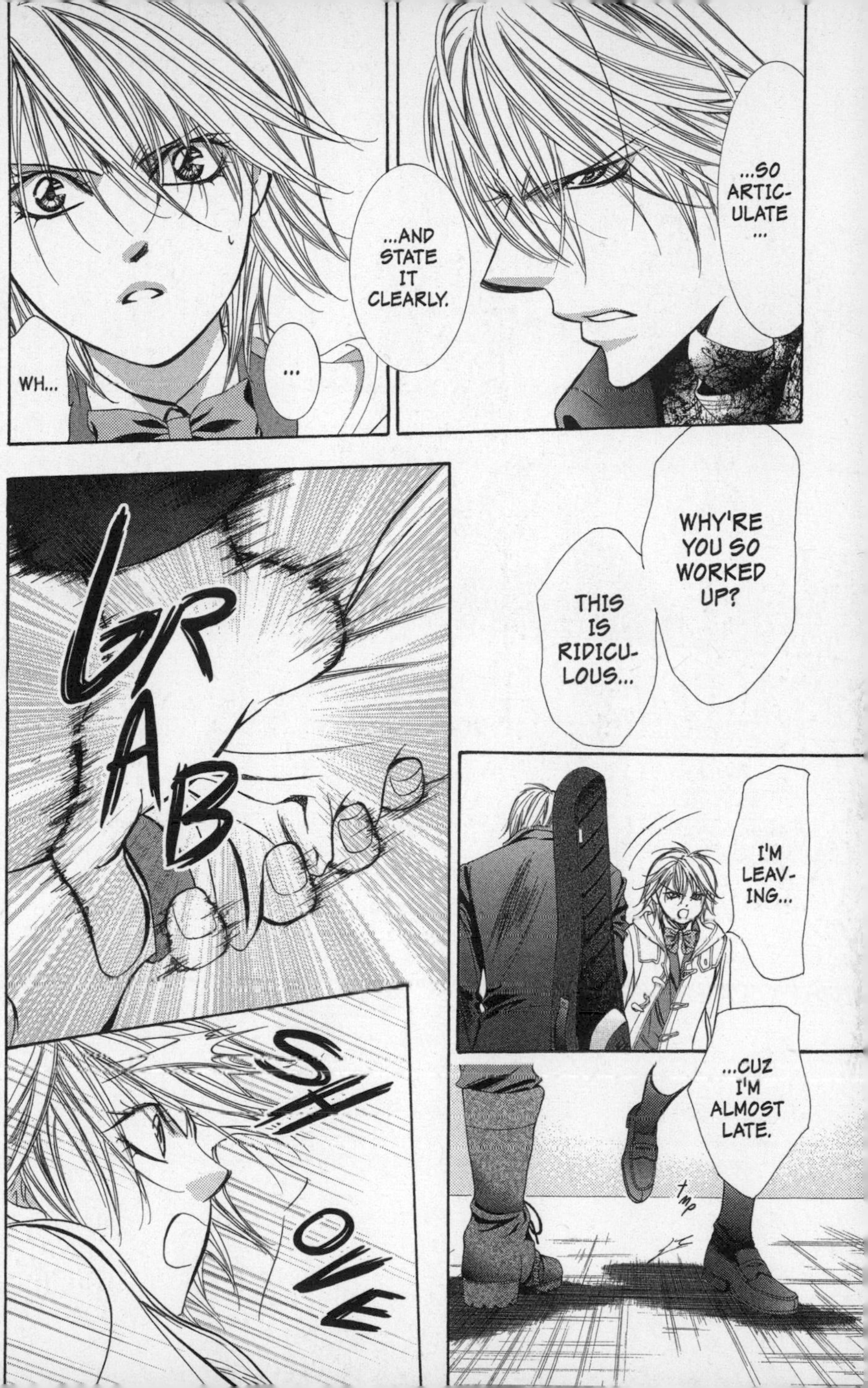
...SO ARTIC-ULATE ...
...AND STATE IT CLEARLY.
...
WH...
WHY'RE YOU SO WORKED UP?
THIS IS RIDICU-LOUS...
I'M LEAV-ING...
...CUZ I'M ALMOST LATE.
tmp
GRAB
SHOVE

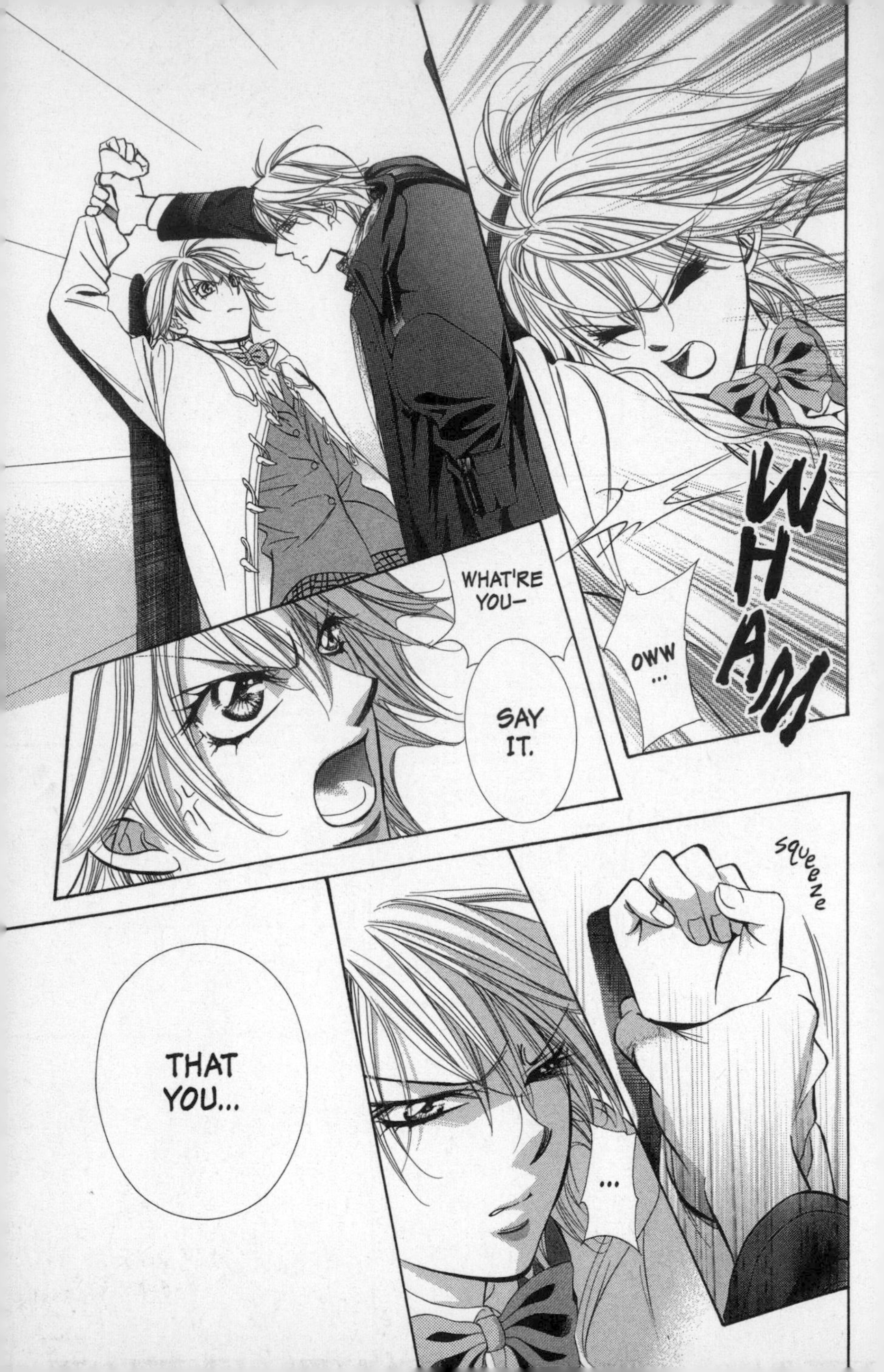
WHAM
OWW ...
WHAT'RE YOU—
SAY IT.
squeeze
...
THAT YOU...

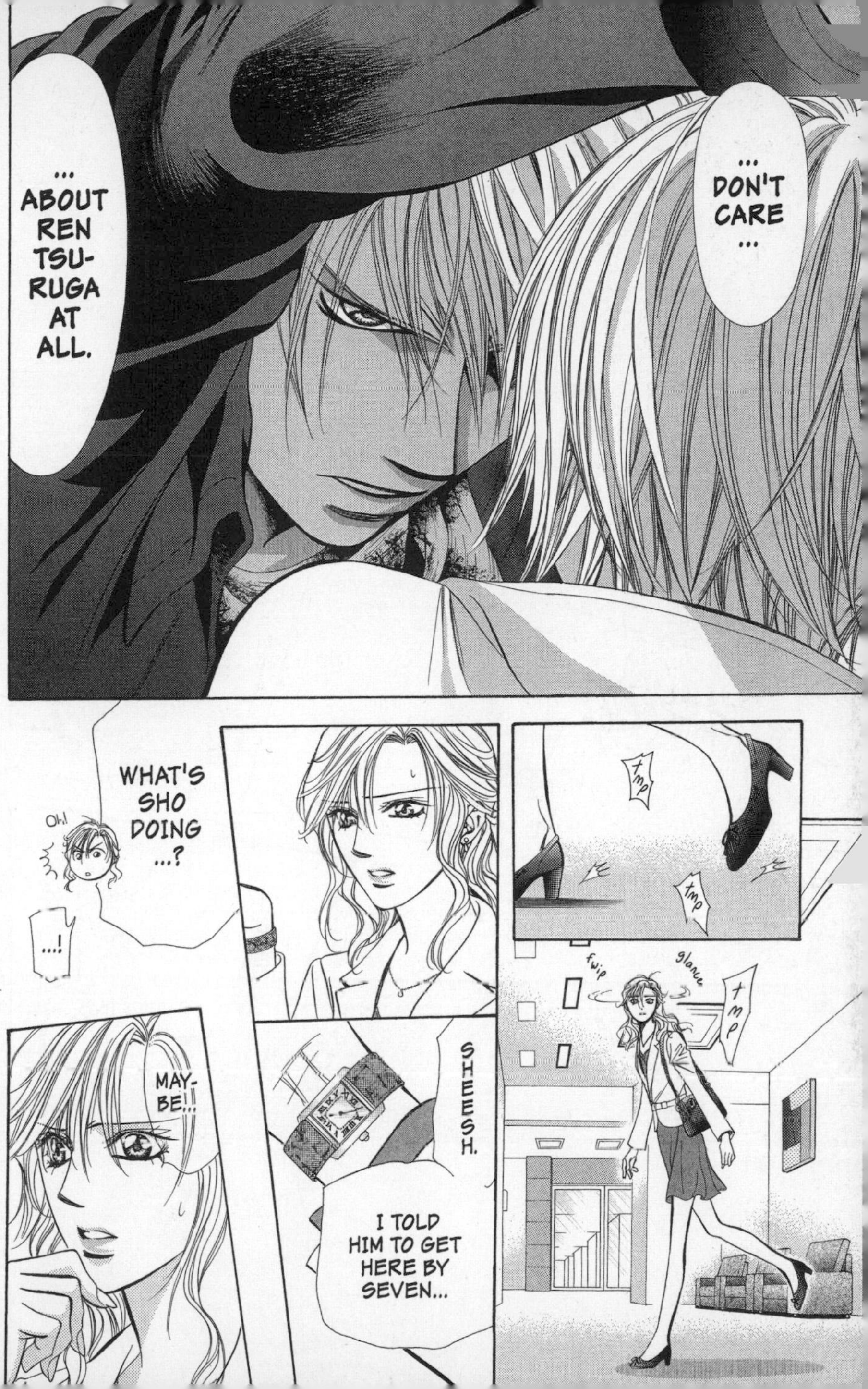
...DON'T CARE...
...ABOUT REN TSURUGA AT ALL.
tmp
tmp
fwip
glance
tmp
SHEESH.
I TOLD HIM TO GET HERE BY SEVEN...
WHAT'S SHO DOING ...?
Oh!
...!
MAY-BE!...

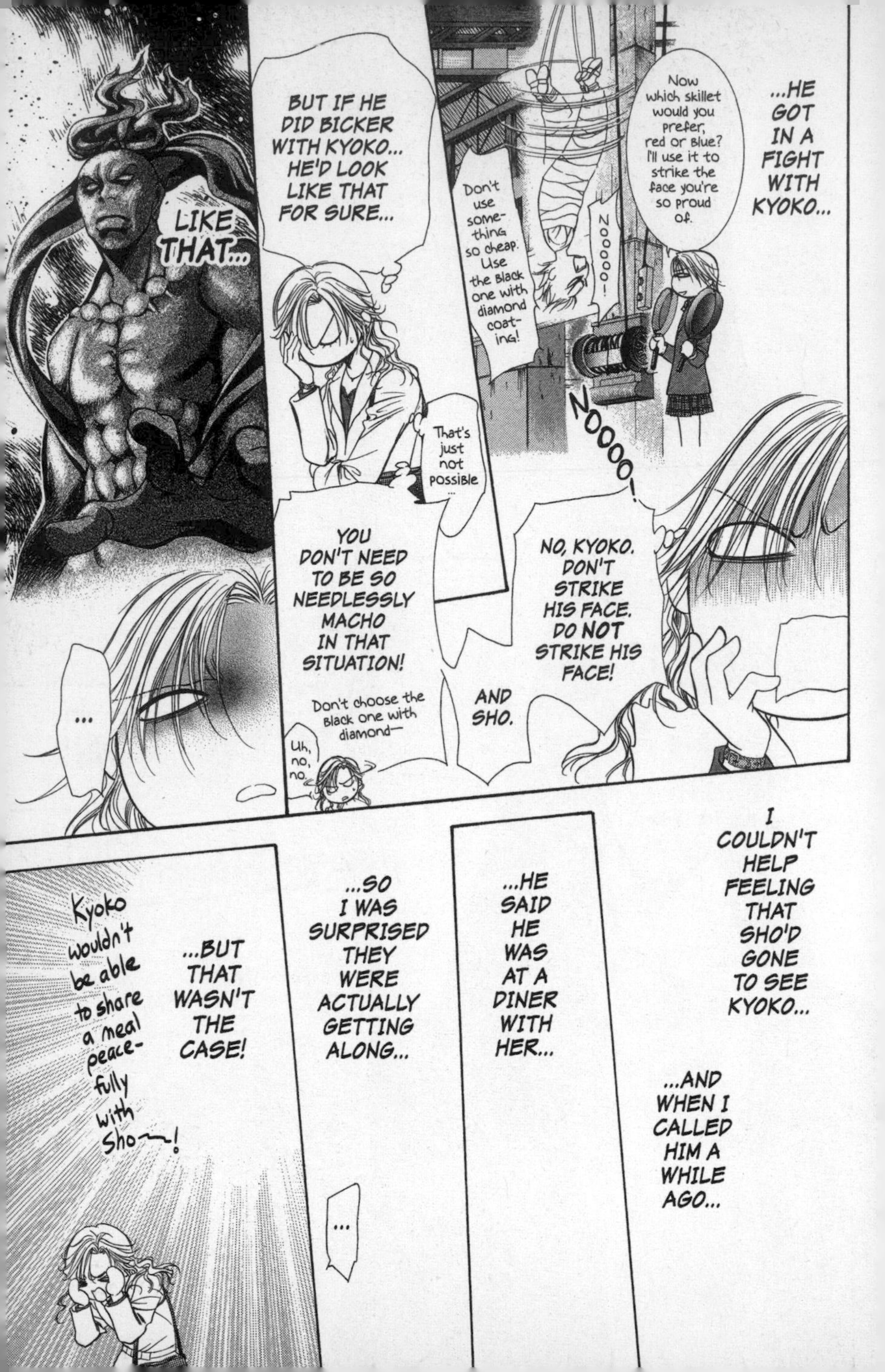
...HE GOT IN A FIGHT WITH KYOKO...
Now which skillet would you prefer, red or blue? I'll use it to strike the face you're so proud of.
Noooooo!
Don't use something so cheap. Use the black one with diamond coating!
NOOOO!
BUT IF HE DID BICKER WITH KYOKO... HE'D LOOK LIKE THAT FOR SURE...
That's just not possible...
LIKE THAT...
NO, KYOKO. DON'T STRIKE HIS FACE. DO NOT STRIKE HIS FACE!
AND SHO.
YOU DON'T NEED TO BE SO NEEDLESSLY MACHO IN THAT SITUATION!
Don't choose the black one with diamond—
Uh, no, no.
...
I COULDN'T HELP FEELING THAT SHO'D GONE TO SEE KYOKO...
...AND WHEN I CALLED HIM A WHILE AGO...
...HE SAID HE WAS AT A DINER WITH HER...
...SO I WAS SURPRISED THEY WERE ACTUALLY GETTING ALONG...
...
...BUT THAT WASN'T THE CASE!
Kyoko wouldn't be able to share a meal peacefully with Sho~!

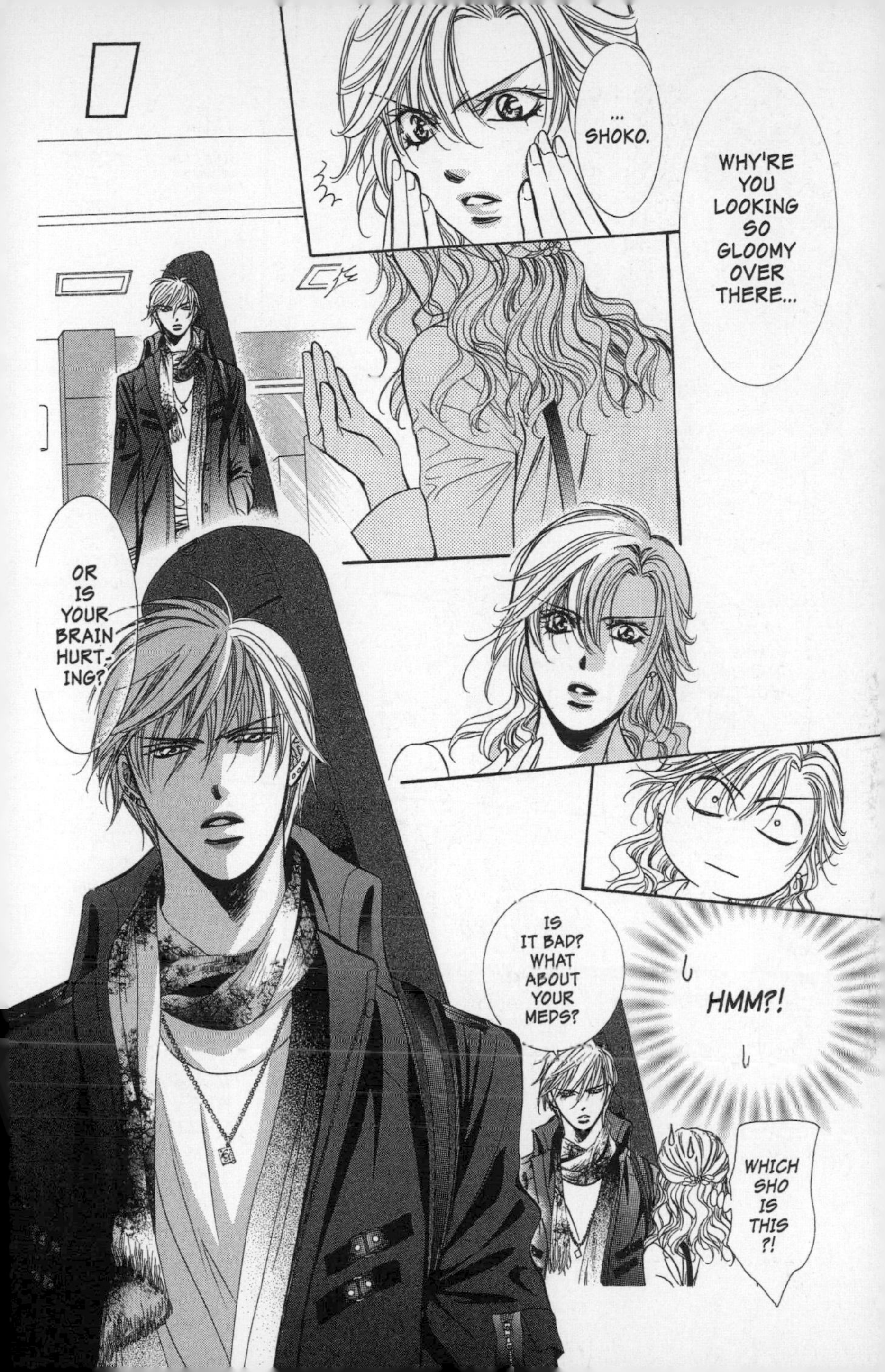

... SHOKO.
WHY'RE YOU LOOKING SO GLOOMY OVER THERE...
OR IS YOUR BRAIN HURTING?
IS IT BAD? WHAT ABOUT YOUR MEDS?
HMM?!
WHICH SHO IS THIS?!

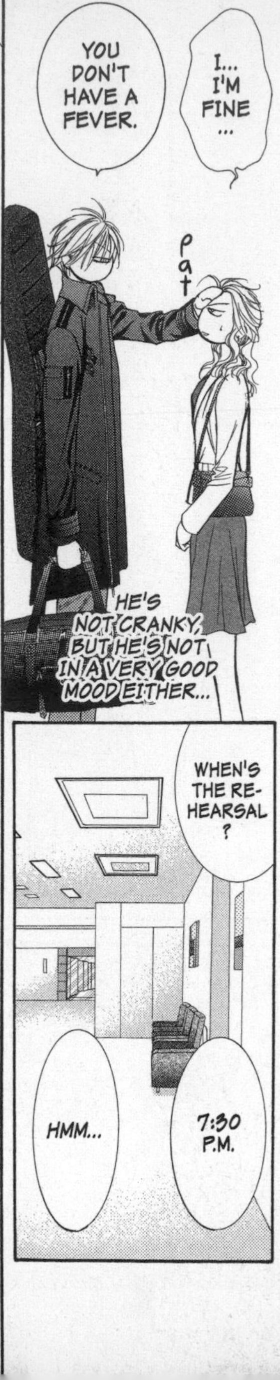
I... I'M FINE...
YOU DON'T HAVE A FEVER.
pat
HE'S NOT CRANKY, BUT HE'S NOT IN A VERY GOOD MOOD EITHER...
WHEN'S THE RE-HEARSAL?
7:30 P.M.
HMM...

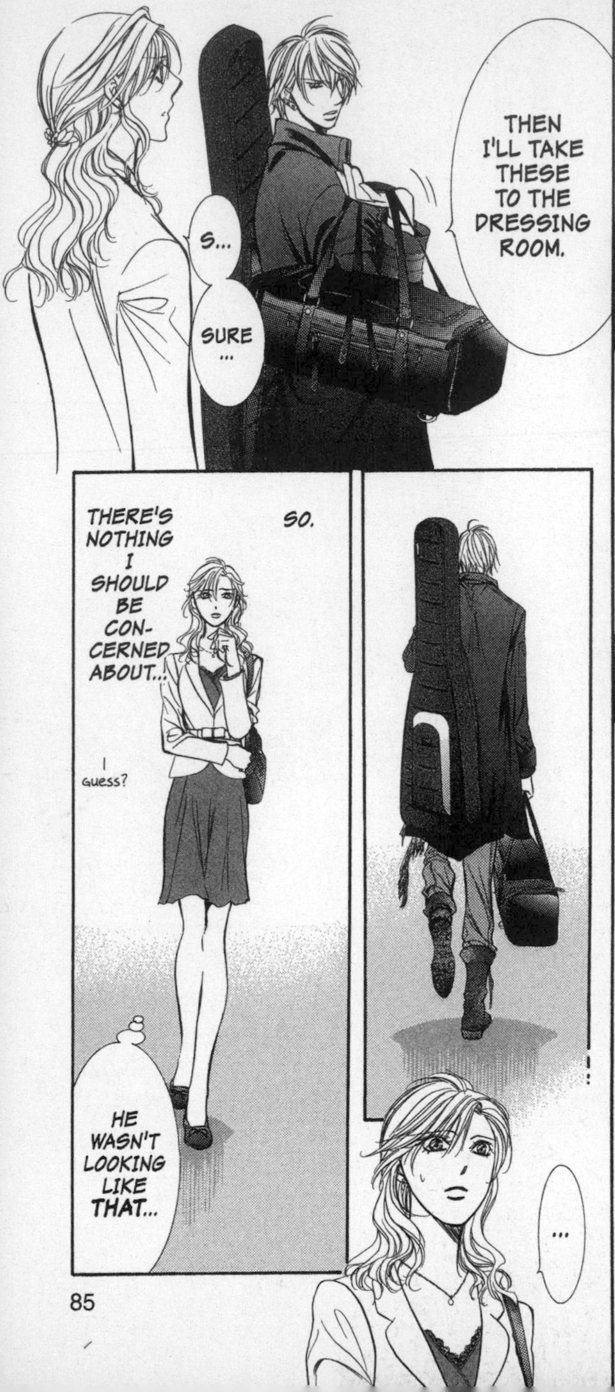
THEN I'LL TAKE THESE TO THE DRESSING ROOM.
S...
SURE...
!
SO.
THERE'S NOTHING I SHOULD BE CON-CERNED ABOUT...
I guess?
HE WASN'T LOOKING LIKE THAT...
...

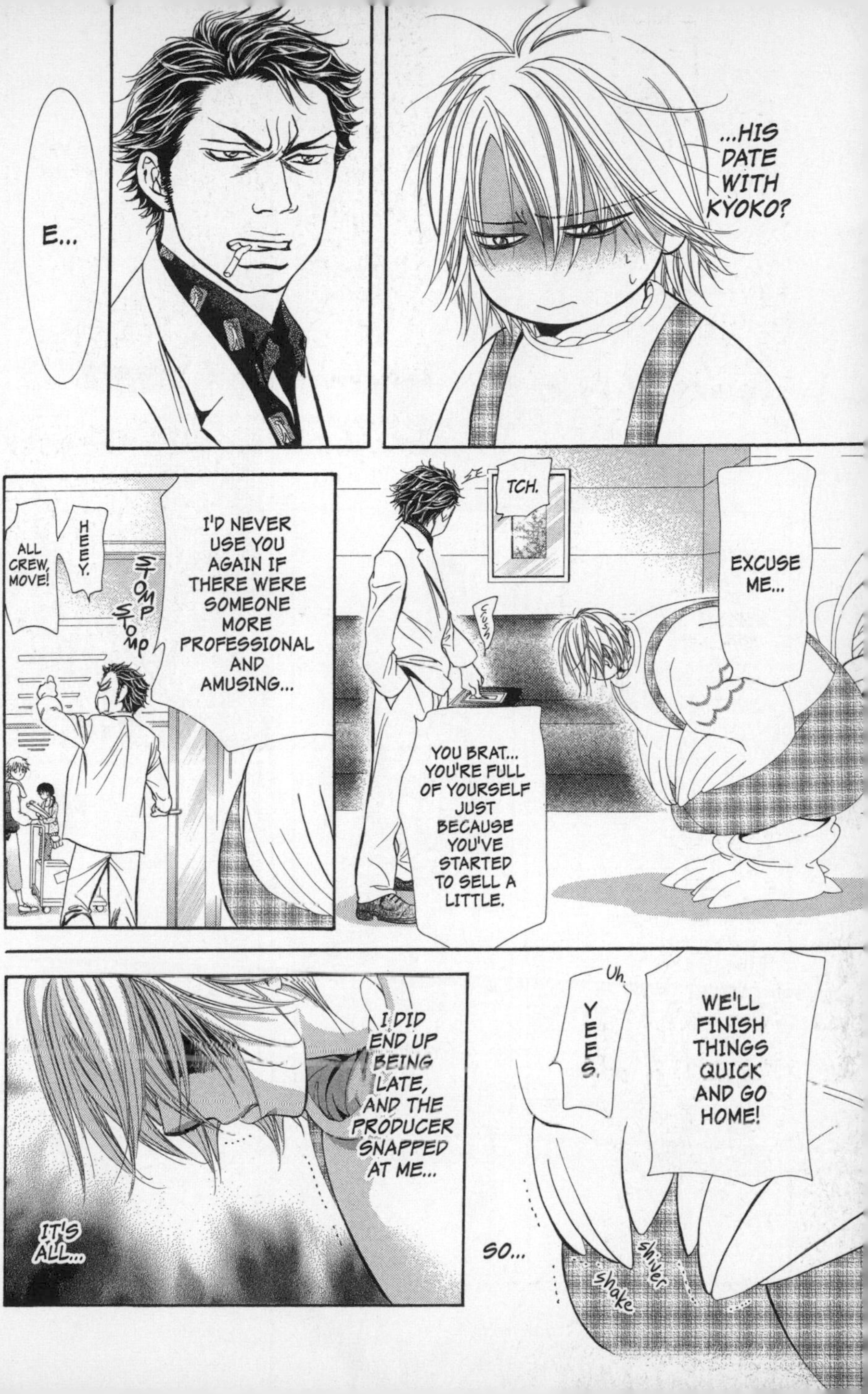
...HIS DATE WITH KYOKO?
E...
EXCUSE ME...
TCH.
YOU BRAT... YOU'RE FULL OF YOURSELF JUST BECAUSE YOU'VE STARTED TO SELL A LITTLE.
I'D NEVER USE YOU AGAIN IF THERE WERE SOMEONE MORE PROFESSIONAL AND AMUSING...
HEEY.
ALL CREW, MOVE!
STOMP STOMP
WE'LL FINISH THINGS QUICK AND GO HOME!
Uh. YEES.
shiver shake
SO...
I DID END UP BEING LATE, AND THE PRODUCER SNAPPED AT ME...
IT'S ALL...

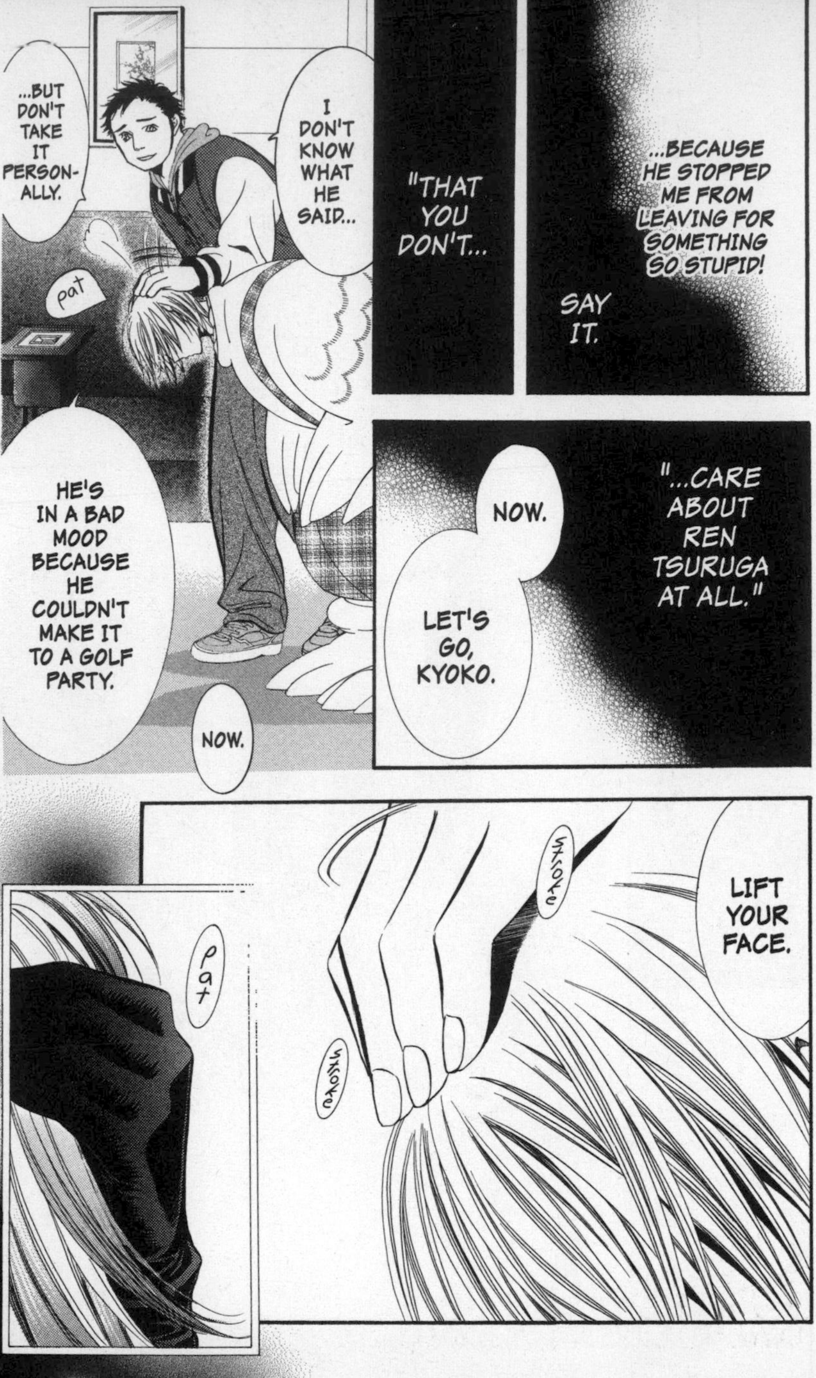
...BECAUSE HE STOPPED ME FROM LEAVING FOR SOMETHING SO STUPID!
SAY IT.
"THAT YOU DON'T...
"...CARE ABOUT REN TSURUGA AT ALL."
NOW.
LET'S GO, KYOKO.
I DON'T KNOW WHAT HE SAID...
...BUT DON'T TAKE IT PERSONALLY.
pat
HE'S IN A BAD MOOD BECAUSE HE COULDN'T MAKE IT TO A GOLF PARTY.
NOW.
LIFT YOUR FACE.
stroke
stroke
pat

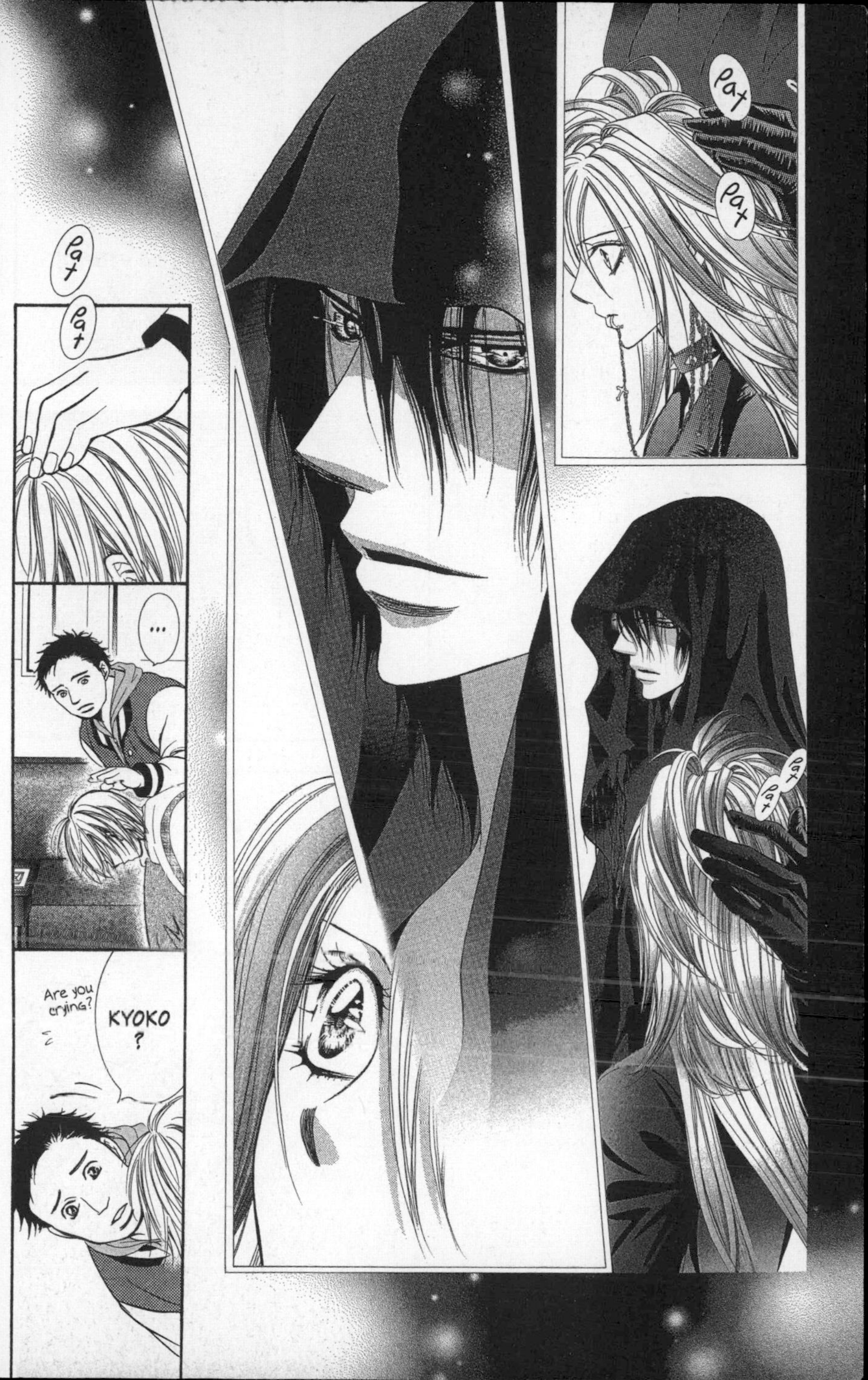
pat
pat
pat
pat
pat
pat
...
KYOKO ?
Are you crying?

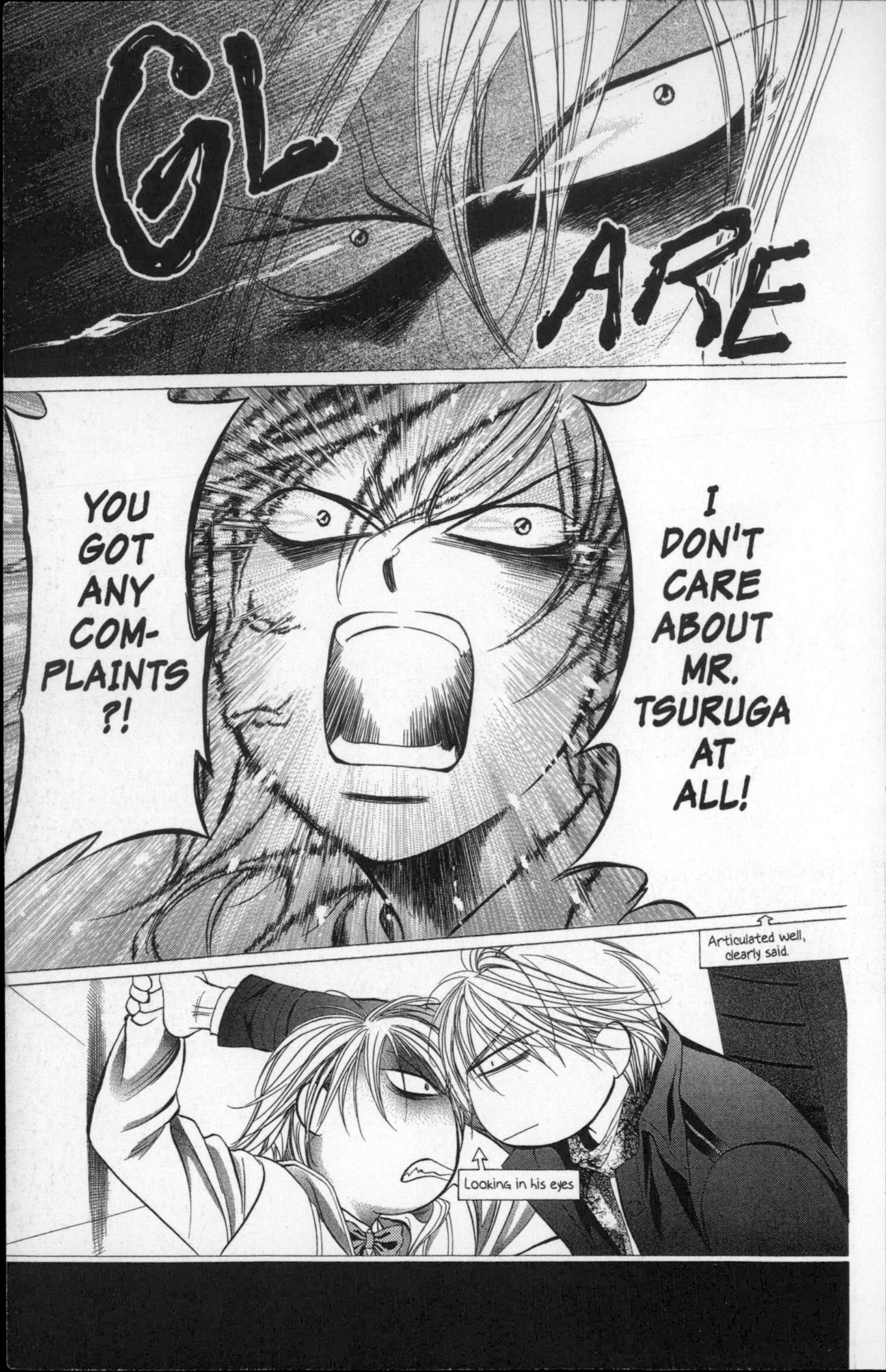
GLARE
I DON'T CARE ABOUT MR. TSURUGA AT ALL!
YOU GOT ANY COM-PLAINTS ?!
Articulated well, clearly said.
Looking in his eyes

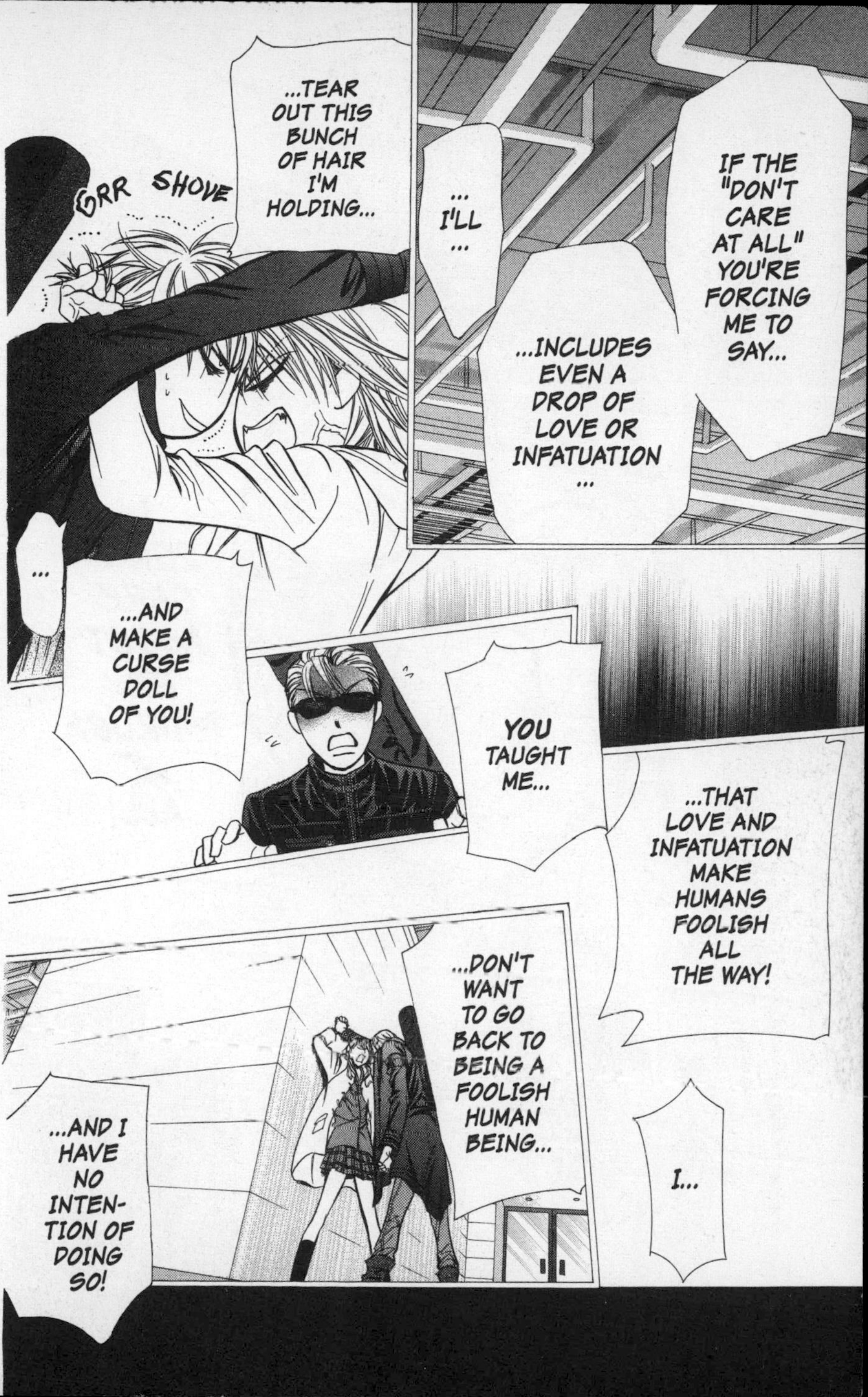
IF THE "DON'T CARE AT ALL" YOU'RE FORCING ME TO SAY...
...INCLUDES EVEN A DROP OF LOVE OR INFATUATION ...
... I'LL ...
...TEAR OUT THIS BUNCH OF HAIR I'M HOLDING...
GRR SHOVE
...
...AND MAKE A CURSE DOLL OF YOU!
YOU TAUGHT ME...
...THAT LOVE AND INFATUATION MAKE HUMANS FOOLISH ALL THE WAY!
I...
...DON'T WANT TO GO BACK TO BEING A FOOLISH HUMAN BEING...
...AND I HAVE NO INTEN-TION OF DOING SO!

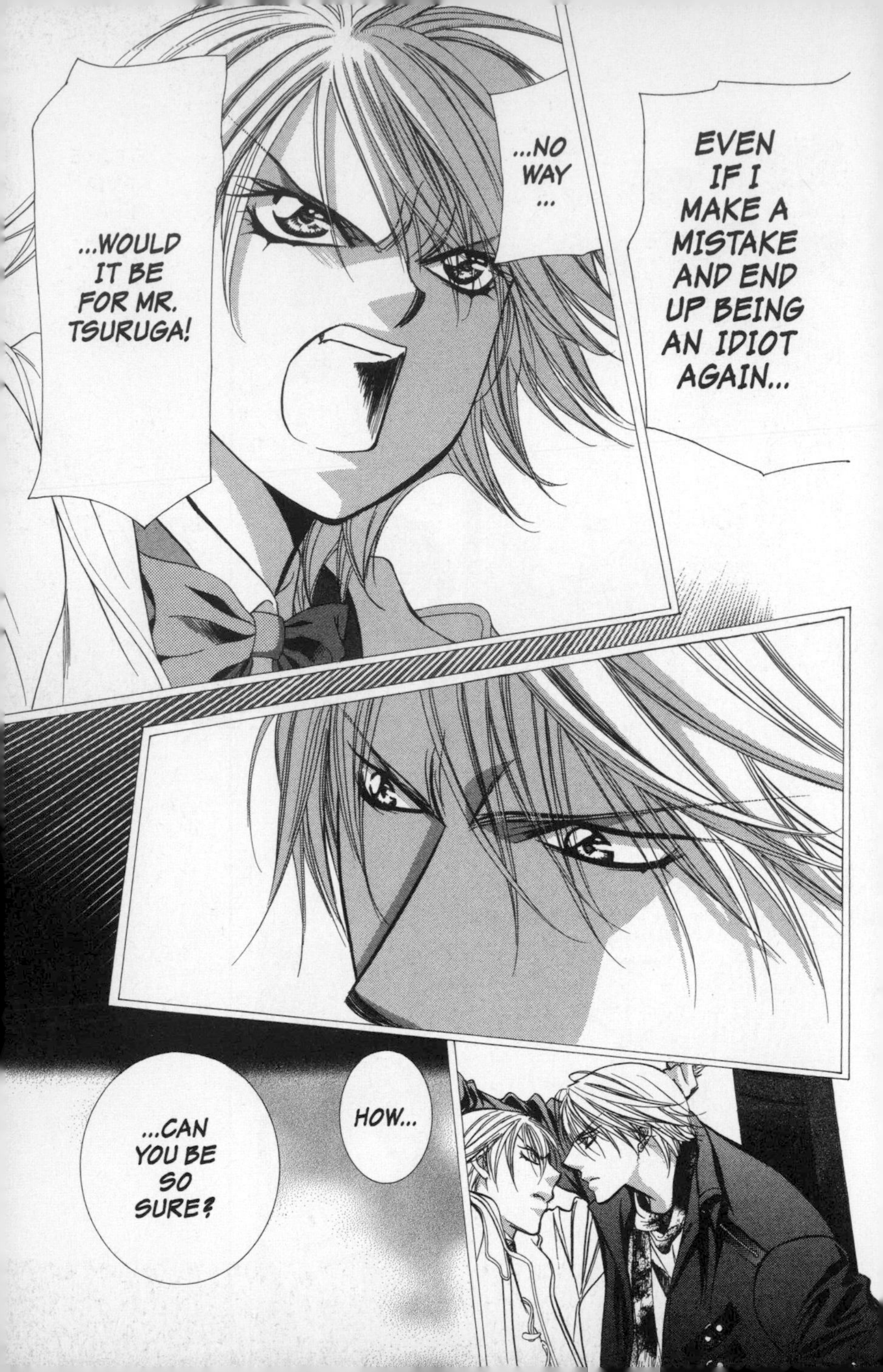
EVEN IF I MAKE A MISTAKE AND END UP BEING AN IDIOT AGAIN...
...NO WAY...
...WOULD IT BE FOR MR. TSURUGA!
HOW...
...CAN YOU BE SO SURE?

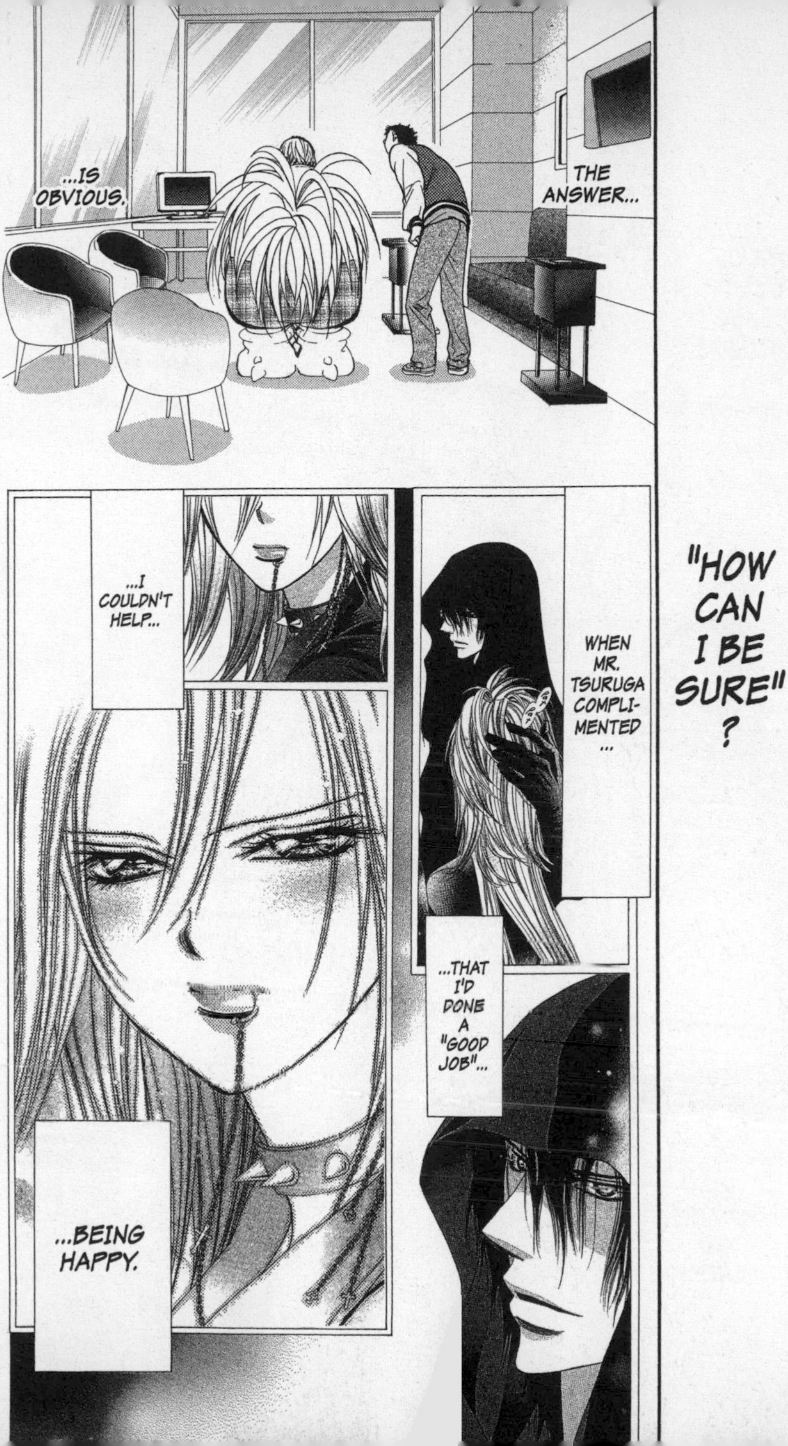
THE ANSWER...
...IS OBVIOUS.
"HOW CAN I BE SURE"?
WHEN MR. TSURUGA COMPLIMENTED...
...THAT I'D DONE A "GOOD JOB"...
...I COULDN'T HELP...
...BEING HAPPY.

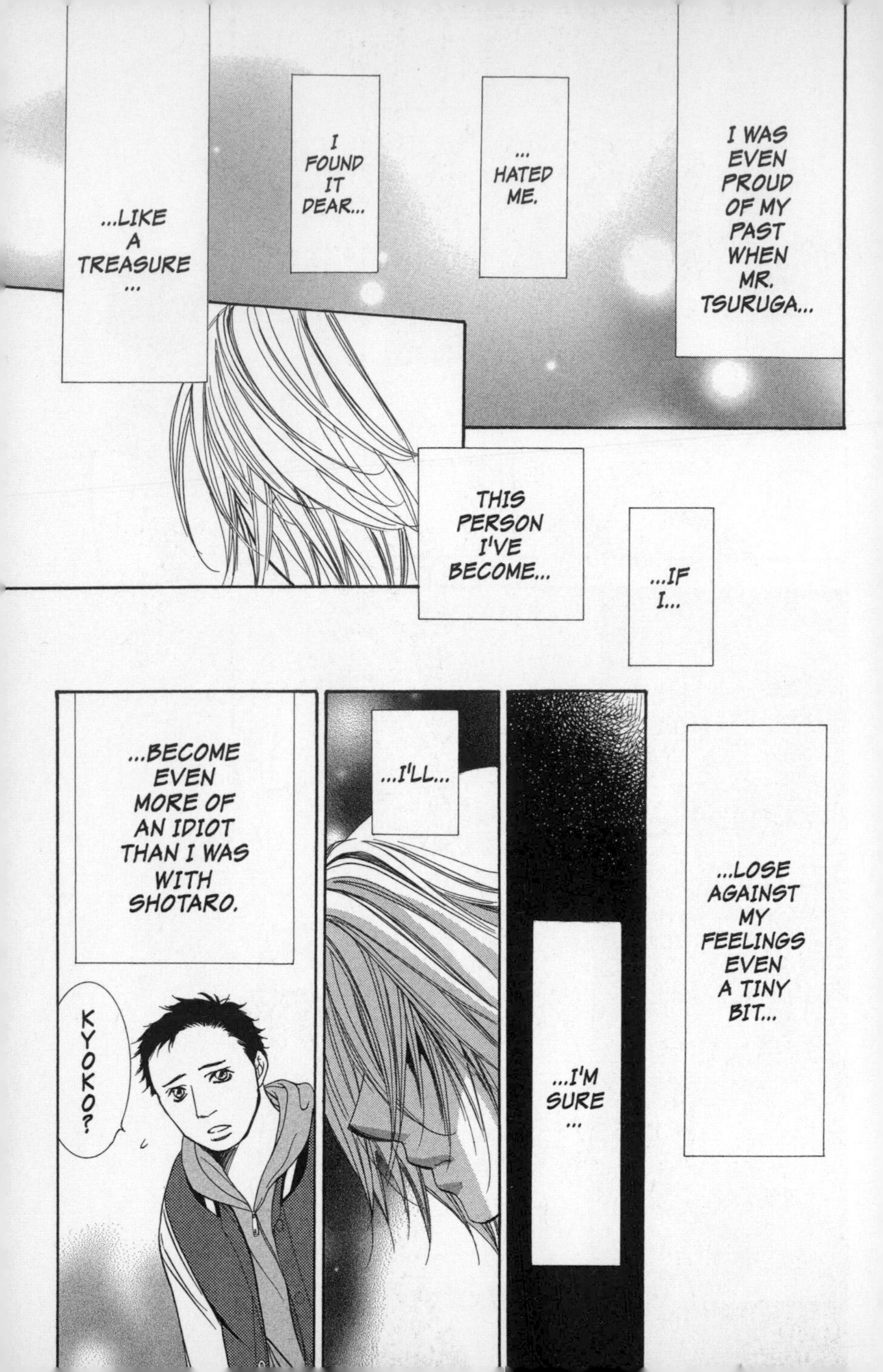
I WAS EVEN PROUD OF MY PAST WHEN MR. TSURUGA...
...HATED ME.
I FOUND IT DEAR...
...LIKE A TREASURE...
THIS PERSON I'VE BECOME...
...IF I...
...LOSE AGAINST MY FEELINGS EVEN A TINY BIT...
...I'M SURE...
...I'LL...
...BECOME EVEN MORE OF AN IDIOT THAN I WAS WITH SHOTARO.
KYOKO?

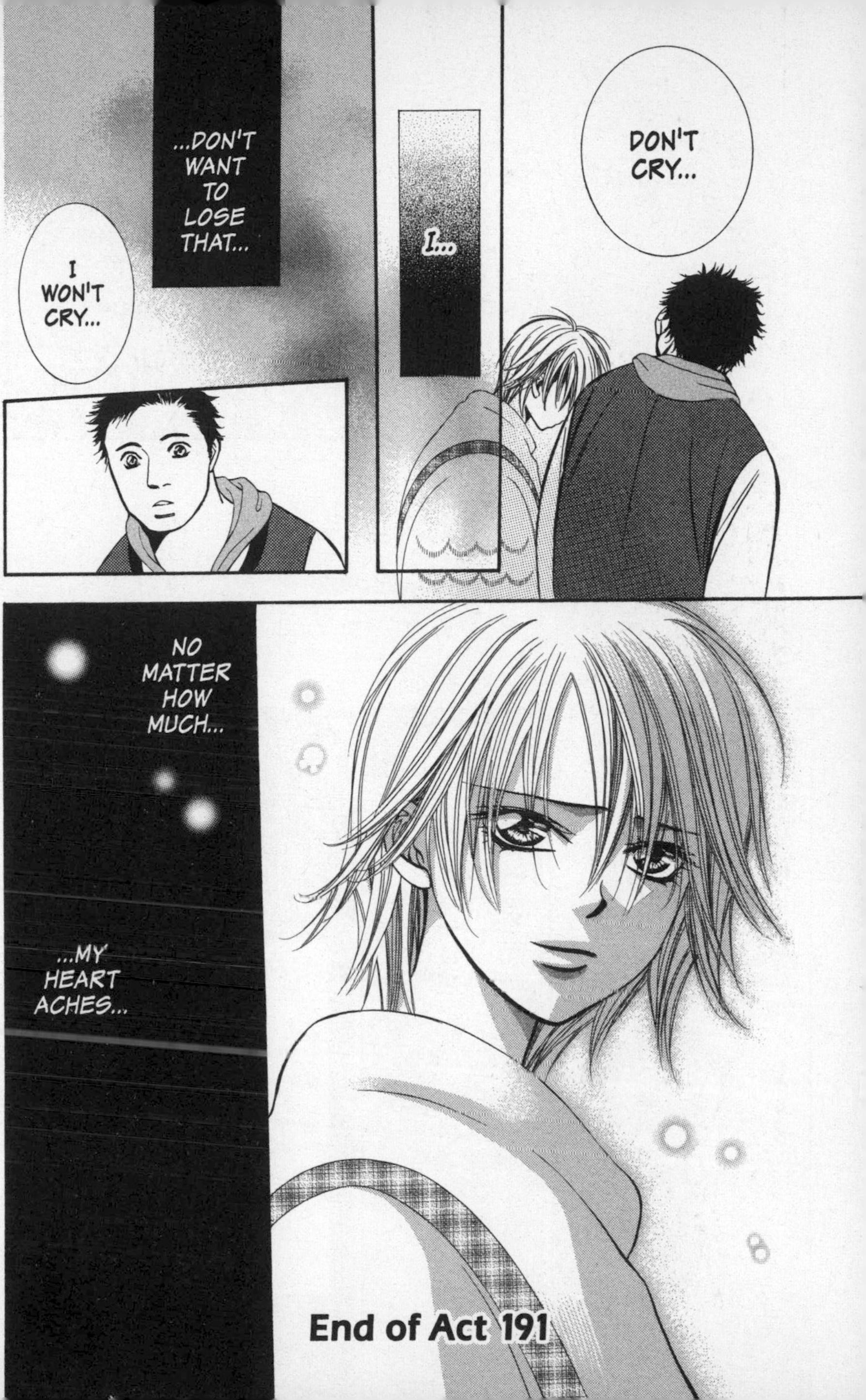
DON'T CRY...
I...
...DON'T WANT TO LOSE THAT...
I WON'T CRY...
NO MATTER HOW MUCH...
...MY HEART ACHES...

End of Act 191

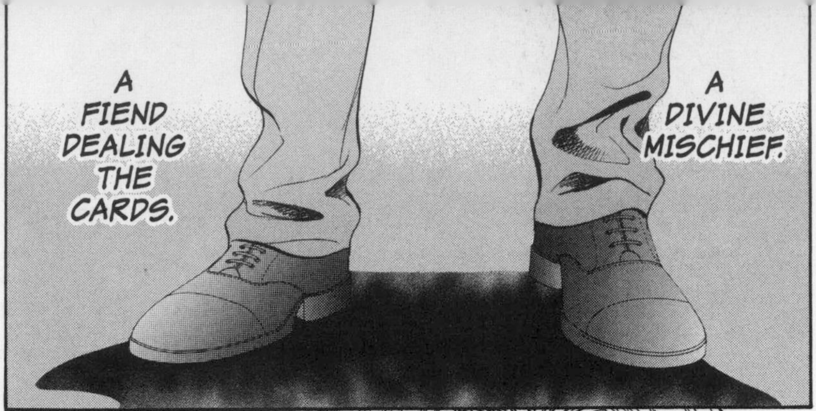
A DIVINE MISCHIEF.
A FIEND DEALING THE CARDS.

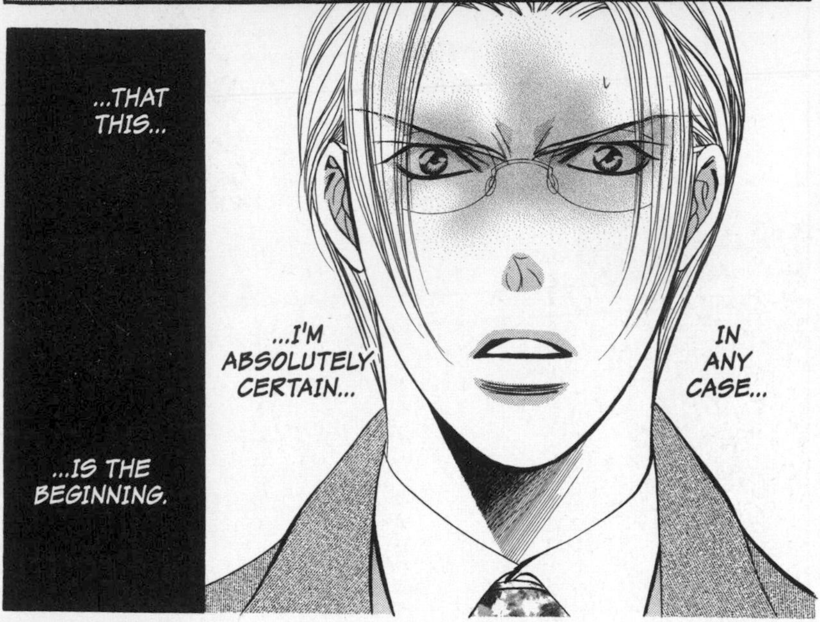
IN ANY CASE...
...I'M ABSOLUTELY CERTAIN...
...THAT THIS...
...IS THE BEGINNING.

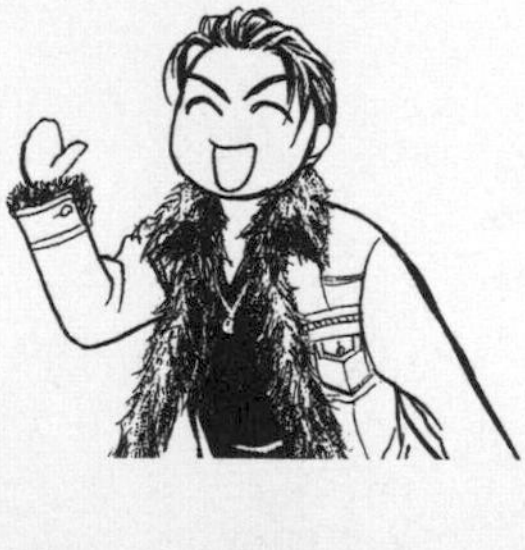

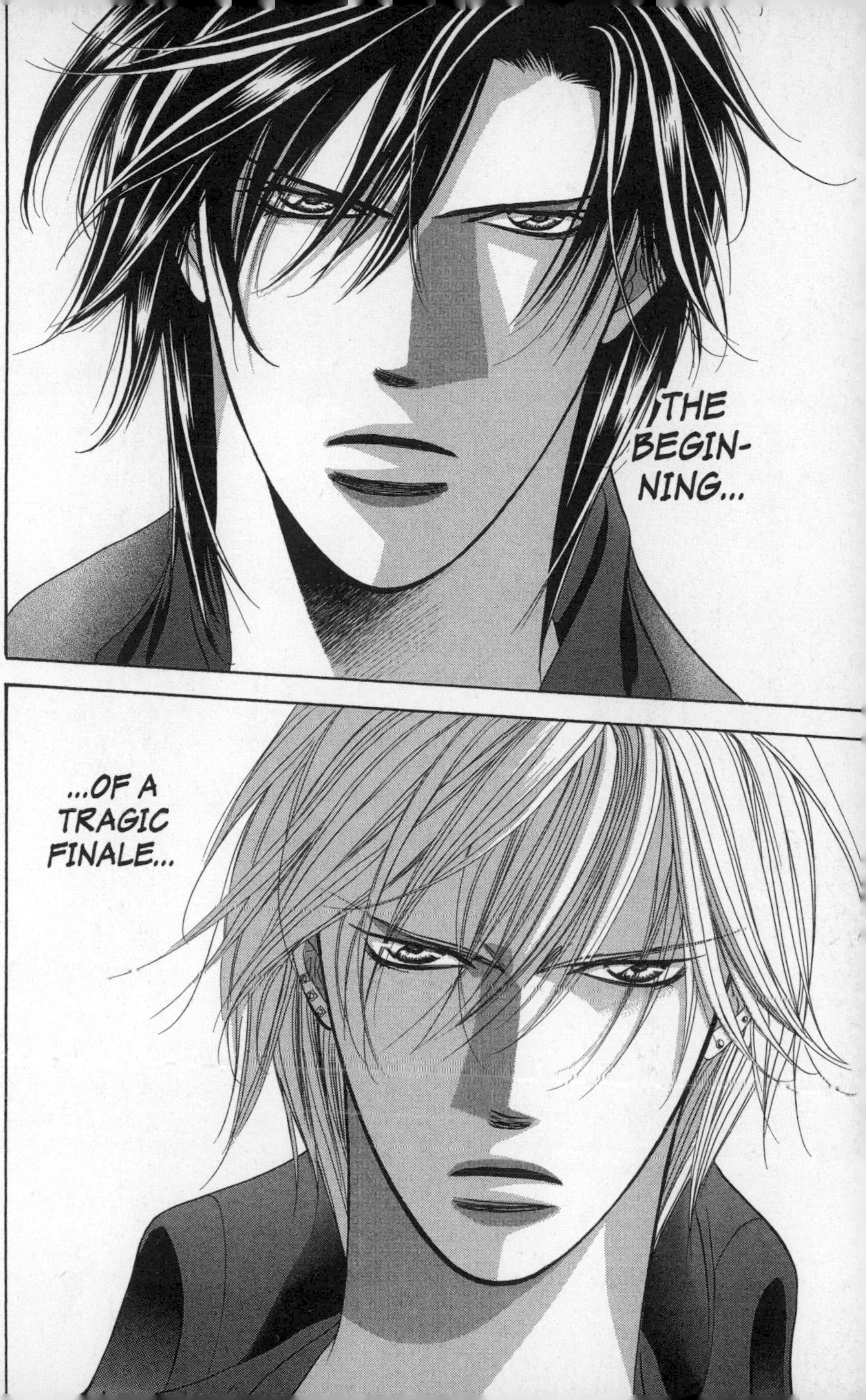
THE BEGIN-NING...
...OF A TRAGIC FINALE...

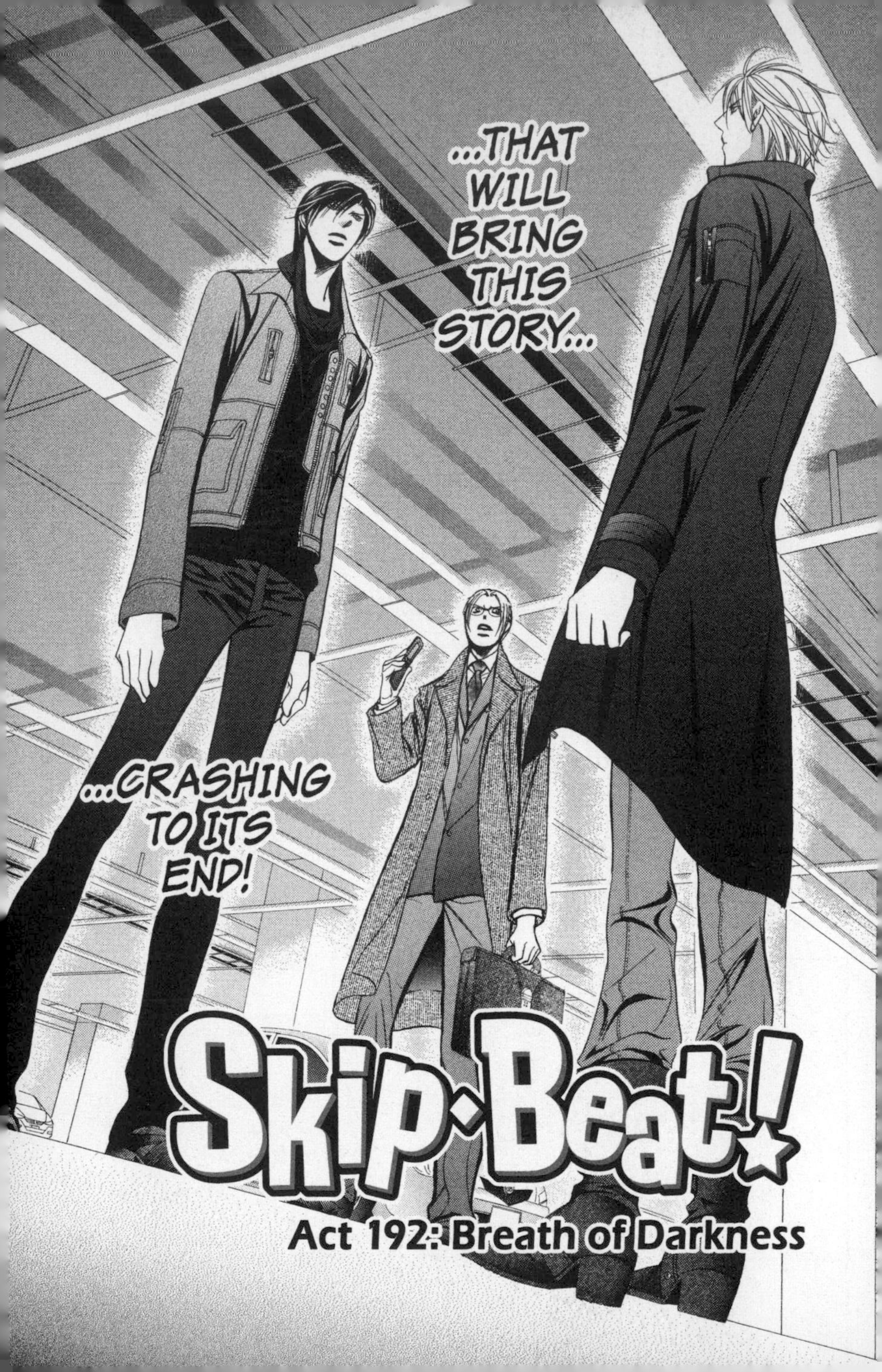
...THAT WILL BRING THIS STORY...
...CRASHING TO ITS END!
Skip·Beat!
Act 192: Breath of Darkness

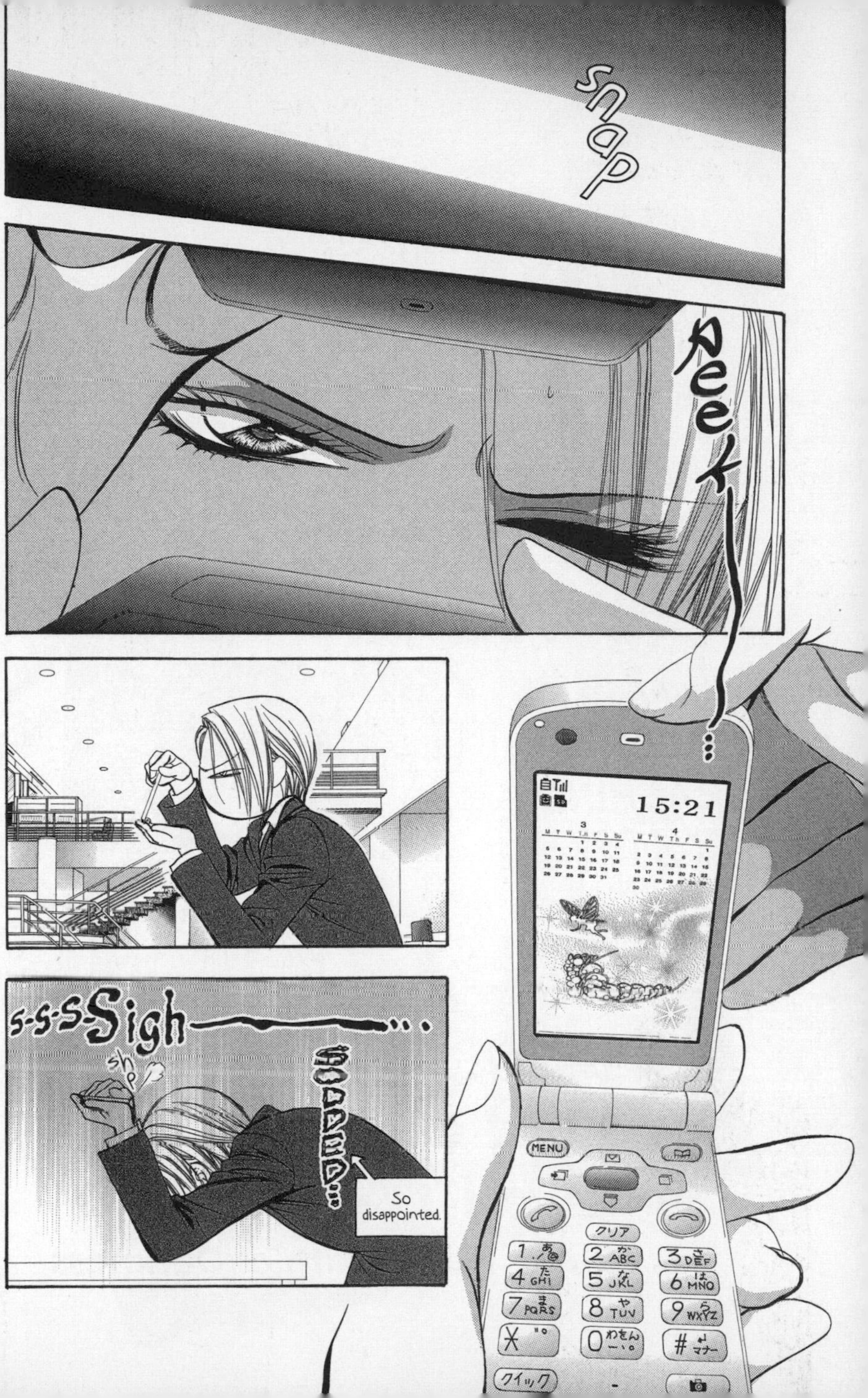
snap
peek...
15:21
s-s-s-Sigh——...
shp
SOBBED..
So disappointed.

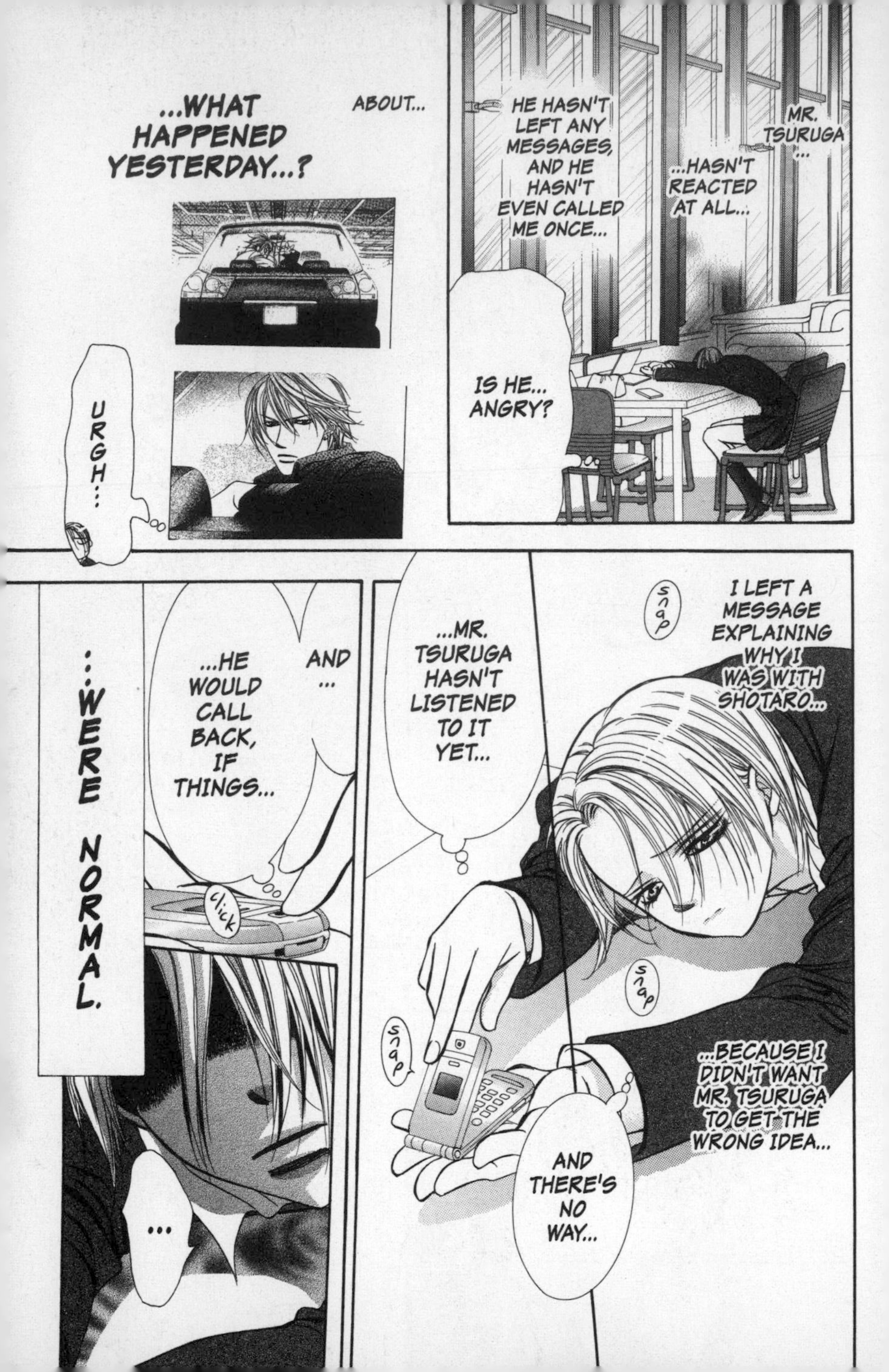
MR. TSURUGA...
...HASN'T REACTED AT ALL...
HE HASN'T LEFT ANY MESSAGES, AND HE HASN'T EVEN CALLED ME ONCE...
ABOUT...
...WHAT HAPPENED YESTERDAY...?
IS HE... ANGRY?
URGH...
I LEFT A MESSAGE EXPLAINING WHY I WAS WITH SHOTARO...
snap
...BECAUSE I DIDN'T WANT MR. TSURUGA TO GET THE WRONG IDEA...
snap
snap
AND THERE'S NO WAY...
...MR. TSURUGA HASN'T LISTENED TO IT YET...
AND...
...HE WOULD CALL BACK, IF THINGS...
...WERE NORMAL.
click
...

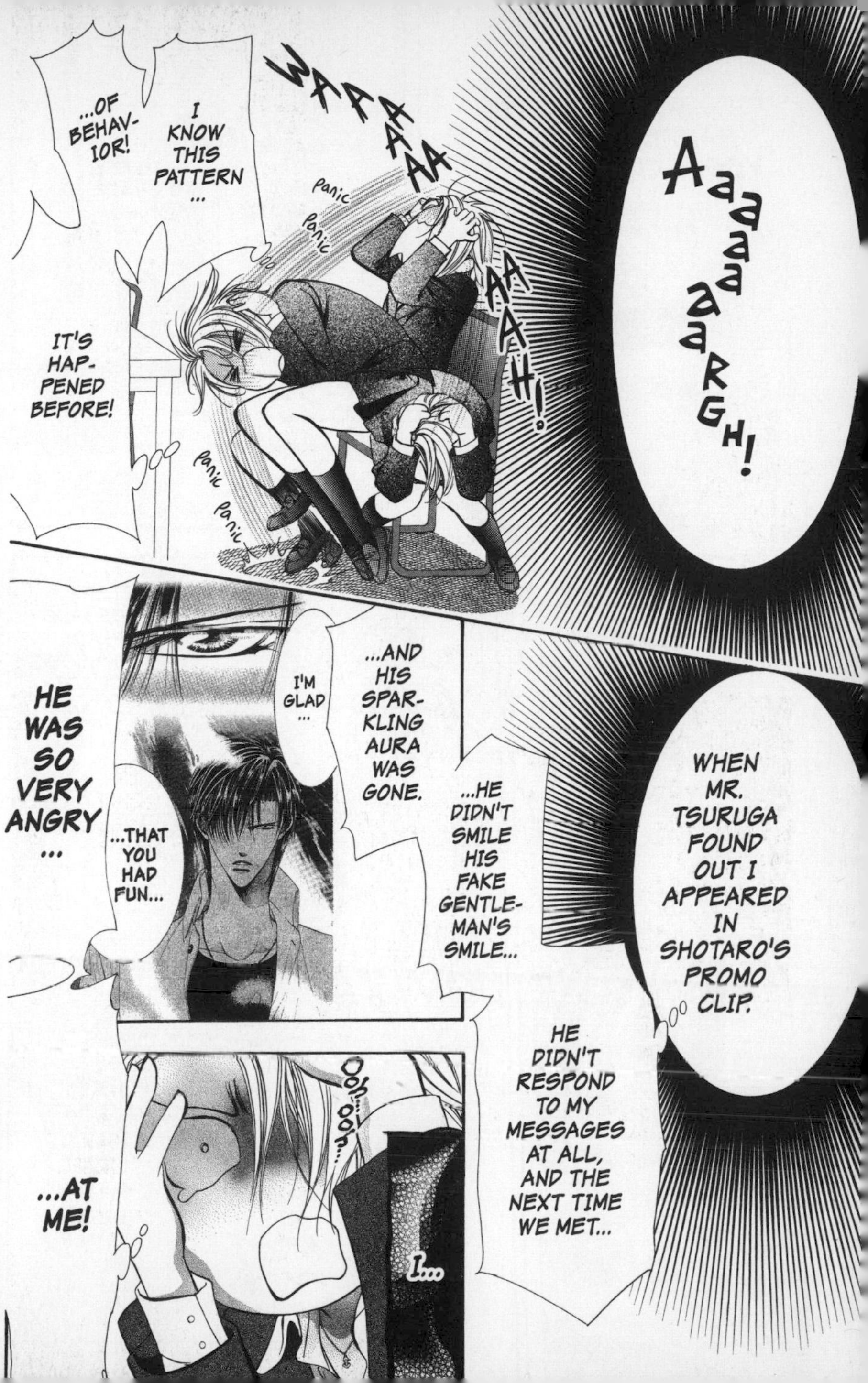

AAAAAAARGH!
WAAAAAAAAH!
panic panic
panic panic
I KNOW THIS PATTERN...
...OF BEHAVIOR!
IT'S HAPPENED BEFORE!
WHEN MR. TSURUGA FOUND OUT I APPEARED IN SHOTARO'S PROMO CLIP.
HE DIDN'T RESPOND TO MY MESSAGES AT ALL, AND THE NEXT TIME WE MET...
...HE DIDN'T SMILE HIS FAKE GENTLEMAN'S SMILE...
...AND HIS SPARKLING AURA WAS GONE.
I'M GLAD...
...THAT YOU HAD FUN...
HE WAS SO VERY ANGRY...
Ooh... ooh...
I...
...AT ME!

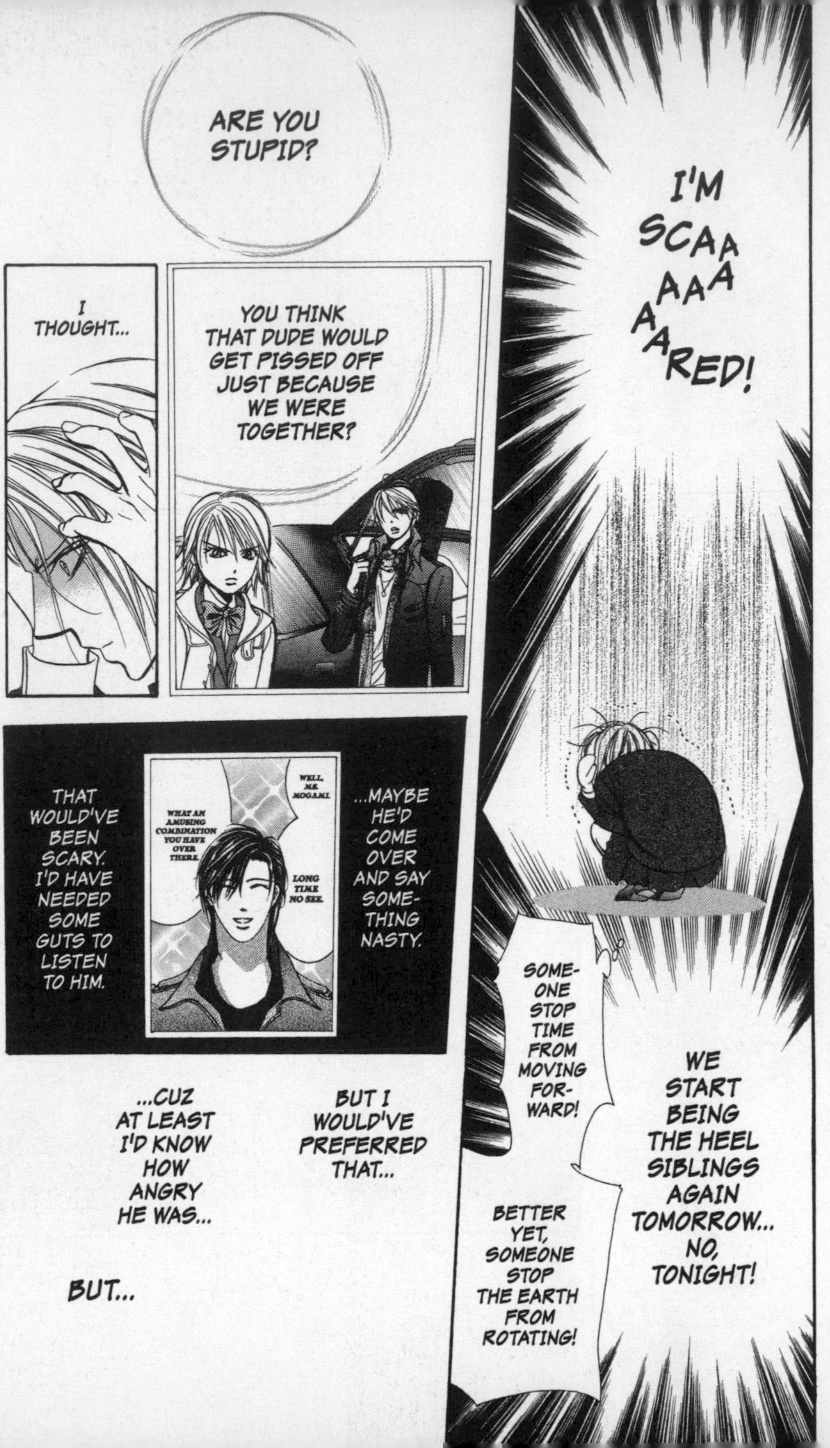
ARE YOU STUPID?
YOU THINK THAT DUDE WOULD GET PISSED OFF JUST BECAUSE WE WERE TOGETHER?
I THOUGHT...
...MAYBE HE'D COME OVER AND SAY SOME-THING NASTY.
WELL, MS. MOGAMI.
WHAT AN AMUSING COMBINATION YOU HAVE OVER THERE.
LONG TIME NO SEE.
THAT WOULD'VE BEEN SCARY. I'D HAVE NEEDED SOME GUTS TO LISTEN TO HIM.
BUT I WOULD'VE PREFERRED THAT...
...CUZ AT LEAST I'D KNOW HOW ANGRY HE WAS...
BUT...
I'M SCAAAAAAARED!
WE START BEING THE HEEL SIBLINGS AGAIN TOMORROW... NO, TONIGHT!
SOME-ONE STOP TIME FROM MOVING FOR-WARD!
BETTER YET, SOMEONE STOP THE EARTH FROM ROTATING!

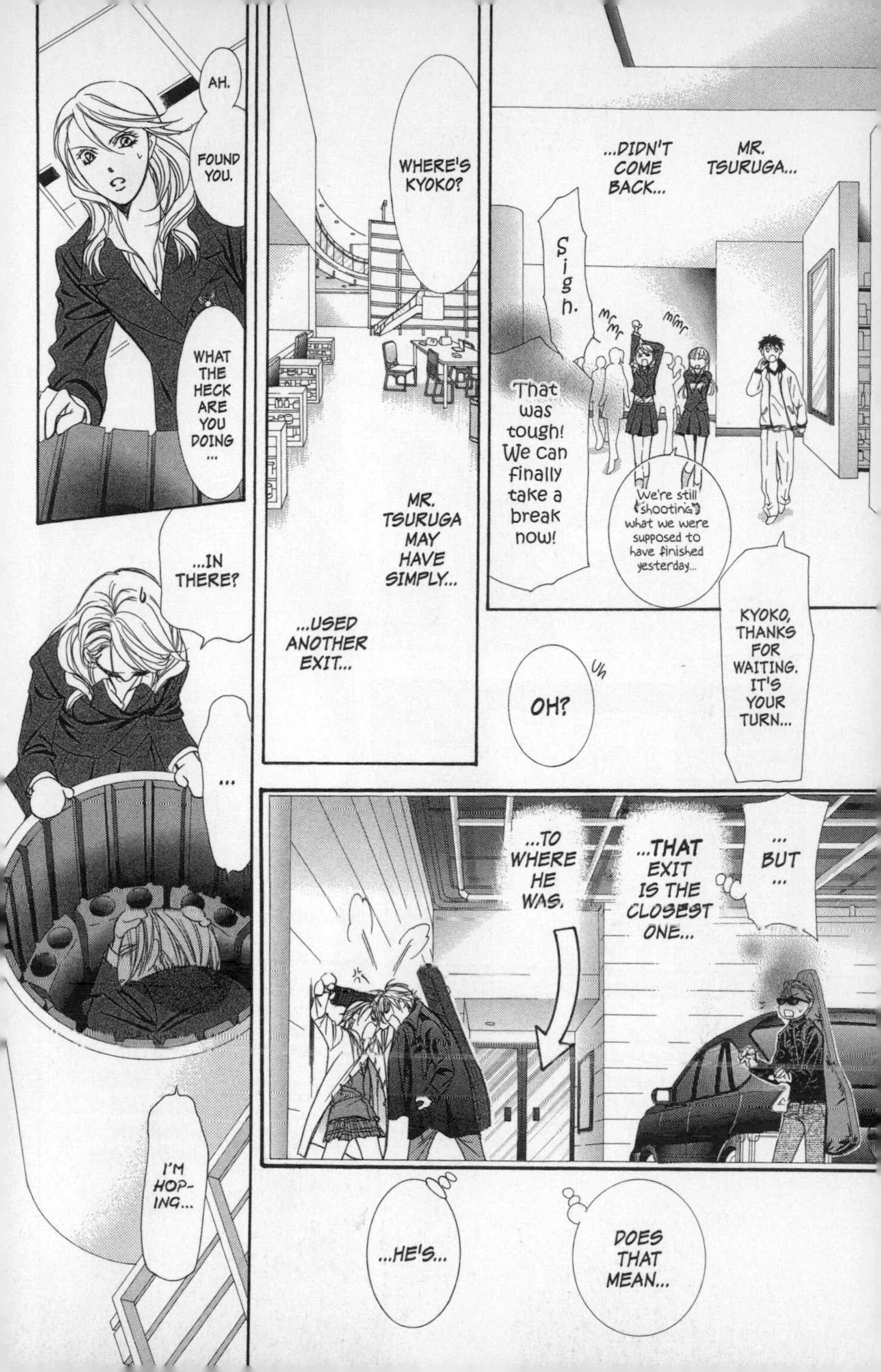
MR. TSURUGA...
...DIDN'T COME BACK...
Sigh.
That was tough! We can finally take a break now!
We're still "shooting" what we were supposed to have finished yesterday...
KYOKO, THANKS FOR WAITING. IT'S YOUR TURN...
Uh
OH?
WHERE'S KYOKO?
MR. TSURUGA MAY HAVE SIMPLY...
...USED ANOTHER EXIT...
... BUT ...
...THAT EXIT IS THE CLOSEST ONE...
...TO WHERE HE WAS.
DOES THAT MEAN...
...HE'S...
AH.
FOUND YOU.
WHAT THE HECK ARE YOU DOING...
...IN THERE?
...
I'M HOPING...

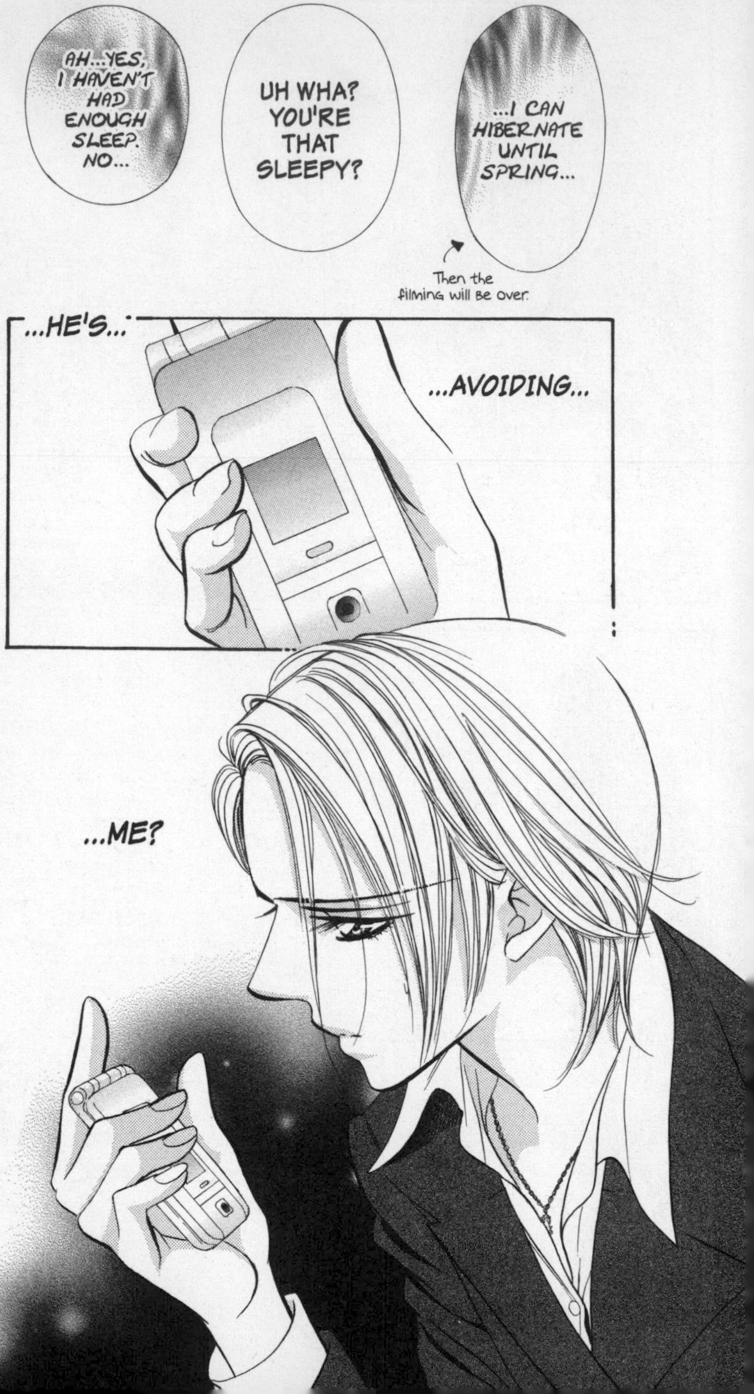
...I CAN HIBERNATE UNTIL SPRING...
Then the filming will be over.
UH WHA? YOU'RE THAT SLEEPY?
AH...YES, I HAVEN'T HAD ENOUGH SLEEP. NO...
...HE'S...
...AVOIDING...
...ME?

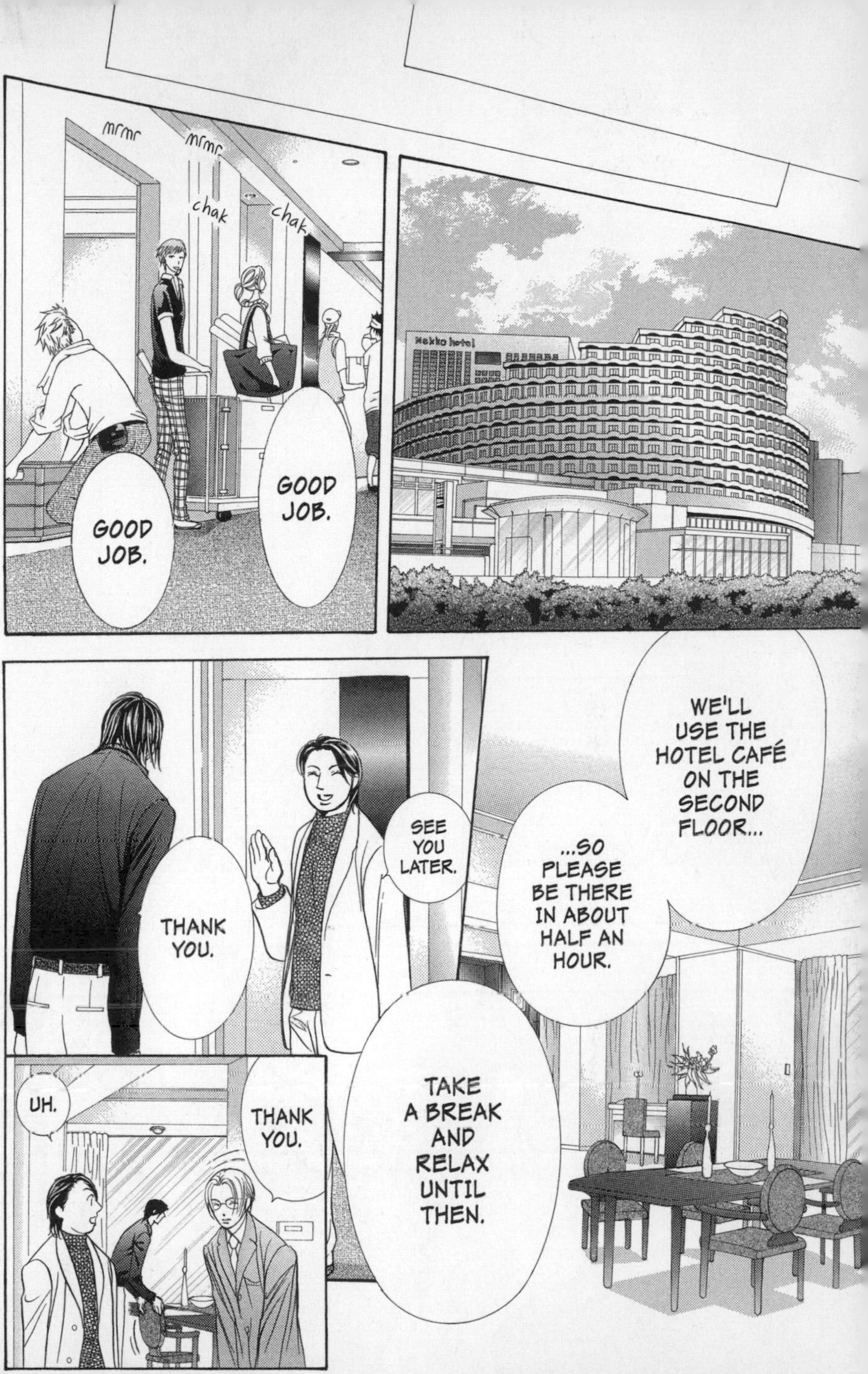
mrmr
mrmr
chak
chak
GOOD JOB.
GOOD JOB.
WE'LL USE THE HOTEL CAFÉ ON THE SECOND FLOOR...
...SO PLEASE BE THERE IN ABOUT HALF AN HOUR.
TAKE A BREAK AND RELAX UNTIL THEN.
SEE YOU LATER.
THANK YOU.
THANK YOU.
UH.

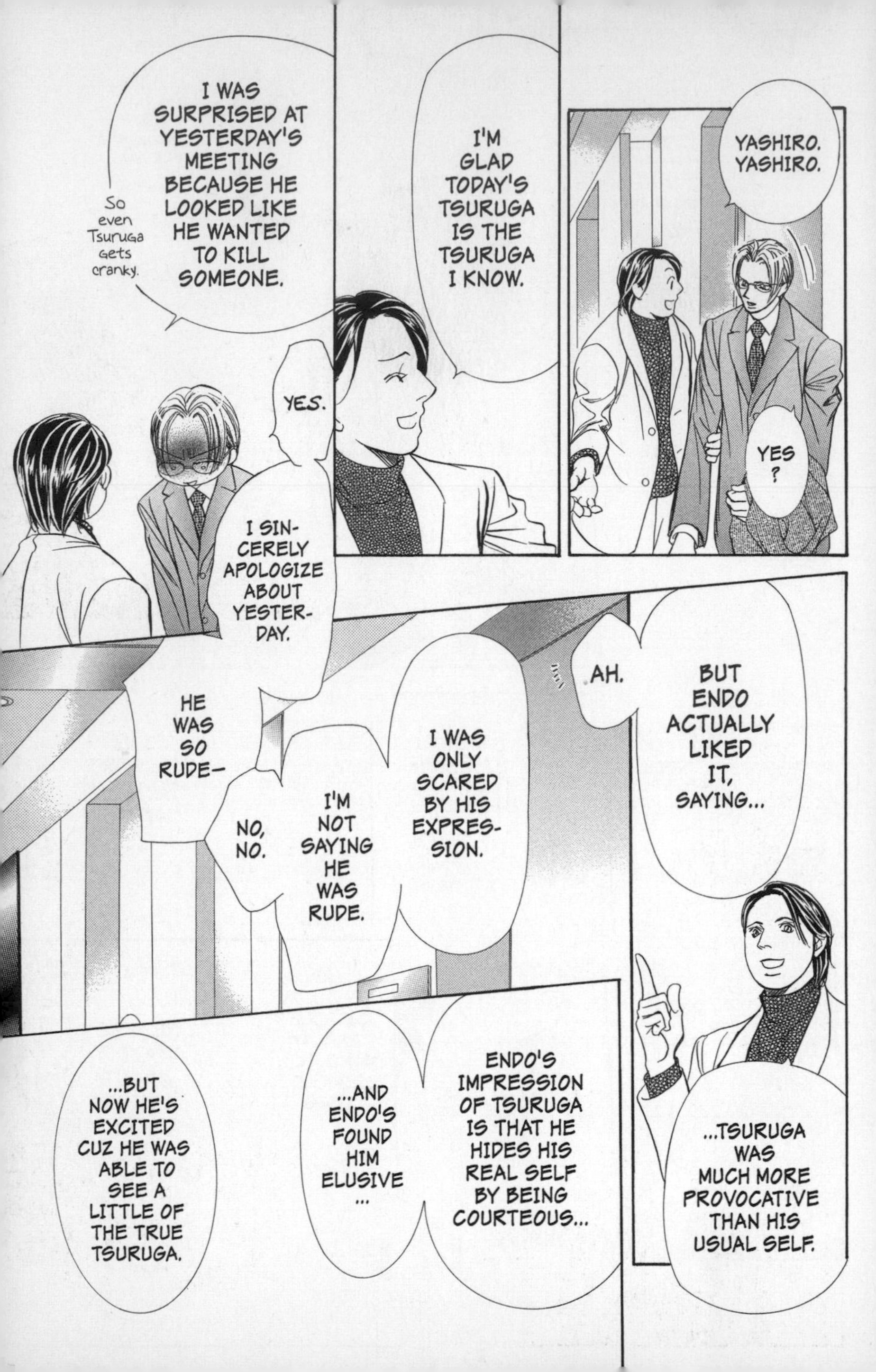
YASHIRO. YASHIRO.
YES?
I'M GLAD TODAY'S TSURUGA IS THE TSURUGA I KNOW.
YES.
I WAS SURPRISED AT YESTERDAY'S MEETING BECAUSE HE LOOKED LIKE HE WANTED TO KILL SOMEONE.
So even Tsuruga gets cranky.
I SINCERELY APOLOGIZE ABOUT YESTERDAY.
HE WAS SO RUDE—
NO, NO.
I'M NOT SAYING HE WAS RUDE.
I WAS ONLY SCARED BY HIS EXPRESSION.
AH.
BUT ENDO ACTUALLY LIKED IT, SAYING...
...TSURUGA WAS MUCH MORE PROVOCATIVE THAN HIS USUAL SELF.
ENDO'S IMPRESSION OF TSURUGA IS THAT HE HIDES HIS REAL SELF BY BEING COURTEOUS...
...AND ENDO'S FOUND HIM ELUSIVE...
...BUT NOW HE'S EXCITED CUZ HE WAS ABLE TO SEE A LITTLE OF THE TRUE TSURUGA.

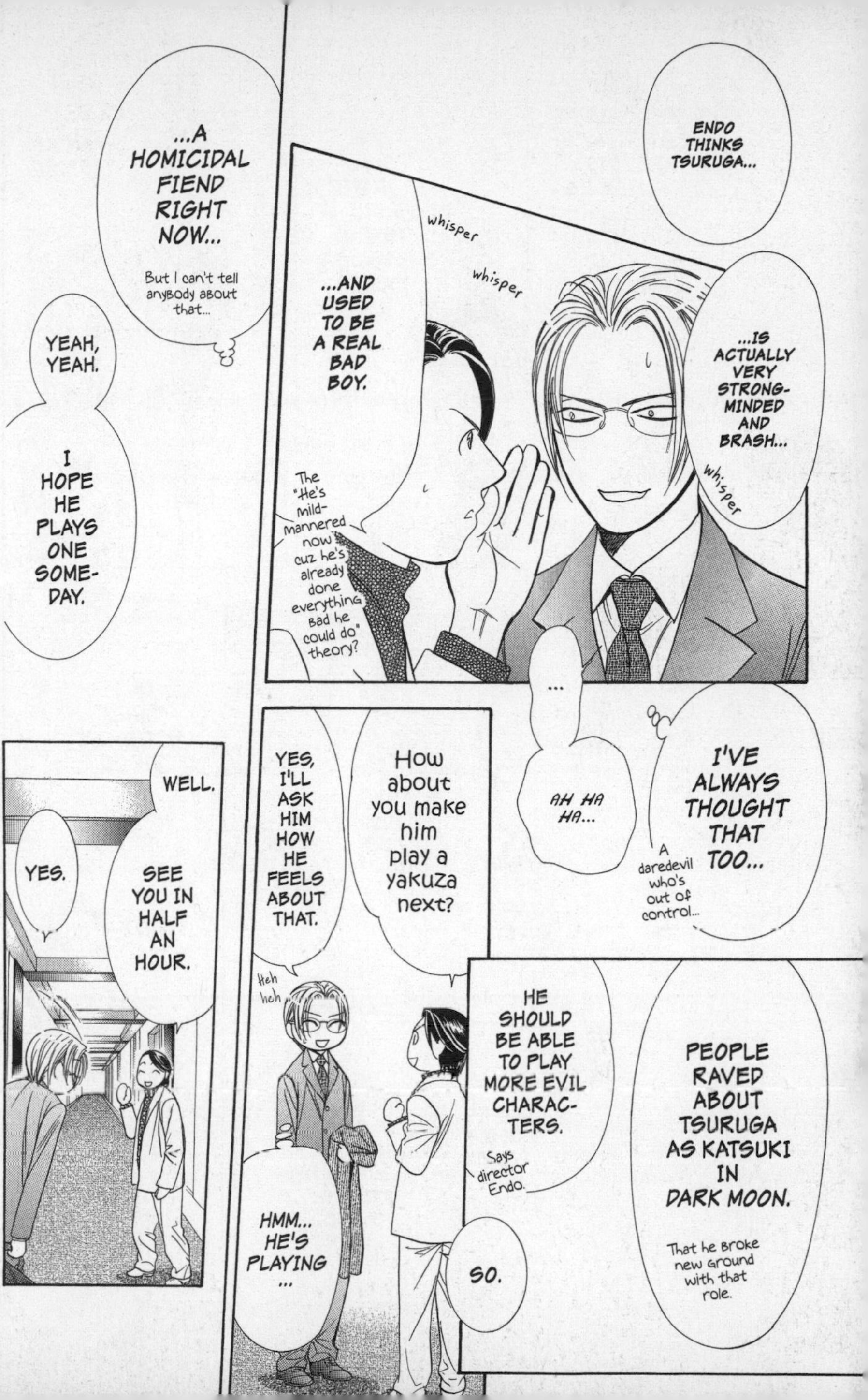

ENDO THINKS TSURUGA...
...IS ACTUALLY VERY STRONG-MINDED AND BRASH...
whisper
...AND USED TO BE A REAL BAD BOY.
whisper
whisper
The "He's mild-mannered now cuz he's already done everything bad he could do" theory?
...
I'VE ALWAYS THOUGHT THAT TOO...
A daredevil who's out of control...
AH HA HA...
PEOPLE RAVED ABOUT TSURUGA AS KATSUKI IN DARK MOON.
That he broke new ground with that role.
HE SHOULD BE ABLE TO PLAY MORE EVIL CHARACTERS.
Says director Endo.
SO.
How about you make him play a yakuza next?
YES, I'LL ASK HIM HOW HE FEELS ABOUT THAT.
Heh heh
HMM... HE'S PLAYING...
...A HOMICIDAL FIEND RIGHT NOW...
But I can't tell anybody about that...
YEAH, YEAH.
I HOPE HE PLAYS ONE SOMEDAY.
WELL.
SEE YOU IN HALF AN HOUR.
YES.

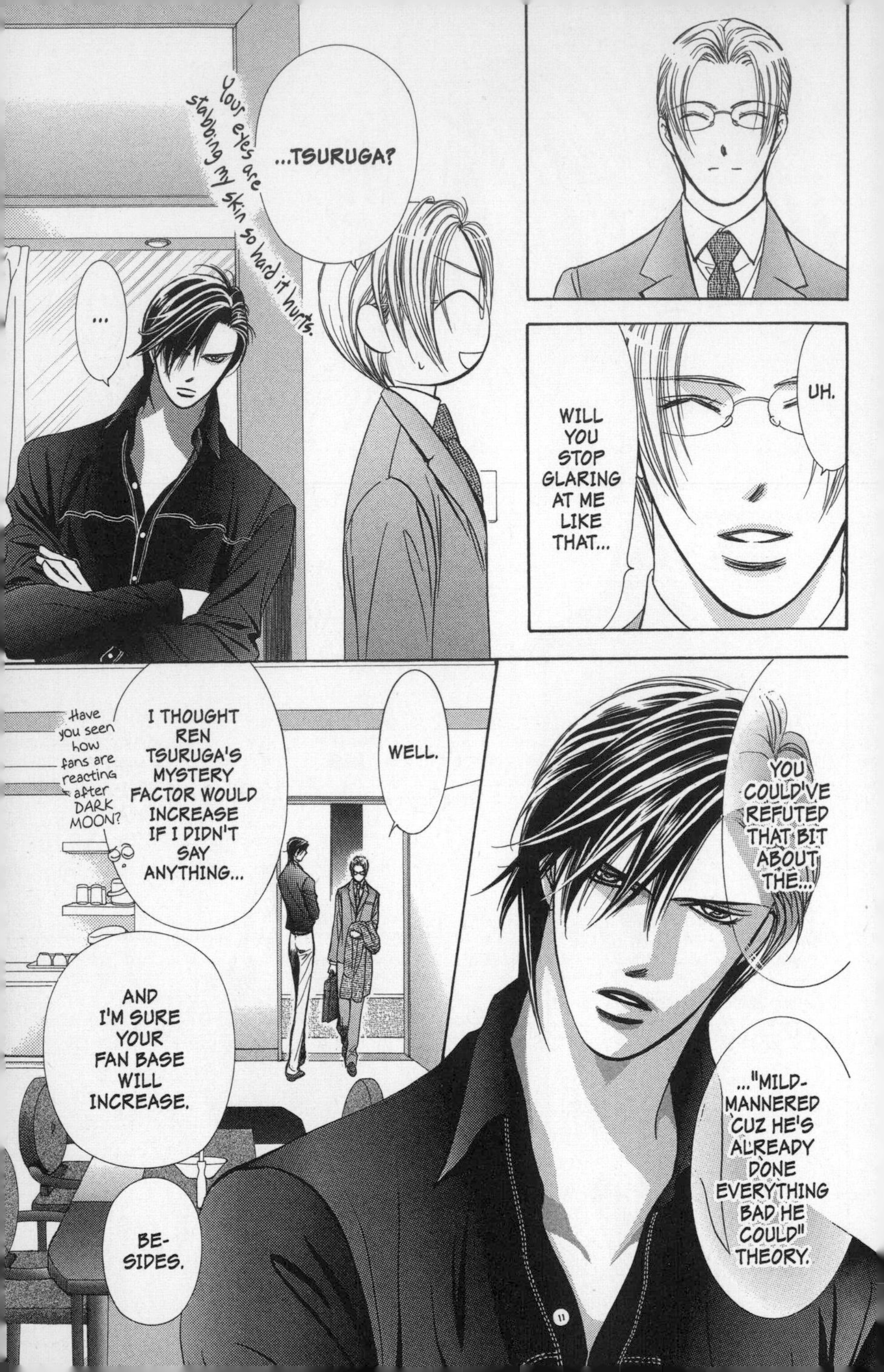
UH.
WILL YOU STOP GLARING AT ME LIKE THAT...
...TSURUGA?
Your eyes are stabbing my skin so hard it hurts.
...
YOU COULD'VE REFUTED THAT BIT ABOUT THE...!
..."MILD-MANNERED CUZ HE'S ALREADY DONE EVERYTHING BAD HE COULD" THEORY.
WELL.
I THOUGHT REN TSURUGA'S MYSTERY FACTOR WOULD INCREASE IF I DIDN'T SAY ANYTHING...
Have you seen how fans are reacting after DARK MOON?
AND I'M SURE YOUR FAN BASE WILL INCREASE.
BE-SIDES.

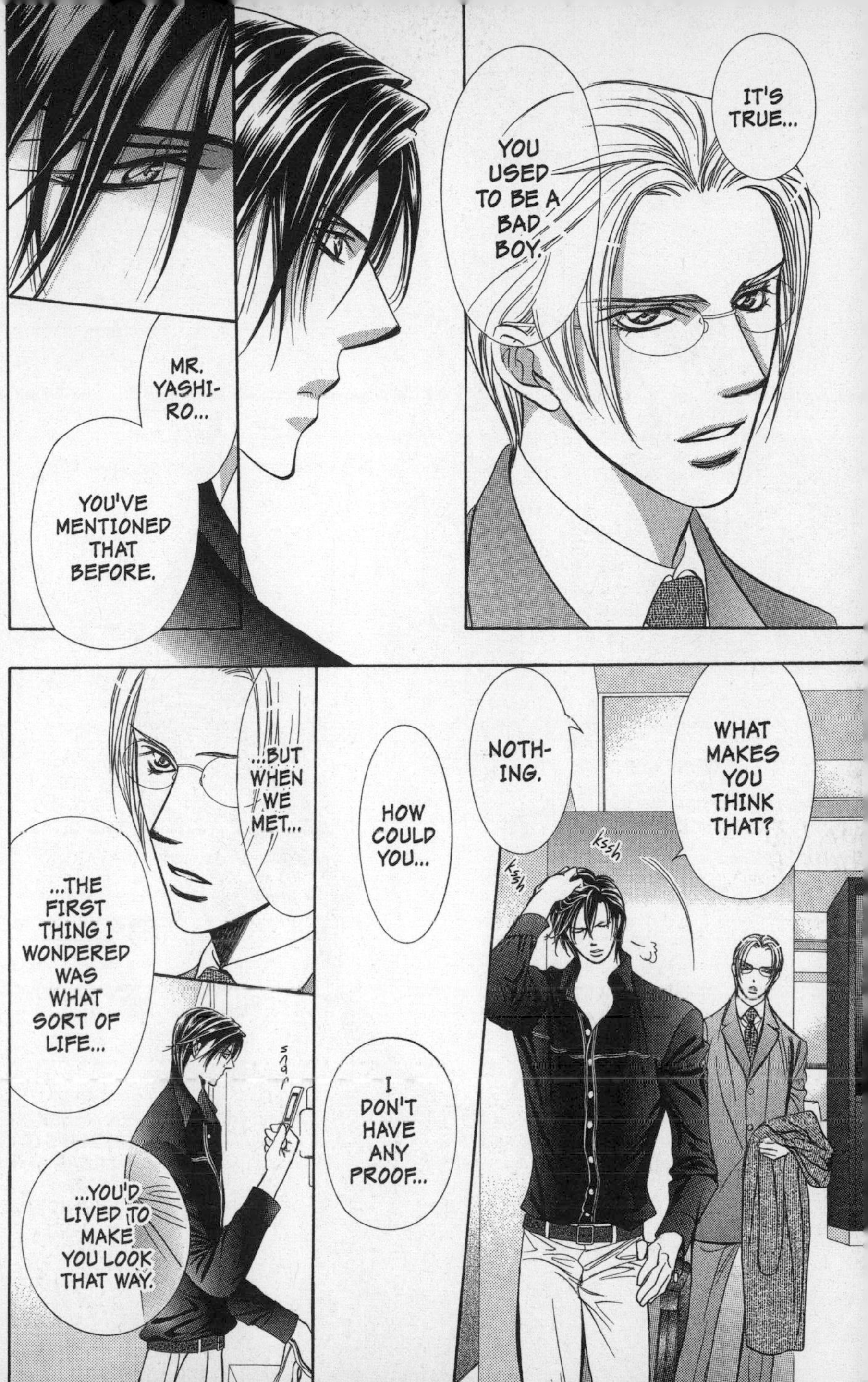
IT'S TRUE...
YOU USED TO BE A BAD BOY.
MR. YASHIRO...
YOU'VE MENTIONED THAT BEFORE.
WHAT MAKES YOU THINK THAT?
NOTHING.
kssh
kssh
HOW COULD YOU...
I DON'T HAVE ANY PROOF...
...BUT WHEN WE MET...
...THE FIRST THING I WONDERED WAS WHAT SORT OF LIFE...
...YOU'D LIVED TO MAKE YOU LOOK THAT WAY.

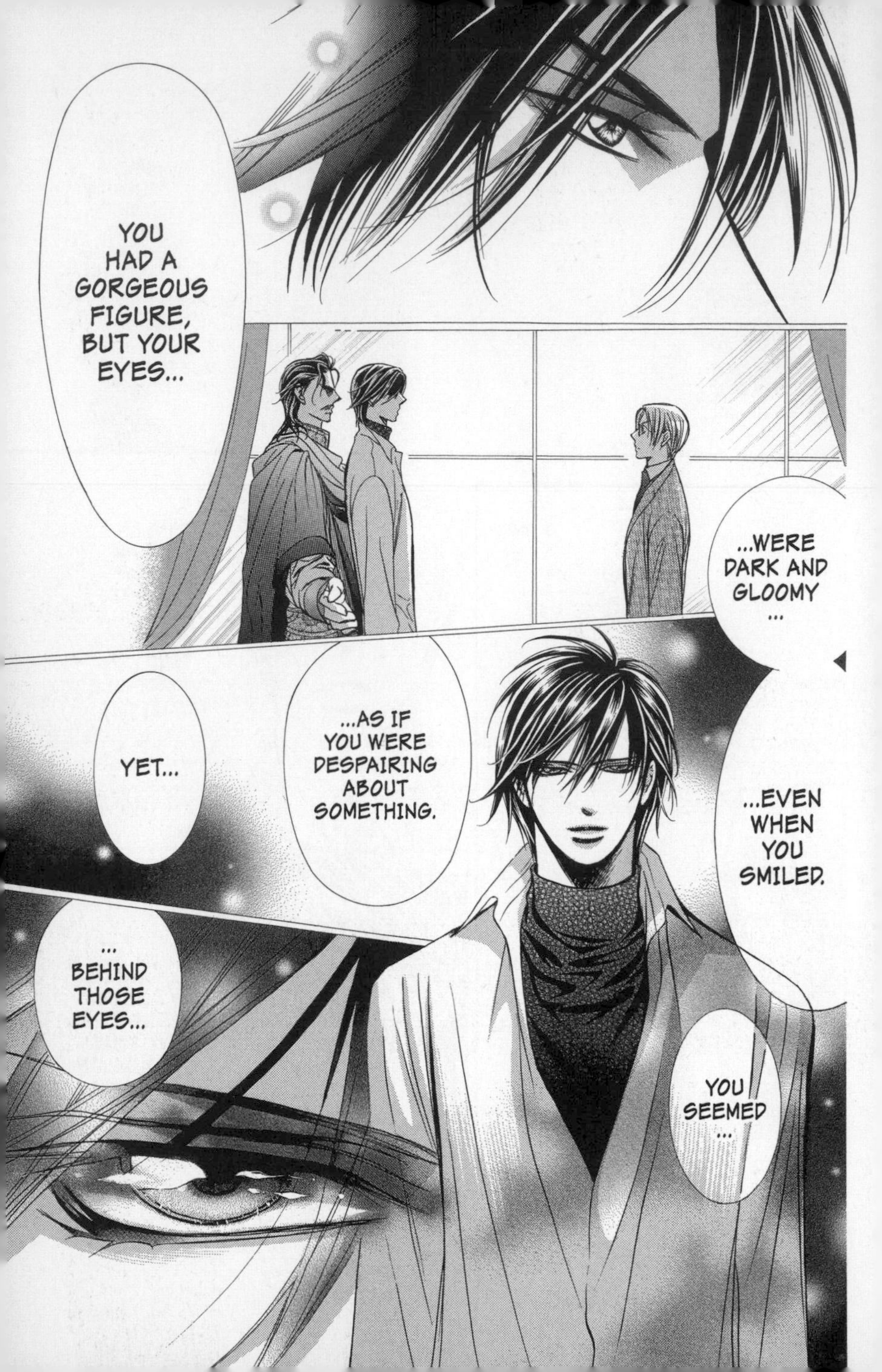
YOU HAD A GORGEOUS FIGURE, BUT YOUR EYES...
...WERE DARK AND GLOOMY ...
...EVEN WHEN YOU SMILED.
YET...
... BEHIND THOSE EYES...
YOU SEEMED ...
...AS IF YOU WERE DESPAIRING ABOUT SOMETHING.

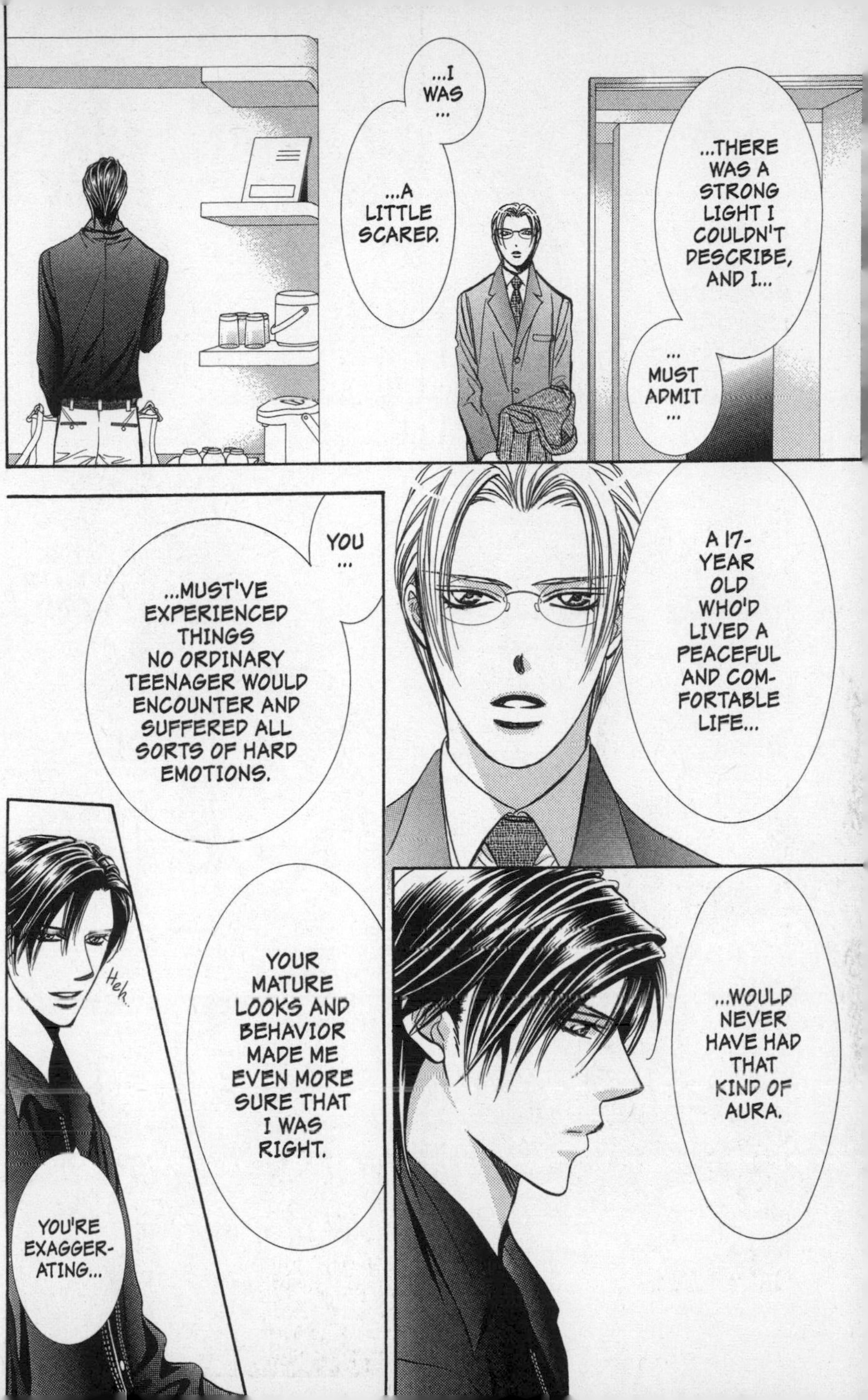
...THERE WAS A STRONG LIGHT I COULDN'T DESCRIBE, AND I...
...MUST ADMIT...
...I WAS...
...A LITTLE SCARED.
A 17-YEAR OLD WHO'D LIVED A PEACEFUL AND COMFORTABLE LIFE...
YOU...
...MUST'VE EXPERIENCED THINGS NO ORDINARY TEENAGER WOULD ENCOUNTER AND SUFFERED ALL SORTS OF HARD EMOTIONS.
...WOULD NEVER HAVE HAD THAT KIND OF AURA.
YOUR MATURE LOOKS AND BEHAVIOR MADE ME EVEN MORE SURE THAT I WAS RIGHT.
Heh.
YOU'RE EXAGGERATING...

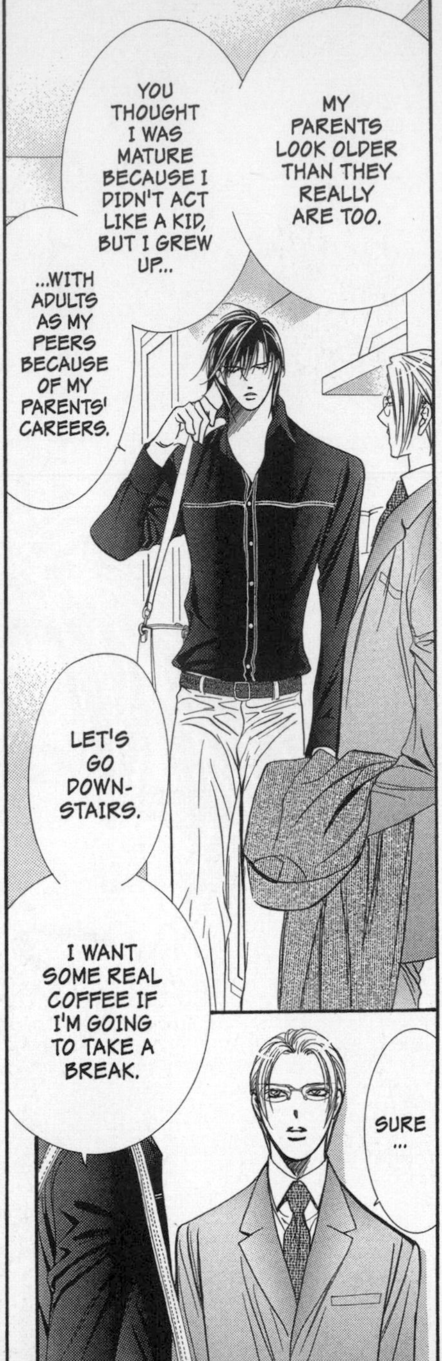
MY PARENTS LOOK OLDER THAN THEY REALLY ARE TOO.
YOU THOUGHT I WAS MATURE BECAUSE I DIDN'T ACT LIKE A KID, BUT I GREW UP...
...WITH ADULTS AS MY PEERS BECAUSE OF MY PARENTS' CAREERS.
LET'S GO DOWN-STAIRS.
I WANT SOME REAL COFFEE IF I'M GOING TO TAKE A BREAK.
SURE...

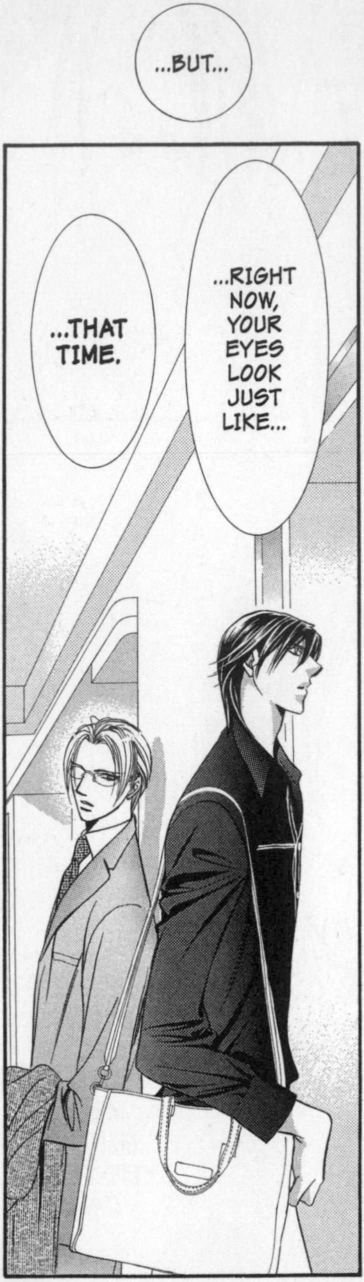
...BUT...
...RIGHT NOW, YOUR EYES LOOK JUST LIKE...
...THAT TIME.

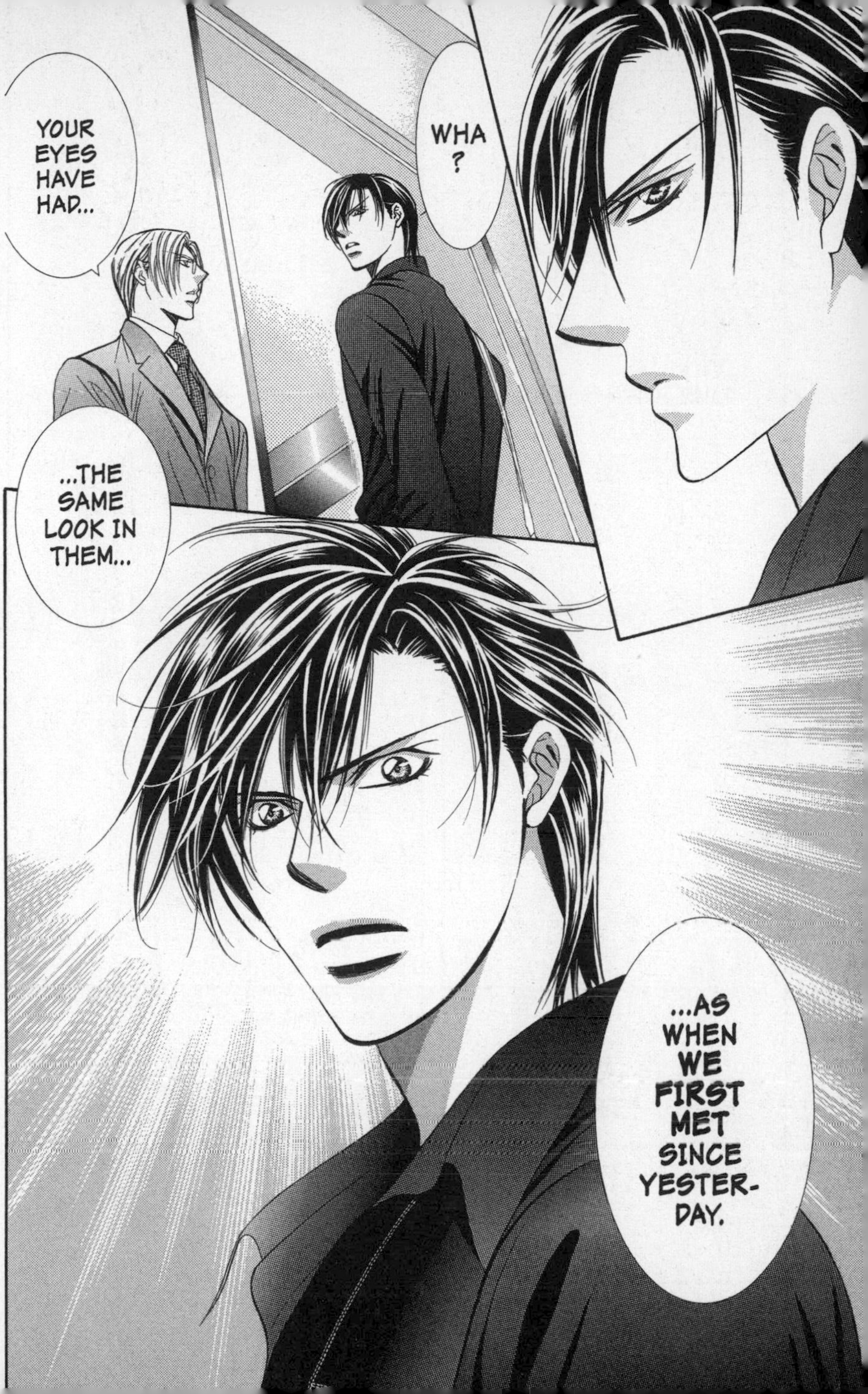
WHA?
YOUR EYES HAVE HAD...
...THE SAME LOOK IN THEM...
...AS WHEN WE FIRST MET SINCE YESTERDAY.

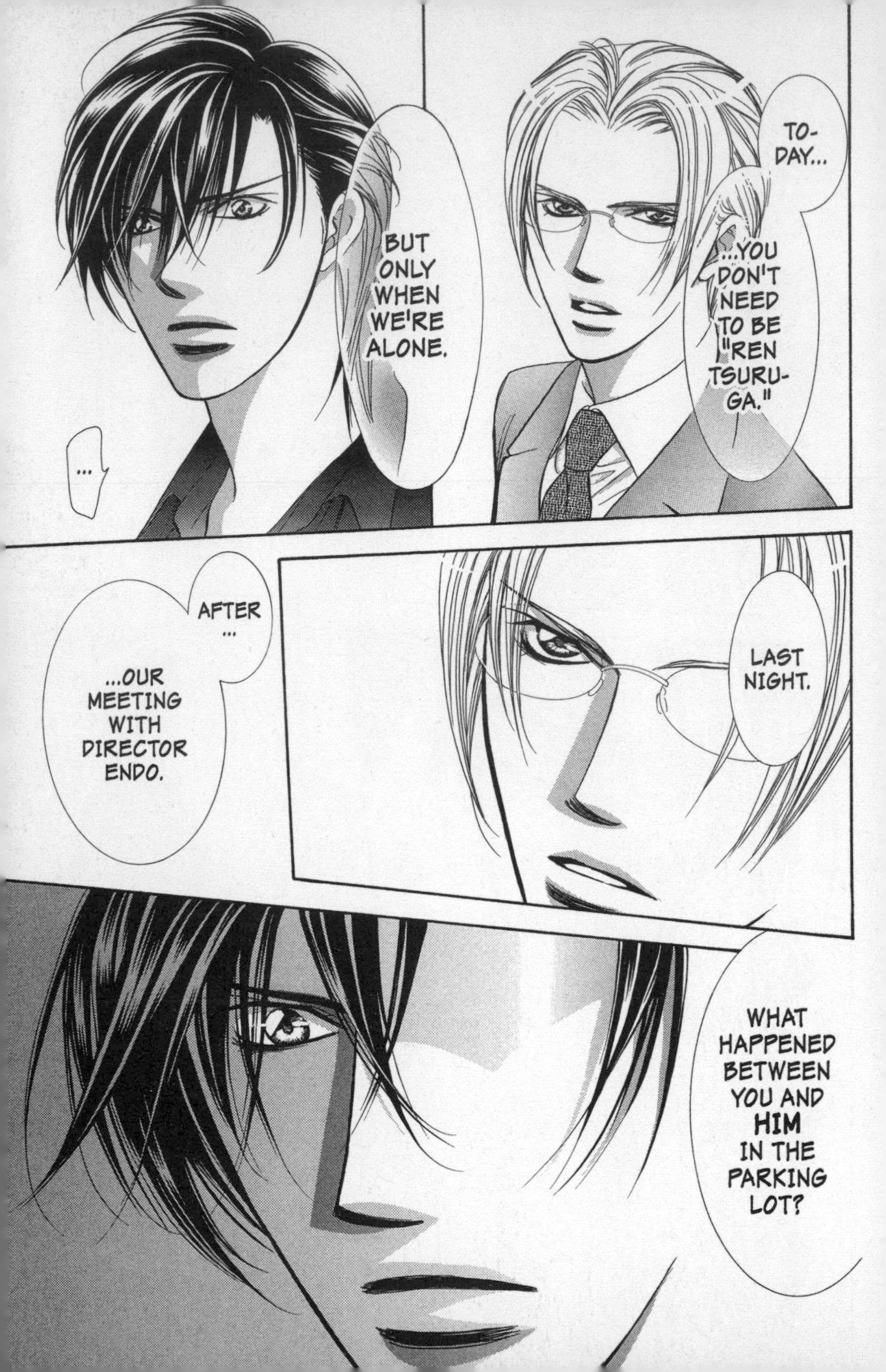
TO-DAY...
...YOU DON'T NEED TO BE "REN TSURUGA."
BUT ONLY WHEN WE'RE ALONE.
...
LAST NIGHT.
AFTER ...
...OUR MEETING WITH DIRECTOR ENDO.
WHAT HAPPENED BETWEEN YOU AND HIM IN THE PARKING LOT?

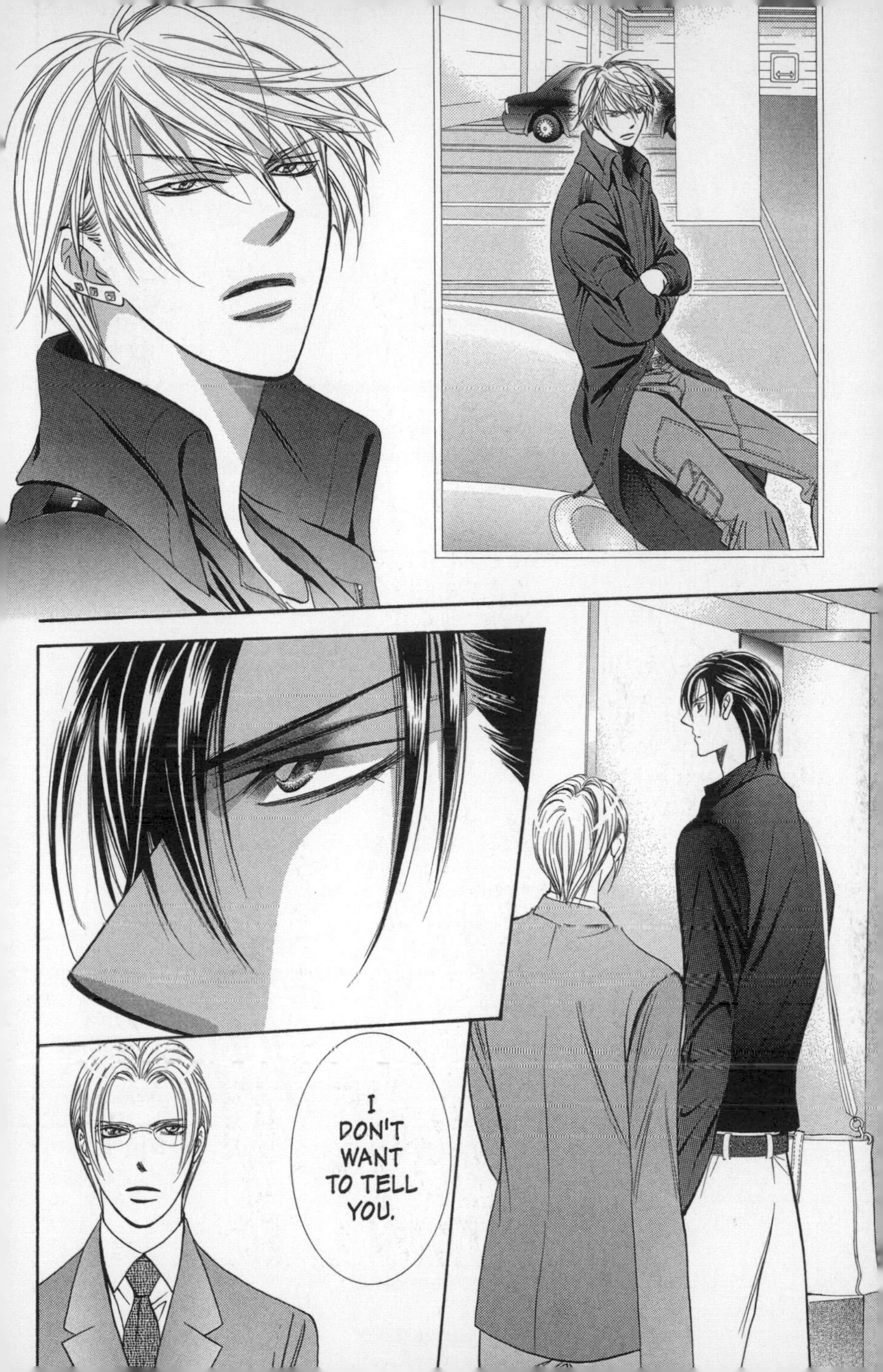
I DON'T WANT TO TELL YOU.

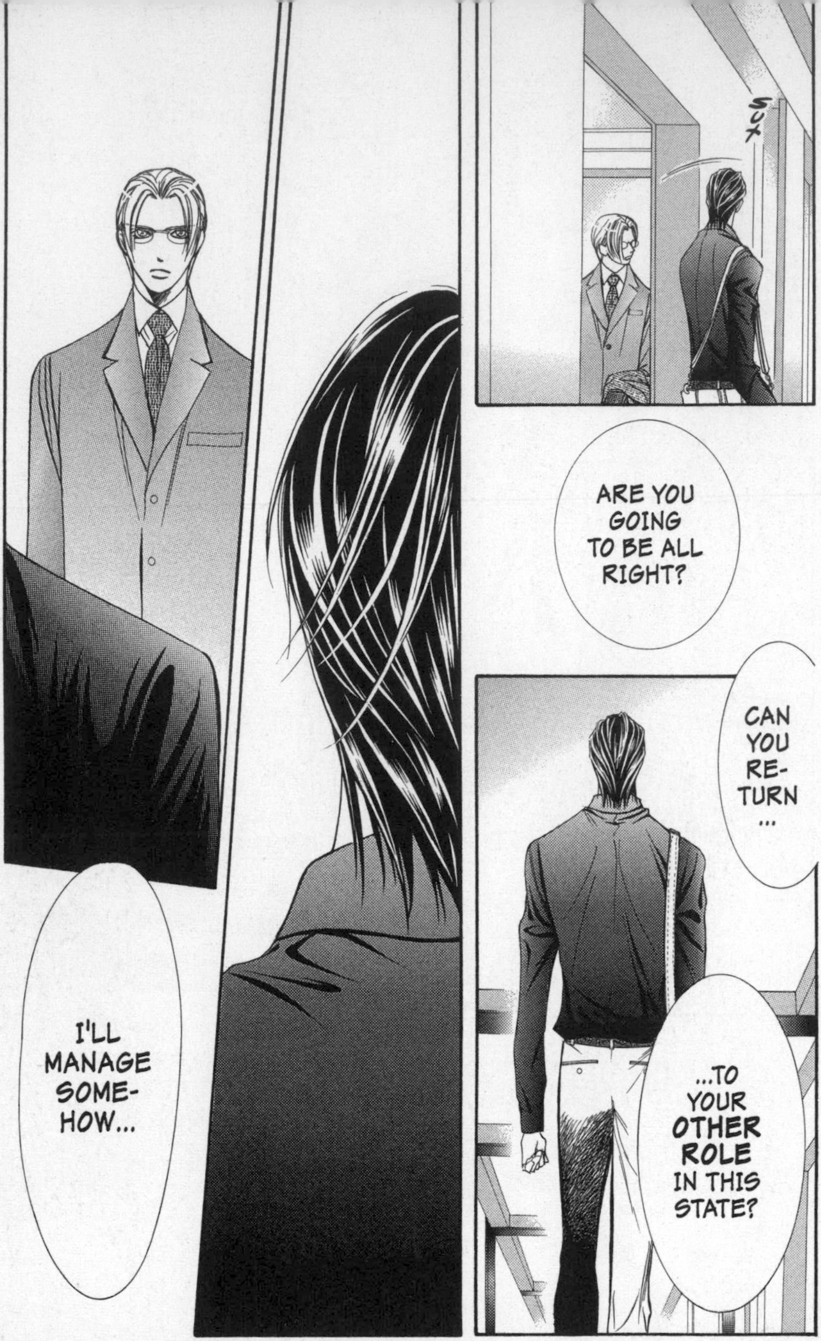
SUX
ARE YOU GOING TO BE ALL RIGHT?
CAN YOU RE-TURN...
...TO YOUR OTHER ROLE IN THIS STATE?
I'LL MANAGE SOME-HOW...

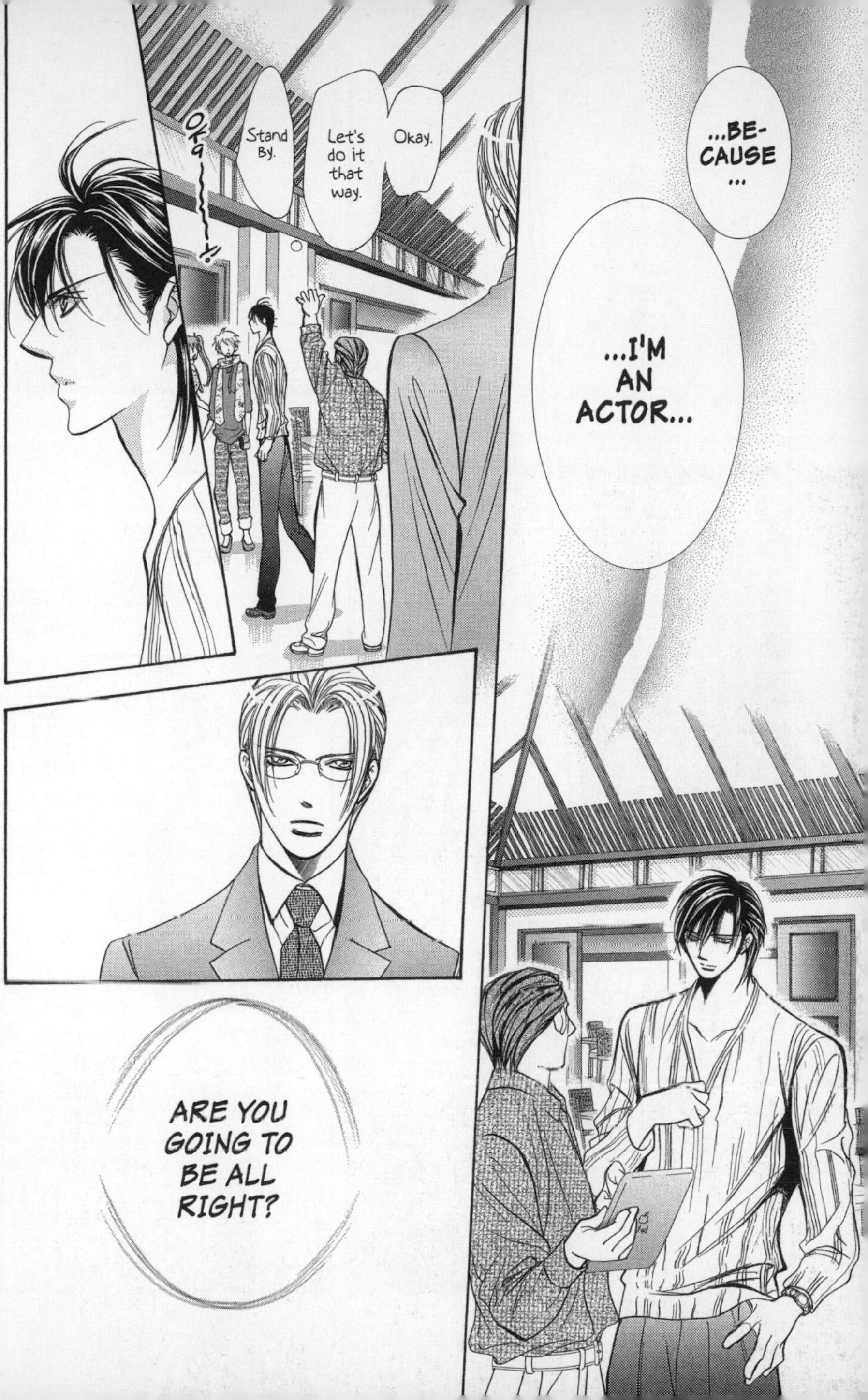
...BE-
CAUSE
...
...I'M AN ACTOR...
Okay.
Let's do it that way.
Stand By.
Okay~~~!!
ARE YOU GOING TO BE ALL RIGHT?

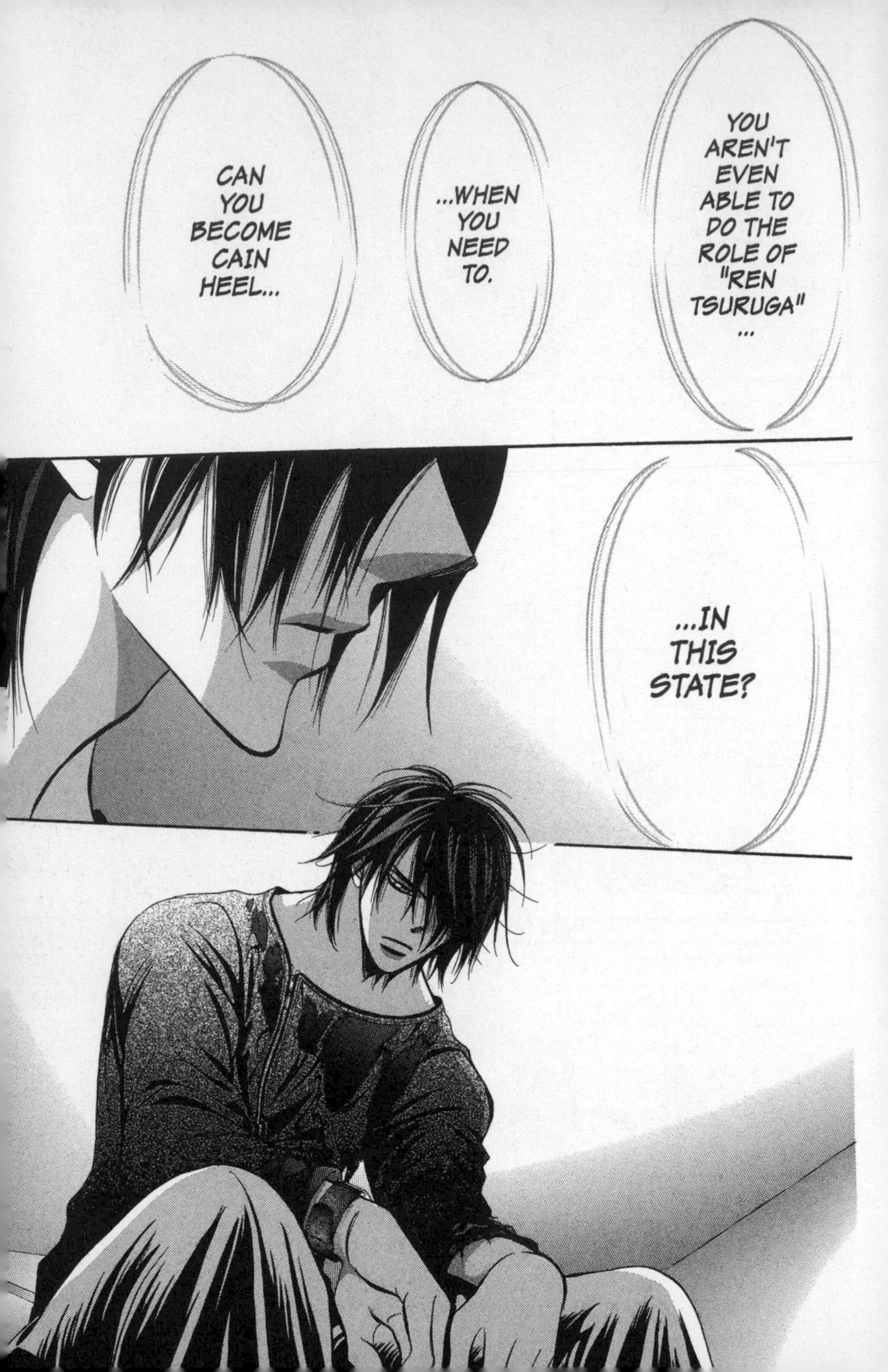
YOU AREN'T EVEN ABLE TO DO THE ROLE OF "REN TSURUGA" ...
...WHEN YOU NEED TO.
CAN YOU BECOME CAIN HEEL...
...IN THIS STATE?

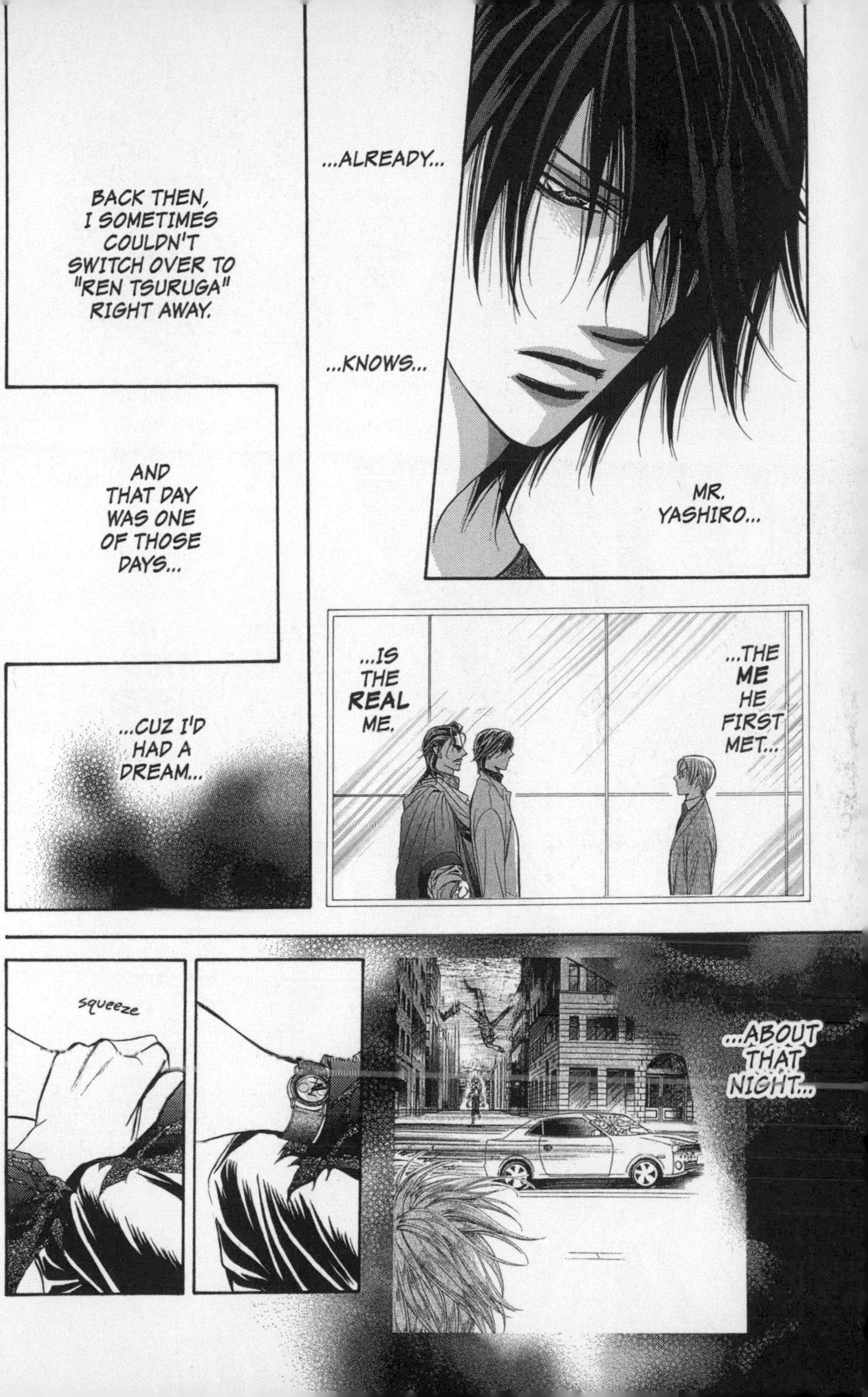
MR. YASHIRO...
...ALREADY...
...KNOWS...
...THE ME HE FIRST MET...
...IS THE REAL ME.
BACK THEN, I SOMETIMES COULDN'T SWITCH OVER TO "REN TSURUGA" RIGHT AWAY.
AND THAT DAY WAS ONE OF THOSE DAYS...
...CUZ I'D HAD A DREAM...
...ABOUT THAT NIGHT...
squeeze

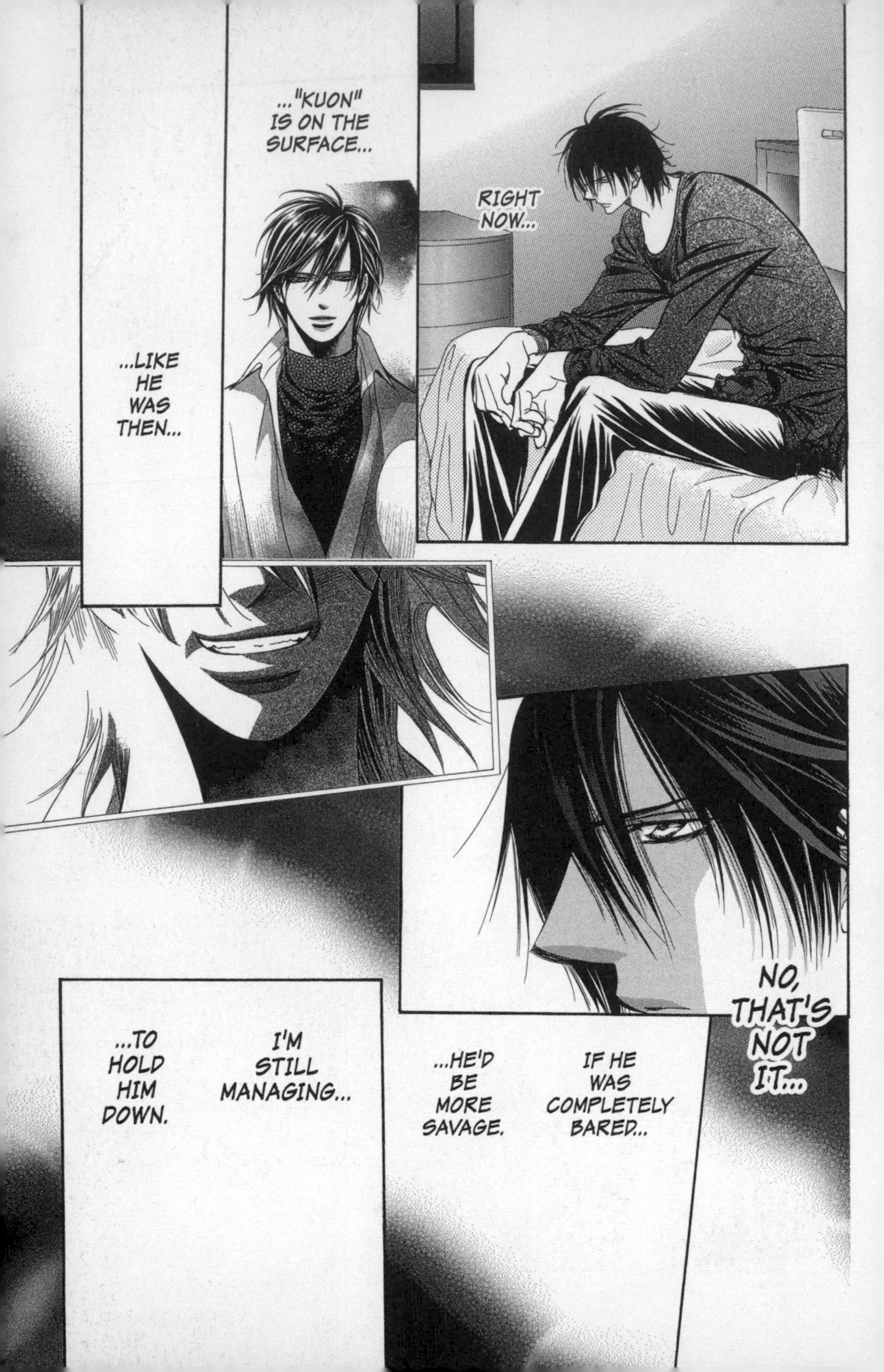
RIGHT NOW...
..."KUON" IS ON THE SURFACE...
...LIKE HE WAS THEN...
NO, THAT'S NOT IT...
IF HE WAS COMPLETELY BARED...
...HE'D BE MORE SAVAGE.
I'M STILL MANAGING...
...TO HOLD HIM DOWN.

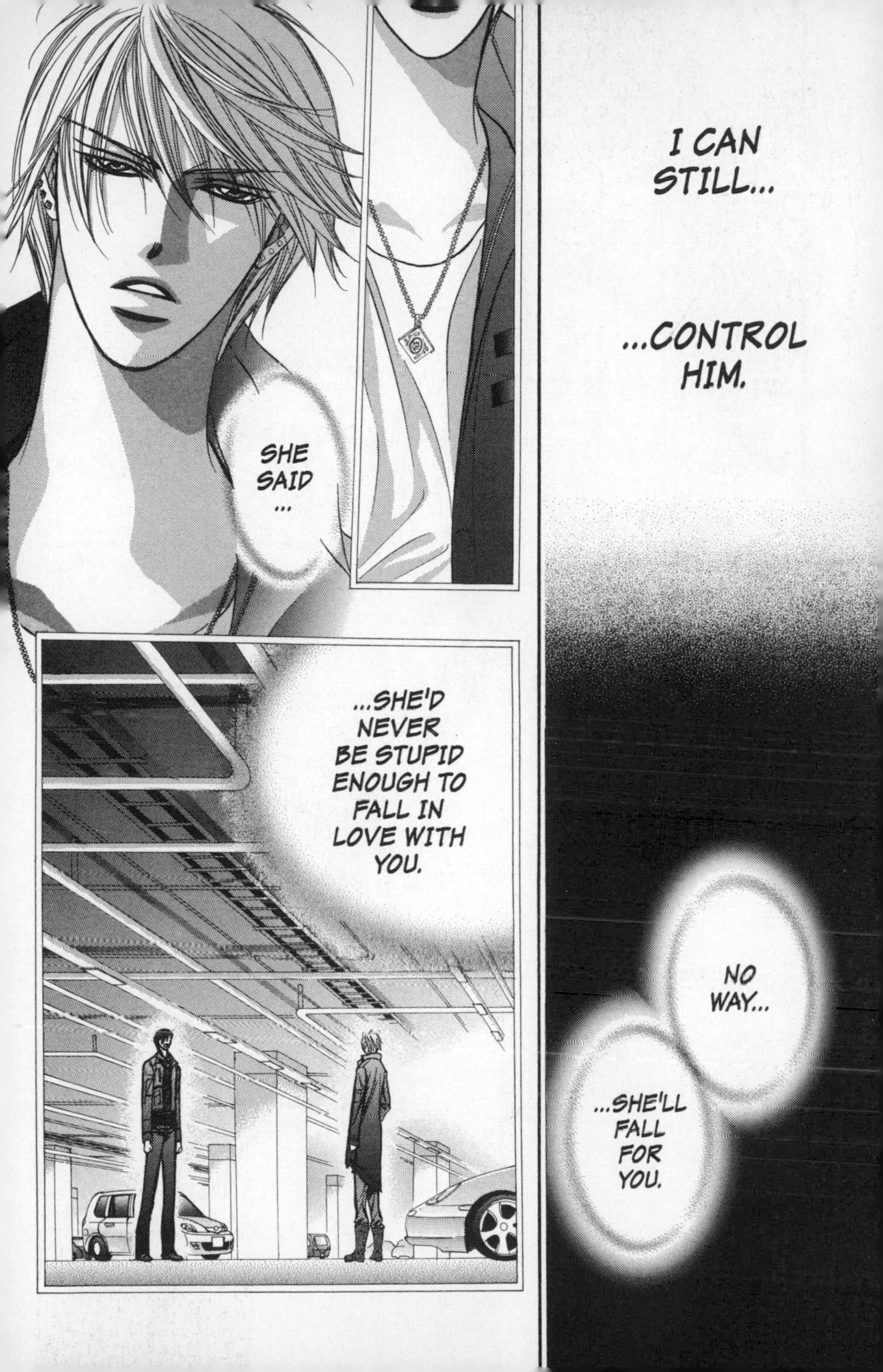
I CAN STILL...
...CONTROL HIM.
NO WAY...
...SHE'LL FALL FOR YOU.
SHE SAID ...
...SHE'D NEVER BE STUPID ENOUGH TO FALL IN LOVE WITH YOU.

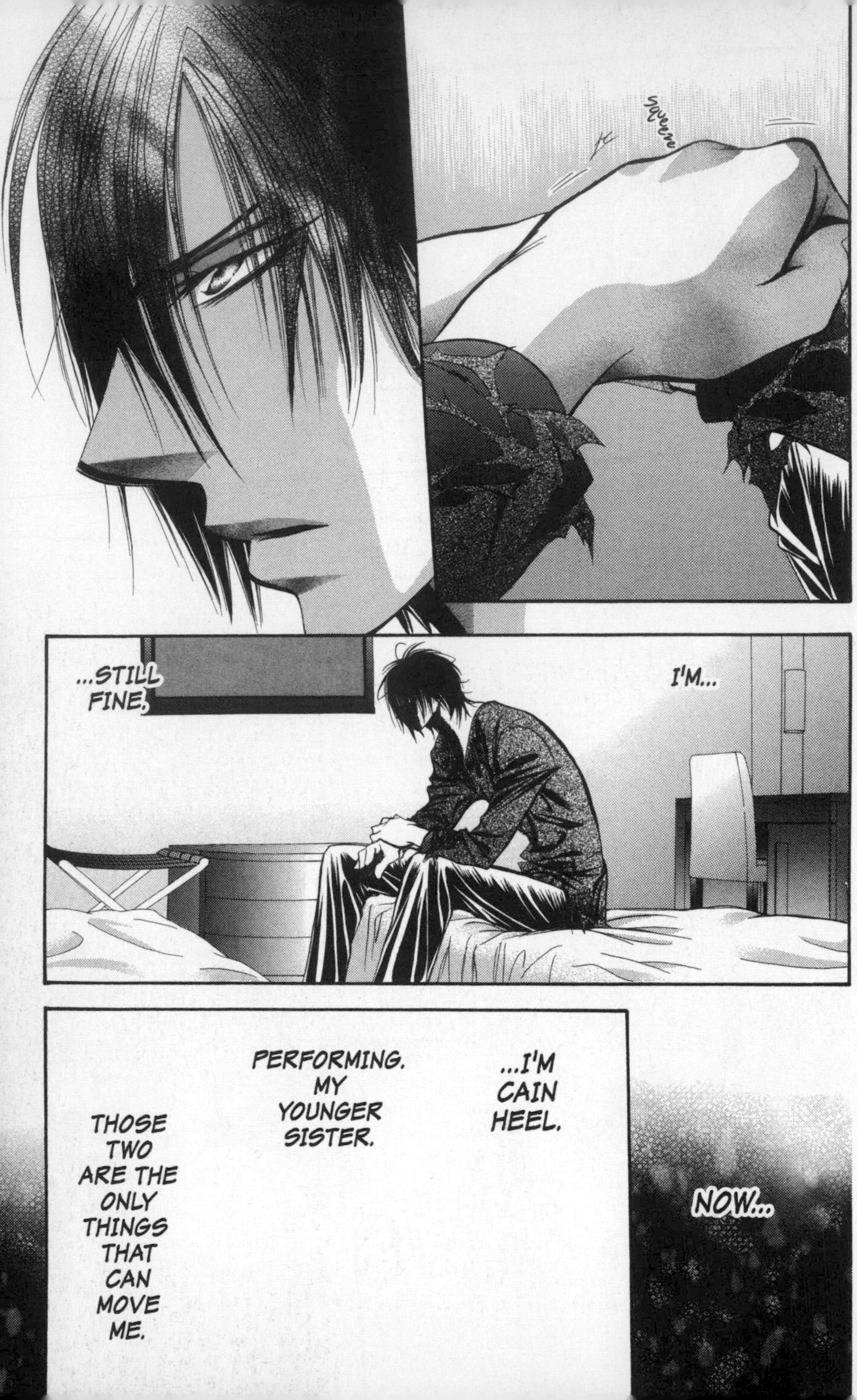
squeeze
I'M...
...STILL FINE.
NOW...
...I'M CAIN HEEL.
PERFORMING. MY YOUNGER SISTER.
THOSE TWO ARE THE ONLY THINGS THAT CAN MOVE ME.

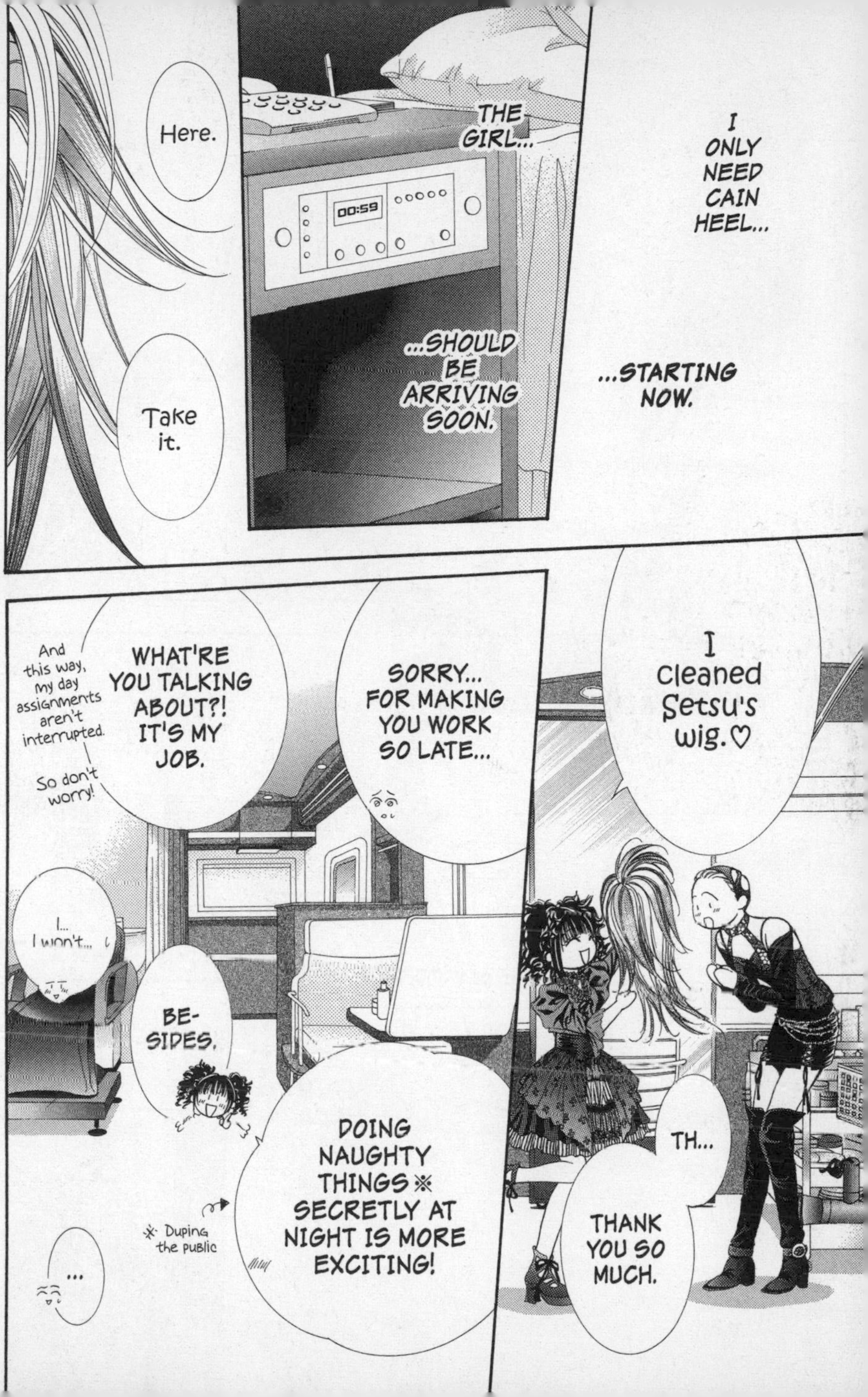
I ONLY NEED CAIN HEEL...
...STARTING NOW.
THE GIRL...
...SHOULD BE ARRIVING SOON.
Here.
Take it.
I cleaned Setsu's wig.♡
TH...
THANK YOU SO MUCH.
SORRY... FOR MAKING YOU WORK SO LATE...
WHAT'RE YOU TALKING ABOUT?! IT'S MY JOB.
And this way, my day assignments aren't interrupted.
So don't worry!
I... I won't...
BE-SIDES.
DOING NAUGHTY THINGS※ SECRETLY AT NIGHT IS MORE EXCITING!
※: Duping the public
...

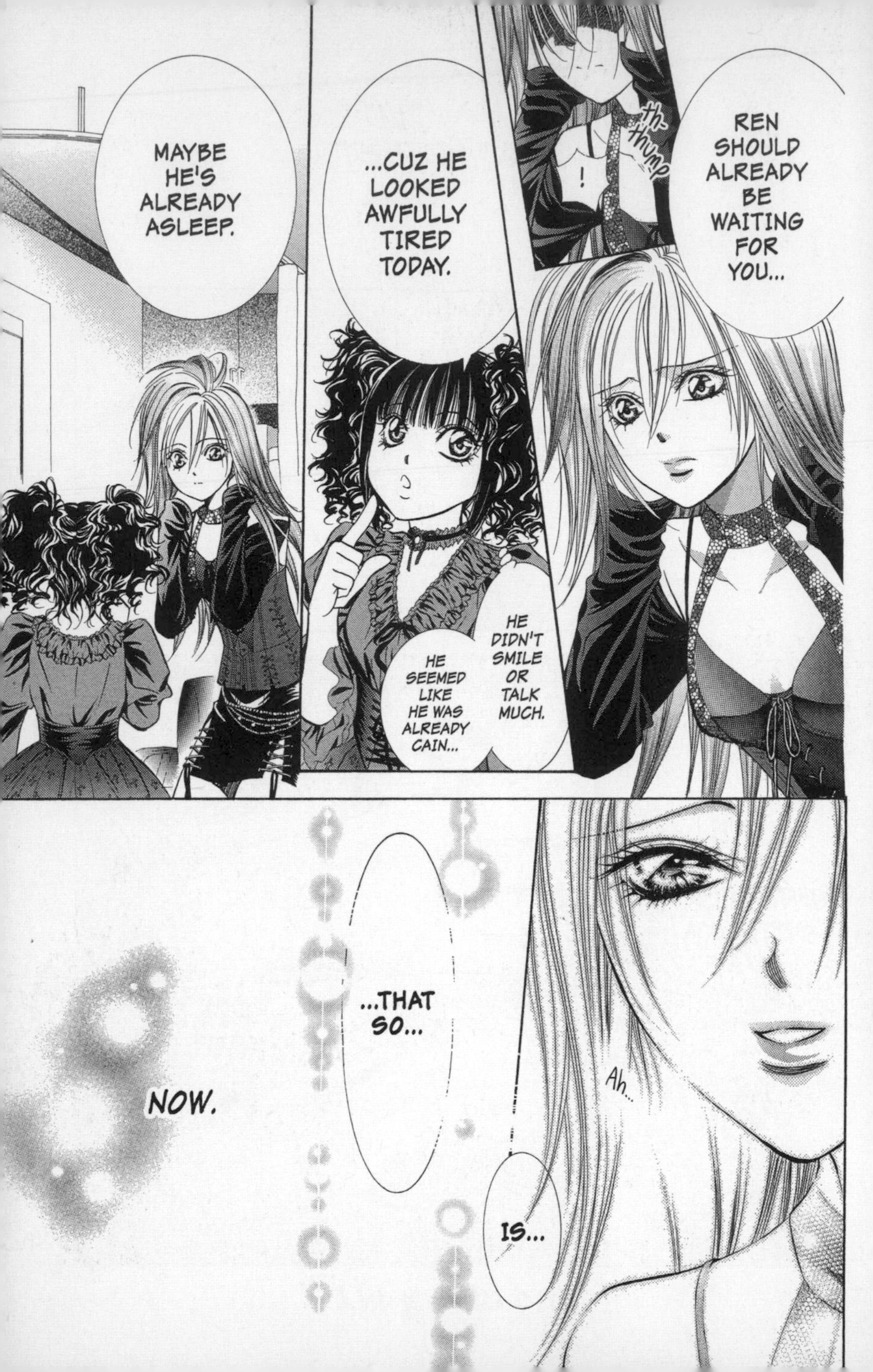
REN SHOULD ALREADY BE WAITING FOR YOU...
th-thump
!
...CUZ HE LOOKED AWFULLY TIRED TODAY.
HE DIDN'T SMILE OR TALK MUCH.
HE SEEMED LIKE HE WAS ALREADY CAIN...
MAYBE HE'S ALREADY ASLEEP.
...THAT SO...
Ah...
IS...
NOW.

I'LL GREET HER.

I SHALL BECOME ...

 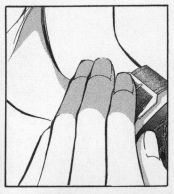

...THE BIG BROTHER SETSUKA LOVES.

s h p

End of Act 192

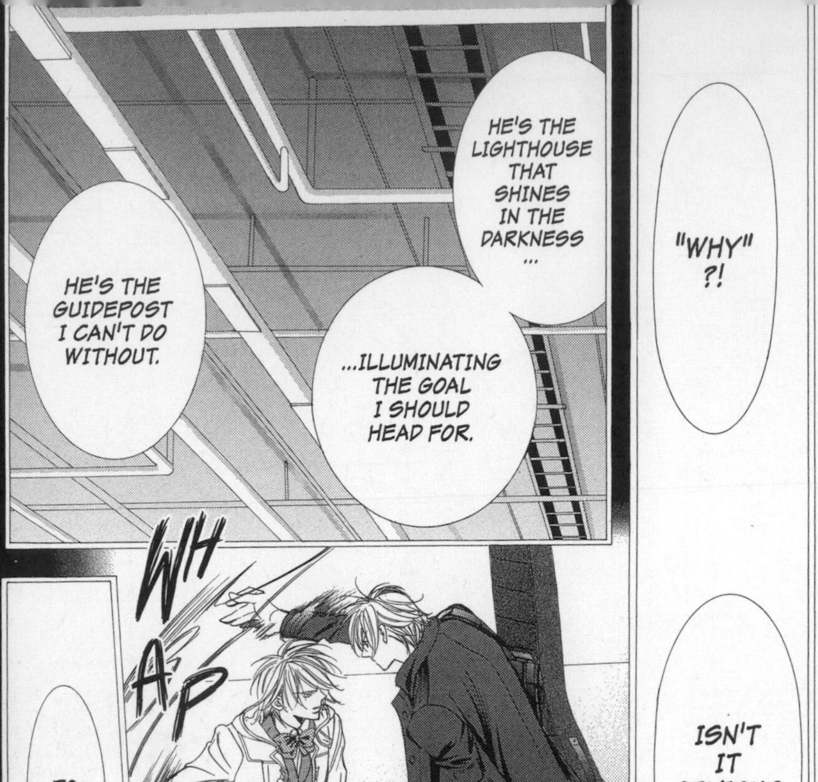
"WHY" ?!
ISN'T IT OBVIOUS ?!
HE'S THE LIGHTHOUSE THAT SHINES IN THE DARKNESS ...
...ILLUMINATING THE GOAL I SHOULD HEAD FOR.
HE'S THE GUIDEPOST I CAN'T DO WITHOUT.
WHAP
TO ME...

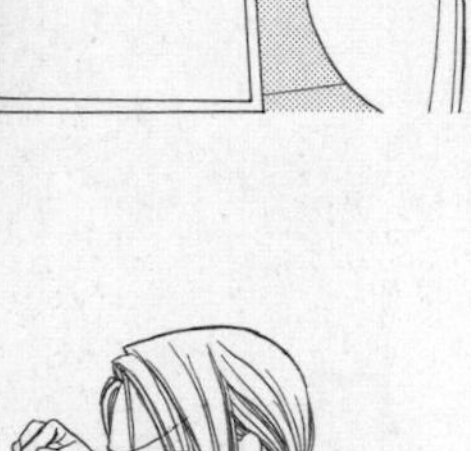

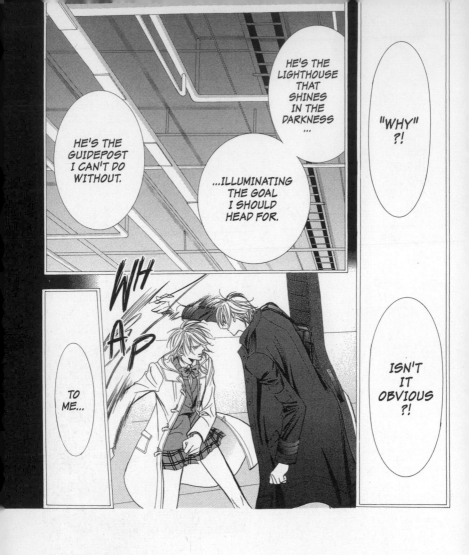

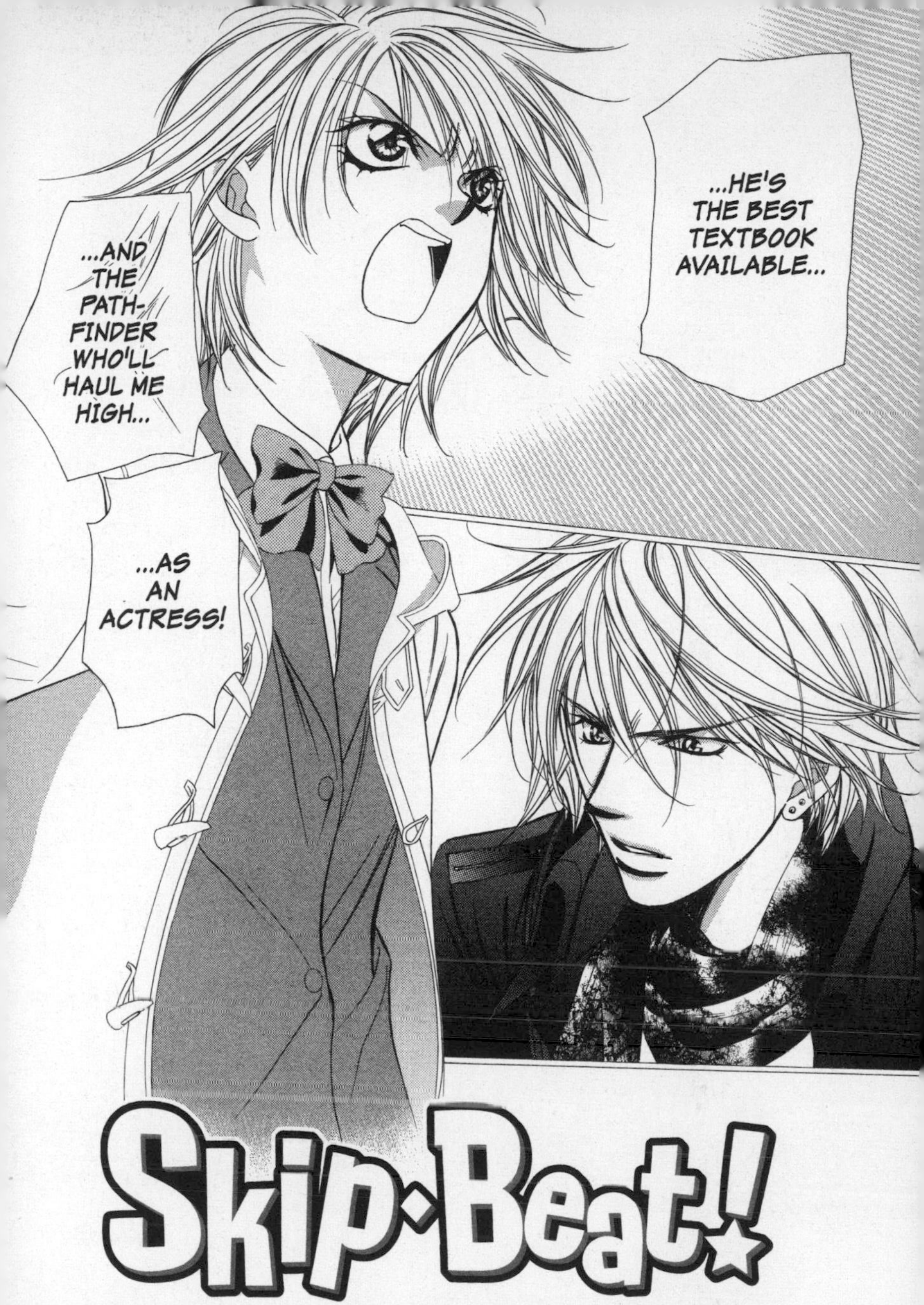
...HE'S THE BEST TEXTBOOK AVAILABLE...
...AND THE PATH-FINDER WHO'LL HAUL ME HIGH...
...AS AN ACTRESS!

Skip·Beat!

Act 193: Breath of Darkness

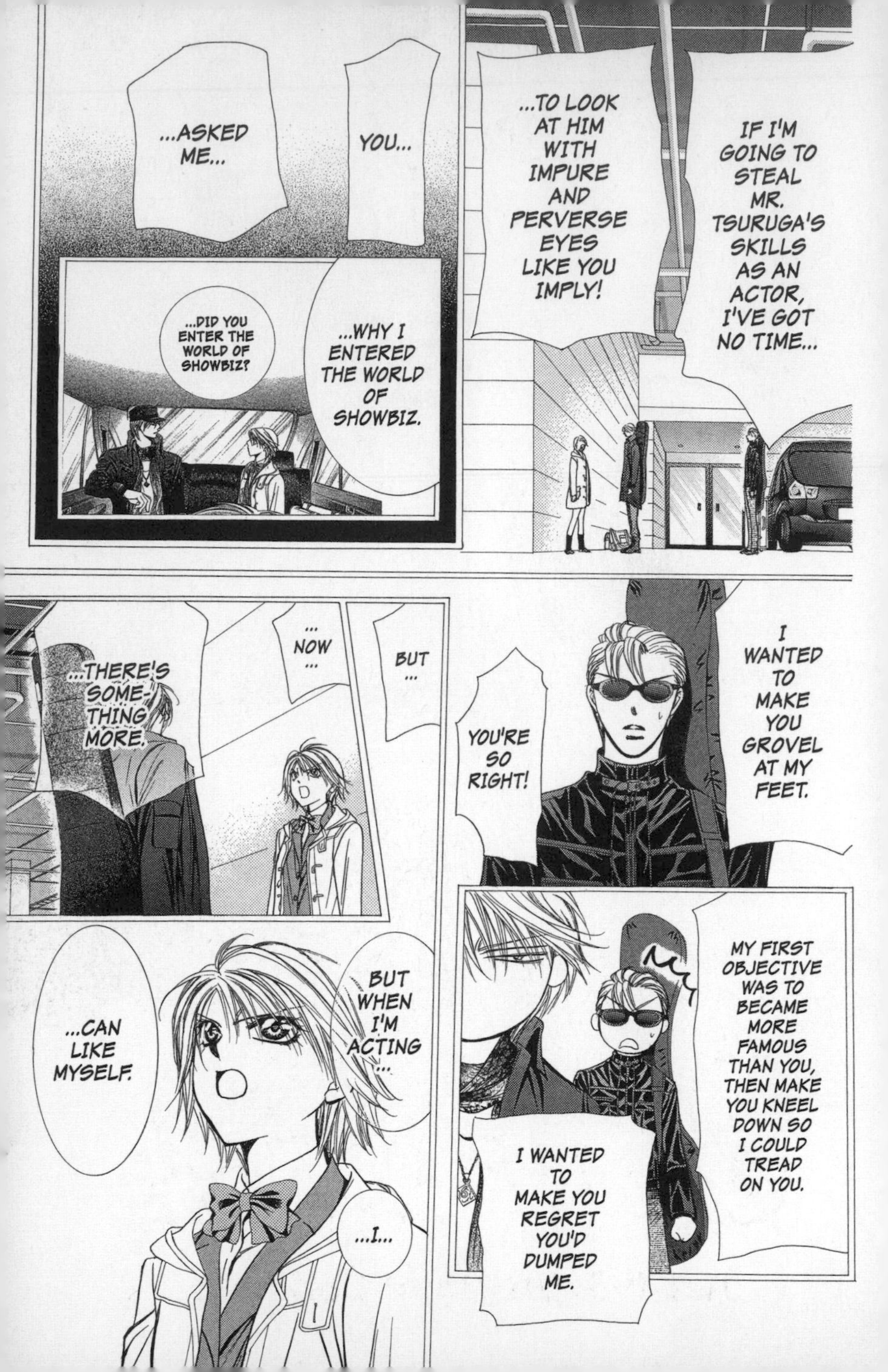
IF I'M GOING TO STEAL MR. TSURUGA'S SKILLS AS AN ACTOR, I'VE GOT NO TIME...
...TO LOOK AT HIM WITH IMPURE AND PERVERSE EYES LIKE YOU IMPLY!
YOU...
...ASKED ME...
...WHY I ENTERED THE WORLD OF SHOWBIZ.
...DID YOU ENTER THE WORLD OF SHOWBIZ?
I WANTED TO MAKE YOU GROVEL AT MY FEET.
YOU'RE SO RIGHT!
BUT...
...NOW...
...THERE'S SOME-THING MORE.
MY FIRST OBJECTIVE WAS TO BECAME MORE FAMOUS THAN YOU, THEN MAKE YOU KNEEL DOWN SO I COULD TREAD ON YOU.
I WANTED TO MAKE YOU REGRET YOU'D DUMPED ME.
BUT WHEN I'M ACTING...
...I...
...CAN LIKE MYSELF.

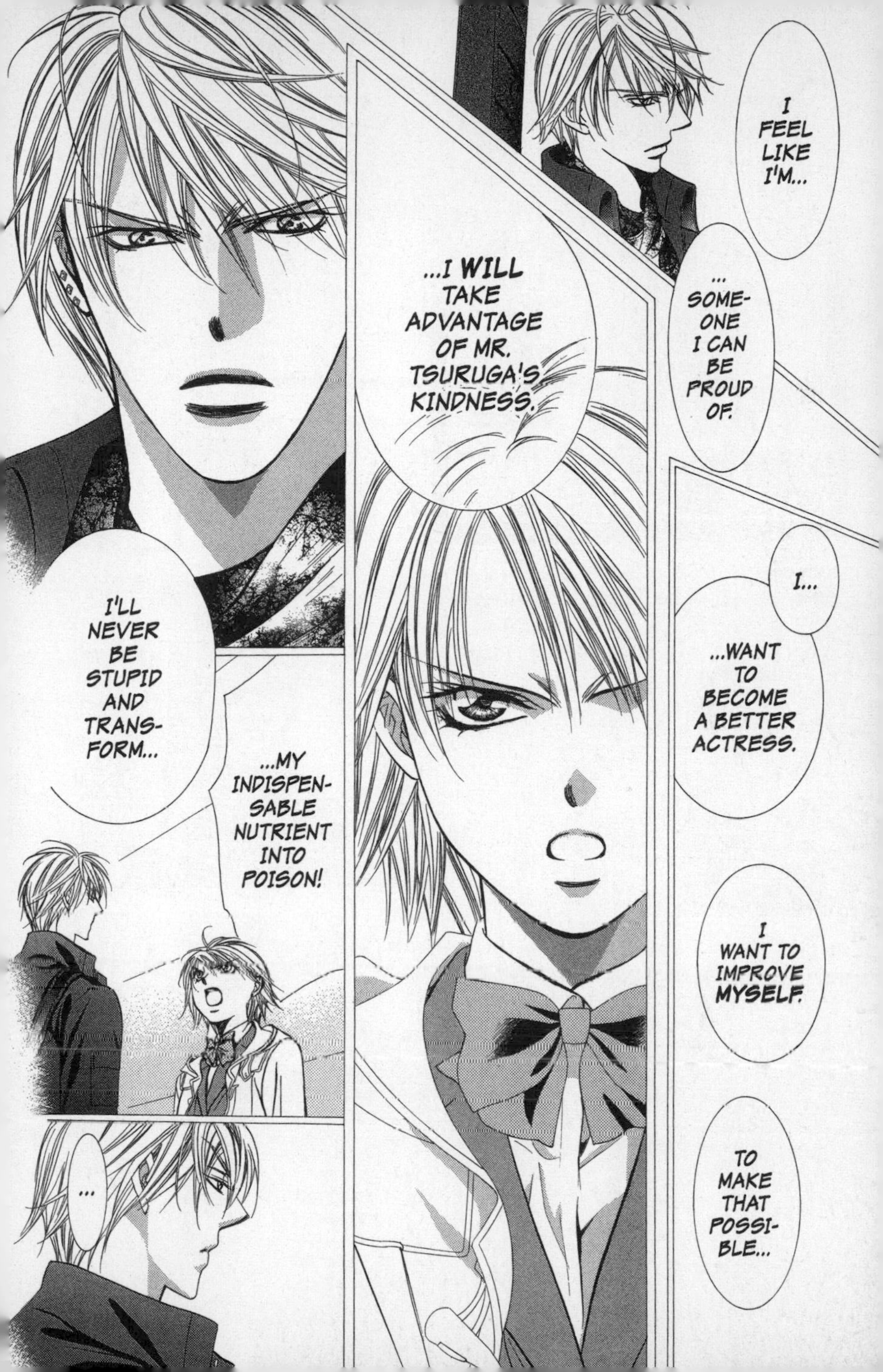
I FEEL LIKE I'M...
...SOMEONE I CAN BE PROUD OF.
I...
...WANT TO BECOME A BETTER ACTRESS.
I WANT TO IMPROVE MYSELF.
TO MAKE THAT POSSIBLE...
...I WILL TAKE ADVANTAGE OF MR. TSURUGA'S KINDNESS.
I'LL NEVER BE STUPID AND TRANSFORM...
...MY INDISPENSABLE NUTRIENT INTO POISON!
...

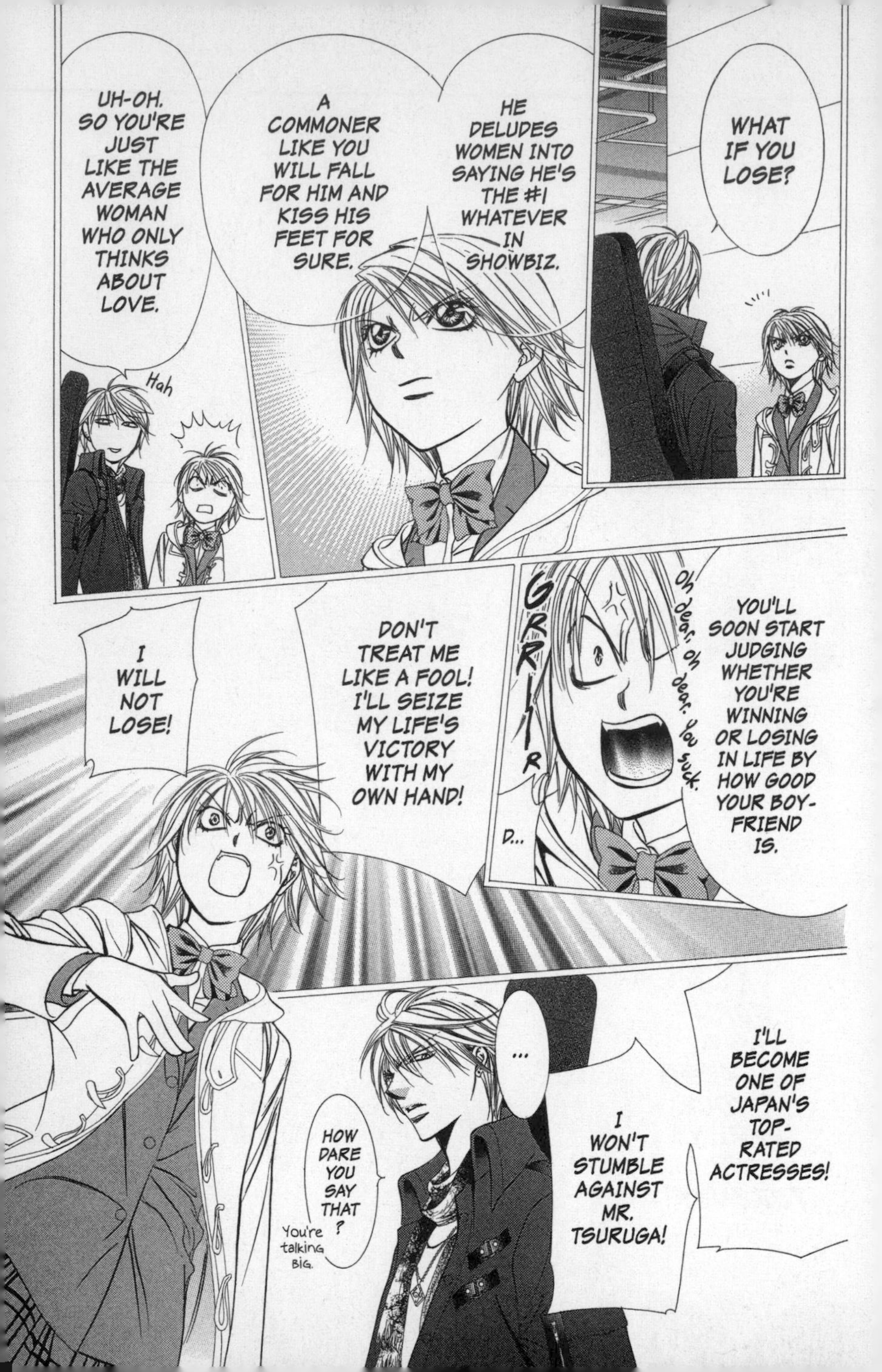
WHAT IF YOU LOSE?
HE DELUDES WOMEN INTO SAYING HE'S THE #1 WHATEVER IN SHOWBIZ.
A COMMONER LIKE YOU WILL FALL FOR HIM AND KISS HIS FEET FOR SURE.
UH-OH. SO YOU'RE JUST LIKE THE AVERAGE WOMAN WHO ONLY THINKS ABOUT LOVE.
Hah
YOU'LL SOON START JUDGING WHETHER YOU'RE WINNING OR LOSING IN LIFE BY HOW GOOD YOUR BOY-FRIEND IS.
Oh dear, oh dear. You suck.
GRRRR
D...
DON'T TREAT ME LIKE A FOOL! I'LL SEIZE MY LIFE'S VICTORY WITH MY OWN HAND!
I WILL NOT LOSE!
I'LL BECOME ONE OF JAPAN'S TOP-RATED ACTRESSES!
I WON'T STUMBLE AGAINST MR. TSURUGA!
...
HOW DARE YOU SAY THAT?
You're talking BIG.

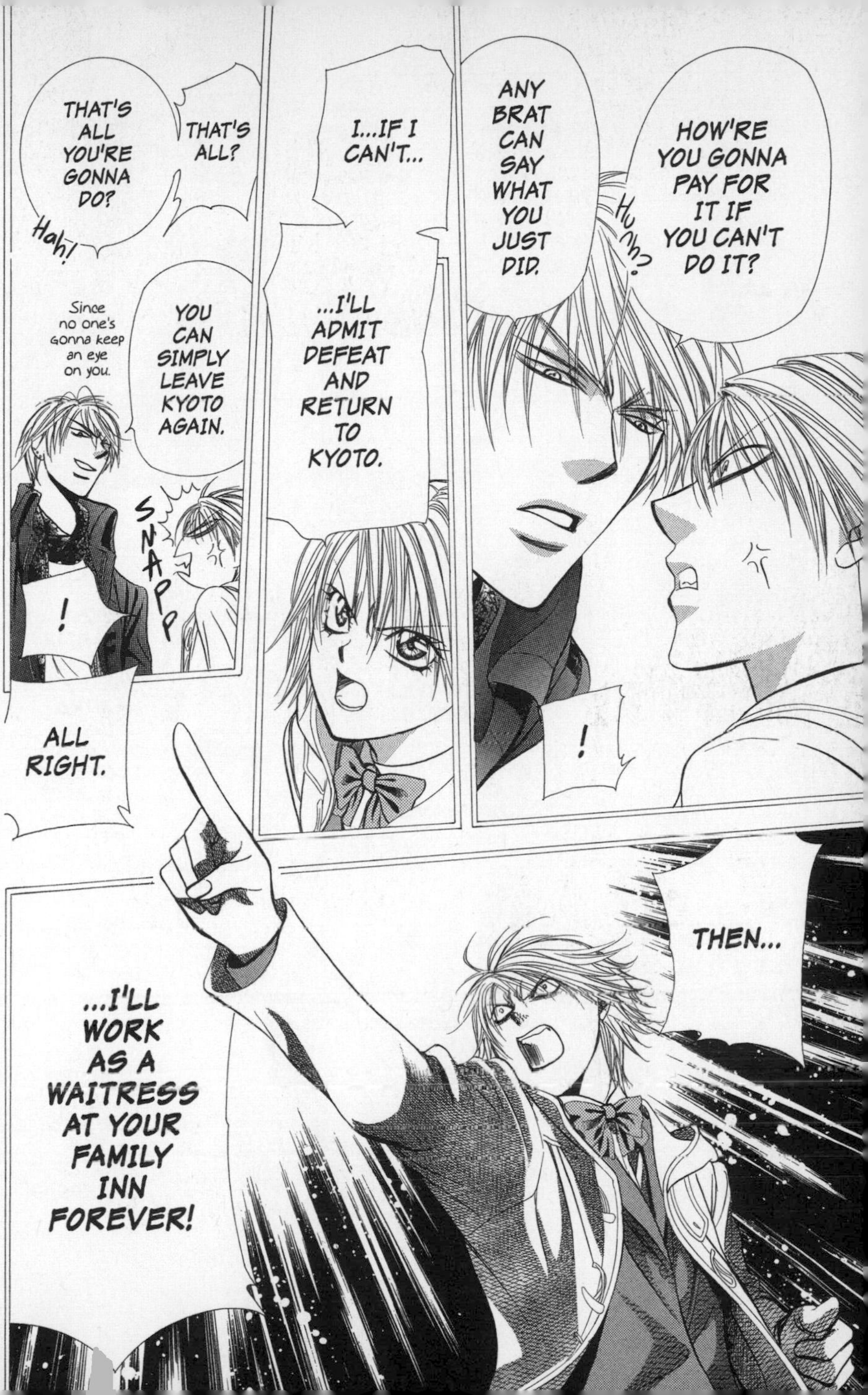
HOW'RE YOU GONNA PAY FOR IT IF YOU CAN'T DO IT?
Hunh?
ANY BRAT CAN SAY WHAT YOU JUST DID.
!
I...IF I CAN'T...
...I'LL ADMIT DEFEAT AND RETURN TO KYOTO.
THAT'S ALL?
THAT'S ALL YOU'RE GONNA DO?
Hah!
YOU CAN SIMPLY LEAVE KYOTO AGAIN.
Since no one's gonna keep an eye on you.
SNAPP
!
ALL RIGHT.
THEN...
...I'LL WORK AS A WAITRESS AT YOUR FAMILY INN FOREVER!

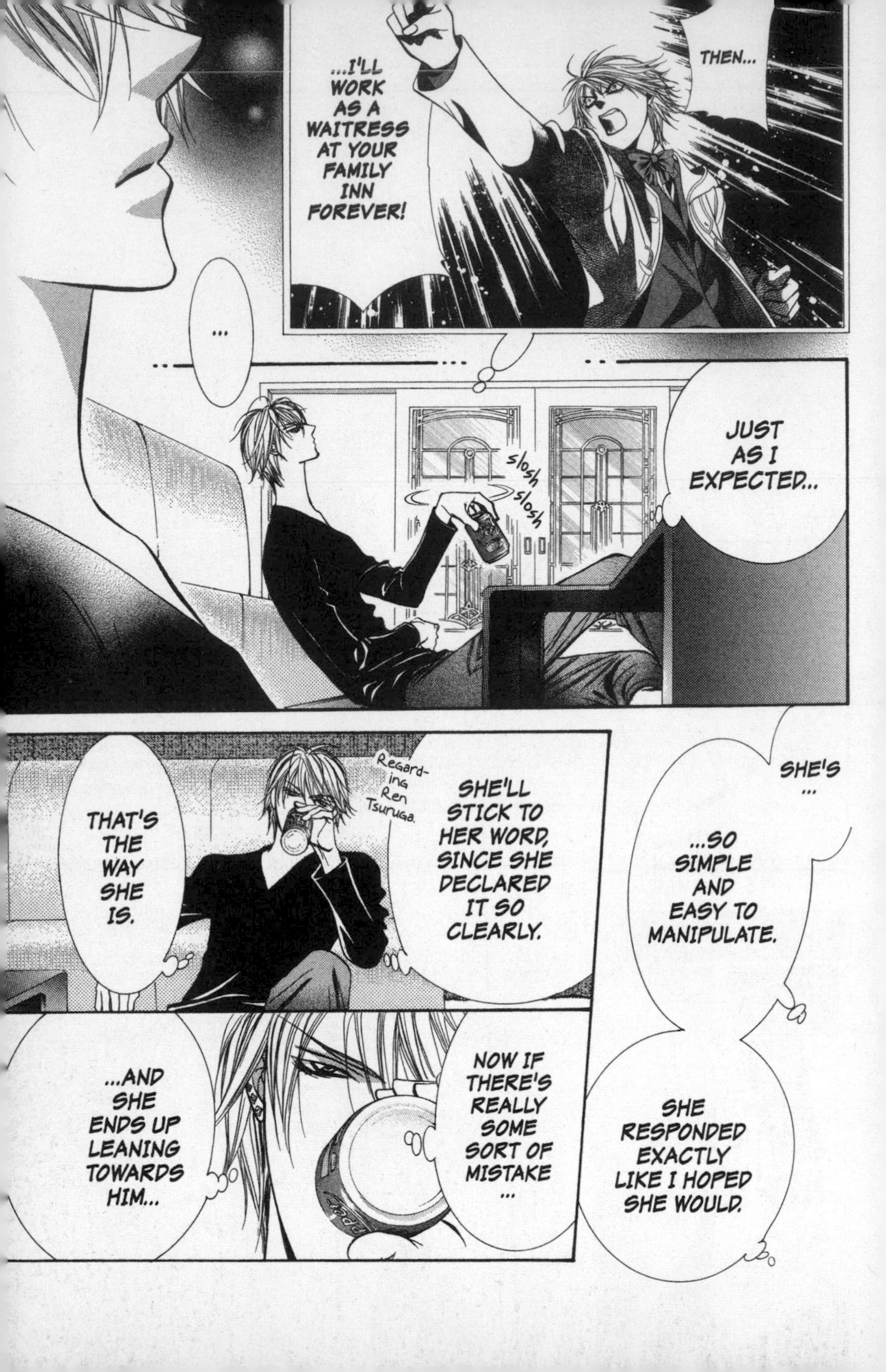

THEN...
...I'LL WORK AS A WAITRESS AT YOUR FAMILY INN FOREVER!
JUST AS I EXPECTED...
slosh slosh
...
SHE'S ...
...SO SIMPLE AND EASY TO MANIPULATE.
SHE'LL STICK TO HER WORD, SINCE SHE DECLARED IT SO CLEARLY.
Regarding Ren Tsuruga.
THAT'S THE WAY SHE IS.
SHE RESPONDED EXACTLY LIKE I HOPED SHE WOULD.
NOW IF THERE'S REALLY SOME SORT OF MISTAKE ...
...AND SHE ENDS UP LEANING TOWARDS HIM...

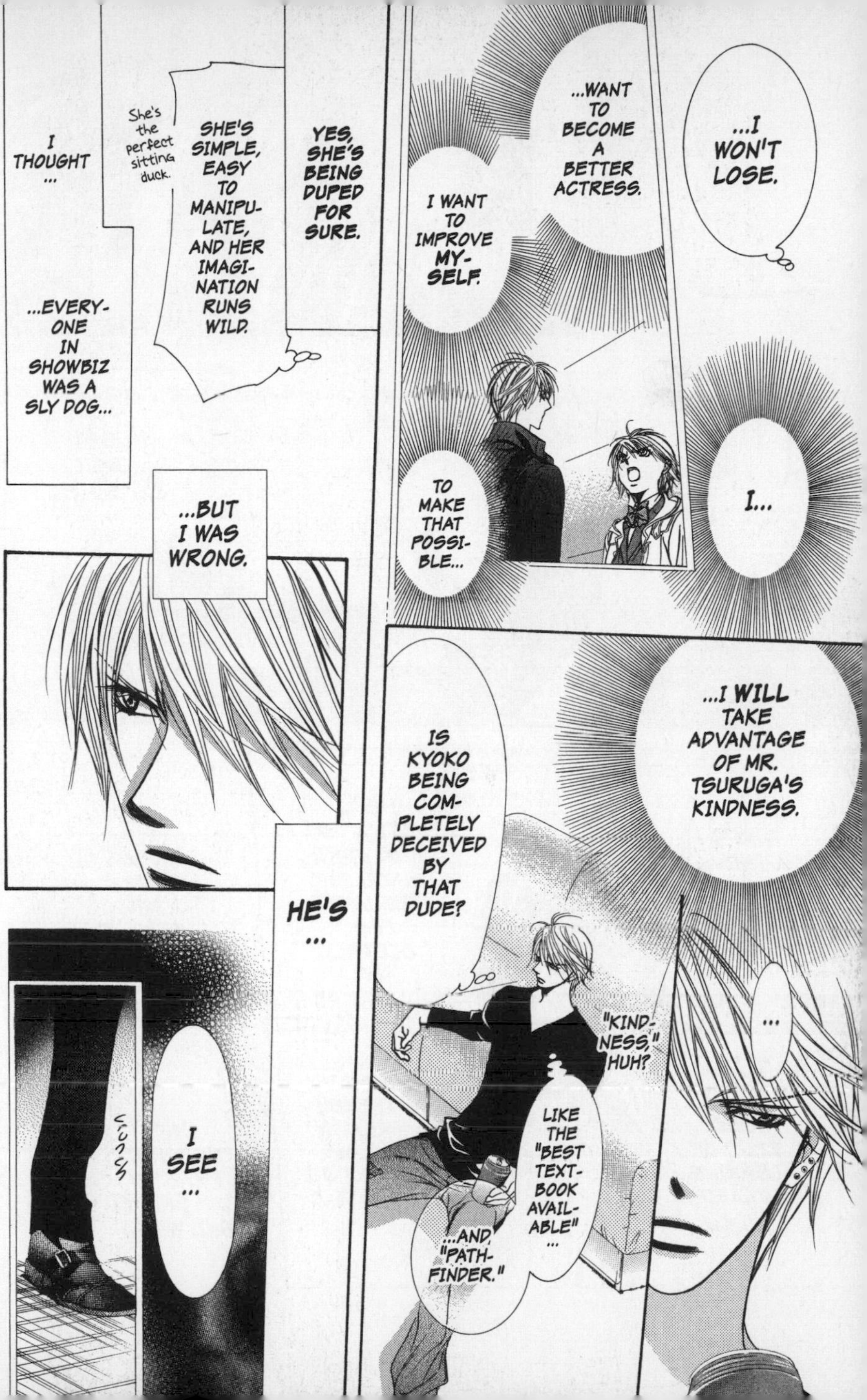
...I WON'T LOSE.
...WANT TO BECOME A BETTER ACTRESS.
I WANT TO IMPROVE MY-SELF.
I...
TO MAKE THAT POSSI-BLE...
...I WILL TAKE ADVANTAGE OF MR. TSURUGA'S KINDNESS.
IS KYOKO BEING COM-PLETELY DECEIVED BY THAT DUDE?
...
"KIND-NESS," HUH?
LIKE THE "BEST TEXT-BOOK AVAIL-ABLE"...
...AND, "PATH-FINDER."
YES, SHE'S BEING DUPED FOR SURE.
SHE'S SIMPLE, EASY TO MANIPU-LATE, AND HER IMAGI-NATION RUNS WILD.
She's the perfect sitting duck.
I THOUGHT...
...EVERY-ONE IN SHOWBIZ WAS A SLY DOG...
...BUT I WAS WRONG.
HE'S...
I SEE...

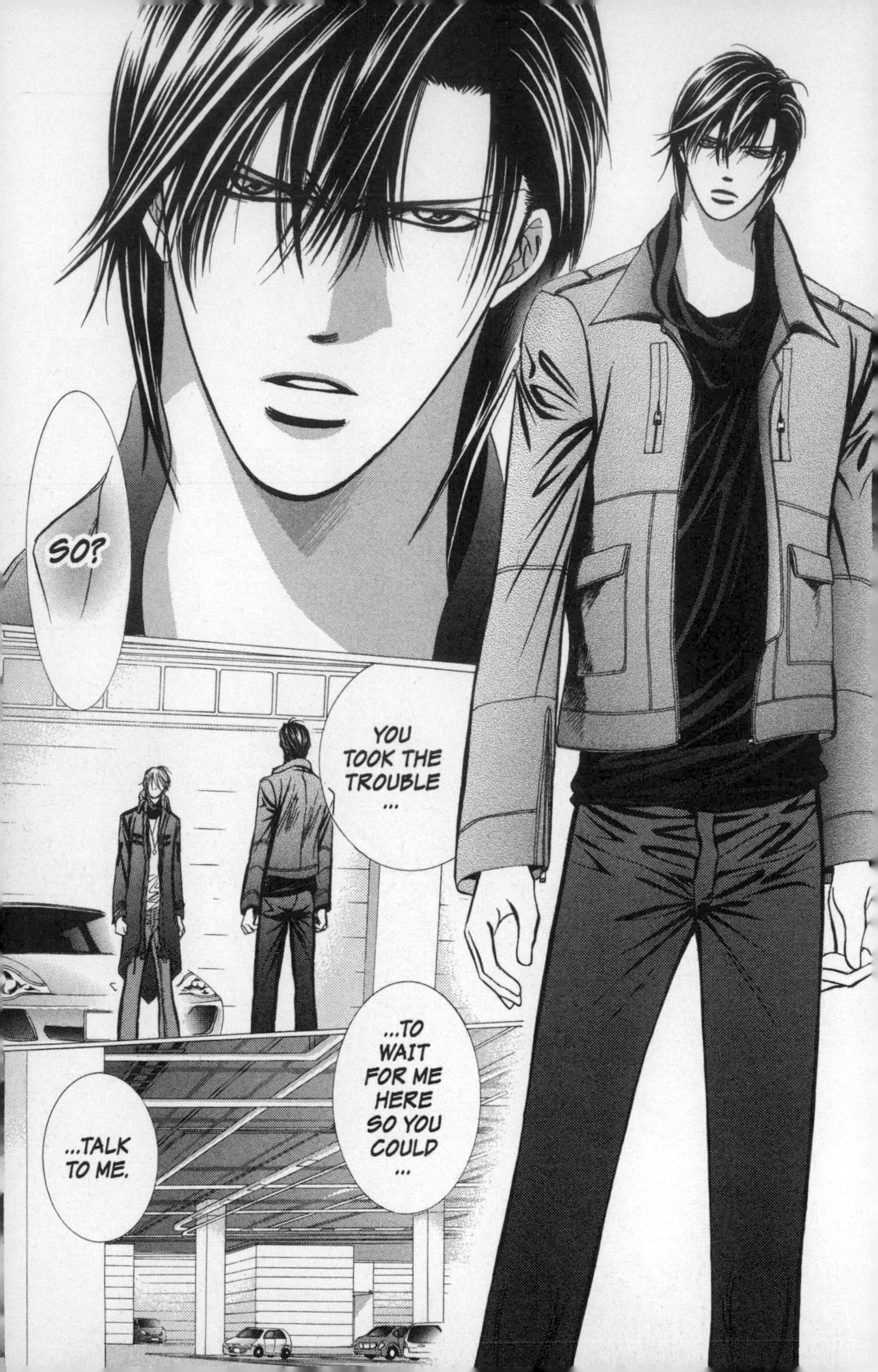
SO?
YOU TOOK THE TROUBLE ...
...TO WAIT FOR ME HERE SO YOU COULD ...
...TALK TO ME.

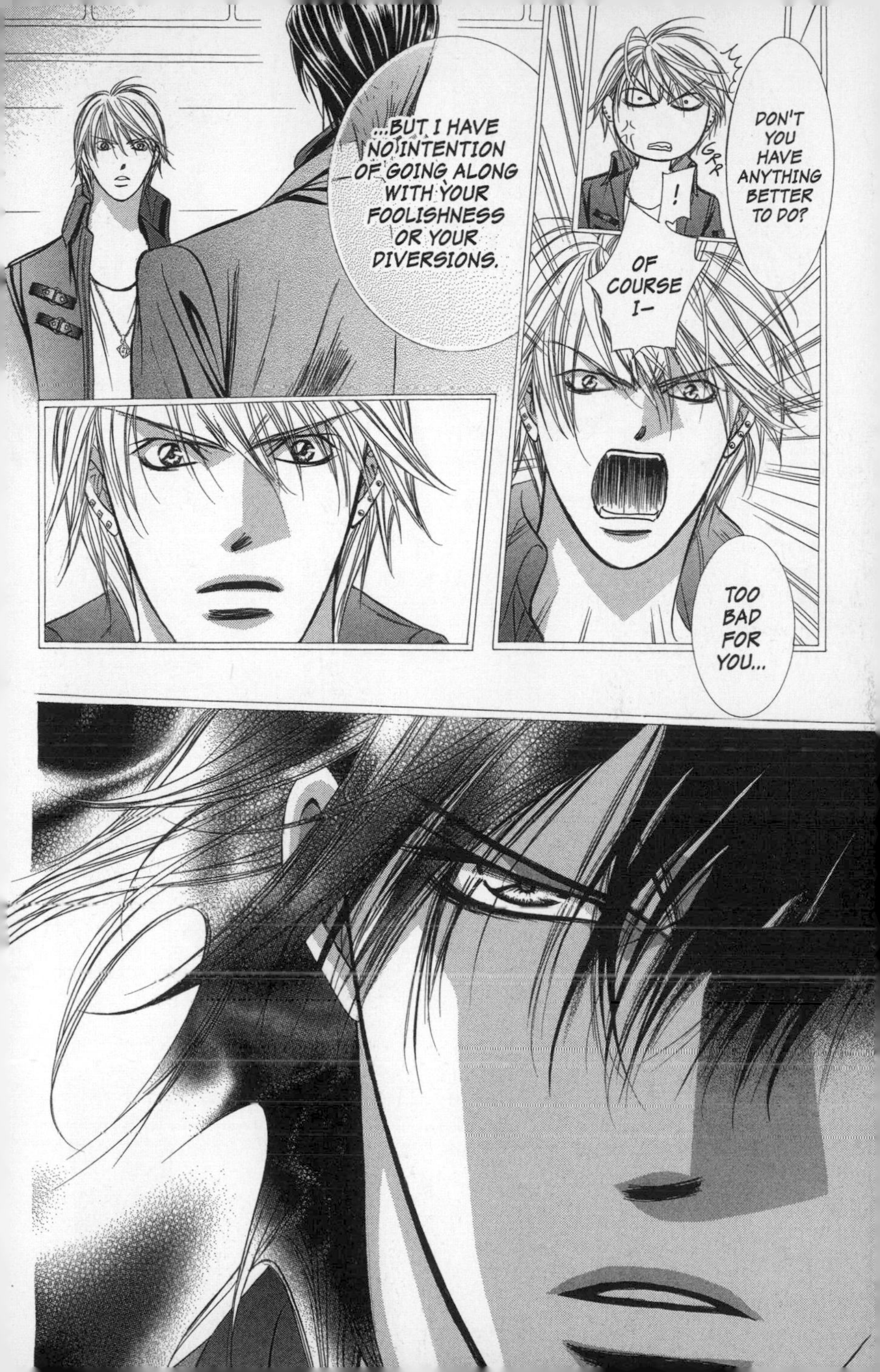
DON'T YOU HAVE ANYTHING BETTER TO DO?
GRR
!
OF COURSE I—
TOO BAD FOR YOU...
...BUT I HAVE NO INTENTION OF GOING ALONG WITH YOUR FOOLISHNESS OR YOUR DIVERSIONS.

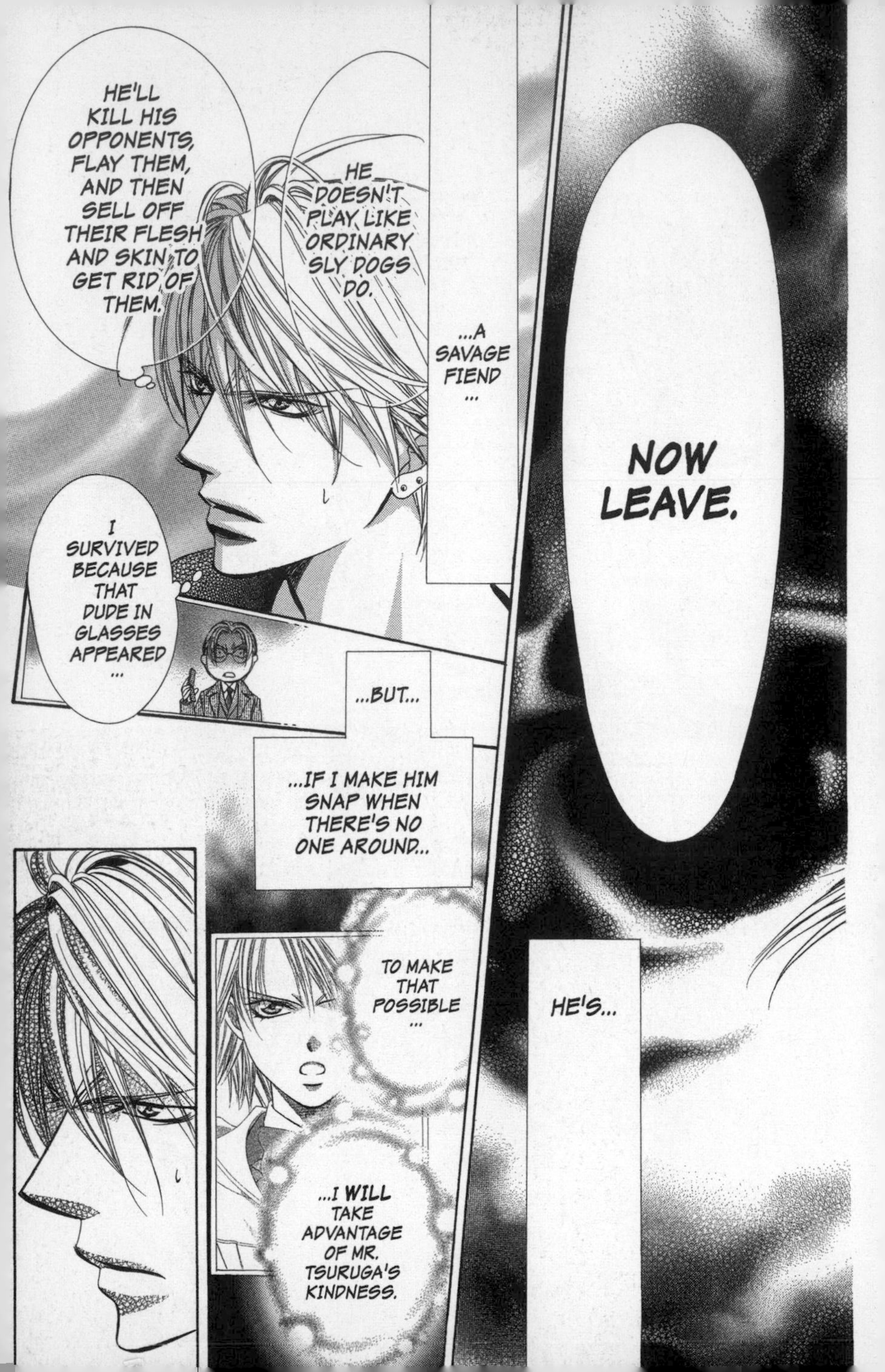
NOW LEAVE.
HE'S...
...A SAVAGE FIEND...
...HE DOESN'T PLAY LIKE ORDINARY SLY DOGS DO.
HE'LL KILL HIS OPPONENTS, FLAY THEM, AND THEN SELL OFF THEIR FLESH AND SKIN TO GET RID OF THEM.
I SURVIVED BECAUSE THAT DUDE IN GLASSES APPEARED...
...BUT...
...IF I MAKE HIM SNAP WHEN THERE'S NO ONE AROUND...
TO MAKE THAT POSSIBLE...
...I WILL TAKE ADVANTAGE OF MR. TSURUGA'S KINDNESS.

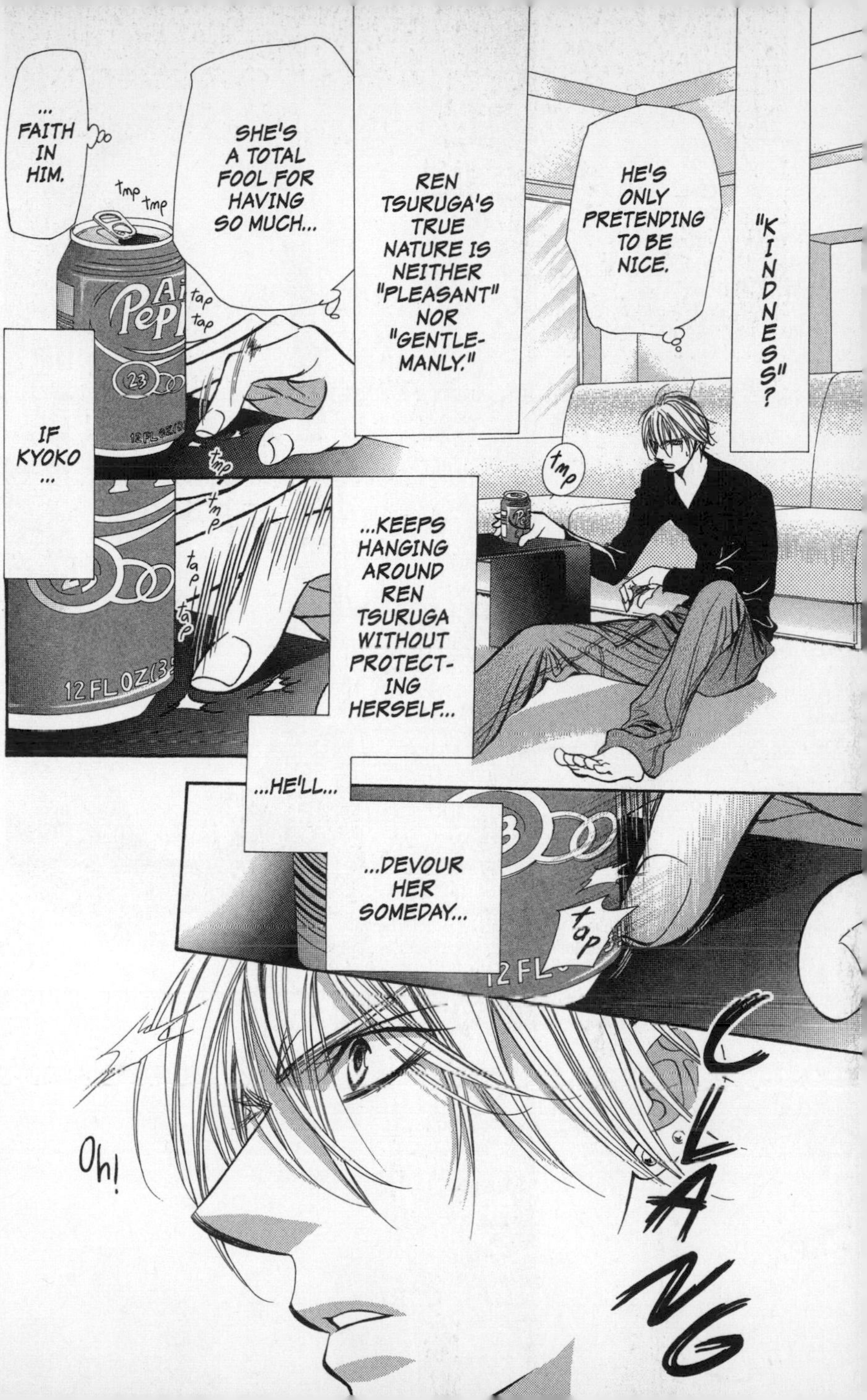
"KINDNESS"?
HE'S ONLY PRETENDING TO BE NICE.
REN TSURUGA'S TRUE NATURE IS NEITHER "PLEASANT" NOR "GENTLE-MANLY."
tmp
SHE'S A TOTAL FOOL FOR HAVING SO MUCH...
... FAITH IN HIM.
tmp tmp
tap tap
tmp
...KEEPS HANGING AROUND REN TSURUGA WITHOUT PROTECT-ING HERSELF...
IF KYOKO ...
tmp
tap tap
...HE'LL...
...DEVOUR HER SOMEDAY...
tap
CLANG
Oh!

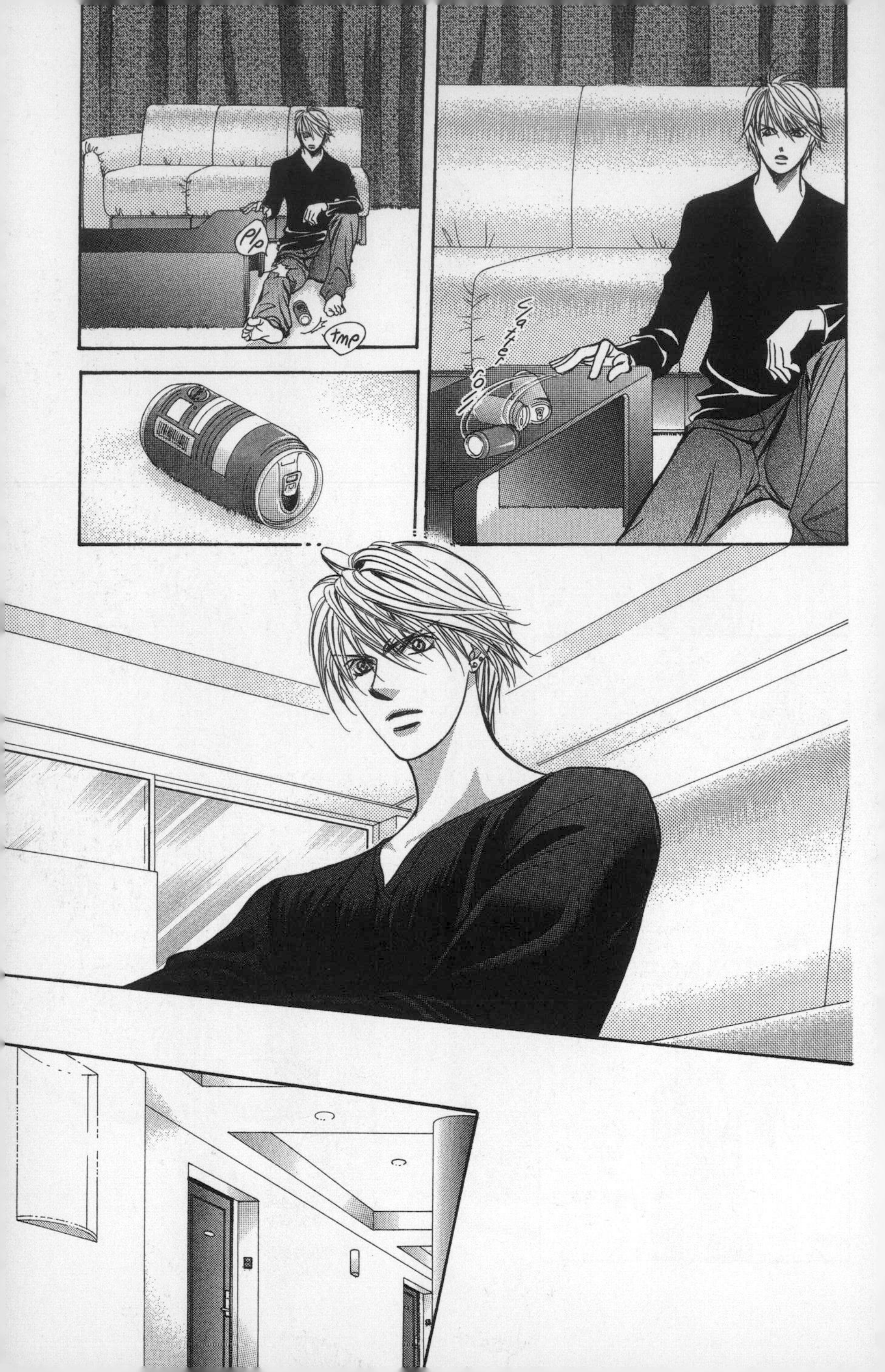
clatter roll
plp
tmp

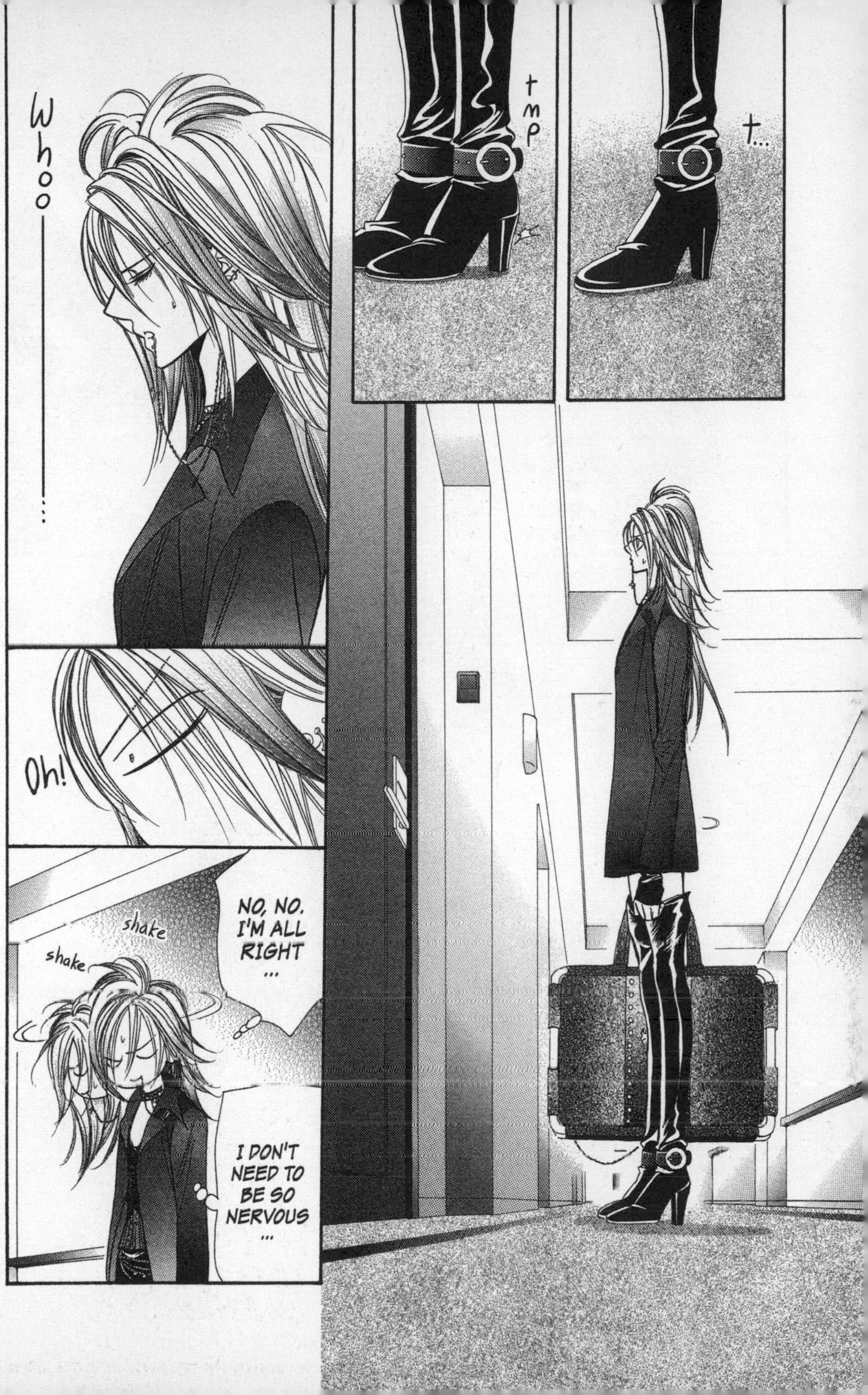
t...
tmp
Whoo——...
Oh!
shake
shake
NO, NO. I'M ALL RIGHT...
I DON'T NEED TO BE SO NERVOUS...

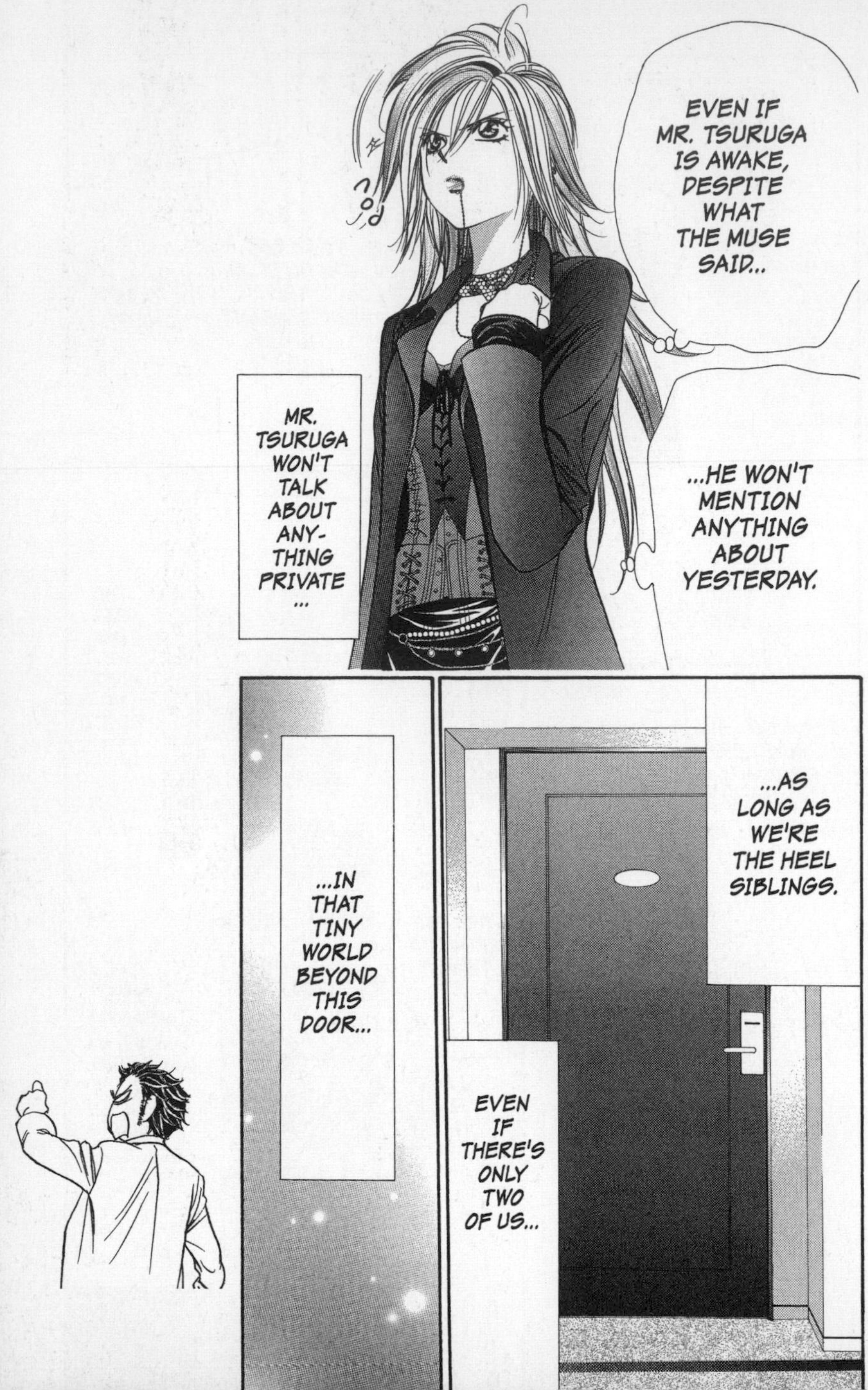
EVEN IF MR. TSURUGA IS AWAKE, DESPITE WHAT THE MUSE SAID...
MR. TSURUGA WON'T TALK ABOUT ANY-THING PRIVATE...
...HE WON'T MENTION ANYTHING ABOUT YESTERDAY.
...AS LONG AS WE'RE THE HEEL SIBLINGS.
EVEN IF THERE'S ONLY TWO OF US...
...IN THAT TINY WORLD BEYOND THIS DOOR...

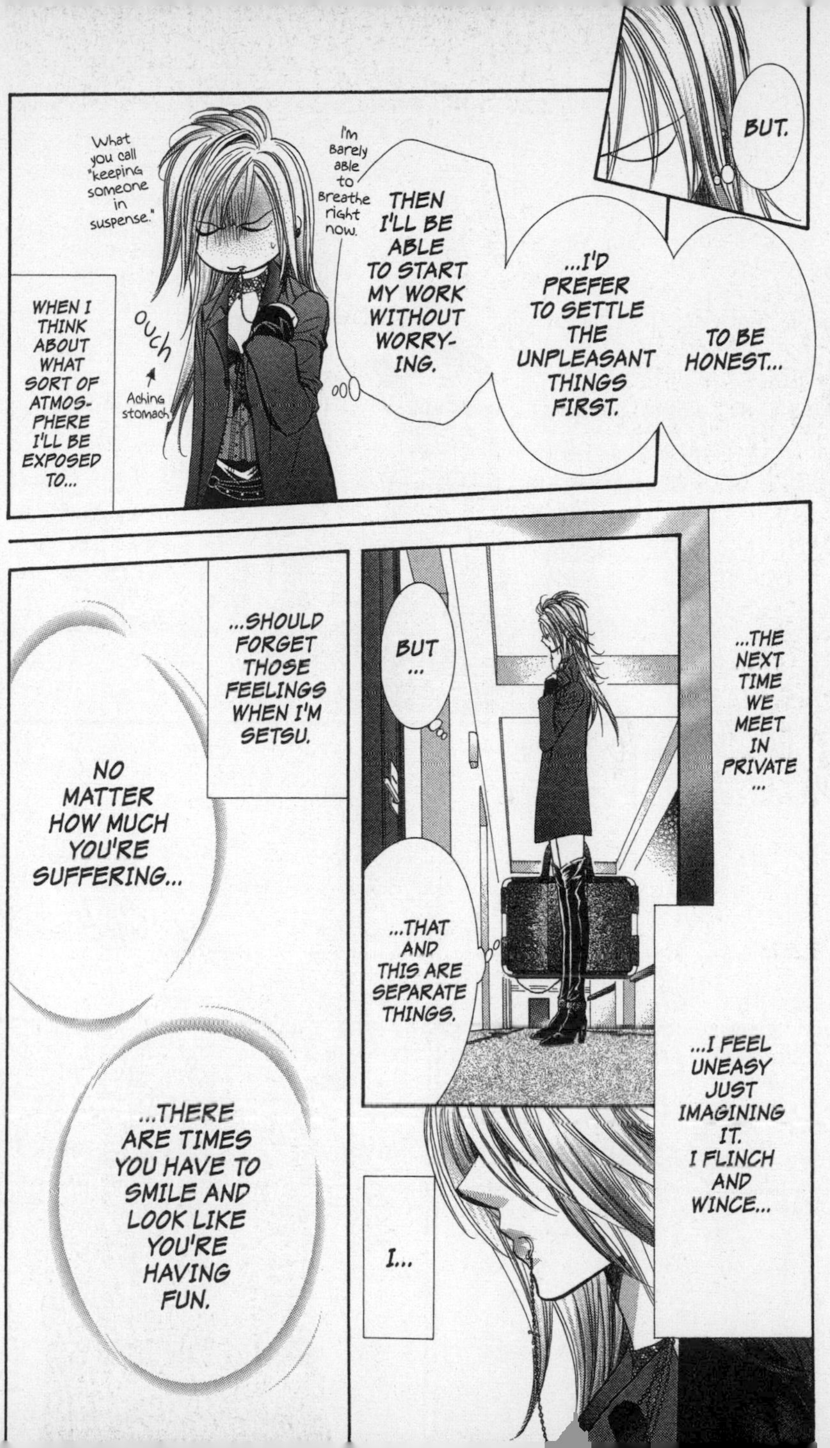
BUT.
TO BE HONEST...
...I'D PREFER TO SETTLE THE UNPLEASANT THINGS FIRST.
THEN I'LL BE ABLE TO START MY WORK WITHOUT WORRY-ING.
I'm Barely able to Breathe right now.
What you call "keeping someone in suspense."
ouch
Aching stomach
WHEN I THINK ABOUT WHAT SORT OF ATMOS-PHERE I'LL BE EXPOSED TO...
...THE NEXT TIME WE MEET IN PRIVATE...
BUT ...
...THAT AND THIS ARE SEPARATE THINGS.
...I FEEL UNEASY JUST IMAGINING IT. I FLINCH AND WINCE...
I...
...SHOULD FORGET THOSE FEELINGS WHEN I'M SETSU.
NO MATTER HOW MUCH YOU'RE SUFFERING...
...THERE ARE TIMES YOU HAVE TO SMILE AND LOOK LIKE YOU'RE HAVING FUN.

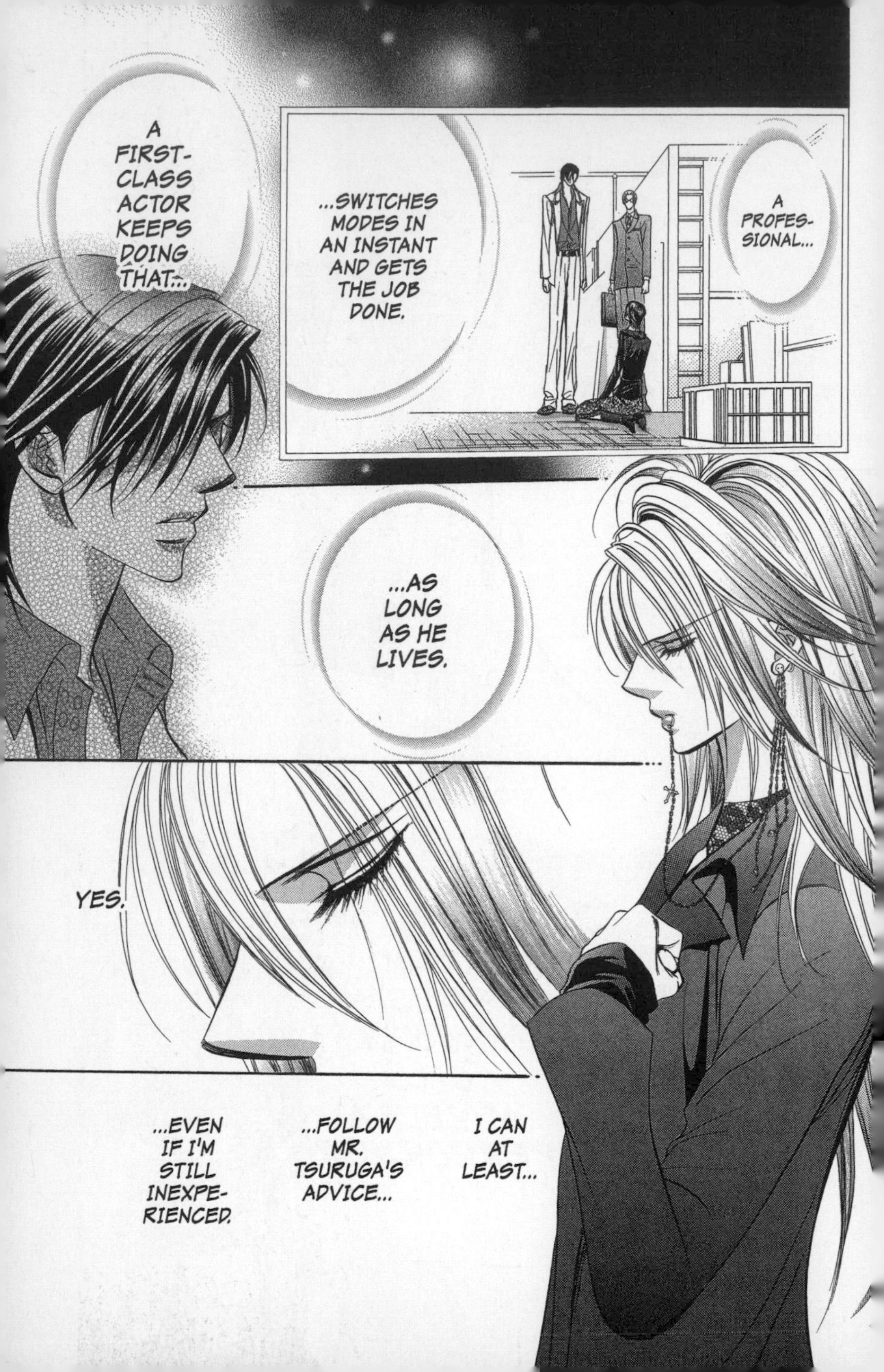
A PROFESSIONAL...
...SWITCHES MODES IN AN INSTANT AND GETS THE JOB DONE.
A FIRST-CLASS ACTOR KEEPS DOING THAT...
...AS LONG AS HE LIVES.
YES.
I CAN AT LEAST...
...FOLLOW MR. TSURUGA'S ADVICE...
...EVEN IF I'M STILL INEXPERIENCED.

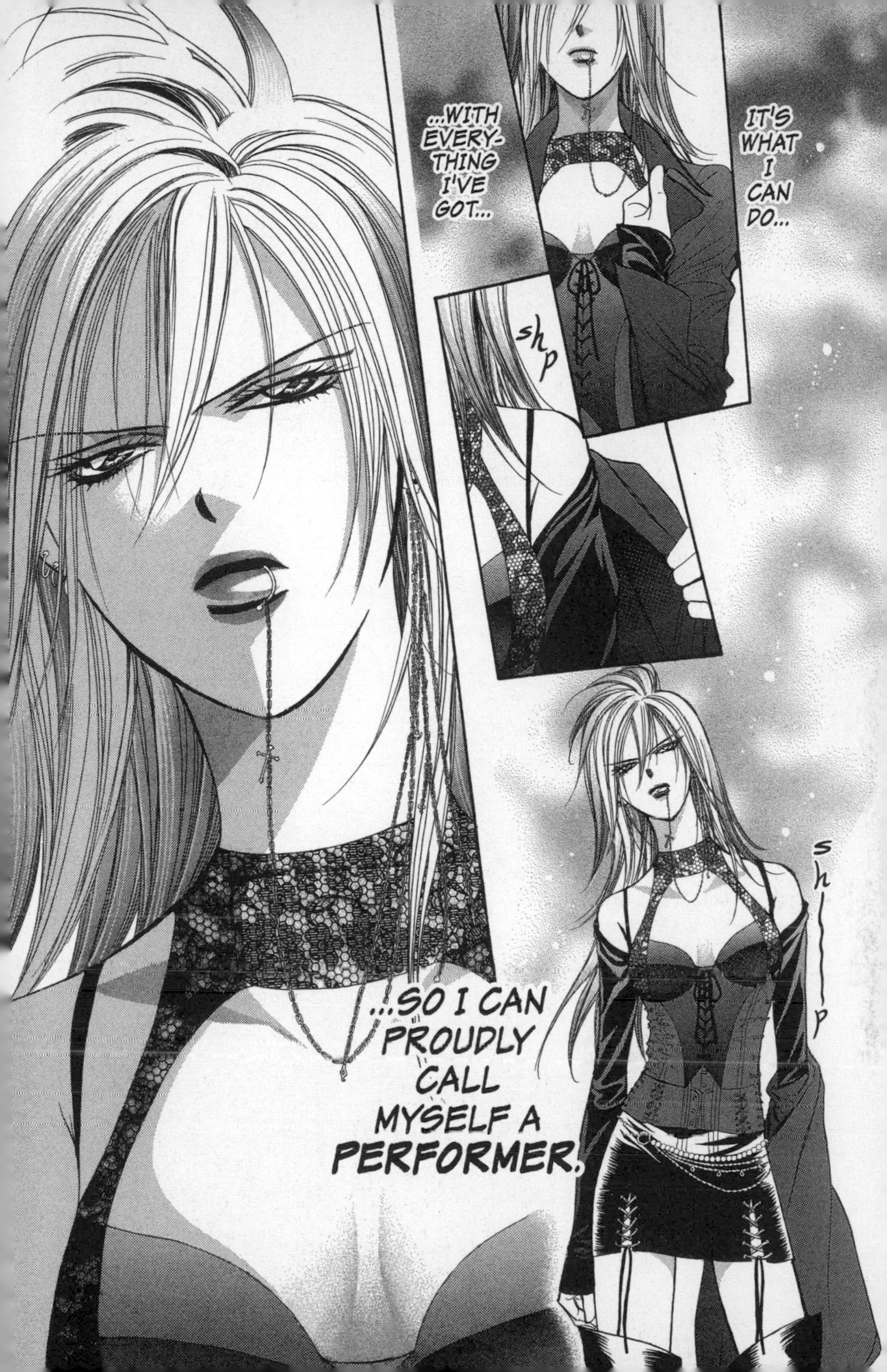

IT'S WHAT I CAN DO...
...WITH EVERYTHING I'VE GOT...
shp
shp
...SO I CAN PROUDLY CALL MYSELF A PERFORMER.

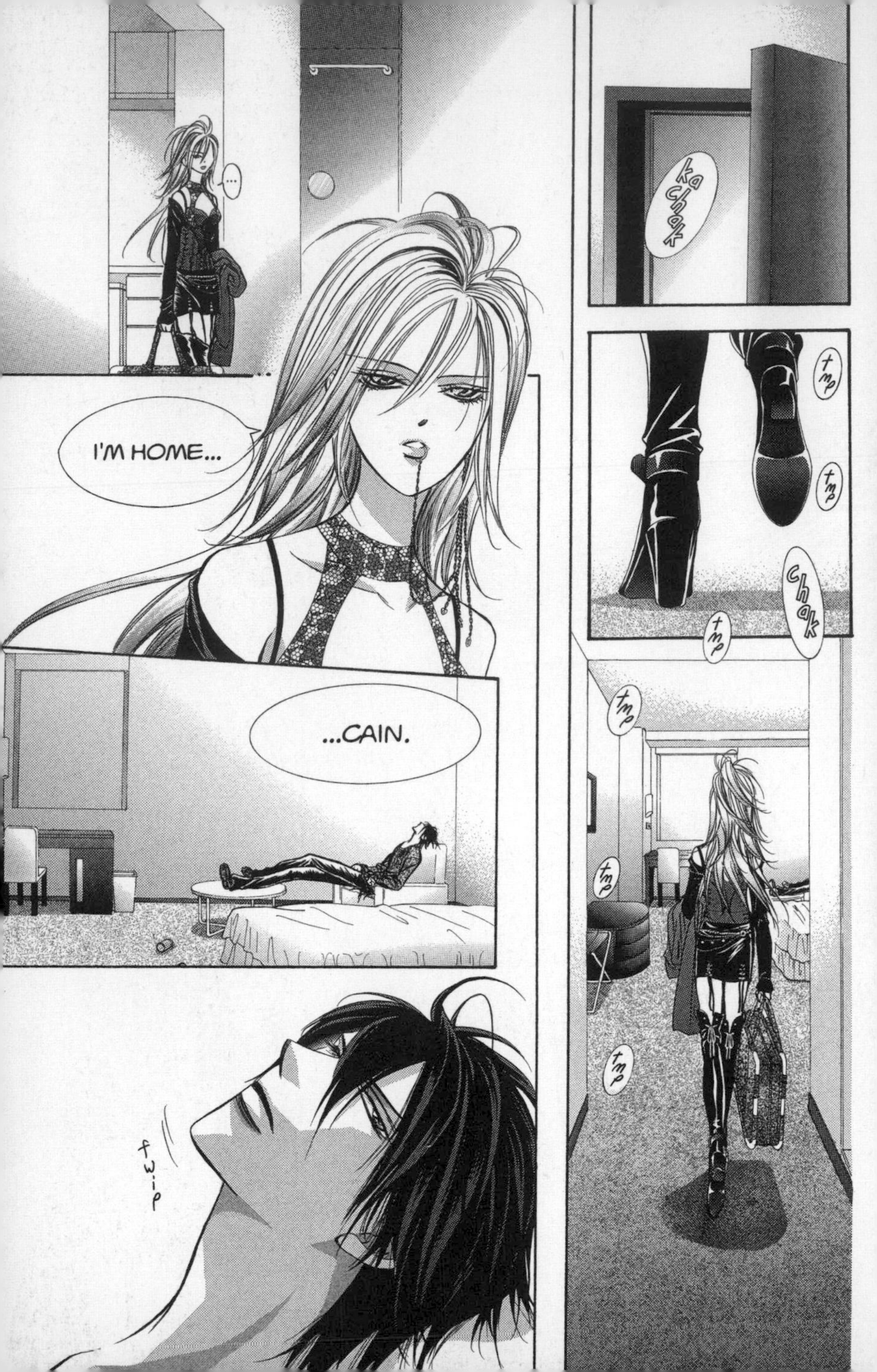
ka chak
tmp
tmp
chak
tmp
tmp
tmp
tmp
...
I'M HOME...
...CAIN.
fwip

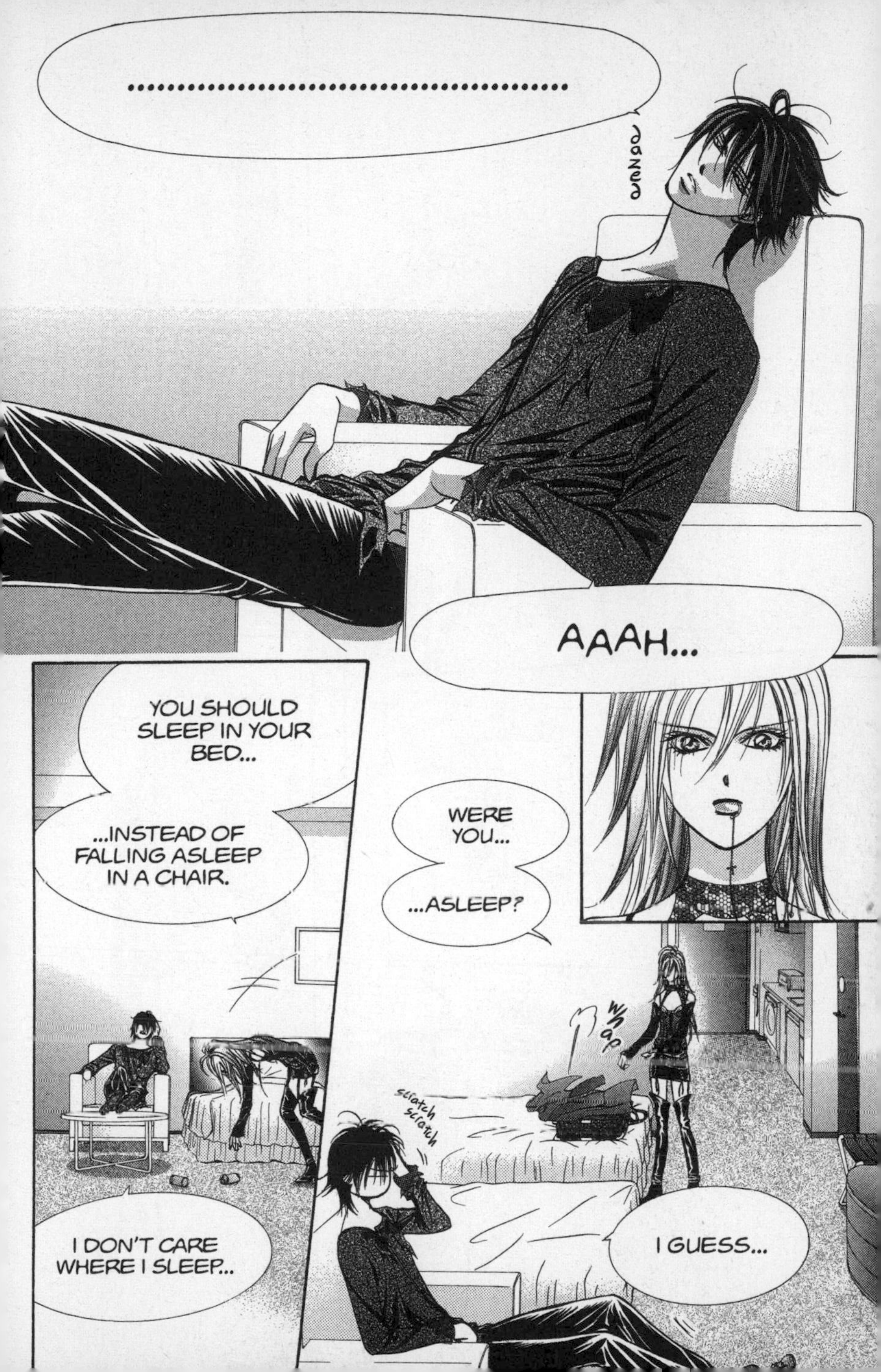
....
AAAH...
WERE YOU...
...ASLEEP?
whap
scratch scratch
I GUESS...
YOU SHOULD SLEEP IN YOUR BED...
...INSTEAD OF FALLING ASLEEP IN A CHAIR.
I DON'T CARE WHERE I SLEEP...

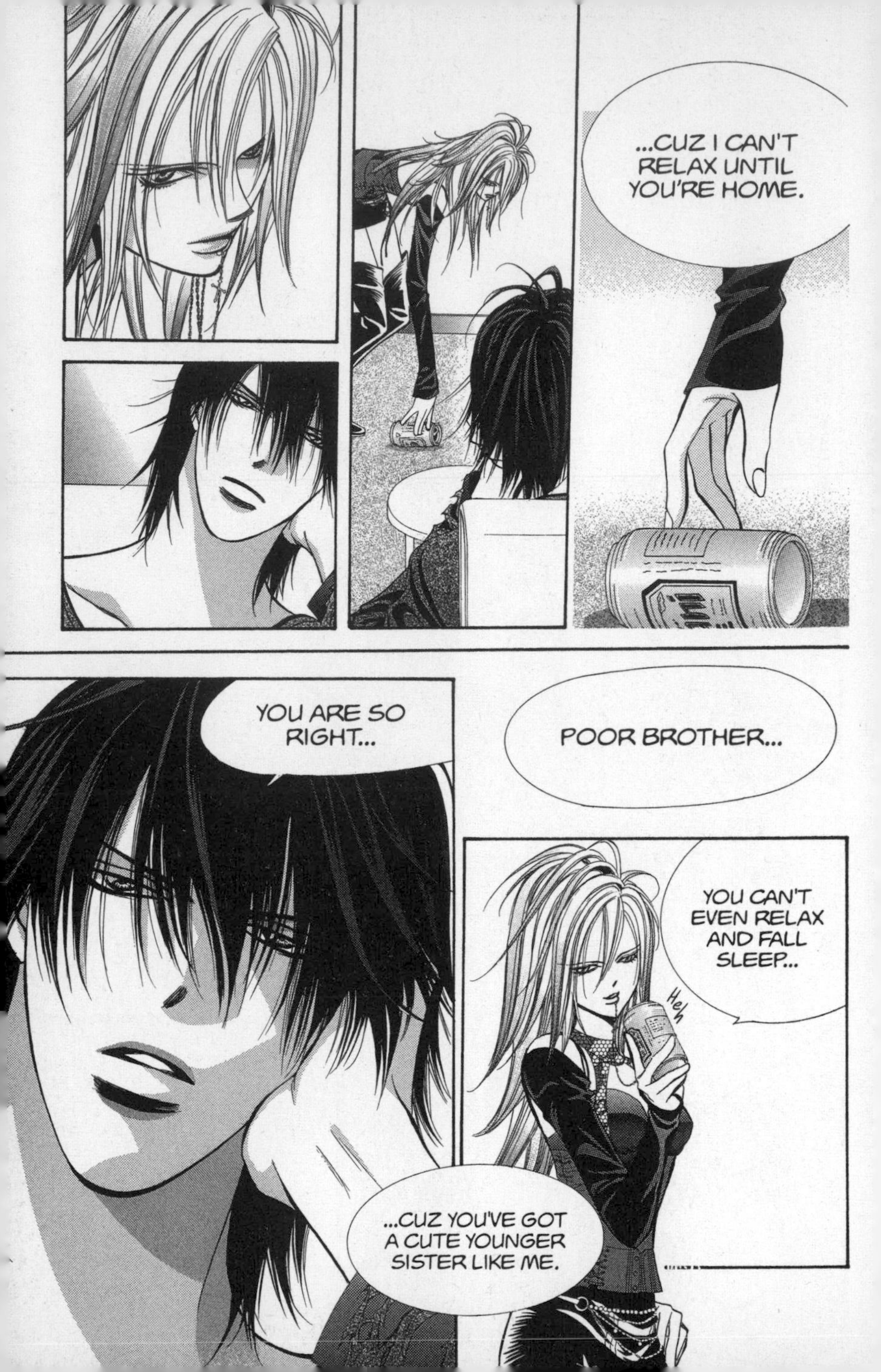
...CUZ I CAN'T RELAX UNTIL YOU'RE HOME.
POOR BROTHER...
YOU ARE SO RIGHT...
YOU CAN'T EVEN RELAX AND FALL SLEEP...
Heh
...CUZ YOU'VE GOT A CUTE YOUNGER SISTER LIKE ME.

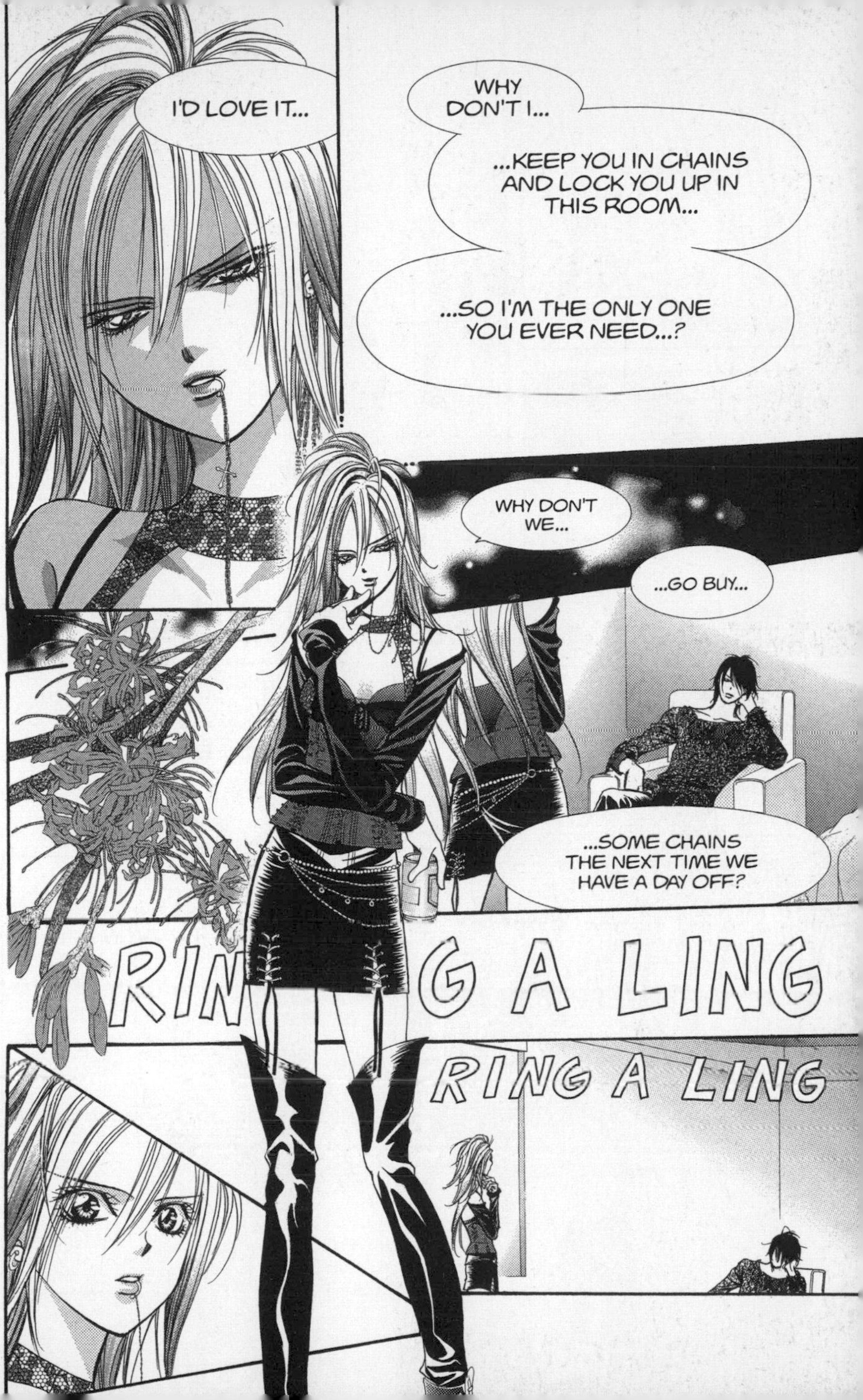
WHY DON'T I...
...KEEP YOU IN CHAINS AND LOCK YOU UP IN THIS ROOM...
...SO I'M THE ONLY ONE YOU EVER NEED...?
I'D LOVE IT...
WHY DON'T WE...
...GO BUY...
...SOME CHAINS THE NEXT TIME WE HAVE A DAY OFF?
RING A LING
RING A LING

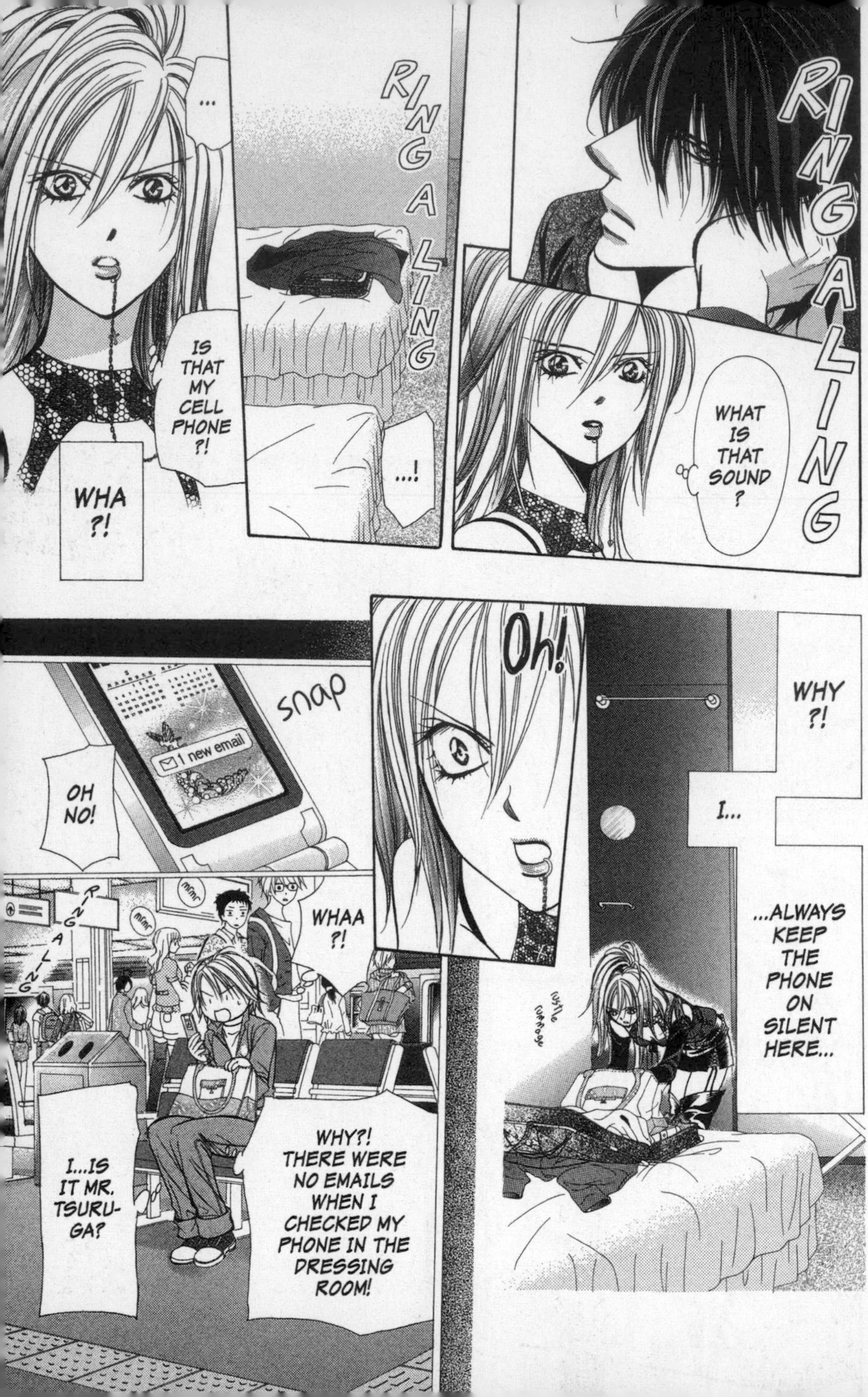
RING A LING
WHAT IS THAT SOUND?
RING A LING
...!
...
IS THAT MY CELL PHONE?!
WHA?!
WHY?!
I...
...ALWAYS KEEP THE PHONE ON SILENT HERE...
rustle rummage
Oh!
snap
1 new email
OH NO!
WHAA?!
RING A LING
WHY?! THERE WERE NO EMAILS WHEN I CHECKED MY PHONE IN THE DRESSING ROOM!
I...IS IT MR. TSURUGA?

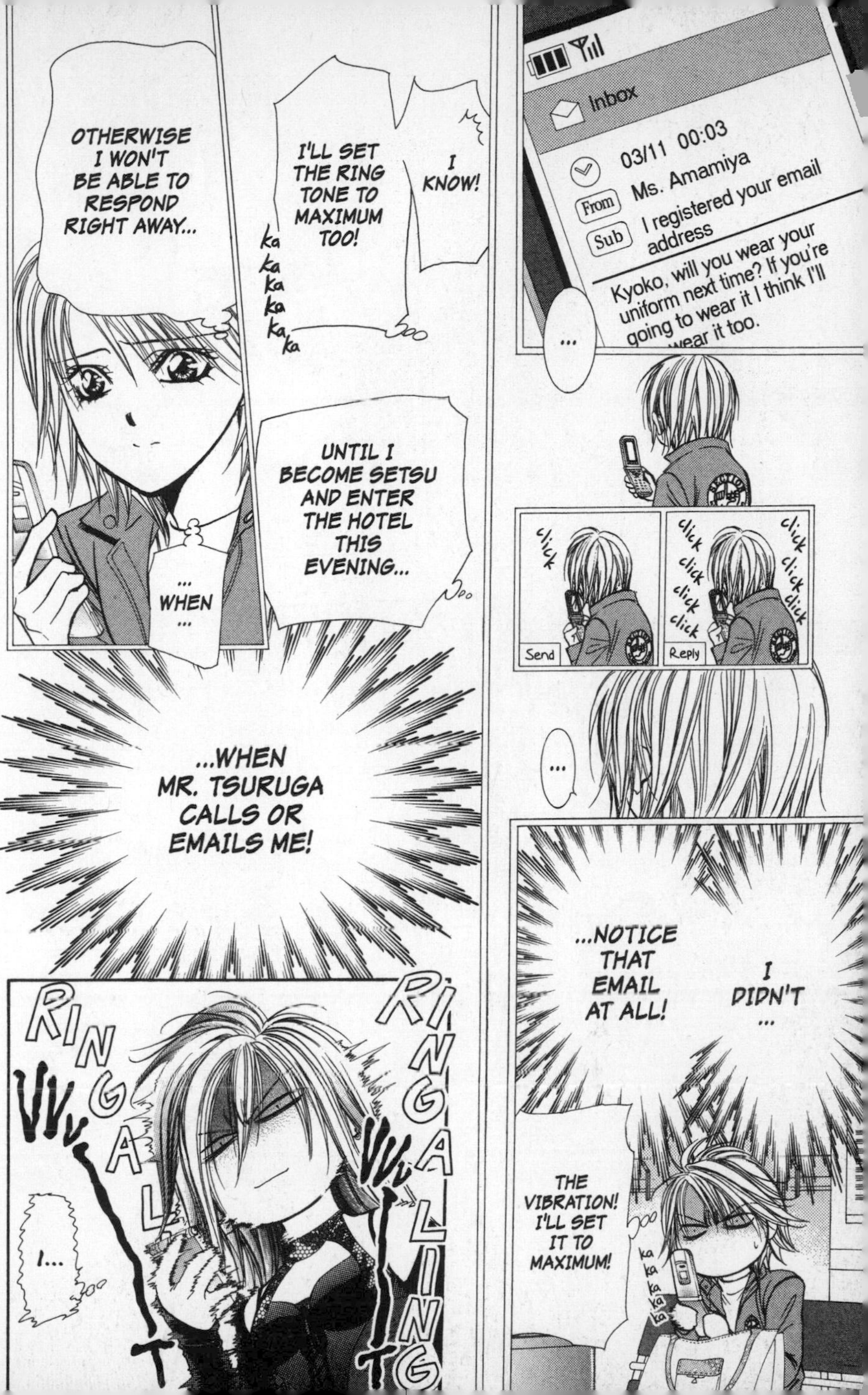
Inbox
03/11 00:03
From Ms. Amamiya
Sub I registered your email address
Kyoko, will you wear your uniform next time? If you're going to wear it I think I'll wear it too.
...
click
click click click click
click click click
Send
Reply
...
I DIDN'T ...
...NOTICE THAT EMAIL AT ALL!
THE VIBRATION! I'LL SET IT TO MAXIMUM!
ka ka ka ka ka
I KNOW!
I'LL SET THE RING TONE TO MAXIMUM TOO!
OTHERWISE I WON'T BE ABLE TO RESPOND RIGHT AWAY...
ka ka ka ka ka ka
UNTIL I BECOME SETSU AND ENTER THE HOTEL THIS EVENING...
... WHEN ...
...WHEN MR. TSURUGA CALLS OR EMAILS ME!
RING A LING
RING A LING
I...

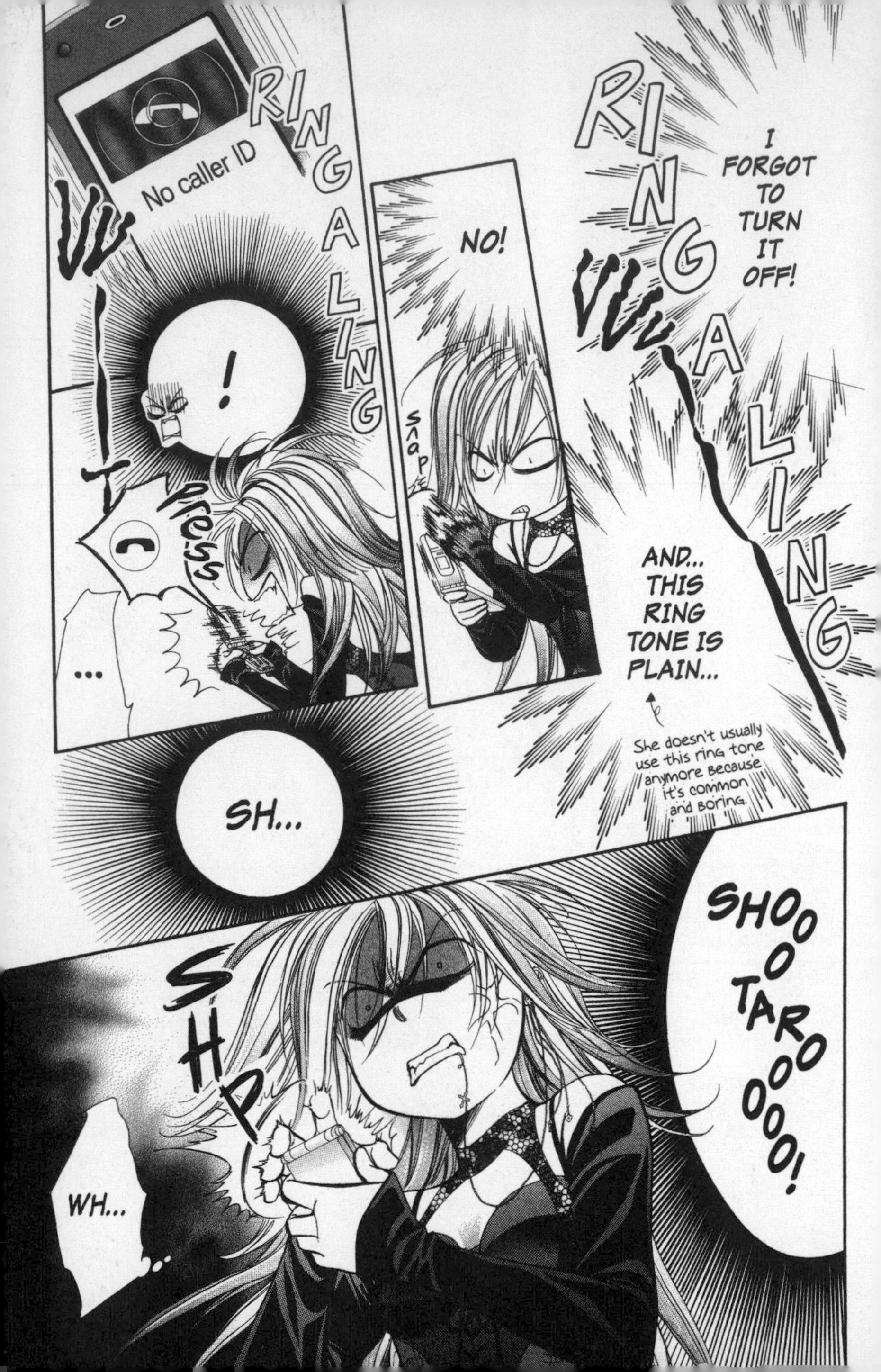
RINGALING
I FORGOT TO TURN IT OFF!
VVV
AND... THIS RING TONE IS PLAIN...
She doesn't usually use this ring tone anymore because it's common and boring.
NO!
snap
No caller ID
RINGALING
VVVIT
!
press
...
SH...
SHOOOTAROOOOOO!
SHP
WH...

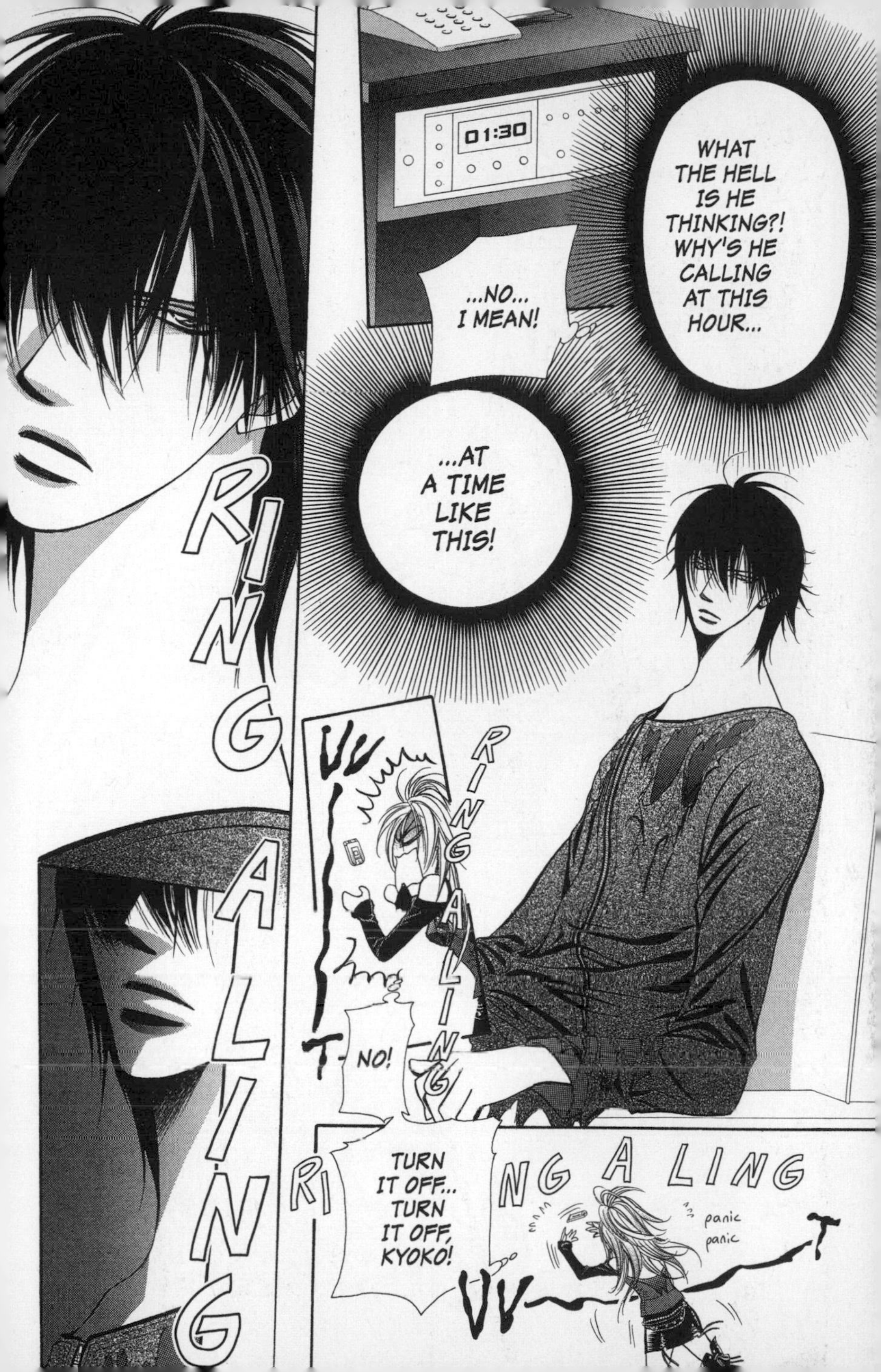
01:30
WHAT THE HELL IS HE THINKING?! WHY'S HE CALLING AT THIS HOUR...
...NO... I MEAN!
...AT A TIME LIKE THIS!
RING A LING
VV
T
NO!
RING A LING
TURN IT OFF... TURN IT OFF, KYOKO!
panic panic
VV
T
RING A LING

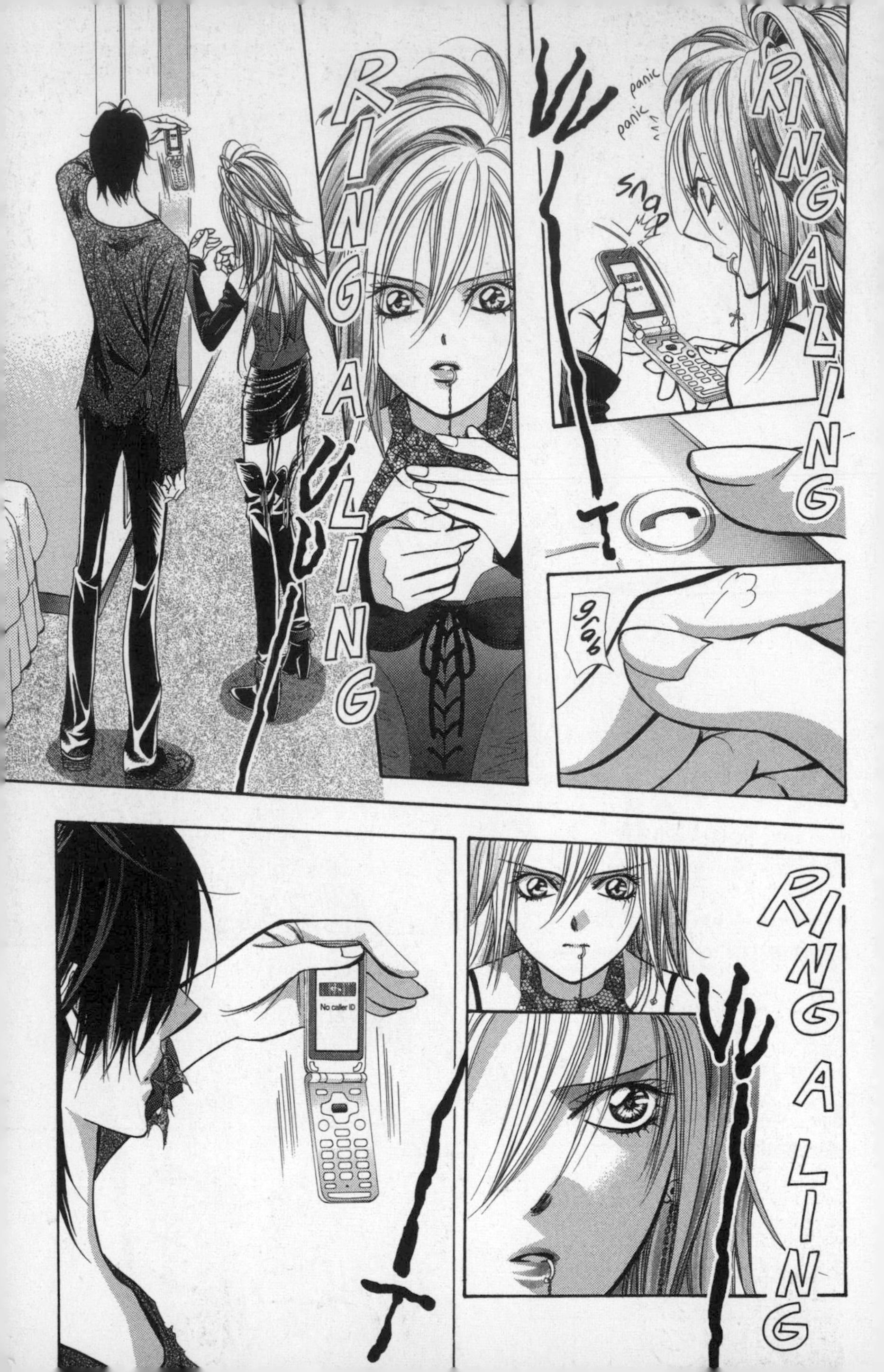
RINGALLING
panic
panic
snap
grab
RING A LING
ALLING
RING A LING
No caller ID

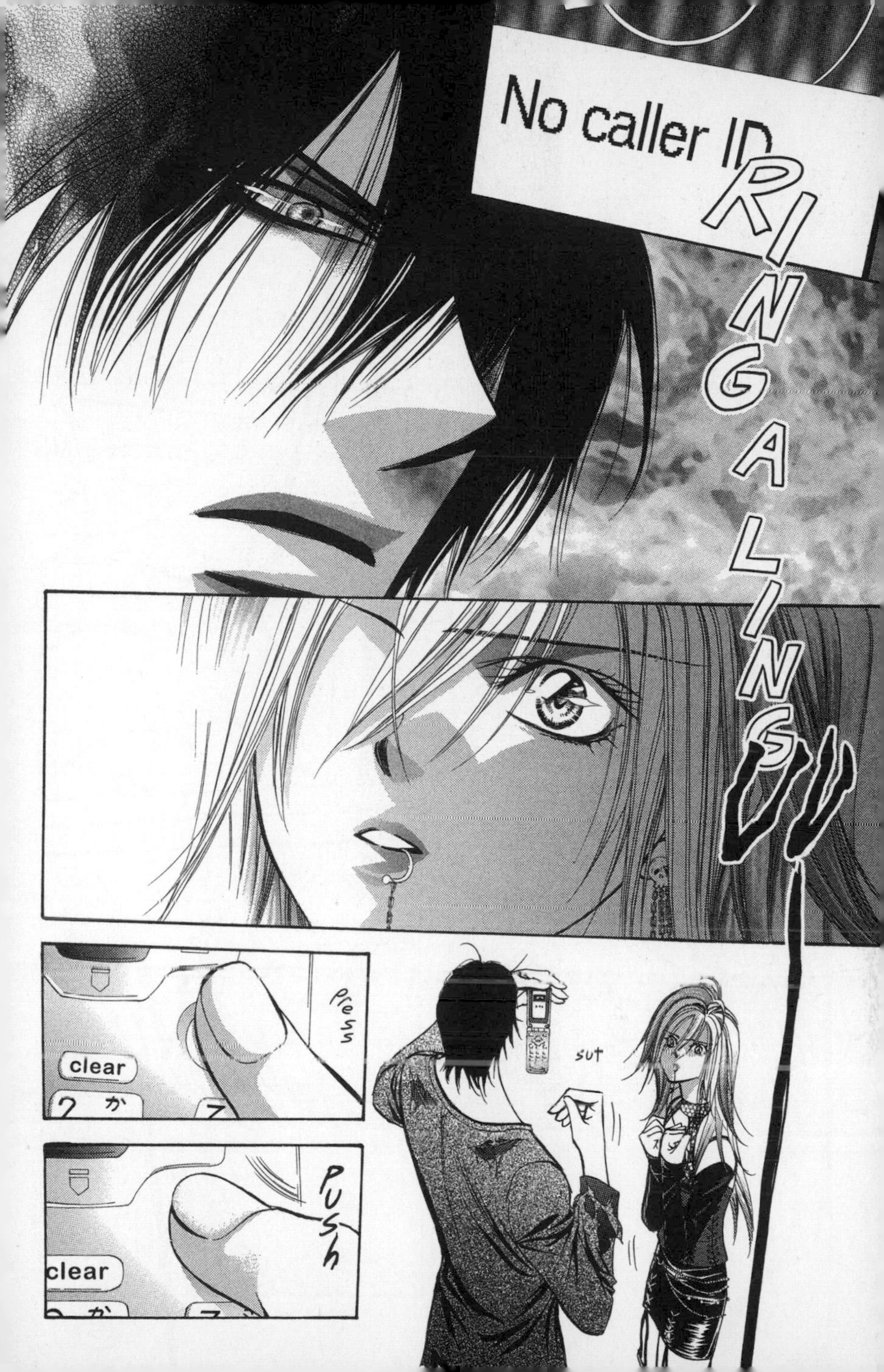
No caller ID
RINGALING
sut
Press
clear
PUSH
clear

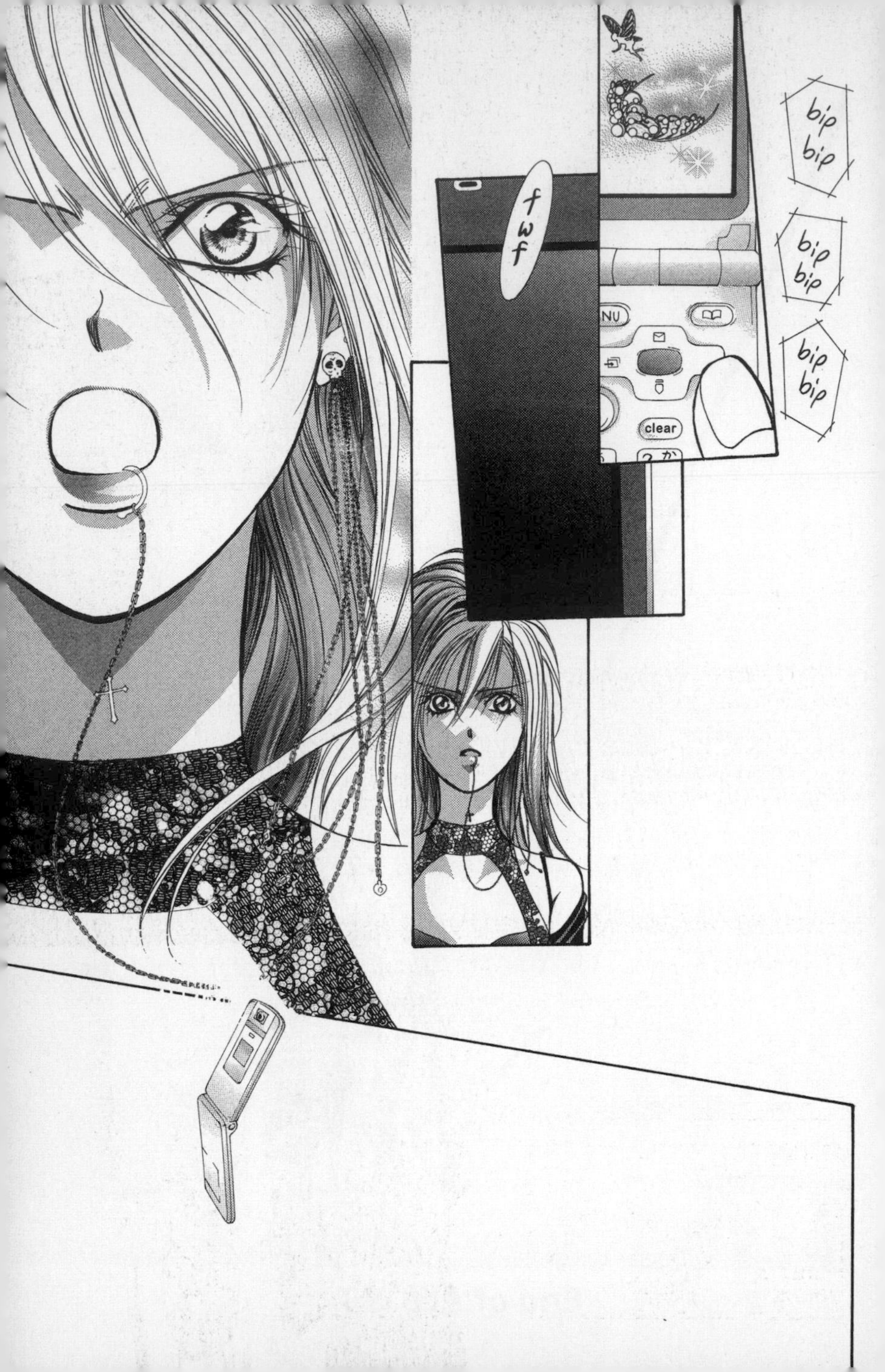
bip bip
bip bip
bip bip
clear
fwf

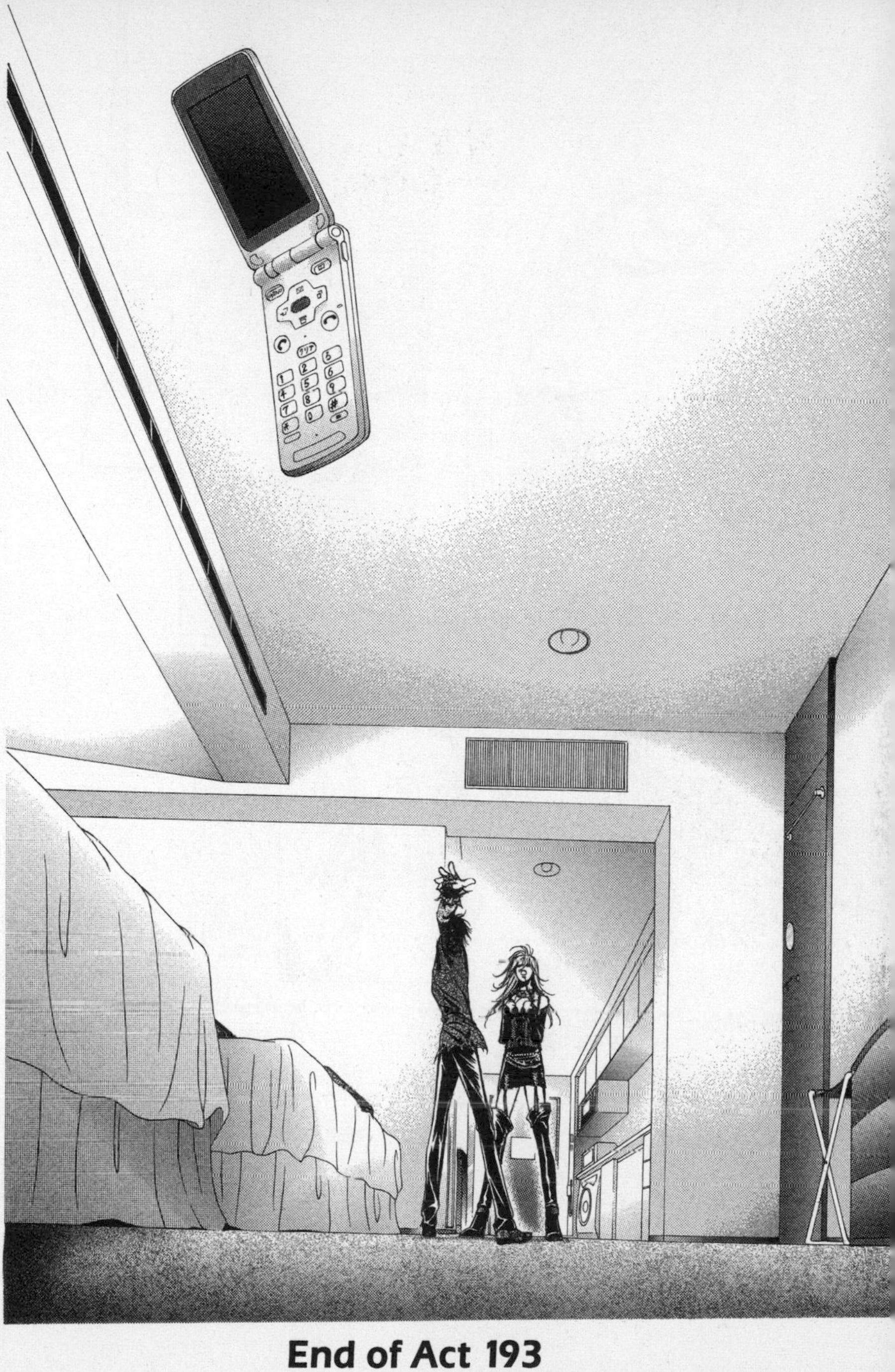

End of Act 193

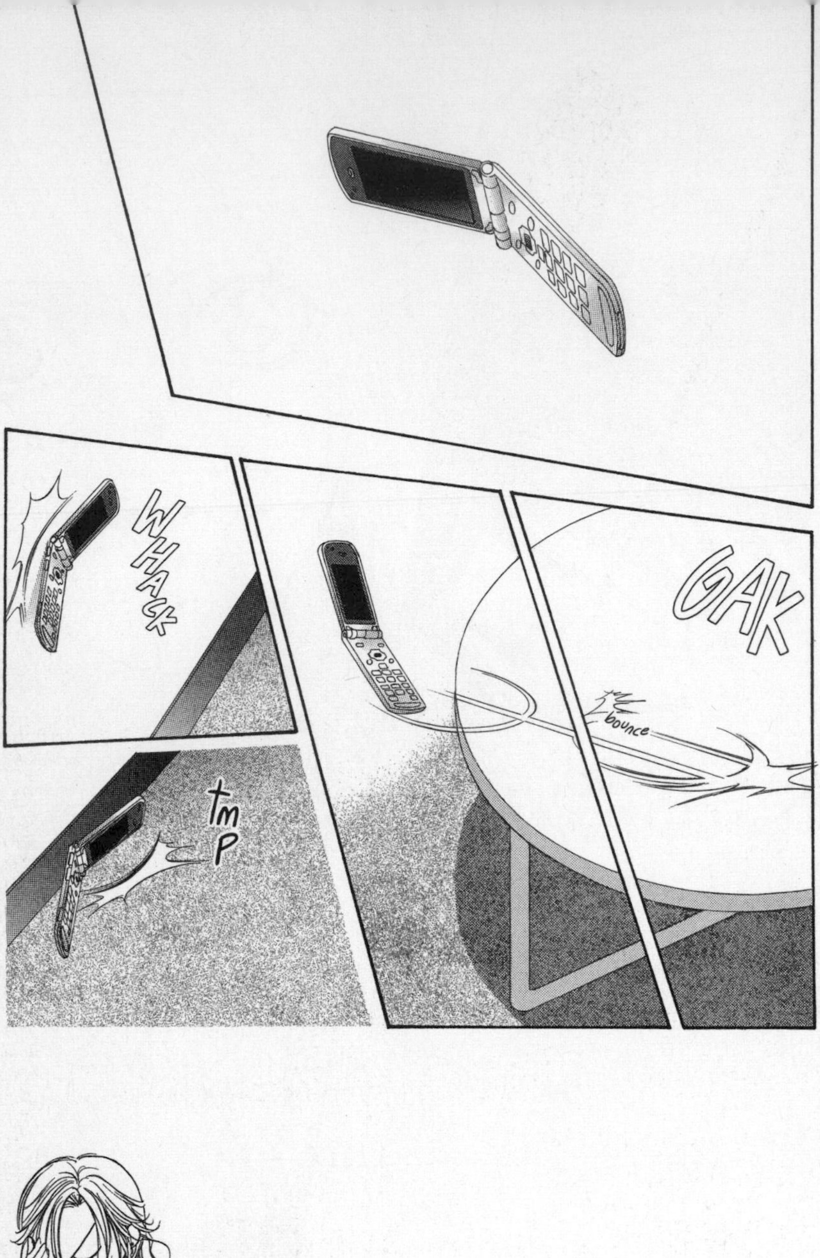
GAK
bounce
WHACK
tmp

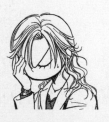

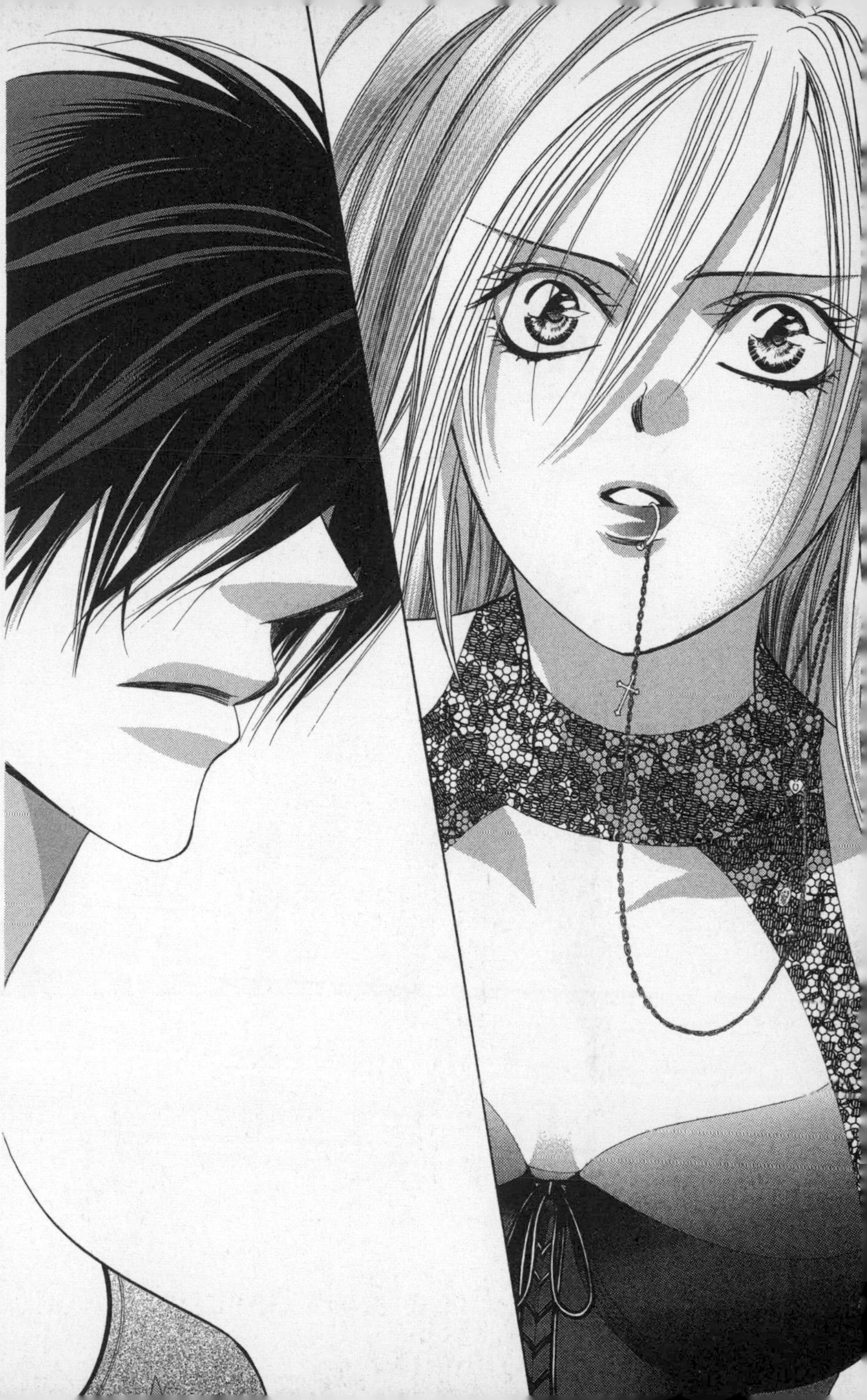

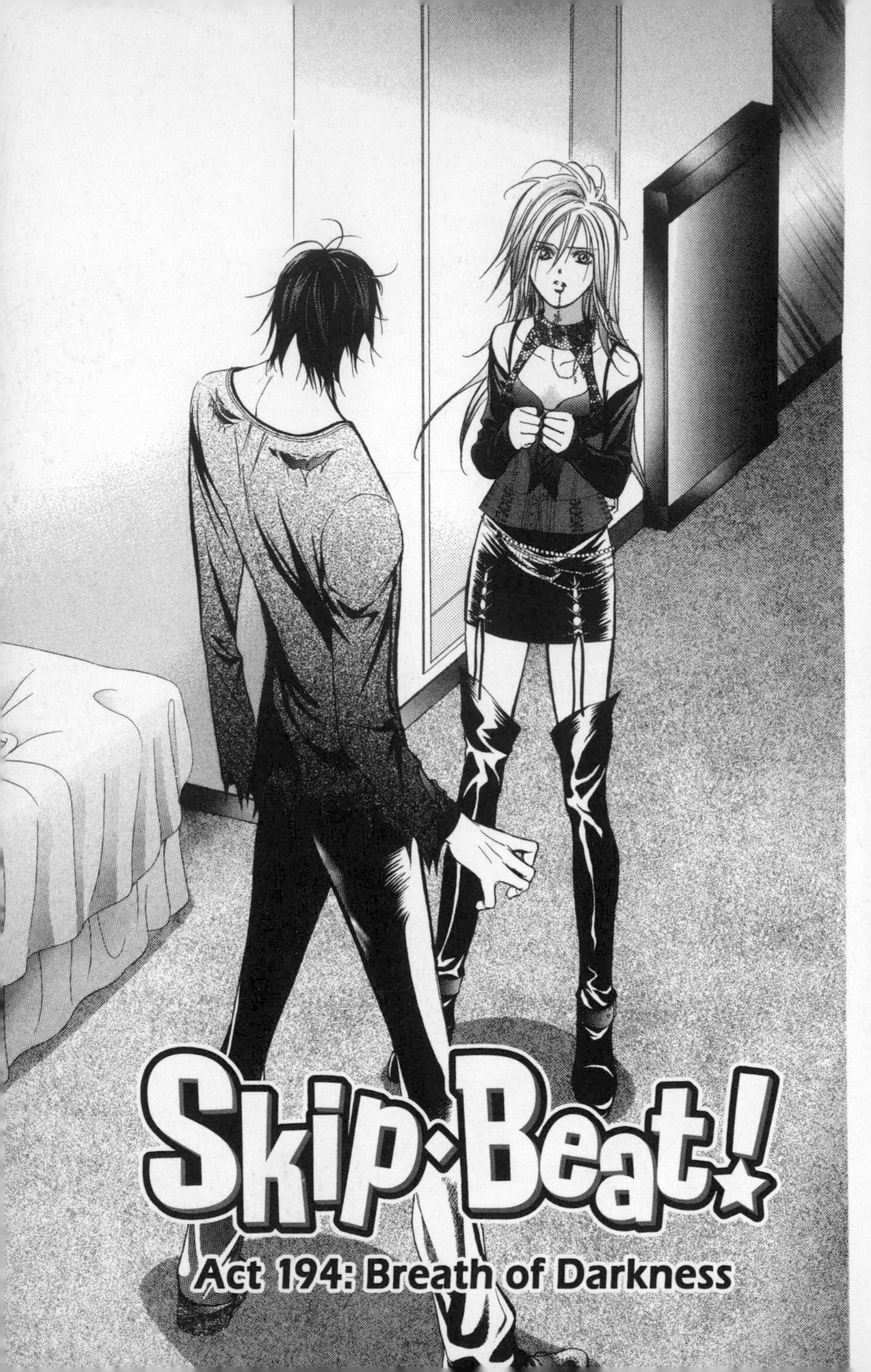
Skip·Beat!
Act 194: Breath of Darkness

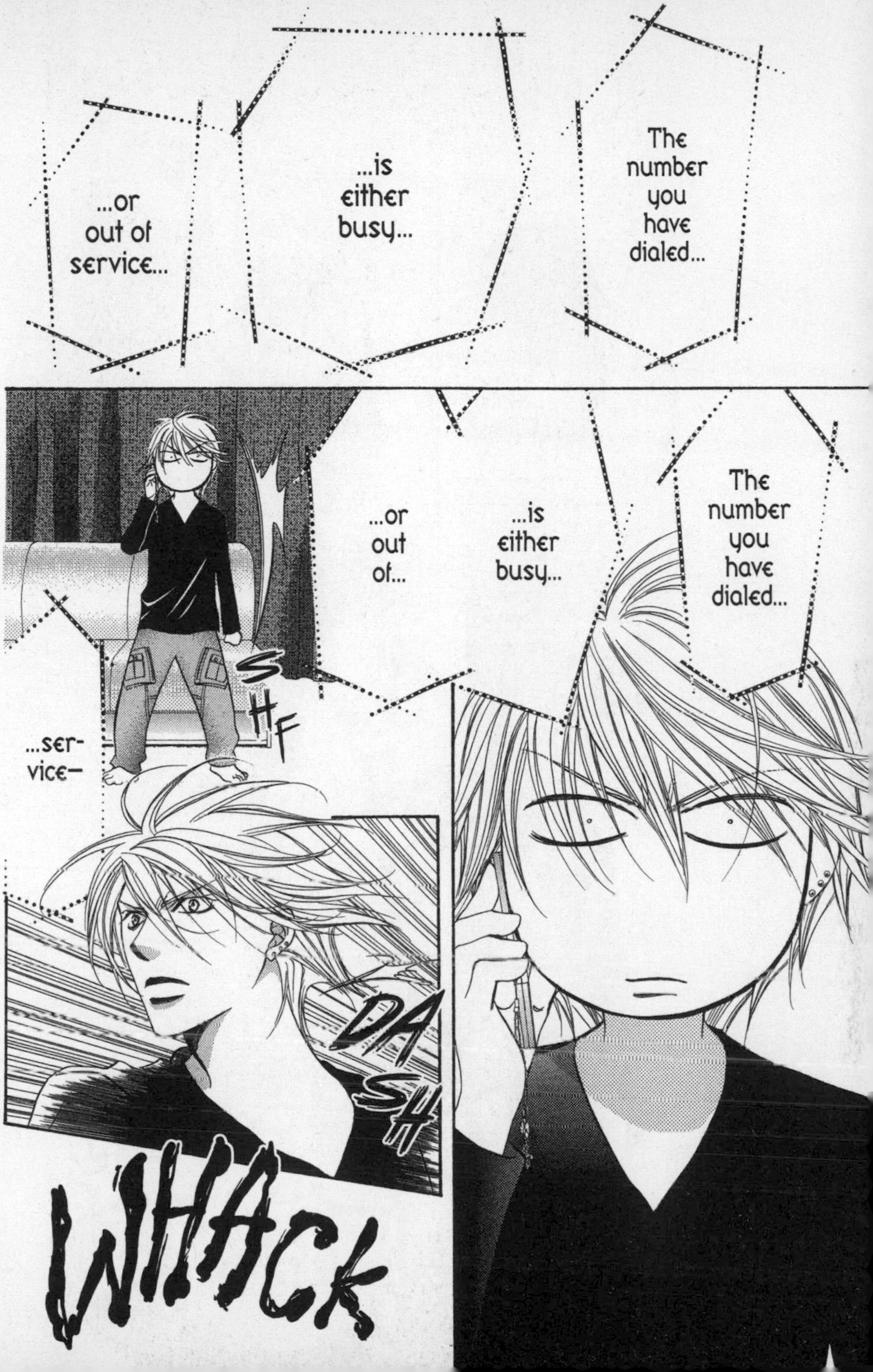
The number you have dialed...
...is either busy...
...or out of service...
The number you have dialed...
...is either busy...
...or out of...
SHF
...ser-vice–
DASH
WHACK

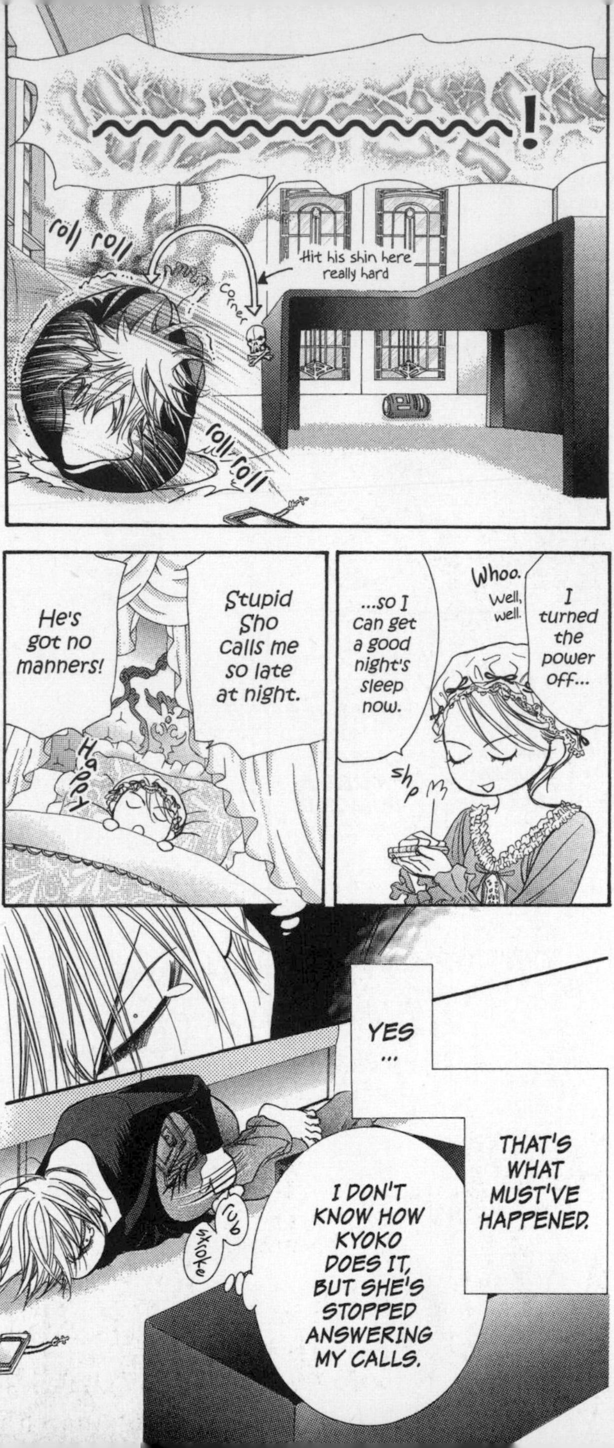
!
roll roll
Hit his shin here really hard
Corner
roll roll
I turned the power off...
Whoo.
Well, well.
...so I can get a good night's sleep now.
shp
Stupid Sho calls me so late at night.
He's got no manners!
Happy
YES...
THAT'S WHAT MUST'VE HAPPENED.
I DON'T KNOW HOW KYOKO DOES IT, BUT SHE'S STOPPED ANSWERING MY CALLS.
rub
stroke

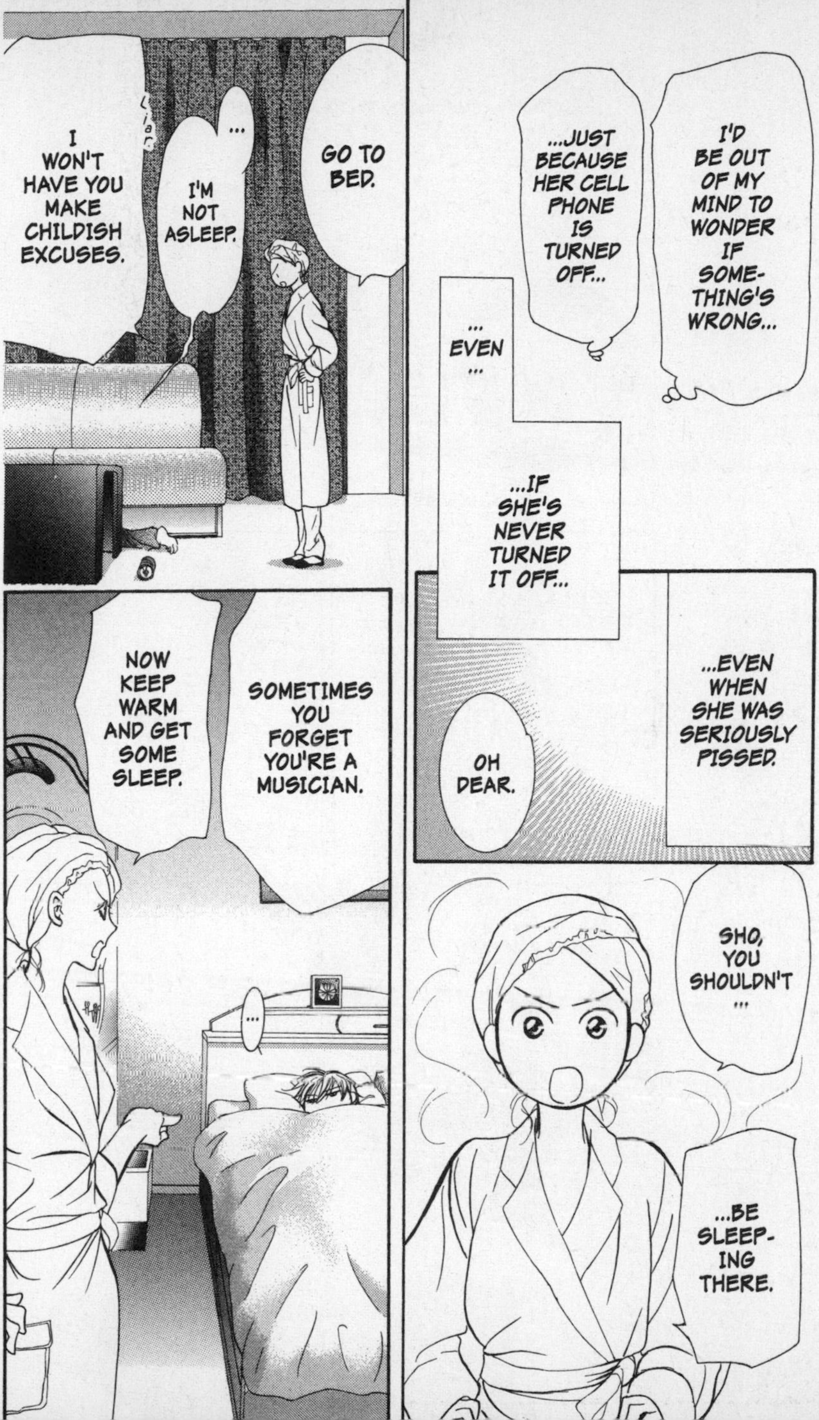
I'D BE OUT OF MY MIND TO WONDER IF SOME-THING'S WRONG...
...JUST BECAUSE HER CELL PHONE IS TURNED OFF...
...EVEN...
...IF SHE'S NEVER TURNED IT OFF...
...EVEN WHEN SHE WAS SERIOUSLY PISSED.
OH DEAR.
SHO, YOU SHOULDN'T...
...BE SLEEP-ING THERE.
GO TO BED.
...
I'M NOT ASLEEP.
Liar.
I WON'T HAVE YOU MAKE CHILDISH EXCUSES.
SOMETIMES YOU FORGET YOU'RE A MUSICIAN.
NOW KEEP WARM AND GET SOME SLEEP.
...

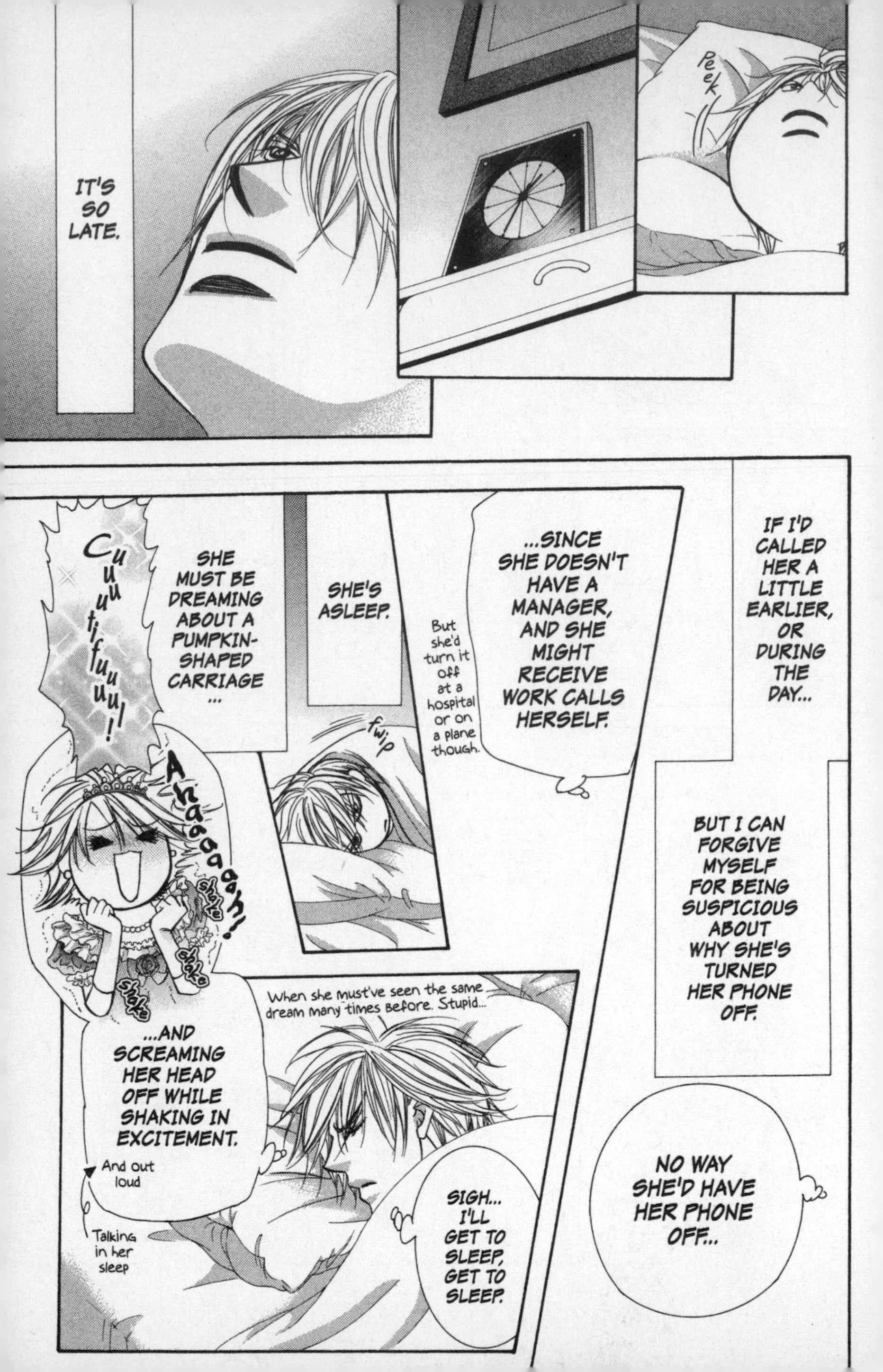
Peek
IT'S SO LATE.
IF I'D CALLED HER A LITTLE EARLIER, OR DURING THE DAY...
BUT I CAN FORGIVE MYSELF FOR BEING SUSPICIOUS ABOUT WHY SHE'S TURNED HER PHONE OFF.
NO WAY SHE'D HAVE HER PHONE OFF...
...SINCE SHE DOESN'T HAVE A MANAGER, AND SHE MIGHT RECEIVE WORK CALLS HERSELF.
But she'd turn it off at a hospital or on a plane though.
fwip
SHE'S ASLEEP.
SHE MUST BE DREAMING ABOUT A PUMPKIN-SHAPED CARRIAGE ...
Cuuutifuuuul!
Ahaaaaaan!!
shake
shake
shake
...AND SCREAMING HER HEAD OFF WHILE SHAKING IN EXCITEMENT.
And out loud
Talking in her sleep
When she must've seen the same dream many times before. Stupid...
SIGH... I'LL GET TO SLEEP, GET TO SLEEP.

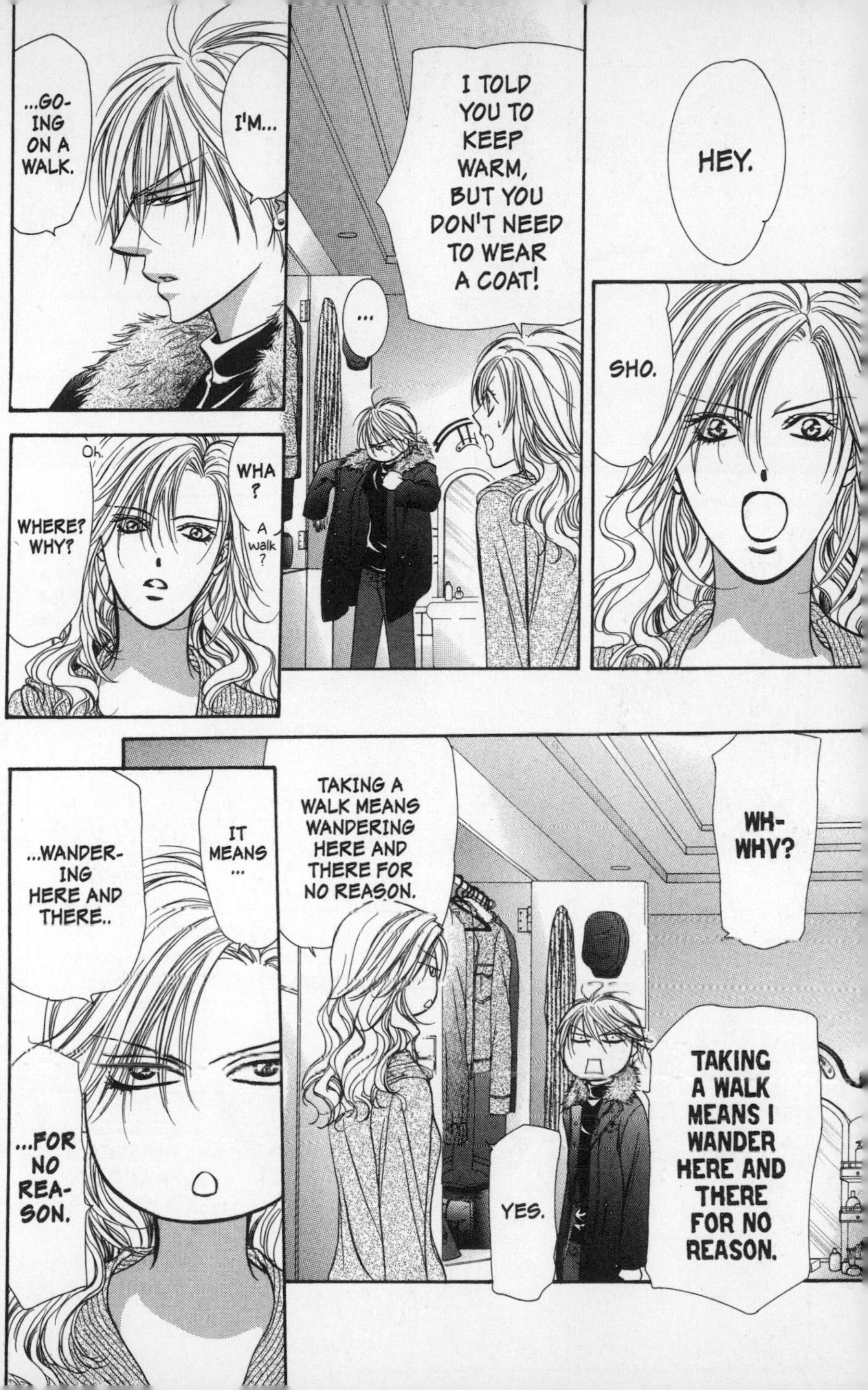
HEY.
SHO.
I TOLD YOU TO KEEP WARM, BUT YOU DON'T NEED TO WEAR A COAT!
...
I'M...
...GO-ING ON A WALK.
WHA?
A walk?
Oh.
WHERE? WHY?
WH-WHY?
TAKING A WALK MEANS WANDERING HERE AND THERE FOR NO REASON.
TAKING A WALK MEANS I WANDER HERE AND THERE FOR NO REASON.
YES.
IT MEANS...
...WANDER-ING HERE AND THERE..
...FOR NO REA-SON.

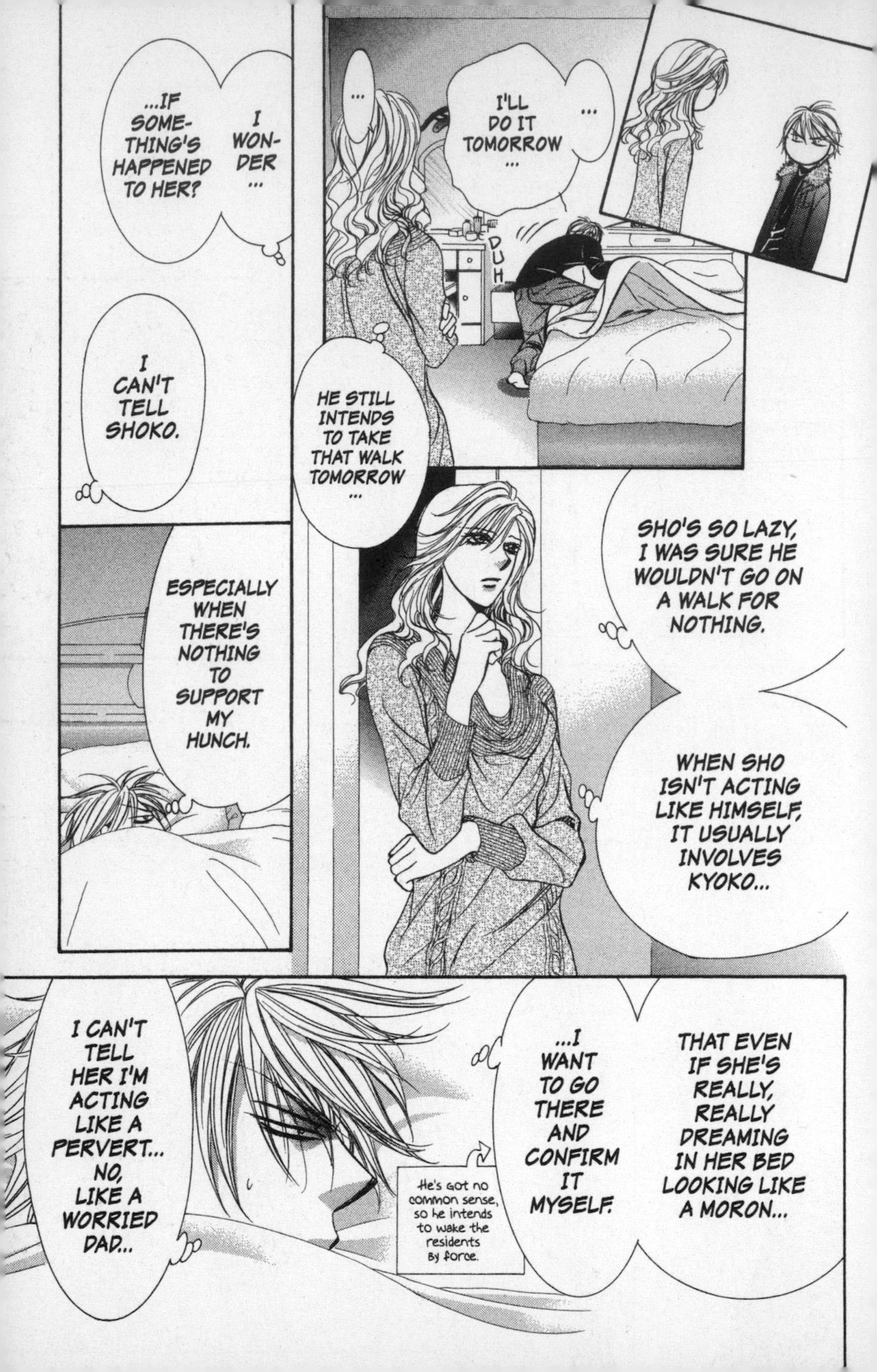
...
I'LL DO IT TOMORROW...
...
DUH
HE STILL INTENDS TO TAKE THAT WALK TOMORROW...
I WONDER...
...IF SOMETHING'S HAPPENED TO HER?
I CAN'T TELL SHOKO.
SHO'S SO LAZY, I WAS SURE HE WOULDN'T GO ON A WALK FOR NOTHING.
WHEN SHO ISN'T ACTING LIKE HIMSELF, IT USUALLY INVOLVES KYOKO...
ESPECIALLY WHEN THERE'S NOTHING TO SUPPORT MY HUNCH.
THAT EVEN IF SHE'S REALLY, REALLY DREAMING IN HER BED LOOKING LIKE A MORON...
...I WANT TO GO THERE AND CONFIRM IT MYSELF.
He's got no common sense, so he intends to wake the residents by force.
I CAN'T TELL HER I'M ACTING LIKE A PERVERT... NO, LIKE A WORRIED DAD...

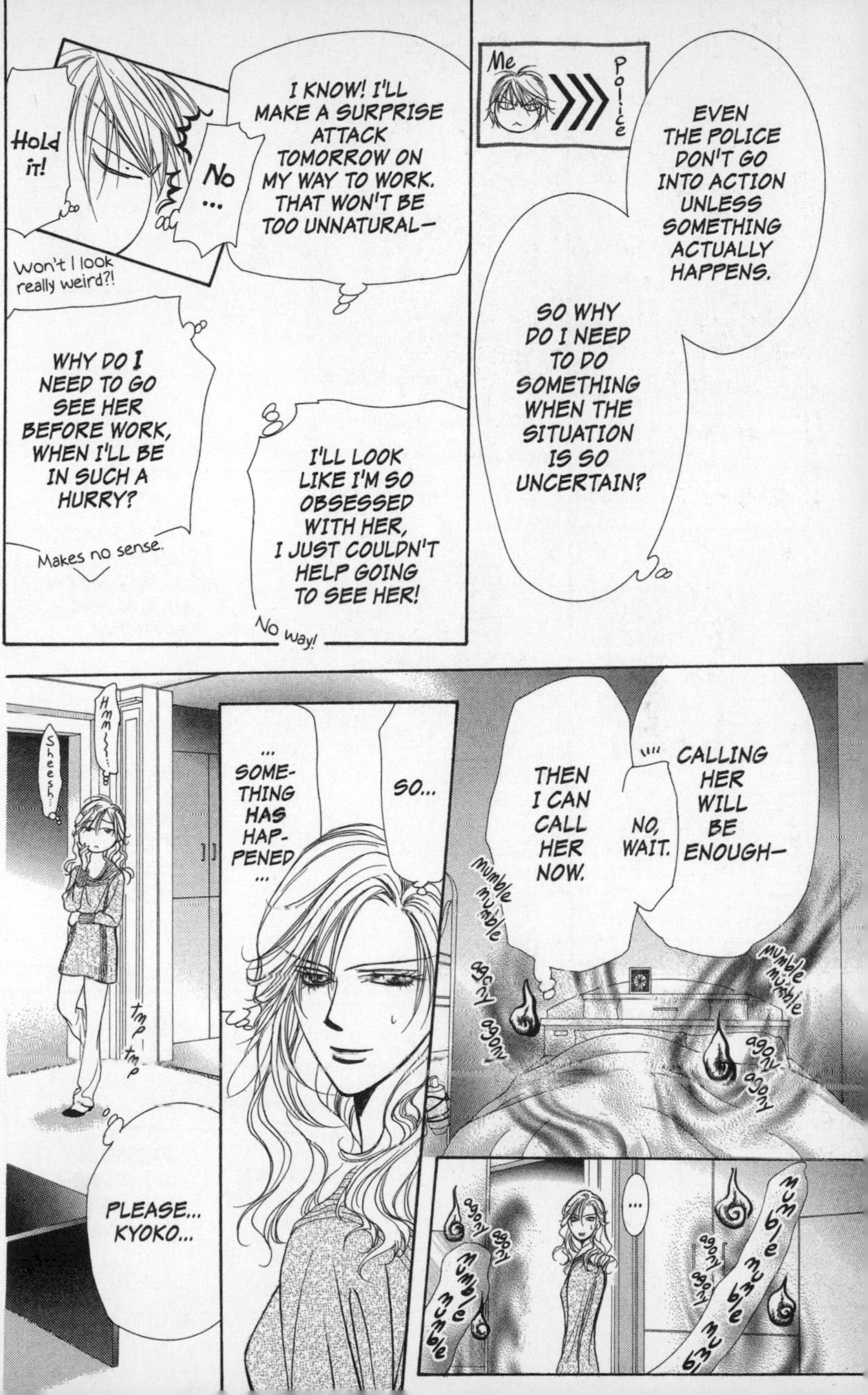

Me
Police
EVEN THE POLICE DON'T GO INTO ACTION UNLESS SOMETHING ACTUALLY HAPPENS.
SO WHY DO I NEED TO DO SOMETHING WHEN THE SITUATION IS SO UNCERTAIN?
I KNOW! I'LL MAKE A SURPRISE ATTACK TOMORROW ON MY WAY TO WORK. THAT WON'T BE TOO UNNATURAL—
No...
Hold it!
Won't I look really weird?!
WHY DO I NEED TO GO SEE HER BEFORE WORK, WHEN I'LL BE IN SUCH A HURRY?
Makes no sense.
I'LL LOOK LIKE I'M SO OBSESSED WITH HER, I JUST COULDN'T HELP GOING TO SEE HER!
No way!
CALLING HER WILL BE ENOUGH—
NO, WAIT.
THEN I CAN CALL HER NOW.
mumble mumble
agony agony
mumble mumble
agony agony
...
agony agony
mumble mumble
agony agony
mumble mumble
SO...
...SOMETHING HAS HAPPENED...
Hmm~~...
Sheesh...
tmp tmp
PLEASE... KYOKO...

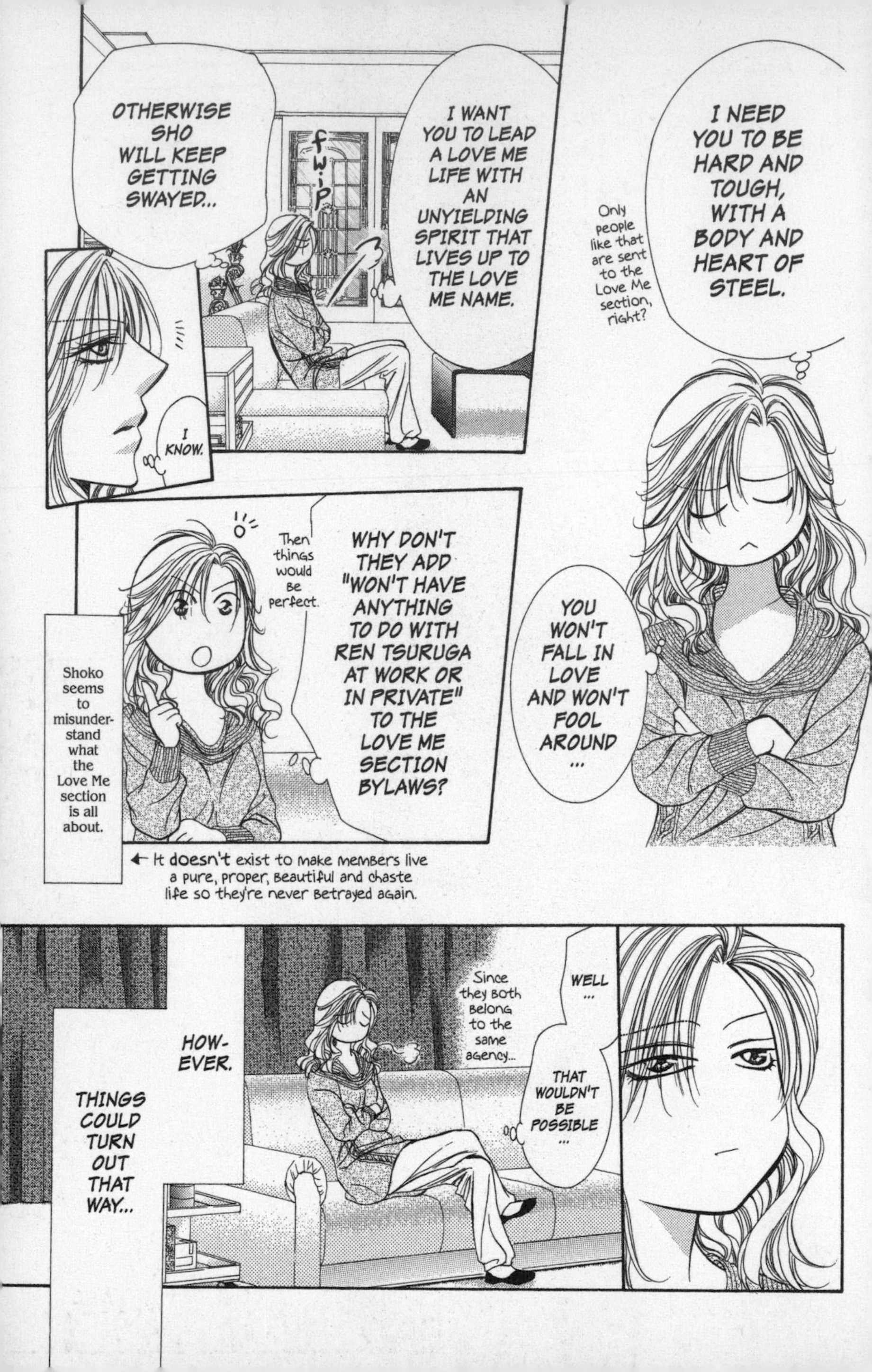
I NEED YOU TO BE HARD AND TOUGH, WITH A BODY AND HEART OF STEEL.
Only people like that are sent to the Love Me section, right?
YOU WON'T FALL IN LOVE AND WON'T FOOL AROUND ...
I WANT YOU TO LEAD A LOVE ME LIFE WITH AN UNYIELDING SPIRIT THAT LIVES UP TO THE LOVE ME NAME.
fwip
OTHERWISE SHO WILL KEEP GETTING SWAYED...
I KNOW.
WHY DON'T THEY ADD "WON'T HAVE ANYTHING TO DO WITH REN TSURUGA AT WORK OR IN PRIVATE" TO THE LOVE ME SECTION BYLAWS?
Then things would be perfect.
Shoko seems to misunderstand what the Love Me section is all about.
← It doesn't exist to make members live a pure, proper, beautiful and chaste life so they're never betrayed again.
WELL ...
THAT WOULDN'T BE POSSIBLE ...
Since they both belong to the same agency...
HOW-EVER.
THINGS COULD TURN OUT THAT WAY...

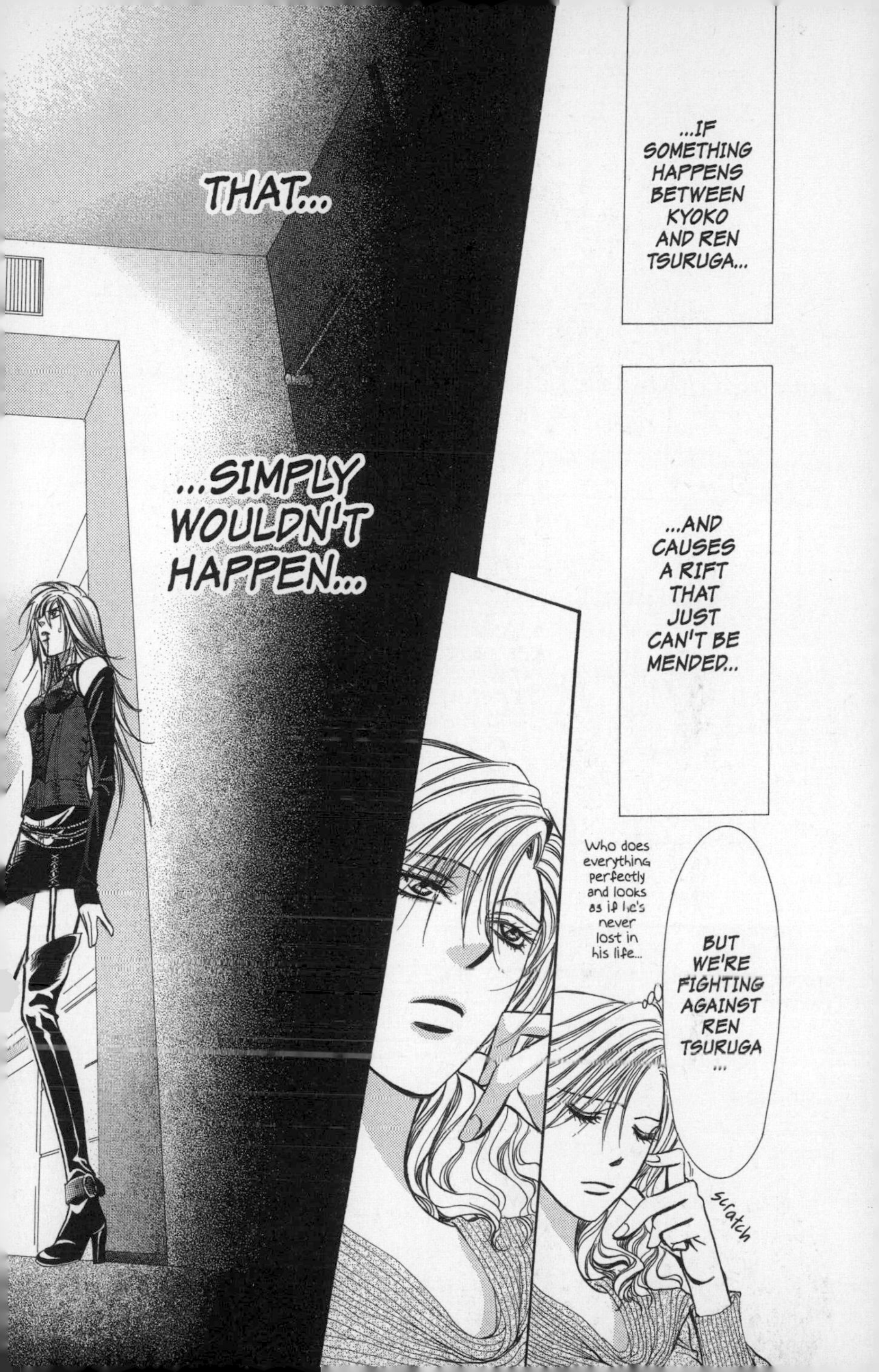
...IF SOMETHING HAPPENS BETWEEN KYOKO AND REN TSURUGA...
...AND CAUSES A RIFT THAT JUST CAN'T BE MENDED...
BUT WE'RE FIGHTING AGAINST REN TSURUGA...
Who does everything perfectly and looks as if he's never lost in his life...
Scratch
THAT...
...SIMPLY WOULDN'T HAPPEN...

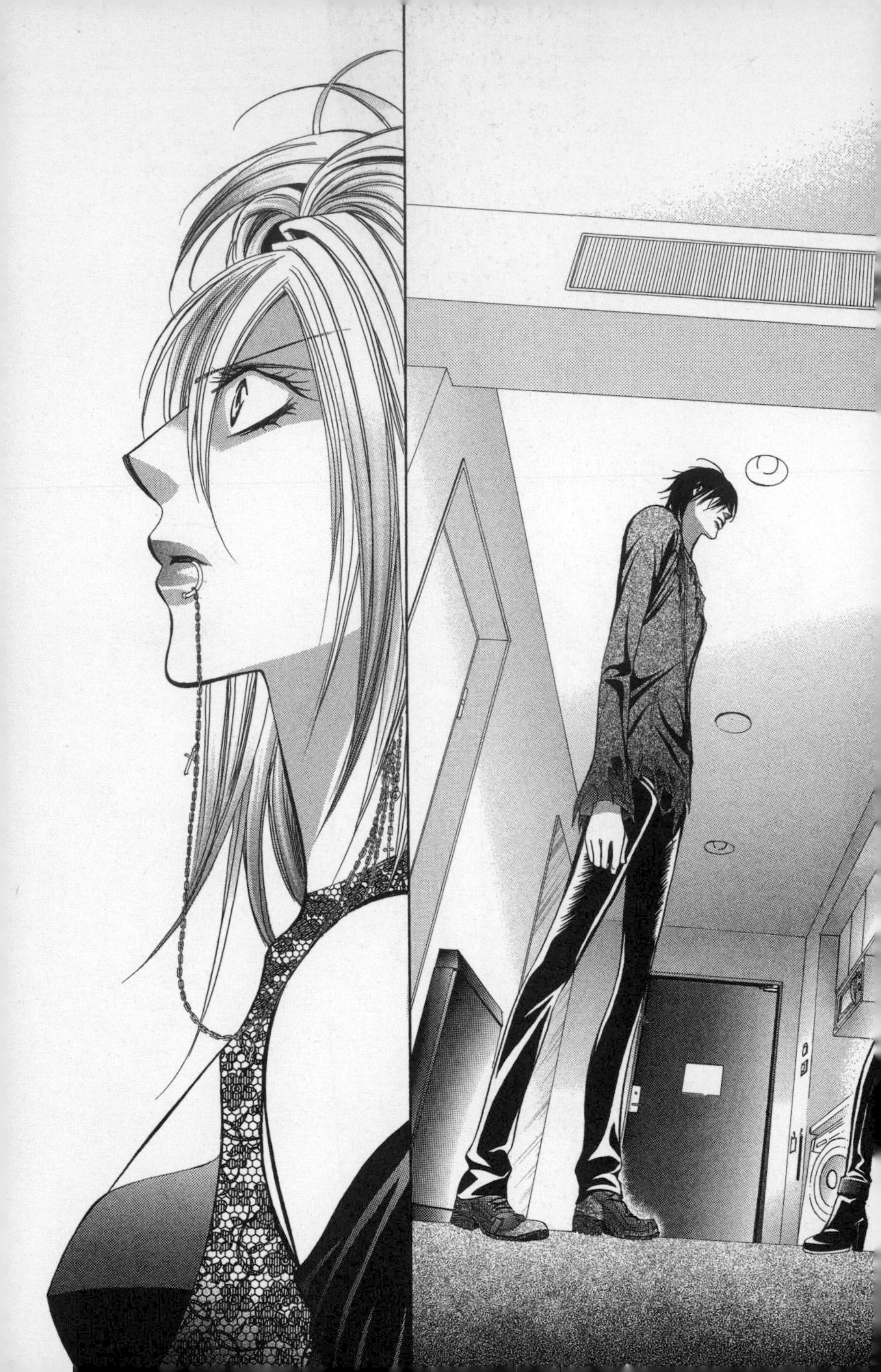

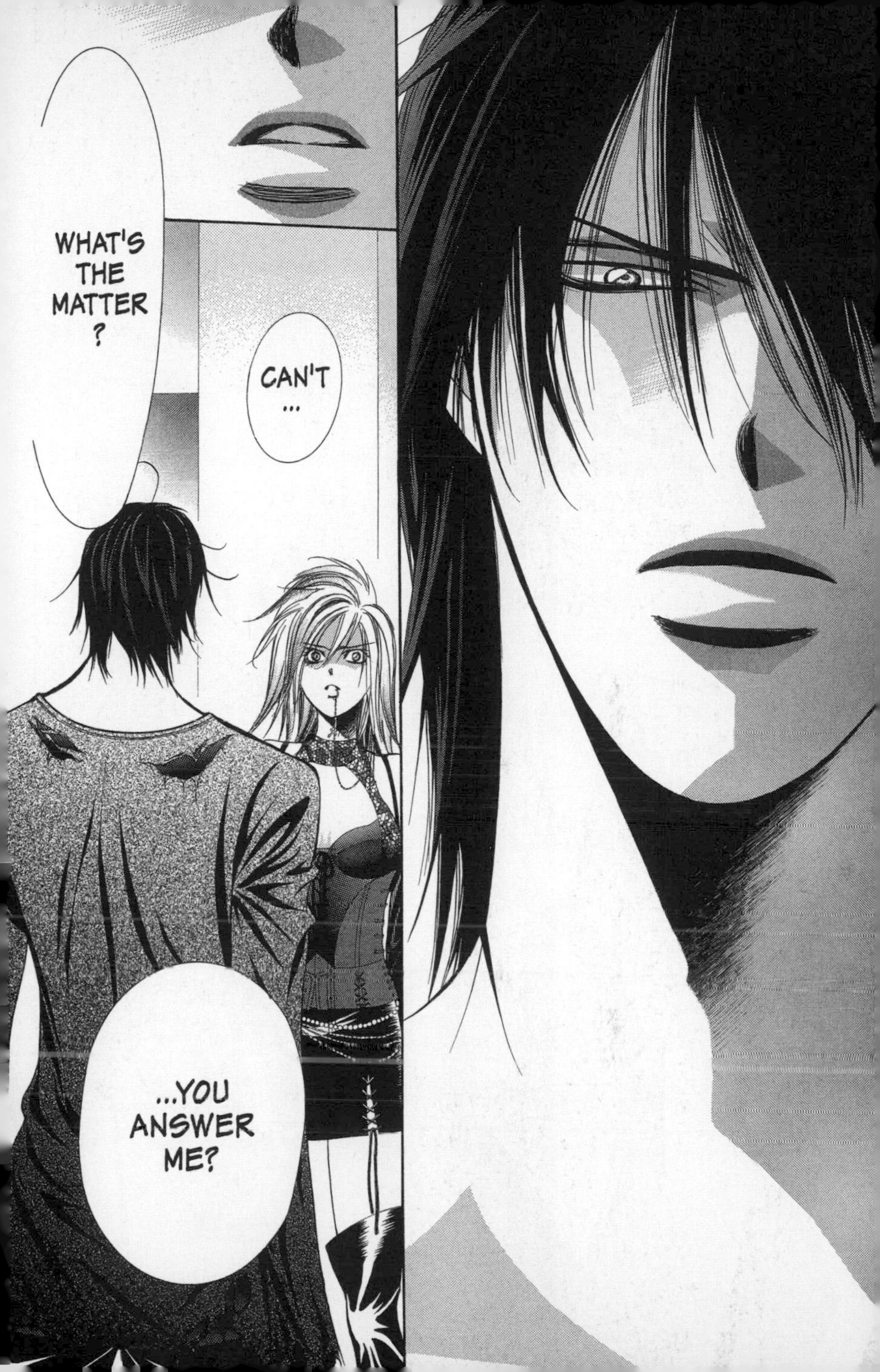
WHAT'S THE MATTER?
CAN'T...
...YOU ANSWER ME?

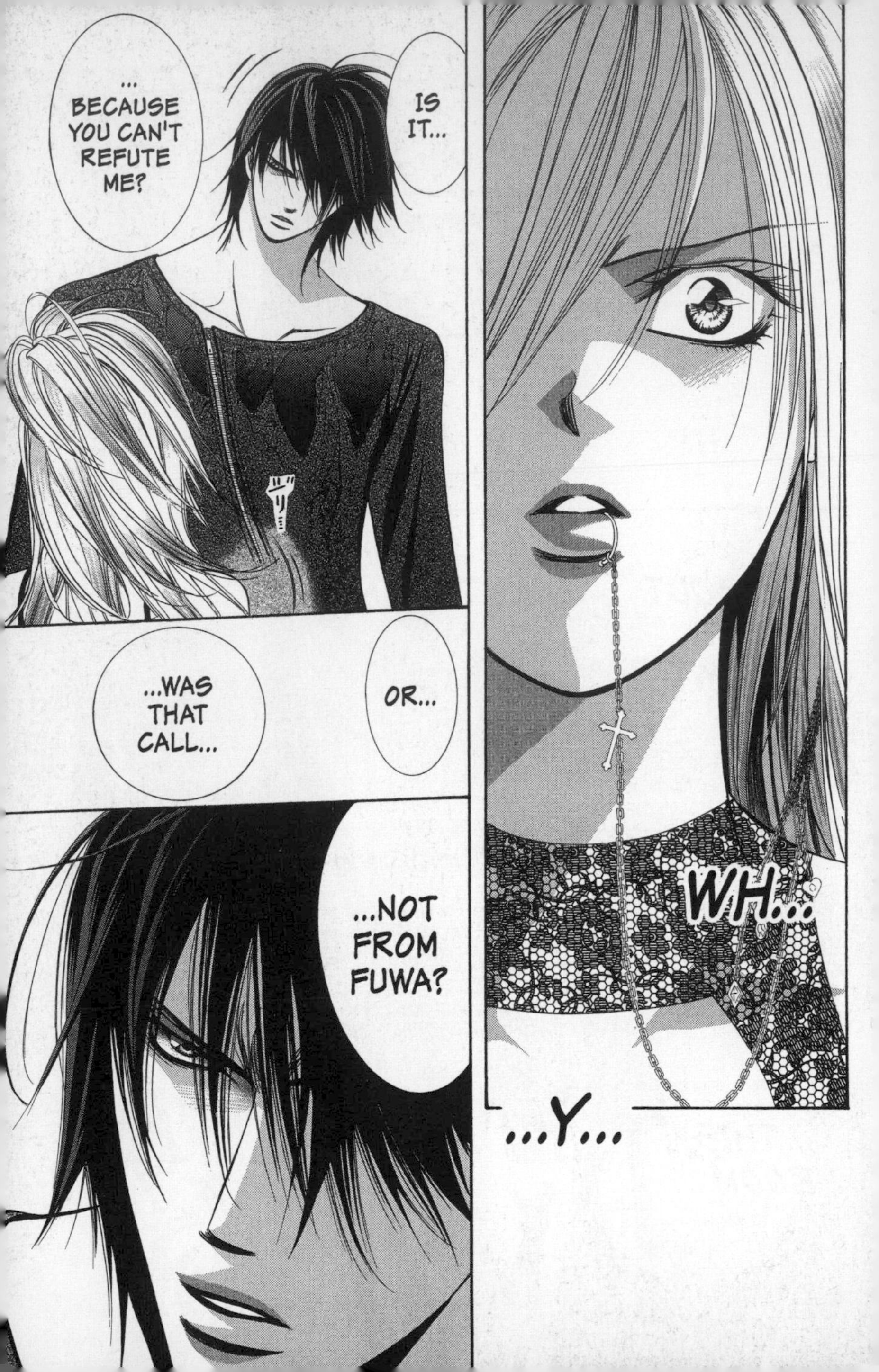
WH...
...Y...
IS IT...
... BECAUSE YOU CAN'T REFUTE ME?
OR...
...WAS THAT CALL...
...NOT FROM FUWA?

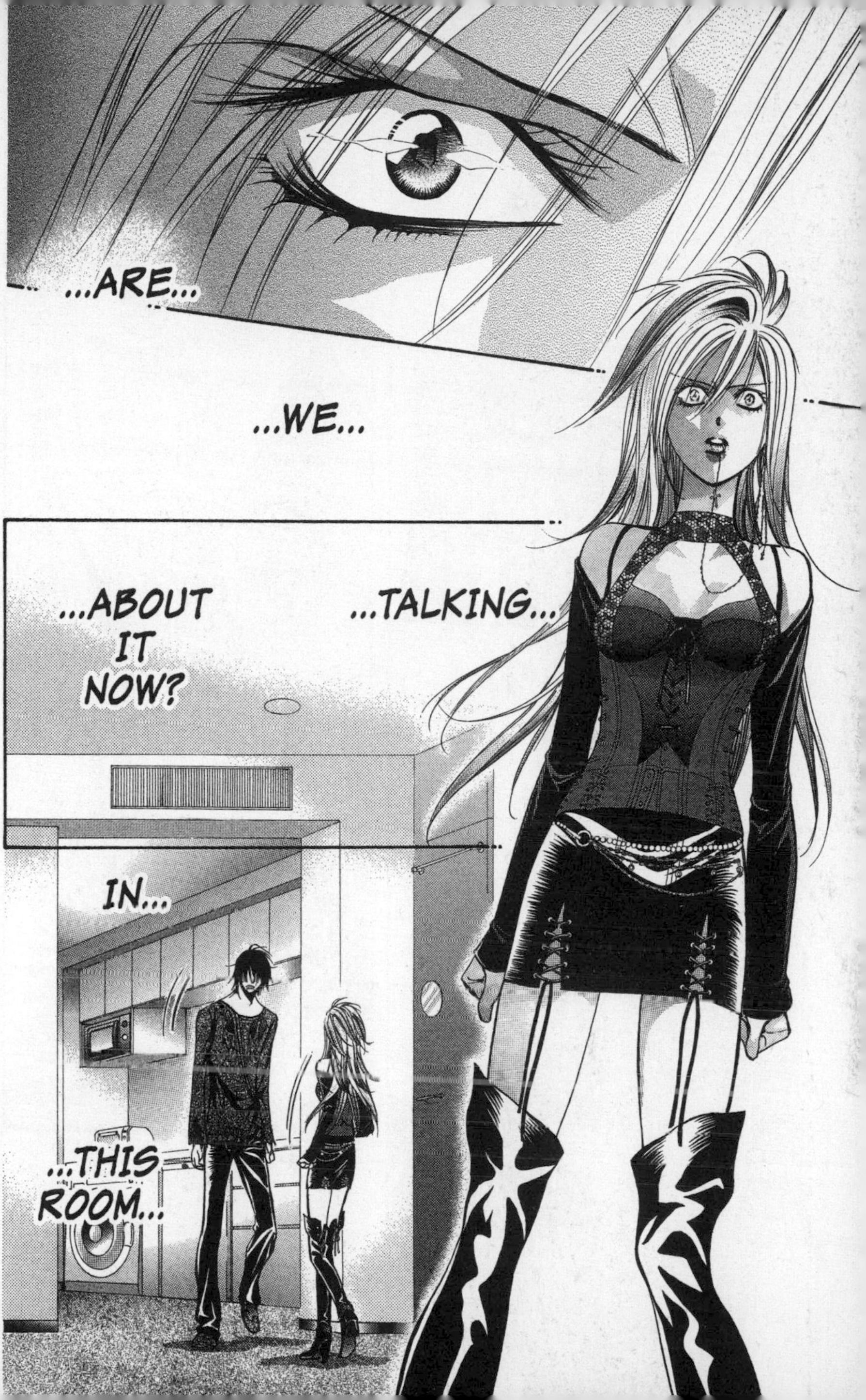
...ARE...
...WE...
...TALKING...
...ABOUT IT NOW?
IN...
...THIS ROOM...

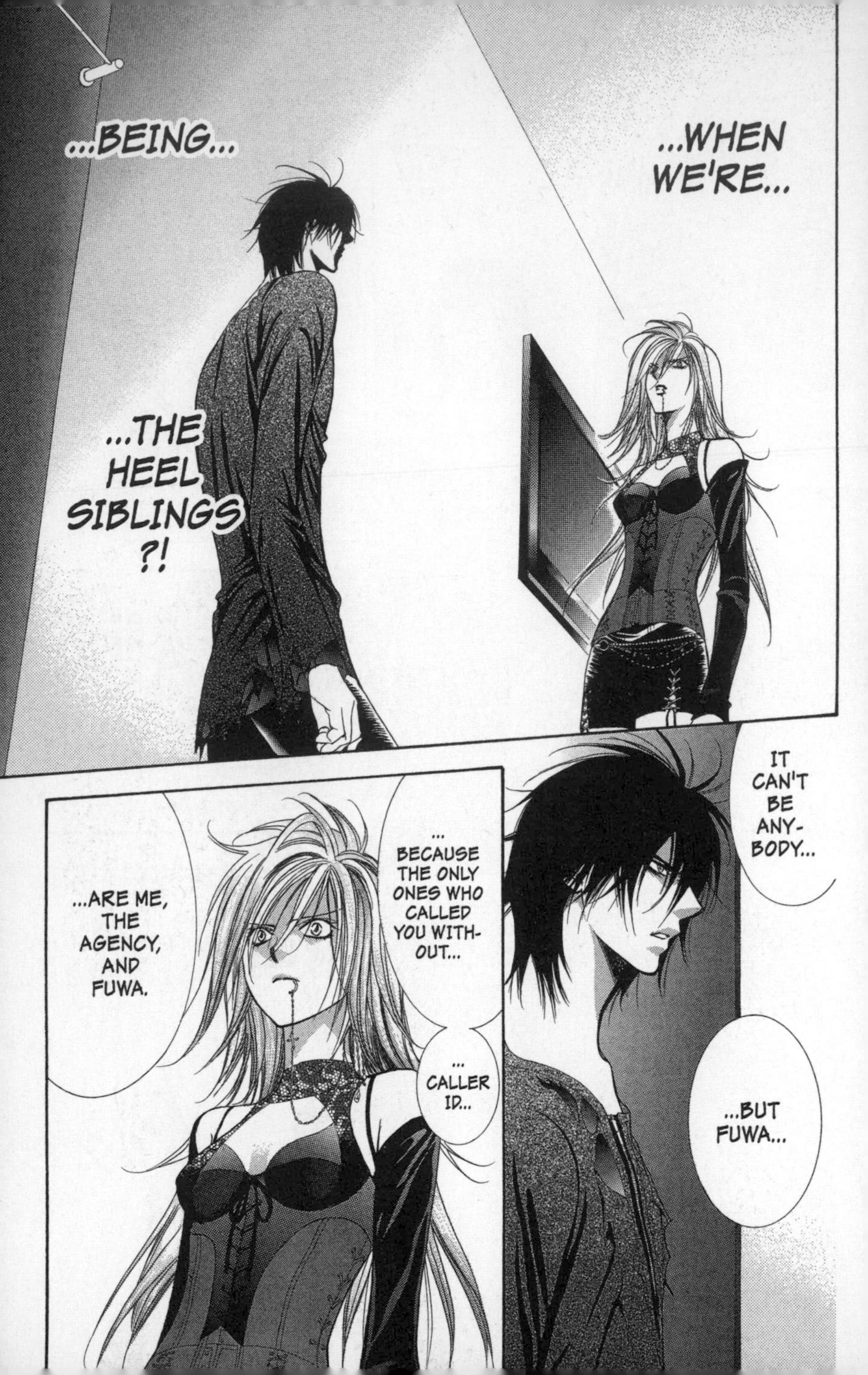
...WHEN WE'RE...
...BEING...
...THE HEEL SIBLINGS ?!
IT CAN'T BE ANYBODY...
...BUT FUWA...
... BECAUSE THE ONLY ONES WHO CALLED YOU WITH-OUT...
... CALLER ID...
...ARE ME, THE AGENCY, AND FUWA.

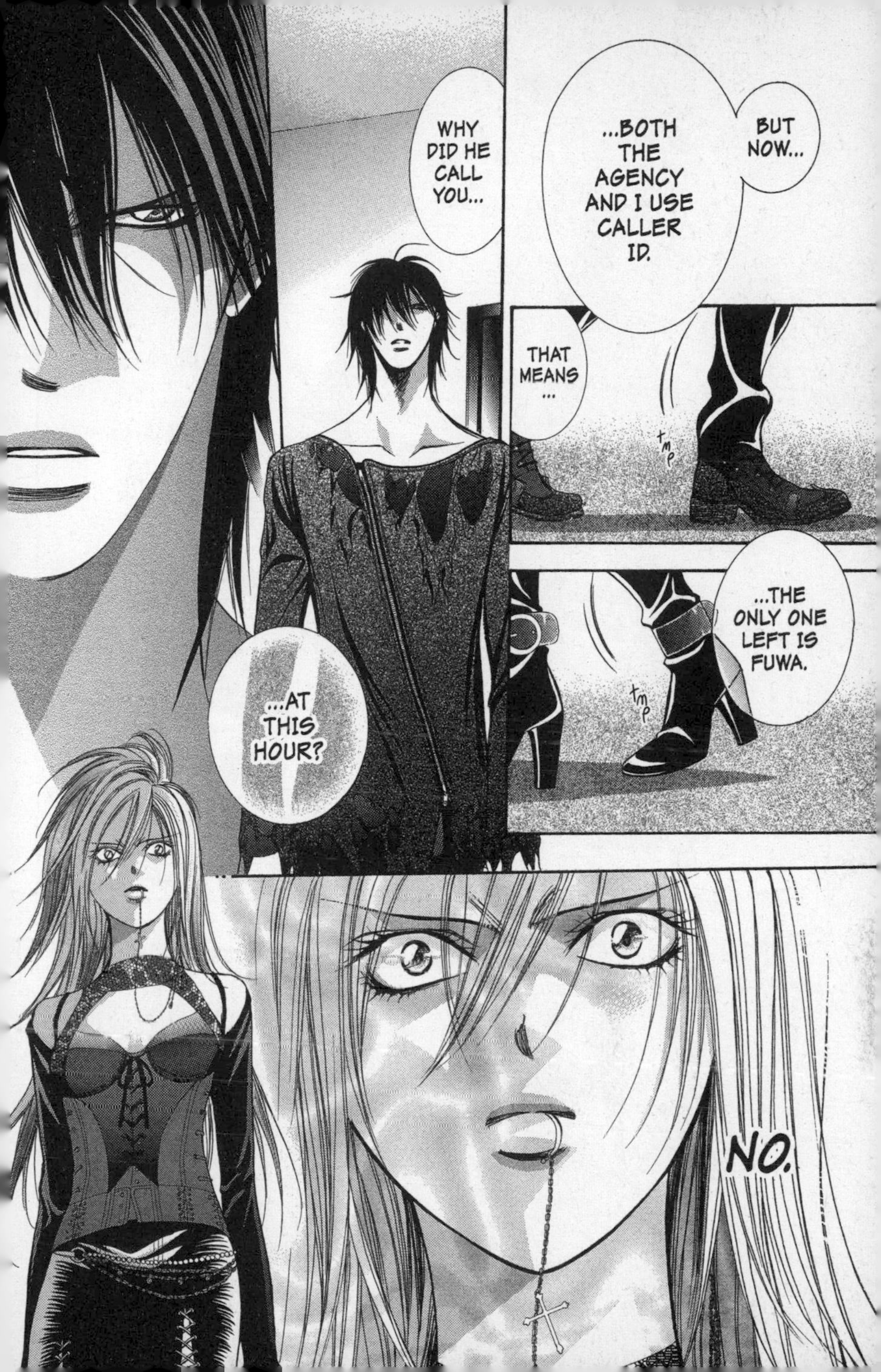
BUT NOW...
...BOTH THE AGENCY AND I USE CALLER ID.
THAT MEANS...
tmp
...THE ONLY ONE LEFT IS FUWA.
tmp
WHY DID HE CALL YOU...
...AT THIS HOUR?
NO.

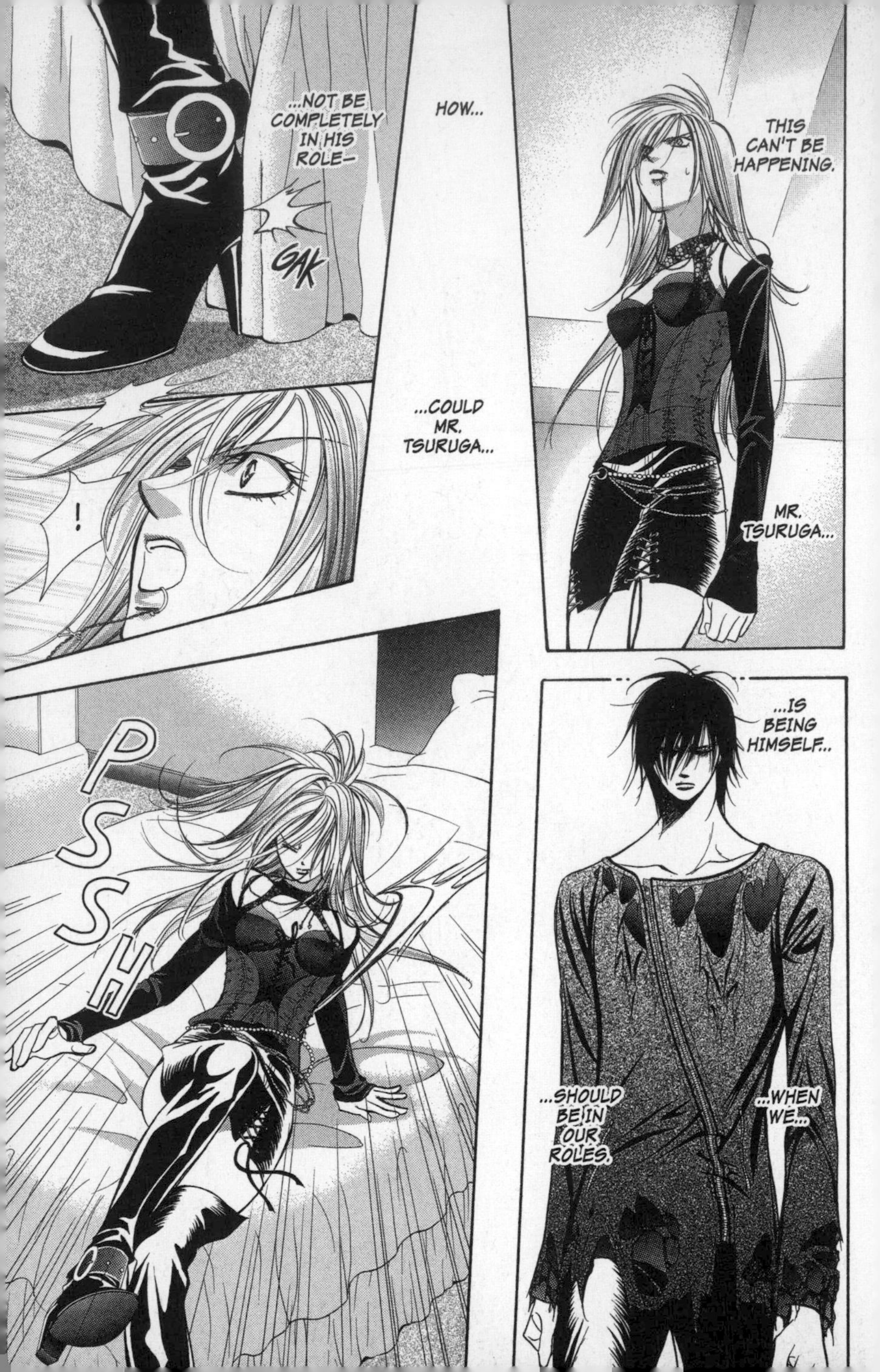
THIS CAN'T BE HAPPENING.
MR. TSURUGA...
HOW...
...COULD MR. TSURUGA...
...NOT BE COMPLETELY IN HIS ROLE—
GAK
!
...IS BEING HIMSELF...
...WHEN WE...
...SHOULD BE IN OUR ROLES.
PSSSH

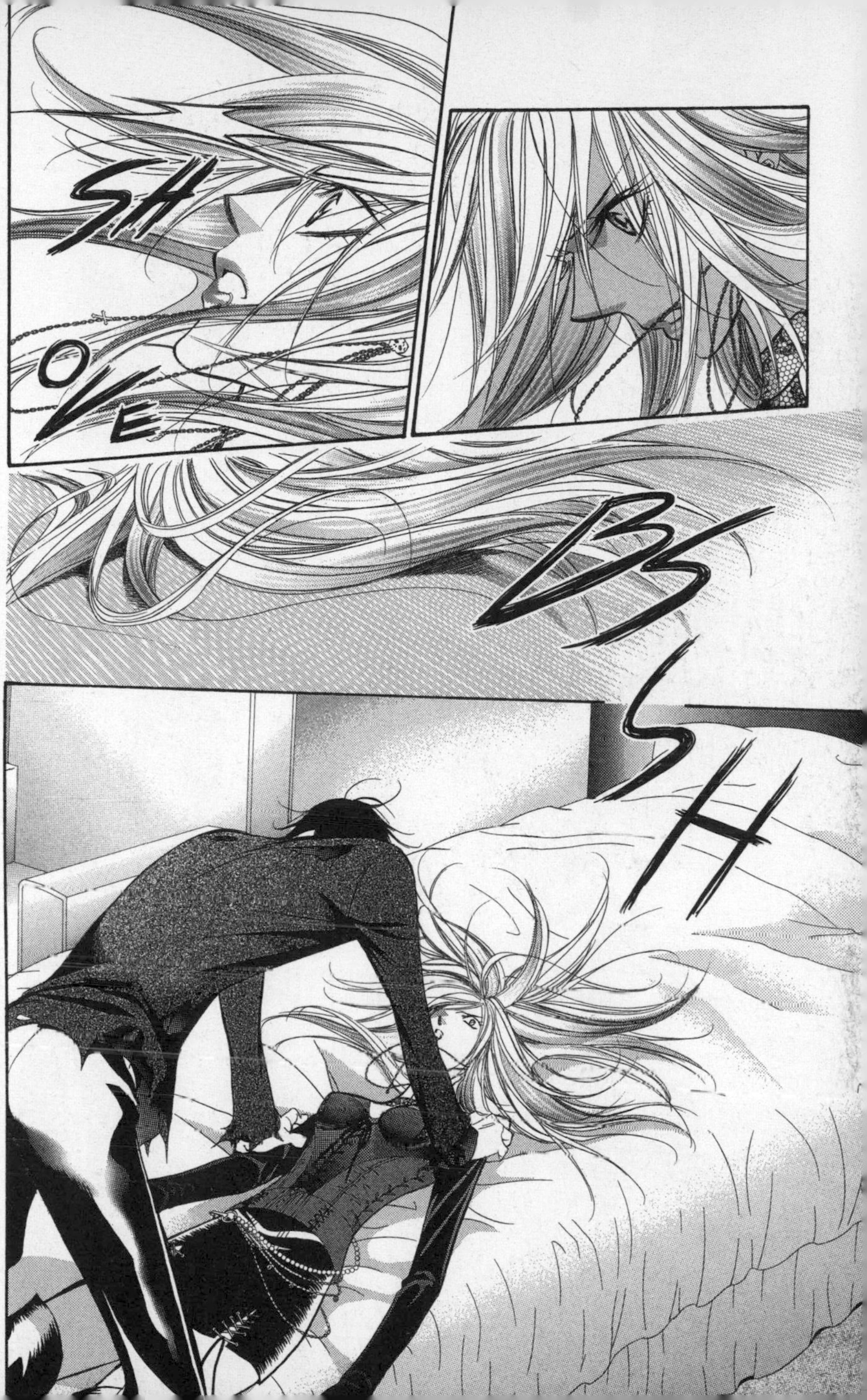
SHOVE
BSSH

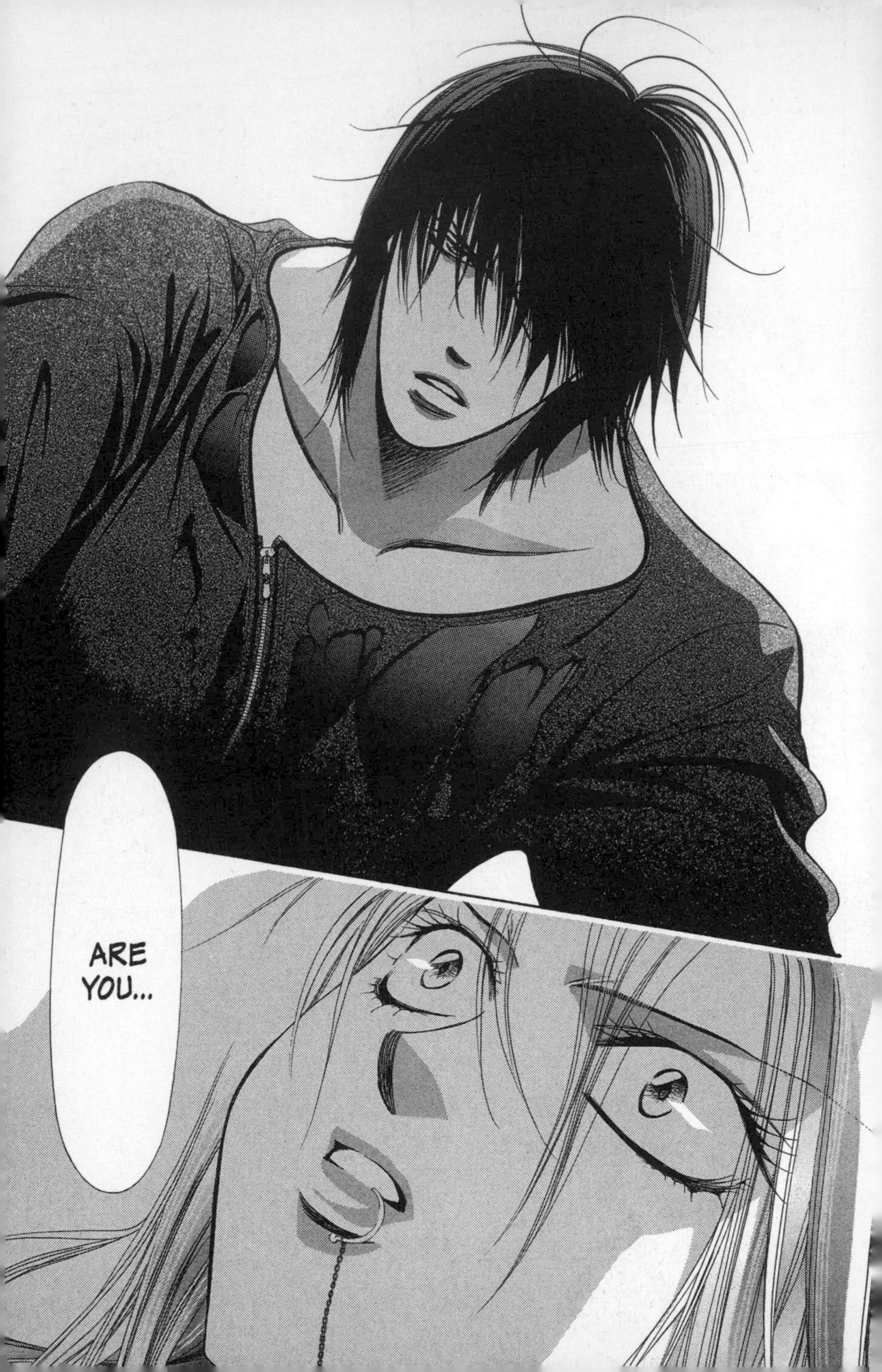
ARE YOU...

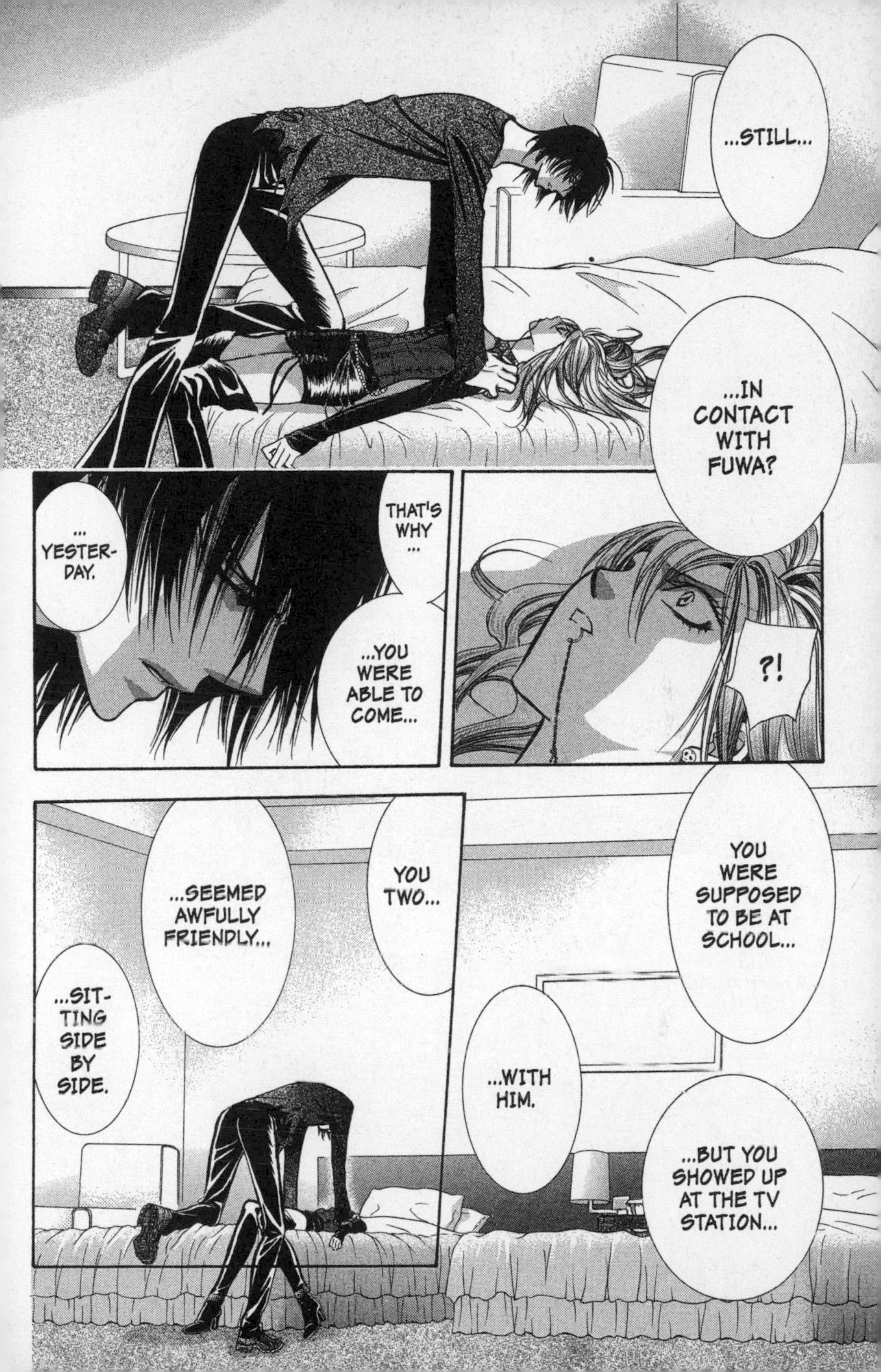
...STILL...
...IN CONTACT WITH FUWA?
?!
THAT'S WHY ...
...YOU WERE ABLE TO COME...
... YESTER-DAY.
YOU WERE SUPPOSED TO BE AT SCHOOL...
...BUT YOU SHOWED UP AT THE TV STATION...
...WITH HIM.
YOU TWO...
...SEEMED AWFULLY FRIENDLY...
...SIT-TING SIDE BY SIDE.

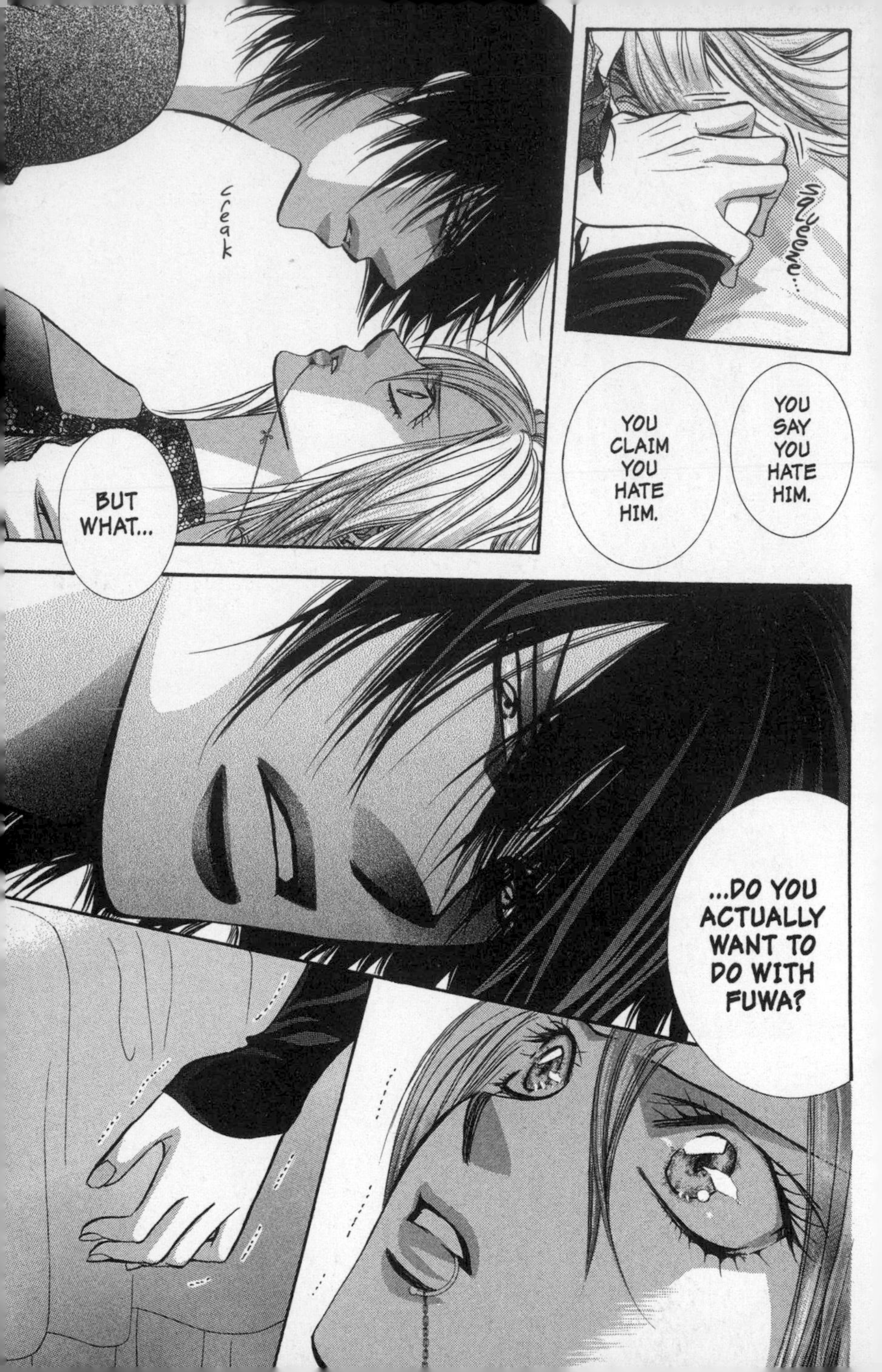
squeeze...
YOU SAY YOU HATE HIM.
YOU CLAIM YOU HATE HIM.
creak
BUT WHAT...
...DO YOU ACTUALLY WANT TO DO WITH FUWA?

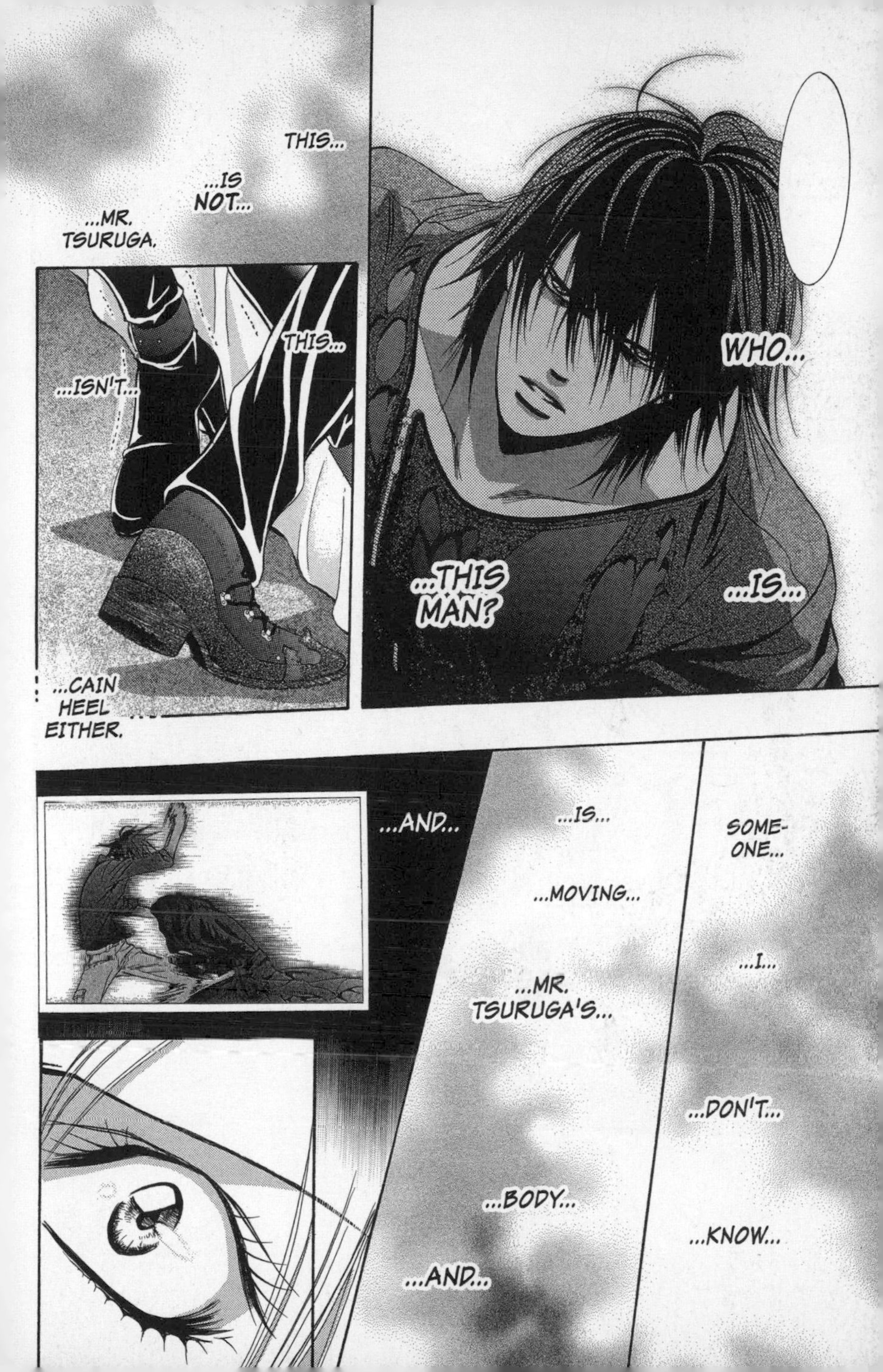
WHO...
...IS...
...THIS MAN?
THIS...
...IS NOT...
...MR. TSURUGA.
THIS...
...ISN'T...
...CAIN HEEL EITHER.
SOME-ONE...
...I...
...DON'T...
...KNOW...
...IS...
...AND...
...MOVING...
...MR. TSURUGA'S...
...BODY...
...AND...

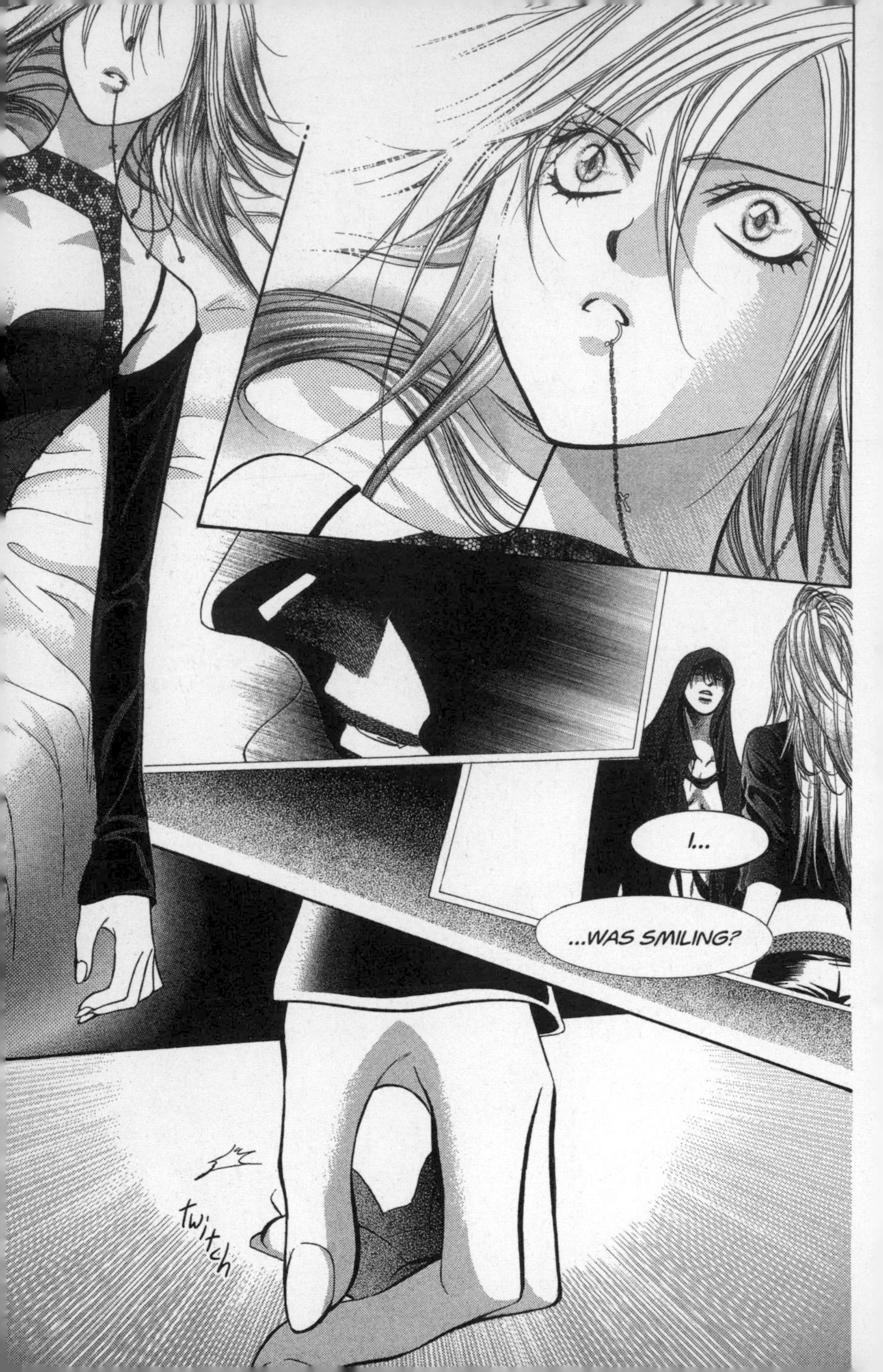
I...
...WAS SMILING?
twitch

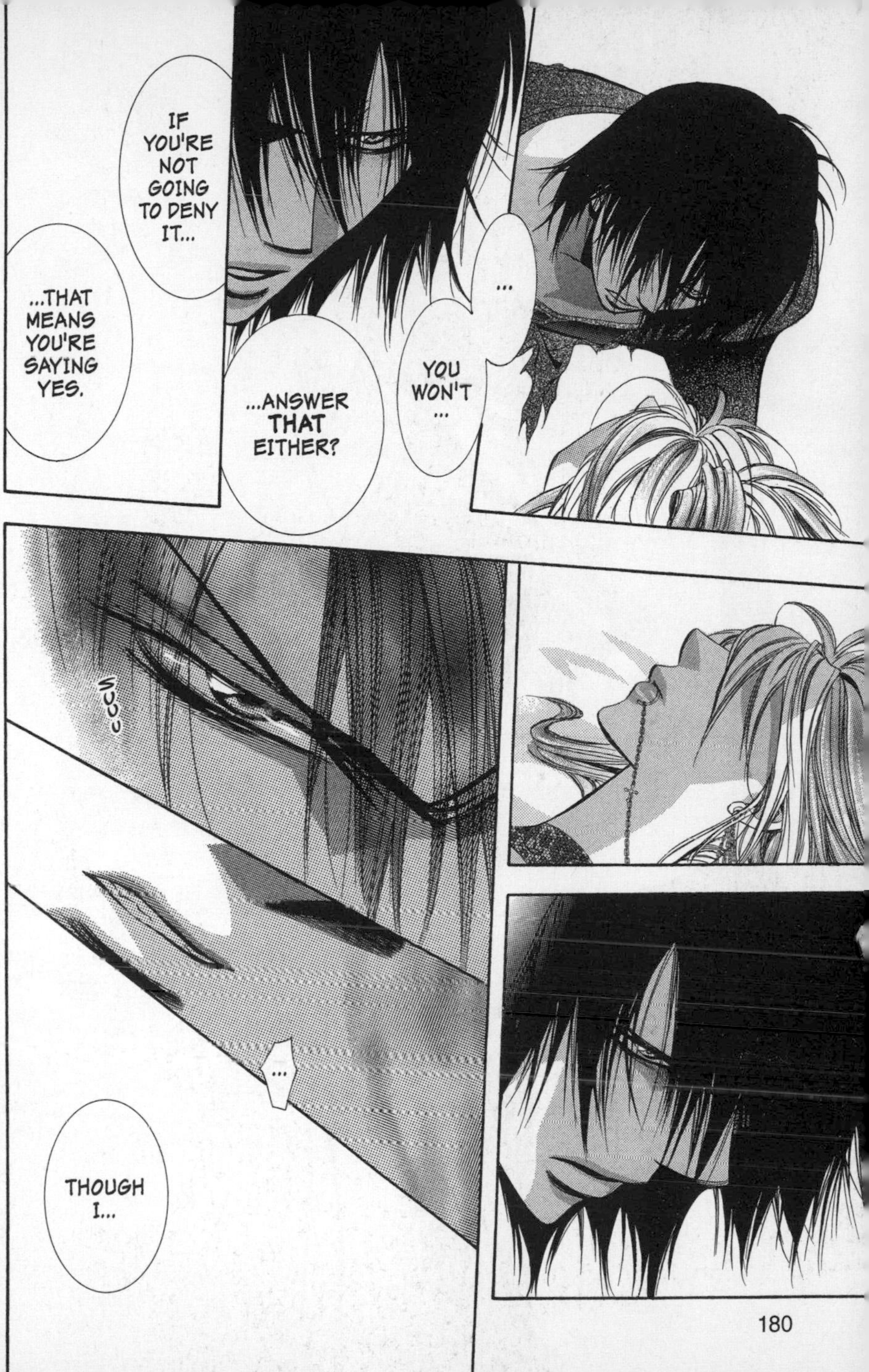
...
YOU WON'T ...
...ANSWER THAT EITHER?
IF YOU'RE NOT GOING TO DENY IT...
...THAT MEANS YOU'RE SAYING YES.
SUUU
...
THOUGH I...

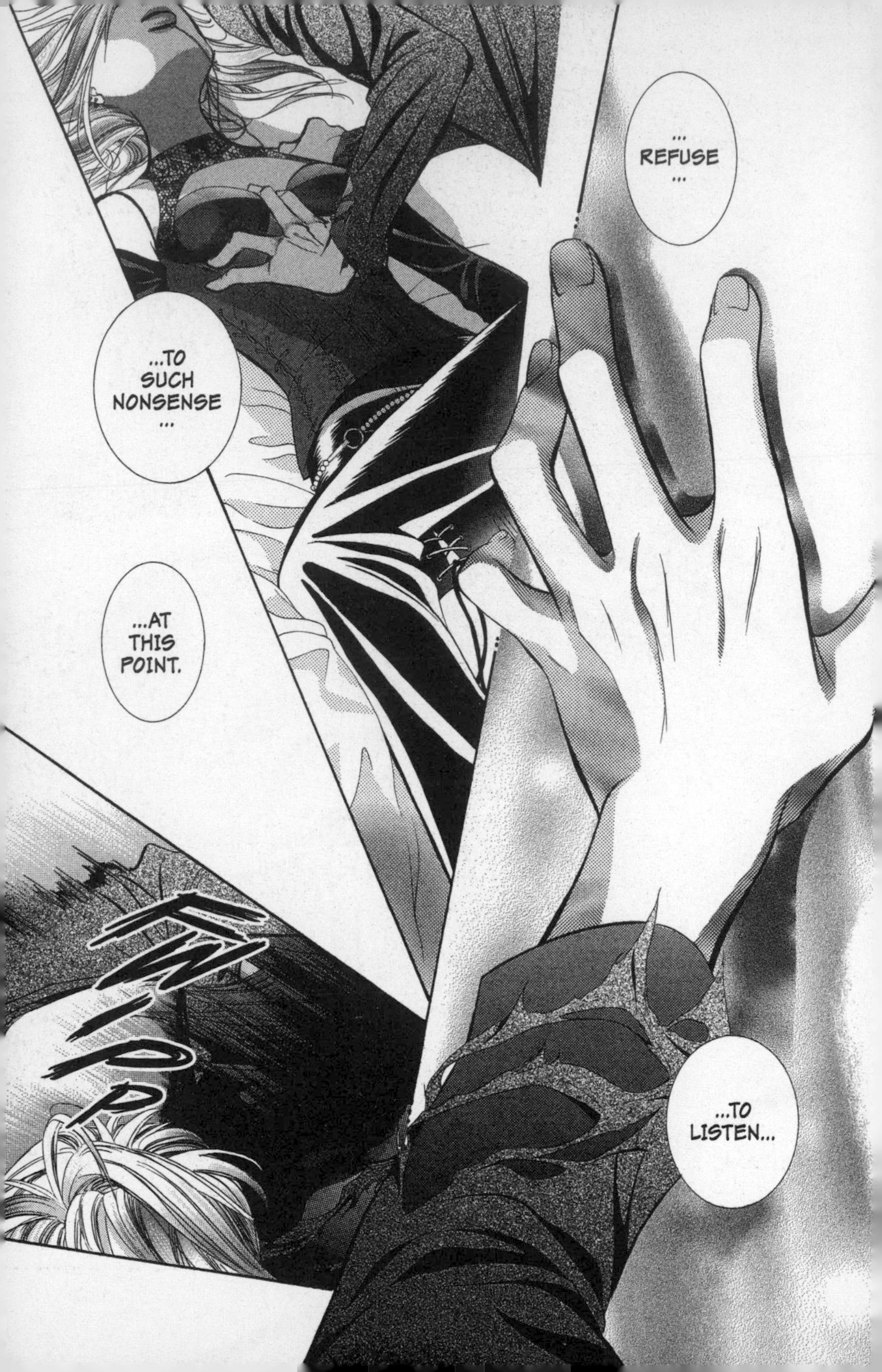
... REFUSE ...
...TO LISTEN...
...TO SUCH NONSENSE ...
...AT THIS POINT.
FWIP

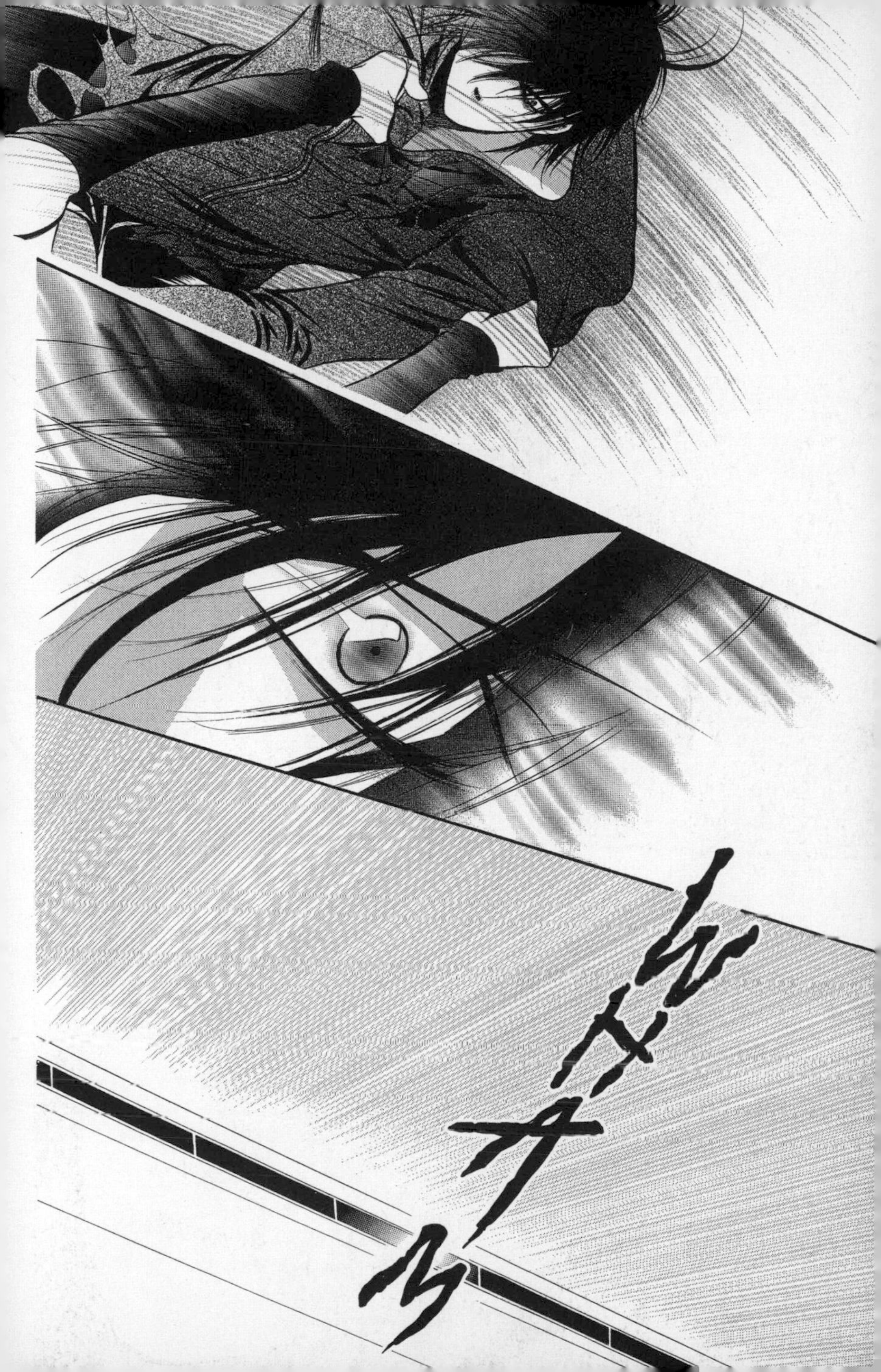
ドサァッ

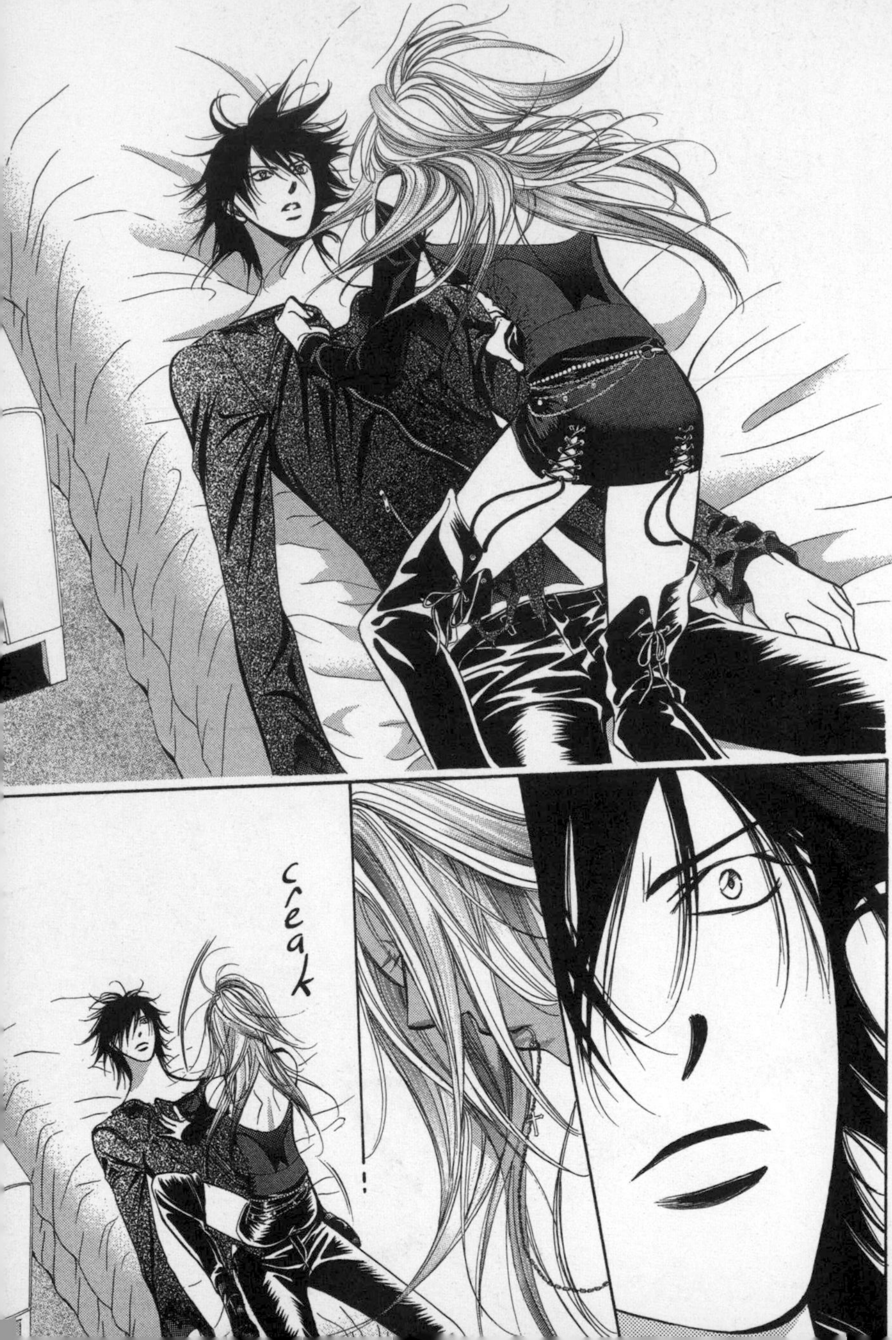
!
creak

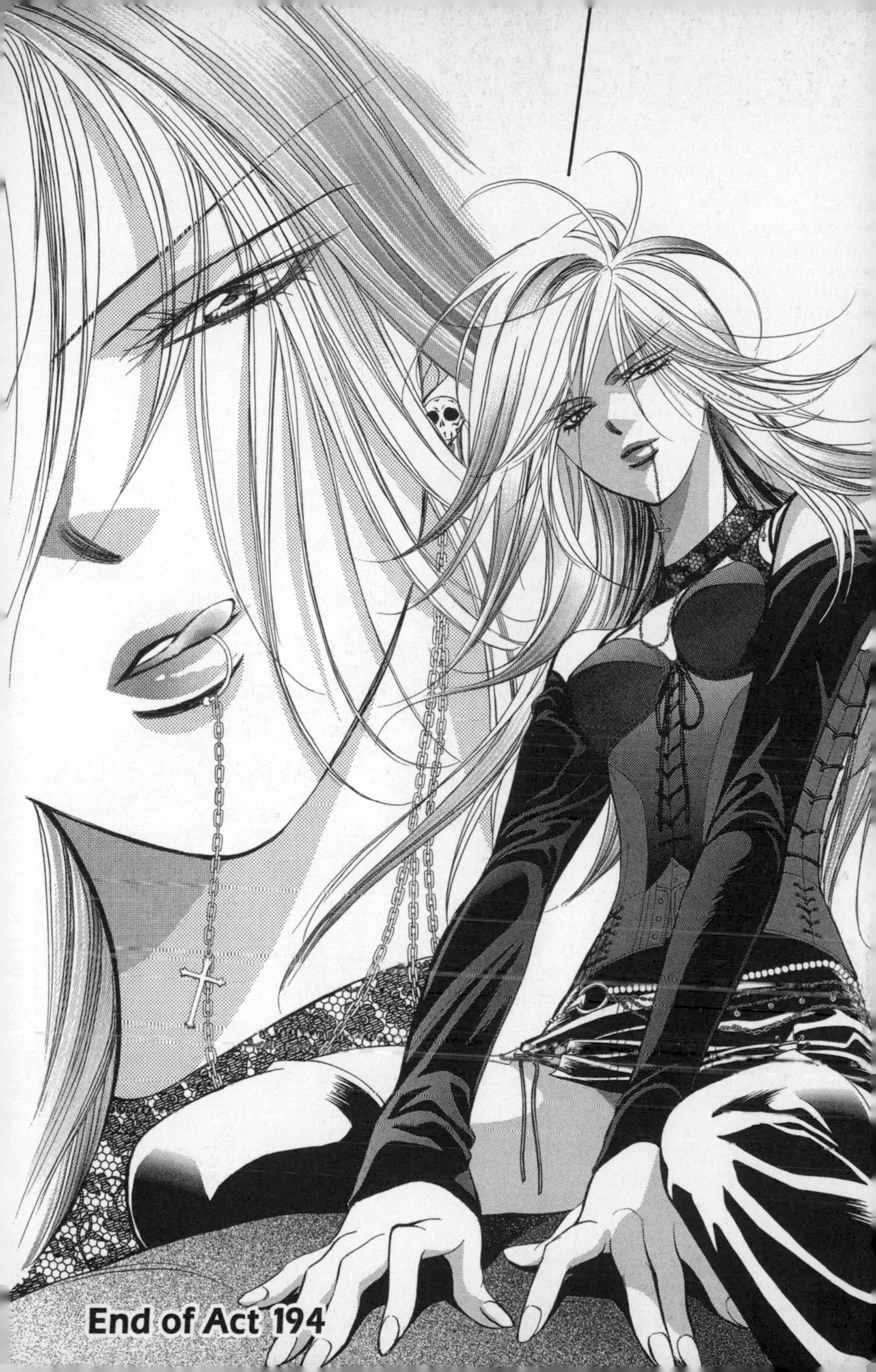
End of Act 194

Yoshiki Nakamura is
originally from Tokushima Prefecture.
She started drawing manga in elementary
school, which eventually led to her 1993 debut of
Yume de Au yori Suteki (Better than Seeing in
a Dream) in *Hana to Yume* magazine. Her other
works include the basketball series *Saint Love,
MVP wa Yuzurenai* (Can't Give Up MVP),
Blue Wars and *Tokyo Crazy Paradise*, a
series about a female bodyguard
in 2020 Tokyo.

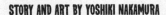

SKIP·BEAT!
Vol. 32
Shojo Beat Edition

STORY AND ART BY YOSHIKI NAKAMURA

English Translation & Adaptation/Tomo Kimura
Touch-up Art & Lettering/Sabrina Heep
Design/Ronnie Casson
Editor/Pancha Diaz

Printed in the U.S.A.

Published by VIZ Media, LLC
P.O. Box 77010
San Francisco, CA 94107

www.viz.com

www.shojobeat.com

10 9 8 7 6 5 4 3 2 1
First printing, December 2013

RATED T FOR TEEN

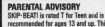

PARENTAL ADVISORY
SKIP·BEAT! is rated T for Teen and is recommended for ages 13 and up. This volume contains a grudge.

ratings.viz.com

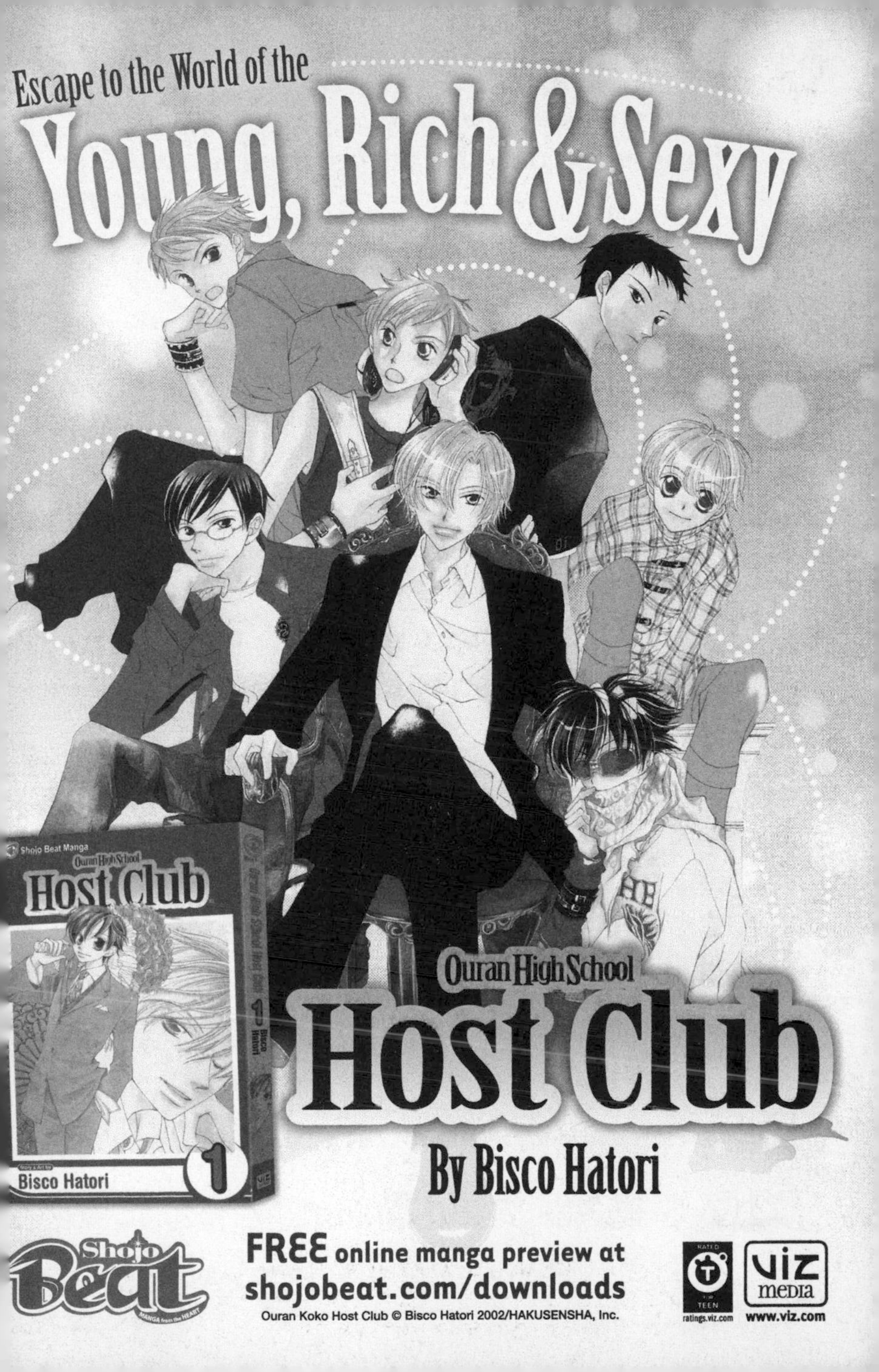
Escape to the World of the
Young, Rich & Sexy
Shojo Beat Manga
Ouran High School
Host Club
1
Bisco Hatori
Ouran High School
Host Club
By Bisco Hatori
Shojo Beat
FREE online manga preview at
shojobeat.com/downloads
Ouran Koko Host Club © Bisco Hatori 2002/HAKUSENSHA, Inc.
TEEN
ratings.viz.com
viz media
www.viz.com

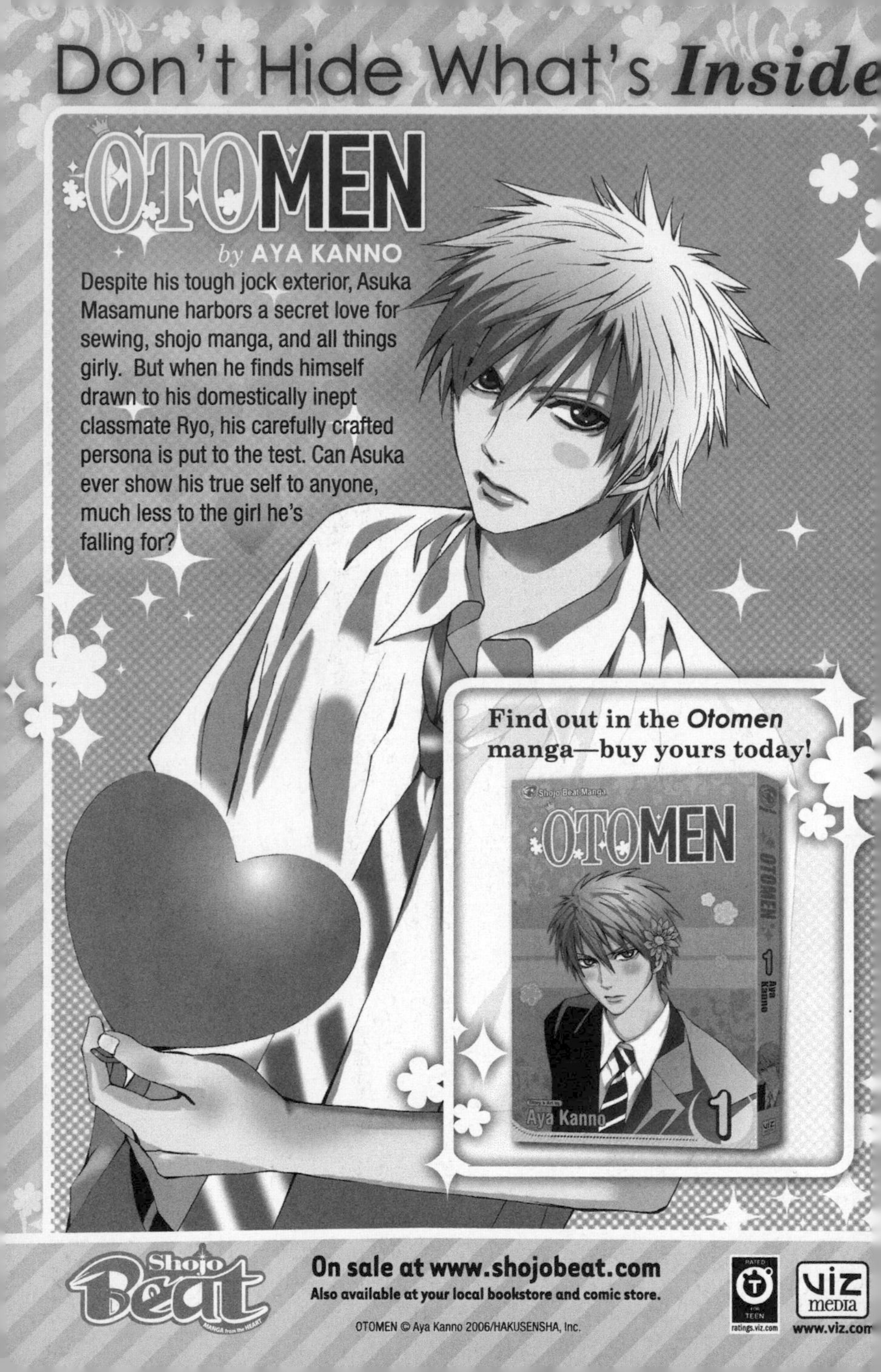
Don't Hide What's Inside
OTOMEN
by AYA KANNO
Despite his tough jock exterior, Asuka Masamune harbors a secret love for sewing, shojo manga, and all things girly. But when he finds himself drawn to his domestically inept classmate Ryo, his carefully crafted persona is put to the test. Can Asuka ever show his true self to anyone, much less to the girl he's falling for?
Find out in the Otomen manga—buy yours today!
Shojo Beat Manga
OTOMEN
1
Aya Kanno
Shojo Beat
MANGA from the HEART
On sale at www.shojobeat.com
Also available at your local bookstore and comic store.
RATED T FOR TEEN
ratings.viz.com
VIZ MEDIA
www.viz.com
OTOMEN © Aya Kanno 2006/HAKUSENSHA, Inc.

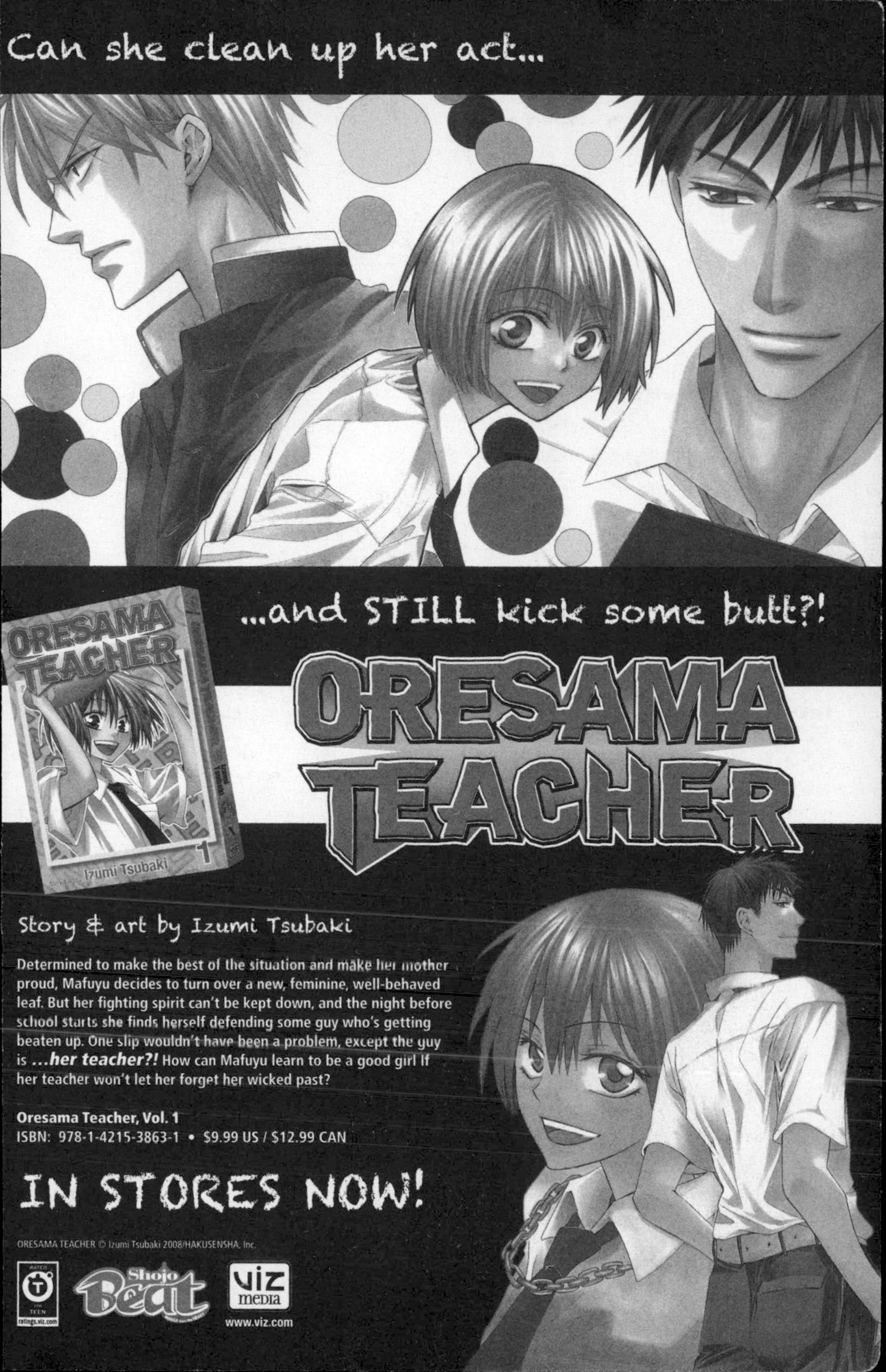
Can she clean up her act...
...and STILL kick some butt?!
ORESAMA TEACHER
ORESAMA TEACHER
Izumi Tsubaki
1
Story & art by Izumi Tsubaki
Determined to make the best of the situation and make her mother proud, Mafuyu decides to turn over a new, feminine, well-behaved leaf. But her fighting spirit can't be kept down, and the night before school starts she finds herself defending some guy who's getting beaten up. One slip wouldn't have been a problem, except the guy is ...her teacher?! How can Mafuyu learn to be a good girl if her teacher won't let her forget her wicked past?
Oresama Teacher, Vol. 1
ISBN: 978-1-4215-3863-1 • $9.99 US / $12.99 CAN
IN STORES NOW!
ORESAMA TEACHER © Izumi Tsubaki 2008/HAKUSENSHA, Inc.
RATED T TEEN ratings.viz.com
Shojo Beat
viz media
www.viz.com

VIZMANGA

Read manga anytime, anywhere!

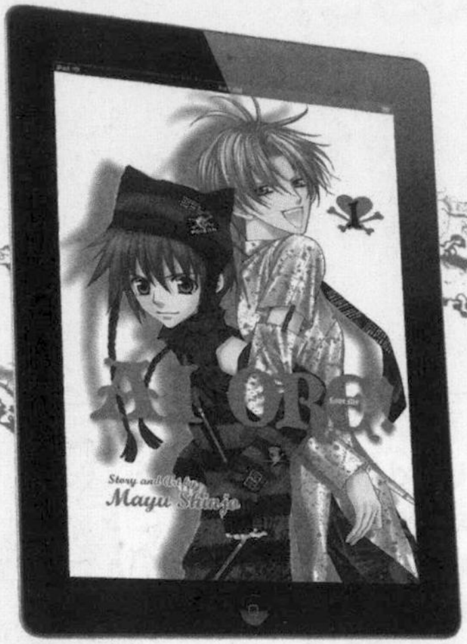

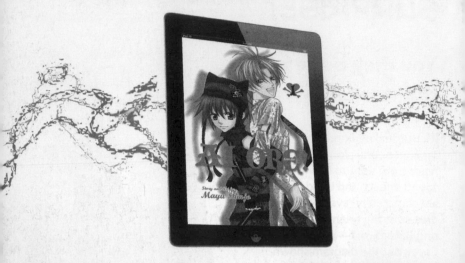

From our newest hit series to the classics you know and love, the best manga in the world is now available digitally. Buy a volume* of digital manga for your:

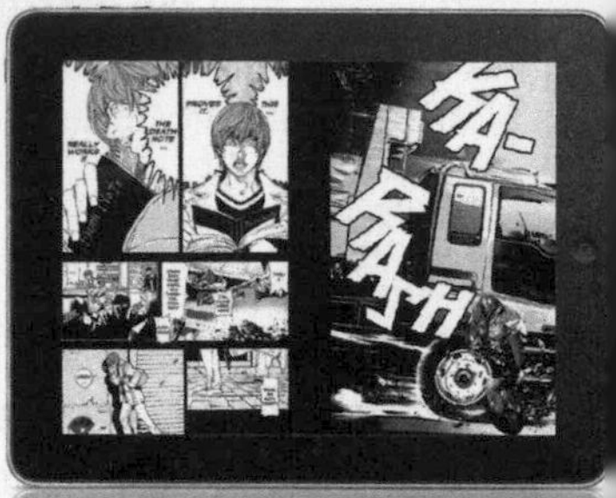

- iOS device (**iPad®**, **iPhone®**, **iPod® touch**) through the **VIZ Manga app**
- Android-powered device (**phone or tablet**) with a browser by visiting VIZManga.com
- **Mac or PC computer** by visiting VIZManga.com

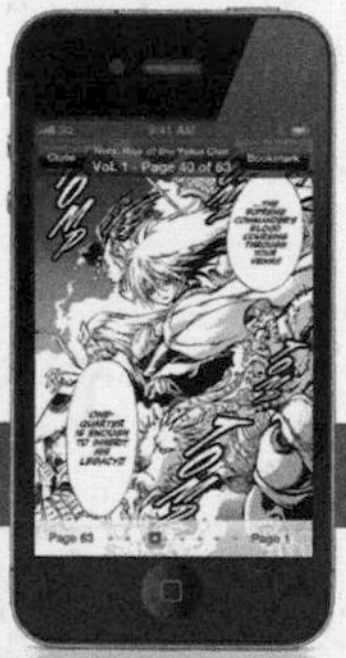

VIZ Digital has loads to offer:

- 500+ ready-to-read volumes
- New volumes each week
- FREE previews
- Access on multiple devices! Create a log-in through the app so you buy a book once, and read it on your device of choice!*

To learn more, visit www.viz.com/apps

*** Some series may not be available for multiple devices. Check the app on your device to find out what's available.**

RATED T+ FOR OLDER TEEN
ratings.viz.com

VIZ media
viz.com/apps

SURPRISE!

You may be reading the wrong way!

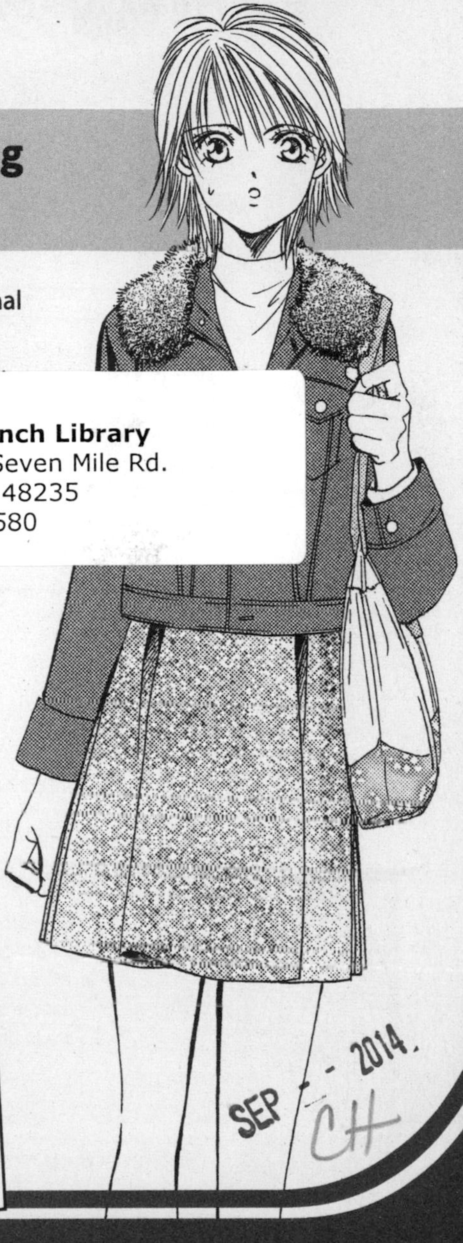

It's true: In keeping with the original Japanese comic format, this book reads from right to left—so action, sound effects, a[...]
are completely [...]
preserves the or[...]
original artwork[...]
Check out the d[...]
here to get the [...]
and then turn to the other side of the book to get started!

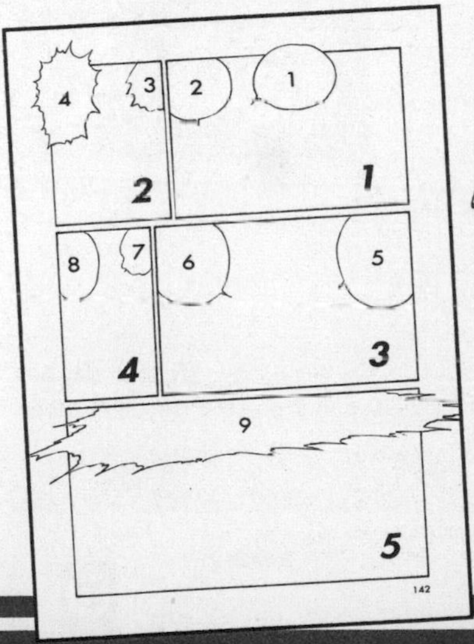
1
2
3
4
1
2
5
6
7
8
3
4
9
5
142